Piers Plowman Studies V

PIERS PLOWMAN: A GLOSSARY OF LEGAL DICTION

Piers Plowman Studies

I   THE THEME OF GOVERNMENT IN PIERS PLOWMAN
Anna Baldwin

II   THE FIGURE OF PIERS PLOWMAN
Margaret E. Goldsmith

III   PERSONIFICATION IN PIERS PLOWMAN
Lavinia Griffiths

IV   THE CLERKLY MAKER: LANGLAND'S POETIC ART
A. V. C. Schmidt

ISSN 0261-9849

Piers Plowman

A Glossary of Legal Diction

JOHN A. ALFORD

D. S. BREWER

© John A. Alford 1988

First published 1988 by D. S. Brewer
240 Hills Road, Cambridge
an imprint of Boydell & Brewer Ltd
PO Box 9, Woodbridge, Suffolk IP12 3DF
and of Boydell & Brewer Inc.
Wolfeboro, New Hampshire 03894-2069, USA

ISBN 0 85991 248 5

British Library Cataloguing in Publication Data

Alford, John A.
   Piers Plowman: a glossary of legal diction
   – (Piers Plowman studies, ISSN 0261-9849;
   V.5).
   1. Langland, William. Piers Plowman
   2. Langland, William – Knowledge – Law.
   I. Title   II. Series
   821′.1   PR2017.L38
   ISBN 0-85991-248-5

Library of Congress Cataloging-in-Publication Data

Alford, John A., 1938–
   Piers Plowman : a glossary of legal diction / John A. Alford.
        p.   cm. – (Piers Plowman studies : 5)
   Bibliography: p.
   ISBN 0-85991-248-5
   1. Langland, William, 1330?–1400? Piers the Plowman.
   2. Langland, William, 1330?–1400? – Knowledge – Law. 3. Langland,
   William, 1330?–1400? – Language – Glossaries, etc. 4. English
   language – Middle English, 1100–1500 – Glossaries, vocabularies, etc.
   5. Law, Medieval – Dictionaries.   I. Title.   II. Series.
   PR2017.L38A44   1988
   821′.1–dc19   87-37533
                                                              CIP

♾ Printed on long life paper
made to the full American Standard

Printed in Great Britain by
St Edmundsbury Press, Bury St Edmunds, Suffolk

Contents

PREFACE

This book began as the appendix to another. In the process of writing discursively on the central role of law in *Piers Plowman*, I came to see, as my argument drew more and more on Langland's diction, that much of the argument itself could be presented more efficiently in the form of a glossary.

The present work has several purposes:

1. To identify the words in *Piers Plowman*, both common and technical, that have reference to the law, and thus to indicate the nature and extent of the poet's legal frame of thought.

2. To provide an index to legal concepts in all three versions of the poem.

3. To expand our appreciation of Langland's place in the history of the language, especially as an importer of French and Latin law terms into English.

4. To confirm many of the definitions given by the *Oxford English Dictionary* and the *Middle English Dictionary* (often neglected by scholars and translators of the poem) and to supplement or correct others therein.

5. To serve as a reference guide for legal historians, for persons concerned with fourteenth-century usage, and for students of other Middle English authors, such as Chaucer, Gower, and the *Pearl* poet, whose diction reflects a similar preoccupation with the law.

In compiling the glossary, I found myself often in agreement with the pioneering work of the *Middle English Dictionary*. George Kane and the late Judson B. Allen provided steady encouragement. For his many helpful suggestions I thank my colleague (and formerly an associate editor of the *MED*) Lister M. Matheson. For financial support, I am grateful to the National Endowment for the Humanities, which funded the original project upon which this glossary is based; the College of Arts and Letters, Michigan State University; and the MSU Foundation. Above all, for so cheerfully tolerating the costs of my obsession with Langland's words, I am indebted to my wife Linda.

vii

INTRODUCTION

The word *law* appears in the surviving records of English around the year 1000, but not until *Piers Plowman* do we read about *lawyers* – or their *clients* or *cases* or *appeals*. In fact the poem provides the earliest testimony in the language of more than a hundred legal terms. Written at a time when knowledge of the law seems to have been the common property of poets,[1] Langland's work stands out as the most saturated in legal concepts and terminology.

This feature of the poem has not gone unnoticed. W. W. Skeat observed long ago, 'William seems to have been very familiar with the courts of law at Westminster'[2]; and more recent scholars such as W. J. Birnes, Anna P. Baldwin, and Myra Stokes have made important contributions to our understanding of the role played by law in Langland's argument.[3] But not since Rudolf Kirk's article, 'References to the Law in *Piers the Plowman*' (1933), has any study focused on the poet's legal diction.[4]

Kirk's interest in the subject was limited by the current controversy over multiple authorship: Were the A, B, and C texts composed by different persons? Basically Kirk wanted to know if an answer to this question might be found in the distribution of legal terminology over the three versions. '[W]hat has not been pointed out,' he stated, 'is that the references to the law which occur in the three texts of the poem reveal a significant increase in legal knowledge from the A-text to the later texts' (322). As proof he offered the following statistics: 'In "A" William uses about thirteen legal words. . . . In "B" . . . the legal vocabulary leaps to at least forty-five words. . . . "C" has half a dozen more

---

[1] See John A. Alford, 'Literature and Law in Medieval England,' *PMLA* 92 (1977), 941–51; and John A. Alford and Dennis P. Seniff, *Literature and Law in the Middle Ages: A Bibliography of Scholarship* (New York: Garland, 1984).
[2] *The Vision of William concerning Piers the Plowman, in Three Parallel Texts*. 2 vols. (Oxford: Oxford Univ. Press, 1886, rpt. 1961), 2:37.
[3] Birnes, 'Christ as Advocate: The Legal Metaphor of *Piers Plowman*,' *Annuale Mediaevale* 16 (1975), 71–93; Baldwin, *The Theme of Government in Piers Plowman* (Cambridge: D. S. Brewer, 1981); Stokes, *Justice and Mercy in Piers Plowman: A Reading of the B Text Visio* (London and Canberra: Croom Helm, 1984).
[4] *PMLA* 48 (1933), 322–27.

legal words than "B"' (322–25). The inference to be drawn from such evidence, however, was inconclusive: 'William may have read law between the time that he wrote "A" and the time that he revised his poem. In this case we have an additional biographical fact. . . . On the other hand, it would have been possible for later writers to have been more versed in the law than the first poet' (327).

Kirk's investigation was far from adequate. Behind the 'scientific' look of his statistics – a mode of argument that was fashionable among literary critics of the period[5] – lay the failure to define precisely what was being counted. In the A text, for example, he says that there are 'about thirteen legal words' (*canonistres*, *consistory*, *fief*, *forestall*, *huckstering*, *loveday*, *meynpernour*, *meynprise*, *provisor*, *regratory*, *sisors*, *sumners*, and *year's gift*), but there are numerous questionable omissions. If *canonistre* is a 'legal word,' then why not *legistre* or, as noted already, *lawyer*? If *consistory*, then why not the names of other courts, such as the *cheker* (exchequer), *chauncelrie*, *counseil* (the king's council), *kinges bench*, or *parlement*? If *fief* (i.e., *feffen*, 'to grant, convey'), then why not the various documents by which this action was accomplished, such as *feffement*, *chartre*, *dede*, *fin* ('fine' or *finalis concordia*), *writ*, *testament*? If *forestall*, *huckstering*, or *regratory*, then why not other commercial terms like *account*, *dette*, *dischargen*, *marchaundie*, *permutacioun*, *rekenen*, or *rental*? If *sisors* and *sumners*, then why not other officers of the law, such as *archedeken*, *baillif*, *bedel*, *commissarie*, *constable*, *dene*, *jugge*, *justice*, *notarie*, *sherreve*, or *stiward*?

In part the answers must lie in Kirk's limited definition of 'legal words.' He speaks at one point of words 'technical enough to need a full explanation in terms of fourteenth-century law' (326). Presumably, modern readers would need an explanation of canonistres but not lawyers, of consistory but not exchequer or parliament, of fief but not charter or deed.

Modern usage, however, is a poor criterion for judging the technical character of Langland's vocabulary. Many words that are now commonplace entered the language as highly specialized in meaning. Consider the word *divorce*. Everybody uses the word nowadays; and in the United States, where a third of all marriages end in divorce, nearly everybody (counting the children and relatives of divorced couples) has personal cause to use it. But this was not so in medieval England.

---

[5] The outstanding example is John M. Manly's Wharton Lecture, 'Chaucer and the Rhetoricians,' *The Proceedings of the British Academy* 12 (1926), 95–113. Manly's statistical argument suffers from the same defect as Kirk's – a failure to specify what is being counted.

Divorce as we know it did not exist.[6] You were married for life, unless some 'impediment' such as consanguinity was later discovered, thus requiring an anulment or *divortium*. Langland is the first writer, so far as we know, to import the word into English.[7] The fact that English has undergone considerable semantic change since the fourteenth century must be kept constantly in mind, even in the case – or rather especially in the case – of the simplest and most familiar words.[8]

The difficulties facing our investigation, however, are not only diachronic but also synchronic. To distinguish between technical and ordinary usage is no simple matter in any period of time, including our own. As David Mellinkoff richly demonstrates, 'the language of the law' today consists both of terminology peculiar to itself (*habeas corpus*, affidavit, felony) and of a vast number of words in everyday use (action, avoid, consideration, hand, letters, prayer, specialty).[9] What makes the latter group of words technical is context alone, particularly the way in which they are joined with other words. The same is true of medieval usage. The following excerpt from a thirteenth-century formulary will illustrate the point: 'Quidam F . . . appellatus est de quodam probatore de societate et recepto,' which the translator renders as, 'One F . . . is appealed by an approver for fellowship and receipt.'[10] In isolation none of these words (the same in Middle as in Modern English) gives any problem; in combination they read like a foreign language. The layman requires a translation of the translation: *appealed*, 'charged or accused'; *approver*, 'one who serves as a witness against a former accomplice in crime, usually in exchange for a reduced penalty'; *fellowship*, 'covin or conspiracy to commit a crime'; *receipt*, 'the harbouring of known criminals.'

6 R. H. Helmholz, *Marriage Litigation in Medieval England* (Cambridge: Cambridge Univ. Press, 1974), 74.
7 The glossary notes numerous other words that may have been borrowed directly from legal sources in Latin or French: for example, aiel, amortise, appurtenance, broker, challengeable, civil, conspire, construe, copy, controller, defraud, disallow, exchange, except, fornicator, impugn, indulgence, intestate, mitigation, panel, parcel, parsonage, pension, permutation, plurality, provisor, register, registrar, taxer, temporalities, testify, transgressor, trespasser, tutor, and many more.
8 The point is illustrated repeatedly in George Kane's 'Poetry and Lexicography in the Translation of *Piers Plowman*,' *Medieval and Renaissance Studies* 9 (1982), 33–54. Kane draws the conclusion: 'The translator will be well advised to adopt as a working principle that historical differentiation of meaning between a fourteenth-century word and its twentieth-century descendant is as likely as not, and never guess.'
9 *The Language of the Law* (Boston: Little, Brown, 1963).
10 *The Court Baron*, ed. F. W. Maitland and William P. Baildon, Selden Society 4 (London: Quaritch, 1891), 91.

Piers Plowman offers an abundance of similar examples. Let me call attention here to just two words from the glossary. They are extremely common: *contree* and *paper*.[11] The first is quoted from C.2.63, 'Simonye and Syuile and sysores of contrees Were most pryue with Mede.' In its general signification as 'a geographical area' (whatever the size), *contree* seems an odd choice of words. Pearsall skews his definition somewhat in order to make it fit: '**contrees** *pl.* districts, areas of jurisdiction.' The true meaning of the word, however, is probably 'juries.' When a person had been indicted for certain crimes, he had the choice of undergoing trial by battle or ordeal or else of 'putting himself upon the country,' that is, of putting the question of his guilt or innocence into the hands of jurors or *sysores*.

Even more common (to our eyes at least) is the word *paper*. In C.13.36–38 Langland says:

> The marchaunt mote nede be ylet lenger then the messager,
> For þe parcel of his paper and oþer pryue dettes
> Wol lette hym, as y leue, the lenghe of a myle.

In this instance Pearsall does not bother to provide a gloss. *Paper* is paper. Yet the meaning of the line is not entirely clear. What is the nature of this 'paper'? The rest of the line offers a clue: the merchant is slowed down by his paper and '*oþer* pryue dettes.' By *paper* Langland seems to refer not to sheets of writing material as such but to a recently introduced way of recording debts, a signed acknowledgement or in colloquial terms 'an IOU.' Thus a statute of 1363 complains that 'many people are grieved and attached by their bodies in the city of London at the suit of men in the same city, surmising to them that they are debtors and that will they prove by their papers [par lour papirs], whereas they have no deed or tally.'[12] This interpretation of *paper* in C.13.37 is strengthened by the association with *parcel*, which means not only a 'piece or segment' but also 'an estreat, abstract, or itemized list of commercial transactions.' Moreover, the sentence contains just two lines earlier the phrase 'rikene . . . a resonable acounte,' a formula repeated over and over in writs of account. Langland uses few words more familiar to us than *paper*; and yet in this context, charged with the specialized language of commerce, it seems to bear a highly technical meaning.

Frequently where a word has both a common and a technical signification, it is impossible to 'prove' what Langland meant. The whole

---

[11] The evidence assumed by this discussion will be found in the glossary under *contree* and *paper*.
[12] Statute 38 Edw. III chap. 5.

issue of legal diction must be kept in perspective. We are dealing not with a writ or statute but with a poem. Legal expression aims for precision. This is the major reason for its conservatism – for its retention of archaic English words like *thence* and *witnesseth* and Latin words like *venire* and *mens rea*, its use of redundancies like *over and above* and *without let or hindrance*, its predilection for such (to the layman) inelegant expressions as *the said property*, *the party of the first part*, and so on. It wants *certainty*; and the following statement by *The Oxford Companion to Law* probably represents the official consensus: 'Law would be much better, not worse, if it had a much larger technical vocabulary' (714). Poets take the opposite point of view. Instead of adhering rigorously to the traditional uses of words, poets deliberately bend and twist and stretch their meanings; far from trying to avoid the ambiguity of language, poets thrive on it.[13]

Of poets writing in Middle English, Langland is arguably the most prone to exploit the double meanings of words, a tendency that has been well documented by several studies.[14] Certain elements of his legal diction operate, and indeed are only recognizable, as part of a larger constellation of puns. The infamous grammatical metaphor in C.3.332–406 provides a good illustration.

> Thus is mede and mercede as two maner relacions,
> Rect and indirect, reninde bothe
> On a sad and a siker semblable to hemsuluen,
> As adiectif and sustantif vnite asken
> And acordaunce in kynde, in case and in nombre,
> And ayther is otheres helpe – of hem cometh retribucoun . . .
> Relacoun rect . . . is a record of treuthe . . .
> Indirect thyng is as ho-so coueytede
> Alle kyn kynde to knowe and to folowe
> And withoute cause to cache and come to bothe nombres;
> In whiche ben gode and nat gode to graunte here neyþer will . . .
> Ac relacoun rect is a ryhtful custume,
> As a kyng to clayme the comune at his wille . . .
> Ac þe moste partie of peple now puyr indirect semeth.
> For they wilnen and wolden as beste were for hemsulue

[13] See, for example, Owen Barfield, 'Poetic Diction and Legal Fiction,' *Essays Presented to Charles Williams*, ed. C. S. Lewis (London: Oxford Univ. Press, 1947), 106–127.

[14] For example, Bernard F. Huppé, '*Petrus, id est, Christus*: Word Play in *Piers Plowman*; the B-Text,' *ELH* 17 (1950), 163–90; A. V. C. Schmidt, '*Lele Wordes* and *Bele Paroles*: Some Aspects of Langland's Word-Play,' *RES* ns 34 (1983), 137–50; Hildegard L. C. Tristram, 'Intertextuelle *Puns* in *Piers Plowman*,' *Neuphilologische Mitteilungen* 84 (1983), 182–91.

Thow the kyng and þe comune al the coest hadde.
Such inparfit peple repreueth alle resoun
And halt hem vnstedefast for hem lakketh case.
As relacoynes indirect reccheth thei neuere
Of the cours of case so thei cache suluer.
Be the peccunie ypaied, thow parties chyde,
He þat mede may lacche maketh lytel tale.
Nyme he a noumbre of nobles or of shillynges,
How þat cliauntes acorde acounteth mede litel.

At the beginning of the metaphor (here drastically reduced), there is no hint that the words *relacion*, *rect*, *acordaunce*, *case*, *cours*, and *partie* have anything other than strictly grammatical referents. By the end, however, these same words clearly have slipped from the school-room into the courtroom. The transfer is not gratuitous. 'Just as grammar defines the rules of *recte loquendi*, so law defines the rules of right living.'[15] The puns implicitly support one of Langland's main arguments. The grammar of 'truth' or 'doing well' has its basis in logic, in reason, in the very nature of things; it is not a matter to be decided by individual wills according to their own convenience and desires.

As Langland's fusion of grammatical and legal terminology suggests, diction may serve as argument. Although the pervasive presence of legal words throughout the poem may reflect the dramatic changes taking place in the law (the consolidation of royal justice at Westminster, the development of the chancery as a court of equity, the emergence of professional pleaders, and so forth), although it may even reflect the background or occupation of the poet himself, undoubtedly it reflects the basic concern of the poem – 'How I may saue my soule.' So intertwined historically are the vocabularies of law and theology that medieval writers found it impossible to explain certain doctrines of Christianity without recourse to legal terminology. The Bible is largely responsible for this intermingling. Not only does it describe the history of mankind as a judicial process – crime, punishment, pardon – but quite naturally it also employs the words of the law itself. John Derrett has demonstrated the pervasive use of legal diction in the New Testament;[16] and Walter Ullmann has stressed that the Vulgate translation is so permeated by 'Roman legal terminology' that during the Middle Ages, 'Roman law was so to speak transmitted

---

[15] John A. Alford, 'The Grammatical Metaphor: A Survey of Its Use in the Middle Ages,' *Speculum* 57 (1982), 759.
[16] *Law in the New Testament* (London: Darton, Longman and Todd, 1970); *Studies in the New Testament* I: *Glimpses of the Legal and Social Presuppositions of the Authors* (Leiden: Brill, 1977).

under cover of the Bible.'[17] Thus in his choice of vocabulary (if indeed he really had a choice), Langland was simply using the words best suited by tradition to his subject matter.

The essential connection between legal diction and the logic of salvation is illustrated dramatically in Chaucer's writings. One of the Canterbury tales contains the following terms: accord, accusen, acquiten, agayns his wille, amercimentz, amortize, apurtenaunce, clayme, *contumax*, creant, decree, enditement, essoyne, extorcion, felonie, forfeted, homicide, lachesse, licence, maintain, manslaughtre, occupien, patrimoyne, pledynge, questmonger, relesse, taillage, trespassen. These words do not belong, as one might have expected, to the Man of Law. The pilgrim who draws most heavily on the language of the law is the Parson in his attempt to explain 'what is Penitence.'

All but two of the words above – essoyne and extorcion – occur also in *Piers Plowman*. The poem owes a great deal to the tradition of penitential writings, and like the Parson's Tale its vocabulary overlaps considerably with works such as *Handlyng Synne*, *The Ayenbite of Inwit*, and *Jacob's Well*.[18] Indeed, whole phrases and sentences often correspond. For example, the author of *Jacob's Well* describes the great justice Herkenbald as follows: 'He sparyd no persone for loue, ne dreed, ne for wrethe, but þat in his demyng he dyde equite' (95/27); Langland says of Justice itself: '*Spiritus iusticie* spareth nat to spille hem þat ben gulty . . . For counteth he no kynges wreth . . . present . . . preyere or eny prinses lettres; He dede equite to alle euene-forth his knowyng' (C.21.309). Of thieves *Jacob's Well* says, 'And þey may noȝt ben assoyled, tyl þei haue made restitucyoun' (17/22); similarly Repentance to the sin of Coveitise, 'I kan þee noȝt assoille Til þow make restitucion' (B.5.271). *Jacob's Well* complains, 'False cysourys gon vp-on qwestys . . . & witnessen aȝens trewthe' (131/8); Langland says of the wench Wanhope, 'Hir sire was a Sysour þat neuere swoor truþe . . . atteynt at ech a queste' (B.20.161).

There can be little doubt that Langland's use of legal terminology was conditioned by the Christian view of salvation, particularly as that view was expressed in penitential writings. But his use of it was far from conventional. What distinguishes Langland from other writers of the period, including Chaucer, is his tendency to press the traditional metaphors of Christian thought to their limit. It was commonplace, for

---

[17] *Law and Politics in the Middle Ages* (Ithaca, N.Y.: Cornell Univ. Press, 1975), 45.

[18] A good survey of vernacular moral treatises will be found in W. A. Pantin, *The English Church in the Fourteenth Century* (Cambridge: Cambridge Univ. Press, 1955), chapter 10.

example, to say that at the Last Judgement, everyone would be required to 'render an account' of his deeds. The phrase comes from the parable of the unjust steward, 'Redde rationem villicationis tuae' (Luke 16:2); it was elaborated by numerous writers and served as the theme of a famous sermon preached by Thomas Wimbledon about 1387 at Paul's Cross, London.[19] Yet the degree to which Langland exploits the literal ramifications of the idea is unparalleled. The final rendering of accounts before the Lord will be like the manorial accountings that took place every year throughout the country. The poor should take heart, Langland says, for 'seruaunt3 þat seruen lordes selde fallen in arerage, But þo þat kepen þe lordes catel, clerkes and Reues' (B.10.476–77); indeed, their very poverty will be entered into the reckoning as a credit:

> I wiste neuere renk þat riche was, þat whan he rekene sholde,
> Whan he drogh to his deeþ day þat he ne dredde hym soore,
> And þat at þe rekenyng in Arrerage fel raþer þan out of dette.
> Ther þe poore dar plede and preue by pure reson
> To haue allowaunce of his lord; by þe lawe he it cleymeþ.
>
> (B.14.106–110)

The word *allowaunce*, unattested in English before its use here, is a bookkeeping term meaning a credit or reimbursement. In rendering his account to the lord (or the lord's steward), a reeve would usually claim an 'allowance' for expenses incurred as part of his service. This was deducted from his receipts, and the balance showed him to be quit, in debt, or even owed something additional from his lord. In Langland's analogy, therefore, what the poor servant of the Lord claims 'by þe lawe' is not 'praise or approval' (Skeat) or 'favour' (Schmidt) but *literally* a credit for what he has paid already in suffering and deprivation.

Such daring literalism has not been generally appreciated (though Robert Adams has shown that Langland's position is not so heterodox as it first appears[20]). The impulse of most critics has been to draw the poet's diction back from perceived extremes toward the center of ordinary usage. The same is true of the dictionaries. Both the *Oxford English Dictionary* and the *Middle English Dictionary* show a tendency, as Fred Robinson notes of Old English lexicography, to 'flatten

---

[19] Ed. Ione Kemp Knight, *Wimbledon's Sermon: Redde Rationem Villicationis Tue* (Pittsburgh: Duquesne Univ. Press, 1967).
[20] 'Piers's Pardon and Langland's Semi-Pelagianism,' *Traditio* 39 (1983), 367–418; 'Langland's Theology,' *A Companion to Piers Plowman*, ed. John A. Alford (Berkeley: Univ. of California Press, 1988), 87–114.

out' the meanings of words in poetic texts.[21] The *OED* does not recognize the technical meaning of *allowaunce* until Langland's use of it later in a more apparently secular environment: 'When thy lord loketh to haue allouaunce of his bestes And of þe moneye thow haddest therwith . . . wo is the thenne!' (C.9.271–73). The *MED* gives as the definition of *allowaunce* in B.14.110 (above): 'Commendation, approbation.'

The tendency of lexicographers to deny or overlook specialized usage in general writings may be traced not only to justifiable conservatism, but also to the practical necessity of working from the immediate contexts of words (usually no more than can be transcribed conveniently on a small piece of paper or 'slip'). However, it is in the very nature of poetry that the immediate context is often inadequate to the purpose. A given word may carry an assigned meaning; it may be part of a motif or recurring metaphor; over the course of a long poem like *Piers Plowman* it may acquire a highly charged meaning or multiplicity of meanings. Given the immediate context of *resonable* in B.13.285 ('Was noon swich as hymself . . . Yhabited as an heremyte, an ordre by hymselue, Religion saunȝ rule and resonable obedience'), the *MED* defines the word as 'Of or pertaining to a rule or statute' and glosses the phrase 'resonable obedience' as 'obedience to a religious rule.' This, it must be said, is not very helpful. Clearly *resonable* 'pertains' in some way to a religious rule, but its essential meaning is left unexplained. To clarify that meaning, however, requires a comparison with other contexts of *resonable* (C.3.336, C.6.33), also of *unresonable* (B.6.151, B.15.461), and above all an understanding of *resoun* itself in the overall design of the poem. As he frequently does with other words, Langland uses *resoun* with its Latin equivalent constantly in mind. 'Resonable' obedience is that which is in accordance with the concept of *ratio*, that is, with law, order, measure.[22] 'Resonable' conduct, in this sense of the word, is especially appropriate to the regulated life of religious, but it is also and emphatically the ideal put forth by Langland for all classes of society.

When all of the points raised above are taken into account – the inherent ambiguity of words in both common and legal usage, the poetic tendency to exploit rather than to resolve such ambiguity, the critical

---

[21] 'Lexicography and Literary Criticism: A Caveat,' *Philological Essays: Studies in Old and Middle English Language and Literature in Honour of Herbert Dean Meritt*. Ed. James L. Rosier (The Hague: Mouton, 1970), 99–110.

[22] See John A. Alford, 'The Idea of Reason in *Piers Plowman*,' *Medieval English Studies Presented to George Kane*. Ed. Donald Kennedy, R. A. Waldron, and Joseph S. Wittig (Cambridge: D. S. Brewer, 1988), 199–215.

importance of context, and so forth – it is clear that compiling a glossary of a complex poem like *Piers Plowman* is necessarily an act of interpretation.[23] Many readers may question the inclusion or omission of certain words, or take issue with some of the definitions. But if the glossary leads to a greater appreciation of the poet's legal diction and its place in the structure of his thought, it will have served its main purpose.

Most entries conform to the following order:

(1) *Entry word*. Each word has been chosen on the basis of its significance in secular or ecclesiastical law. The selection, unavoidably subjective, includes terms peculiar to the law (*supersedeas*, intestate, mainpernour), references to officers of the law (sherreve, commissarie) and other persons defined by a legal relationship (patroun, client), words that signify legal procedures, instruments, etc. (alleggen, trien, patente) and actions subject to legal endorsement or penalty (biquethen, defrauden), ordinary words that have technical meanings in legal usage (imaginen, preiere, tale), and legal phrases and maxims (licence and leve, reles and remissioun, *intentio iudicat hominem*). A small number of words have no legal significance in themselves (e.g., faitour, lunatik, pestilence, salarie), but their association with specific legal documents or doctrines may illuminate their use in the poem. The spelling of entry words conforms usually to that of the *MED*, including the use of *th* for thorn, *gh* for medial yogh, *y* for initial yogh, and *i* for *y*. For alphabetical purposes, phrases are treated like single words (apeiren, *a poena et a culpa*, apostata, and so forth). Verbs are given in the infinitive form. Many entries are preceded by an asterisk, indicating that the word is unattested by the *OED* and *MED* for any source earlier than the presumed date of the version cited (that is, about 1370 for the A text, 1377 for B, 1385 for C[24]); that some of these words were introduced into the manuscript tradition by later scribes is possible.

(2) *Definition*. On the whole the definitions coincide with those given by the *OED* and *MED*. But often they are more specific or technical (for example, allowen, fin, love, maken, pensioun, procuratour, ravishen, recoveren, shewen, stoppen, tale, tenen, visiting, writen); and a good number are original (for example, apeiren [I], communes [I], curtesie, devoutour, glosen, knowen [II], macere, Paulines). The order of multiple definitions is usually from specific to

---

[23] Similarly, Kane says of the art of translation: 'The essential beginning must be interpretation' ('Poetry and Lexicography,' 6).

[24] The dates are approximate. For an authoritative discussion, see George Kane, 'The Text,' *A Companion to Piers Plowman* (cited above), 184–86.

general, since in most cases the general definition does not fall within the scope of the glossary. Thus *marien* is defined only in the rare senses of 'to endow a daughter' and 'to witness a marriage,' without notice of the more ordinary senses of 'to marry off (a daughter),' 'to get married,' and so forth. An asterisk immediately before a definition indicates that this particular meaning is unattested by any earlier record of the word.

(3) *Citations*. Quotations are from the following editions of *Piers*: the A version, George Kane, ed. (London: Athlone, 1960); the B version, George Kane and E. Talbot Donaldson, eds. (London: Athlone, 1975); the C version, Derek Pearsall, ed. (London: Arnold, 1978). As of press time for this book, the Athlone edition of the C version, edited by George Russell, had not appeared; in most cases, however, its readings do not vary significantly from those given here. Passages cited from W. W. Skeat's parallel-text edition (Oxford, 1886) are indicated by the abbreviation 'Sk.' Quotations are often given, after the example of the *OED* and *MED*, in shortened form. Ellipses are marked, but changes from lower to upper case letters at the beginning of a citation are not. Each quotation is followed by cross-references, in parentheses, to one or both of the other versions of the poem.

(4) *Additional citations*. Additional uses of the word in *Piers* may be cited but not quoted. These citations include examples that firmly support the definition, examples in which the legal associations are tenuous or uncertain, and examples that serve for comparison or contrast. They do not represent a full concordance. The citations given for terms peculiar to the law (chalengeable, eschete, merciment) are complete; but those given for words more common and frequent (demen, justice, leaute, treuthe) represent only a generous sampling.

(5) *Citations from other Middle English works*. These are meant not only to clarify Langland's usage but also to connect it with literary tradition. The heavy representation of didactic and penitential treatises is deliberate. For the most part the citations are additional to those given in the *OED* and *MED*.

(6) *Citations from legal sources*. Where useful or appropriate, citations from legal sources (writs, charters, pleas, yearbooks, treatises, etc.) are included. Dates are not. They are sometimes interesting but nearly always irrelevant to the purpose. Legal usage is highly conservative; and for every instance cited from fourteenth-century sources in Latin and French, there are usually countless earlier instances of the word in thirteenth- and even twelfth-century documents. Statutes are cited, in the conventional way, by regnal year (e.g., 13 Edw. III). The list of primary sources is varied – exemplifying the uses of the manorial

xix

courts, the courts of Westminster, the law merchant, borough customs, the law of the church – but it is not a list for constructing the history of English law or jurisprudence. Of the fanciful *Mirror of Justices*, for example, F. W. Maitland says indignantly, '[O]ur author chooses to regard every breach of the law as sin. . . . Religion, morality, law, these are for him all one; they are for him law. . . . But it was no more the fashion in the middle ages than it is the fashion nowadays for a lawyer or for anyone else to speak habitually as if law and law-courts and parliaments existed for the purpose of saving the souls of sinners.'[25] It was not the fashion. Yet this is precisely the way in which Langland also speaks.

(7) *Synonyms and related words*. These appear in capital letters, principally at the foot of the entry but frequently (in order to avoid unnecessary repetition) within the definition itself. They are a selective, not complete, guide to similar concepts elsewhere in the poem.

(8) *Commentary*. At various points in numerous entries, relevant comments by legal historians and by Langland scholars are cited or quoted. However, no attempt has been made to cite all the relevant comments that appear in editions of the poem. The notes of Skeat, Bennett, Pearsall, and Schmidt remain indispensable. The present work is merely a supplement.

[25] *The Mirror of Justices*, ed. W. J. Whittaker, with an Introduction by F. W. Maitland, Selden Society 7 (London: Quaritch, 1893), xxviii–xxx.

ABBREVIATIONS

adj.	adjective
adv.	adverb
AF	Anglo-French
c.	chapter
es	extra series
esp.	especially
fig.	figurative(ly)
Fr.	French
gen.	general(ly)
L	Langland
Lat.	Latin
ME	Middle English
ML	Medieval Latin
ns	new series
OE	Old English
OF	Old French
pl.	plural
p.pl.	past participle
sb.	somebody
specif.	specifically
st.	statute
sth.	something

ABBREVIATIONS OF WORKS CITED

Primary Sources

Abbey of H.G.	*The Charter of the Abbey of the Holy Ghost*, in Carl Horstman, ed., *Yorkshire Writers: Richard Rolle of Hampole ... and His Followers*, 2 vols. London: Sonnenschein, 1895. 2:337–362.
Assembly	*The Assembly of Ladies*, ed. Derek Pearsall, *The Floure and the Leafe and the Assembly of Ladies*. London: Thomas Nelson, 1962.
Ayenbite	Dan Michel, *Ayenbite of Inwyt*, ed. Richard Morris. EETS 23 (1866), newly collated by Pamela Gradon and reissued in 1965.
Bennett	J. A. W. Bennett, ed. *Piers Plowman: The Prologue and Passus I–VII of the B Text*. Oxford: Clarendon Press, 1972.
Bor. Cust.	*Borough Customs*, 2 vols., ed. Mary Bateson. Selden Society 18, 21. London: Quaritch, 1904, 1906.
Bracton	Henry de Bracton, *On the Laws and Customs of England*. 4 vols. Ed. and trans. by Samuel E. Thorne. Cambridge, Mass.: Belknap Press of Harvard Univ., in association with the Selden Society, 1968–77.
Britton	*Britton*, ed. F. M. Nichols, 2 vols. Oxford, 1865.
Brown XIV	Carleton Brown, ed. *Religious Lyrics of the XIVth Century*, 2nd edn rev. by G. V. Smithers. Oxford: Clarendon Press, 1952, rpt. 1965.
Brown XV	Carleton Brown, ed. *Religious Lyrics of the XVth Century*. Oxford: Clarendon Press, 1939, rpt. 1967.
Catholicon	*Catholicon Anglicum, An English-Latin Wordbook*, ed. Sidney J. H. Herrtage. EETS 75 (1881).
Chateau d'Amour	Kari Sajavaara, ed., *The Middle English Translations of Robert Grosseteste's 'Chateau d'Amour'*. Helsinki: Société Néophilologique, 1967.
Chancery	*Select Cases in Chancery*, ed. William Paley Baildon. Selden Society 10. London: Quaritch, 1896.
CIC	*Corpus Iuris Canonici*, 2 vols., ed. A. Friedberg. Graz: Akademische Druck- und Verlagsanstalt, 1955.

Court Baron	*The Court Baron*, ed. F. W. Maitland and William Paley Baildon. Selden Society 4. London: Quaritch, 1891.
Cov. Leet	*Coventry Leet Book*, ed. Mary Dormer Harris. EETS 134, 135, 138, 146 (1907–1913).
CT.	Geoffrey Chaucer, *The Canterbury Tales*, ed. F. N. Robinson, in *The Works of Geoffrey Chaucer*, 2nd edn Boston: Houghton Mifflin, 1957. (Individual tales are abbreviated *CT. Friar*, *CT. Pars.*, etc.)
D&P	*Dives and Pauper*, ed. Priscilla Barnum, 2 vols. EETS 275 (1976) and 280 (1980).
Durandus	William Durandus, *Speculum Iudiciale*, 2 vols. Basel, 1574; rpt. Aalen: Scientia Verlag, 1975.
Engl. Canons	*A Collection of the Laws and Canons of the Church of England*, trans. John Johnson, 2 vols. Oxford: Parker, 1850–51. (Unless noted otherwise, all quotations are from vol. 2.)
Eyre	*Year Books of Edward II (The Eyre of London, 14 Edward II, A. D. 1321)*, ed. Helen M. Cam. Selden Society 85. London: Quaritch, 1968.
Farmer	J. S. Farmer, *Lost Tudor Plays*. London: Early English Drama Society, 1907; rpt. Guildford: Traylen, 1966.
Fisher	John H. Fisher, Malcolm Richardson, and Jane L. Fisher. *An Anthology of Chancery English*. Knoxville: Univ. of Tennessee Press, 1984. (Cited by document and line, e.g., 32/6.)
Fleta	*Fleta*, ed. H. G. Richardson and G. O. Sayles. Selden Society 72. London: Quaritch, 1955 (books 1–2); Selden Society 89. London: Selden Society, 1972 (books 3–4). (Cited by book and chapter.)
Fortescue	John Fortescue, *De Laudibus Legum Anglie*, ed. and trans. by S. B. Chrimes. Cambridge: Cambridge University Press, 1942.
Gratian	Gratian, *Concordia Discordantium Canonum* (*CIC*, vol. 1).
Gamelyn	*Gamelyn*, ed. Donald B. Sands, *Middle English Verse Romances*. New York: Holt, Rinehart and Winston, 1966 (pp. 156–181).
Gower, *CA*	John Gower, *Confessio Amantis*, ed. G. C. Macaulay. EETS extra ser. 81 (1900, rpt. 1969).
Hall	Hubert Hall, ed. *A Formula Book of English Official Historical Documents*, 2 vols. 1908–9; rpt. New York: Burt Franklin, 1969.
Hand. Synne	Robert of Brunne, *Handlyng Synne*, ed. Frederick J. Furnivall. EETS 119, 123 (1901, 1903); rpt. as one vol. by Kraus Reprint, Millwood, NY, 1975.
Helmholz, *Defamation*	*Select Cases on Defamation to 1600*, ed. R. H. Helmholz. Selden Society 101. London: Selden Society, 1985.

Henryson	Robert Henryson, *The Moral Fables of Aesop*, ed. George D. Gopen. Notre Dame: Univ. of Notre Dame Press, 1987.
Hist. Poems	Rossell Hope Robbins, ed. *Historical Poems of the XIVth and XVth Centuries*. New York: Columbia Univ. Press, 1959.
Jac. Well	*Jacob's Well* (part 1), ed. Arthur Brandeis. EETS 115 (1900).
Kail	J. Kail, ed. *Twenty-Six Political and Other Poems*. EETS 124 (1904).
Kane	George Kane, ed. *Piers Plowman: The A Version*. London: Athlone, 1960.
K. Bench 5	*Select Cases in the Court of King's Bench under Edward III*, vol. 5, ed. G. O. Sayles. Selden Society 76. London: Quaritch, 1958.
K. Bench 6	*Select Cases in the Court of King's Bench under Edward III*, vol. 6, ed. G. O. Sayles. Selden Society 82. London: Quaritch, 1965.
K. Bench 7	*Select Cases in the Court of King's Bench under Richard II, Henry IV and Henry V*, vol. 7, ed. G. O. Sayles. Selden Society 88. London: Quaritch, 1971.
K. Counc.	*Select Cases before the King's Council 1243–1482*, ed. I. S. Leadam and J. F. Baldwin. Selden Society 35. Cambridge, Mass.: Harvard University Press, 1918.
K-D	George Kane and E. Talbot Donaldson, eds. *Piers Plowman: The B Version*. London: Athlone, 1975.
Launfal	*Sir Launfal*, ed. Donald B. Sands, *Middle English Verse Romances*. New York: Holt, Rinehart and Winston, 1966 (pp. 203–32).
LawMerch. 1	*Select Cases Concerning the Law Merchant*, vol. 1 (Local Courts), ed. Charles Gross. Selden Society 23. London: Quaritch, 1908.
LawMerch. 2	*Select Cases Concerning the Law Merchant*, vol. 2 (Central Courts), ed. Hubert Hall. Selden Society 46. London: Quaritch, 1930.
Lib. Alb.	*Liber Albus*, ed. Henry Thomas Riley, *Munimenta Gildhallae Londoniensis*, Rolls Series No. 12:1 (trans. 12:3). London: Longman, Brown, Green, Longmans, and Roberts, 1859.
Lib. Cust.	*Liber Custumarum*, ed. Henry Thomas Riley, *Munimenta Gildhallae Londoniensis*. Rolls Series No. 12:2. London: Longman, Green, Longman, and Roberts, 1860.
Lud. Cov.	*Ludus Coventriae*, ed. K. S. Block. EETS es 120 (1922, for 1917; rpt. 1960).
Lyndwood	William Lyndwood, *Provinciale*. Oxford: Hall, 1679.
Mankind	*Mankind*, ed. Mark Eccles, *The Macro Plays*. EETS 262 (1969).

Mirror	*The Mirror of Justices*, ed. William J. Whittaker, with an Introduction by Frederic William Maitland. Selden Society 7. London: Quaritch, 1893.
Moots	*Readings and Moots at the Inns of Court in the Fifteenth Century*, vol. 1, ed. Samuel E. Thorne. Selden Society 71. London: Quaritch, 1954.
Myrour	*A Myrour to Lewde Men and Wymmen*, ed. Venetia Nelson. Heidelberg: Carl Winter, 1981.
Nov. Narr.	*Novae Narrationes*, ed. Elsie Shanks. Selden Society 80. London: Quaritch, 1963.
Pearsall	Derek Pearsall, ed. *Piers Plowman: An Edition of the C-text*. London: Arnold, 1978; Berkeley and Los Angeles: Univ. of California Press, 1979.
Pr. Cons.	*The Pricke of Conscience*, ed. Richard Morris. Berlin: Asher, 1863; rpt. New York: AMS Press, 1973.
Pride of Life	Ed. Norman Davis, *Non-Cycle Plays and Fragments*. EETS supp. ser. 1 (1970), 90–105.
Respublica	Ed. Farmer (above).
Reynes	*The Commonplace Book of Robert Reynes of Acles: An Edition of Tanner MS 407*, ed. by Cameron Louis. New York: Garland, 1980.
Rigg-Brewer	A. G. Rigg and Charlotte Brewer, eds. *Piers Plowman: The Z Version*. Toronto: Pontifical Institute of Mediaeval Studies, 1983.
Robbins	Rossell Hope Robbins, ed. *Secular Lyrics of the XIVth and XVth Centuries*. 2nd edn Oxford: Clarendon Press, 1955, rpt. 1968.
Ross	*Middle English Sermons*, ed. W. O. Ross. EETS 209 (1940, for 1938; rpt. 1960).
RR	*Richard the Redeless* (see Skeat).
Ruffhead	Owen Ruffhead, ed., *The Statutes at Large from Magna Charta to the End of the Last Parliament, 1761*. 8 vols. London, 1763.
Schmidt	A. V. C. Schmidt, ed. *The Vision of Piers Plowman* (B Text). London: Dent, 1978.
Simonie	*The Simonie*, ed. Wright (see below), pp. 323–345.
Sisam	Celia and Kenneth Sisam, eds. *The Oxford Book of Medieval Verse*. Oxford: Clarendon, 1970.
Skeat	W. W. Skeat, ed. *The Vision of William Concerning Piers the Plowman ... together with Richard the Redeless*, 2 vols. Oxford: Oxford Univ. Press, 1886, rpt. 1961.
Skelton	John Skelton, *The Complete Poems*, ed. Philip Henderson. 4th edn London: Dent, 1964.
Spalding	Mary Caroline Spalding, ed. *The Middle English Charters of Christ*. Bryn Mawr College Monographs 15. Bryn Mawr: Bryn Mawr College, 1914.

SGGK	*Sir Gawain and the Green Knight*, ed. J. R. R. Tolkien and E. V. Gordon. 2nd edn rev. by Norman Davis. Oxford: Clarendon Press, 1967.
Spec. Sacerdot.	*Speculum Sacerdotale*, ed. Edward H. Weatherly. EETS 200 (1936).
ST	Thomas Aquinas, *Summa Theologica*, 6 vols. Rome, 1886–87. Trans. by Fathers of the English Dominican Province, 22 vols. London: Burns, Oates & Washbourne, 1920–25.
Statute, *Statutes*	*The Statutes of the Realm*. 9 vols. London: Eyre and Strahan, 1810–22.
St. Germ.	Christopher St. German, *Doctor and Student*, ed. T. F. T. Plucknett and J. L. Barton. Selden Society 91. London: Selden Society, 1974.
Stubbs	William Stubbs, *Select Charters*, 9th edn, rev. H. W. C. Davis. Oxford: Clarendon, 1929.
Upland	*Jack Upland, Friar Daw's Reply and Upland's Rejoinder*, ed. P. L. Heyworth. Oxford: Oxford Univ. Press, 1968.
Usk	Thomas Usk, *The Testament of Love*, ed. W. W. Skeat in *Chaucerian and Other Pieces*, vol. 7 (suppl.) of *The Complete Works of Geoffrey Chaucer*. Oxford: Oxford Univ. Press, 1897.
Vices	*The Book of Vices and Virtues*, ed. W. Nelson Francis. EETS 217 (1942, rpt. 1968).
Wilson	Thomas Wilson, *A Discourse on Usury* (1572), with intro. by R. H. Tawney. London: Bell, 1925; rpt. New York: Kelley, 1963.
Wright	Thomas Wright, ed. *The Political Songs of England*. London: Camden Society, 1839.
Writs	Elsa de Haas and G. D. G. Hall, eds., *Early Registers of Writs*. Selden Society 87. London: Quaritch. 1970.
Yrbk. Edw. II	*Yearbooks of 12 Edward II (1319)*, ed. J. P. Collas and T. F. T. Plucknett. Selden Society 70. London: Quaritch, 1951.
Yrbk. Edw. III	*Year Books of the Reign of King Edward the Third. Years XVIII and XIX*, ed. and trans. by Luke Owen Pike. Rolls Series 31b, vol. 12. London, 1905.

Secondary Works

Addleshaw G. W. O. Addleshaw, *Rectors, Vicars and Patrons in Twelfth and Early Thirteenth Century Canon Law*. London and New York: St. Anthony's Press, 1956.

Alford 1975 John A. Alford, 'Some Unidentified Quotations in *Piers Plowman*', *Modern Philology* 72 (1975), 390–99.

Alford 1982 John A. Alford, 'The Grammatical Metaphor: A Survey of Its Use in the Middle Ages', *Speculum* 57 (1982), 728–60.

Alford 1984 John A. Alford, 'More Unidentified Quotations in *Piers Plowman*', *Modern Philology* 81 (1984), 278–85.

Alford 1988 John A. Alford, ed. *A Companion to Piers Plowman*. Berkeley: Univ. of California Press, 1988.

Baldwin Anna P. Baldwin, *The Theme of Government in Piers Plowman*. Cambridge: D. S. Brewer, 1981.

Baldwin, J.W. John W. Baldwin, *The Medieval Theories of the Just Price: Romanists, Canonists, and Theologians in the Twelfth and Thirteenth Centuries*. Philadelphia: American Philosophical Society, 1959.

Barbour W. T. Barbour, *The History of Contract in Early English Equity*. Oxford Studies in Social and Legal History, vol. 7, ed. Paul Vinogradoff. Oxford: Clarendon, 1914.

Barraclough Geoffrey Barraclough, *Public Notaries and the Papal Curia*. London: Macmillan, 1934.

Bellamy J. G. Bellamy, *The Law of Treason in England in the Later Middle Ages*. Cambridge: Cambridge University Press, 1970.

Bennett, H.S. H. S. Bennett, *Life on the English Manor*. Cambridge: Cambridge Univ. Press, 1948.

Bethurum Dorothy Bethurum, 'Stylistic Features of the Old English Laws', *Modern Language Review* 27 (1932), 263–279.

Black Henry Campbell Black, *Black's Law Dictionary*, 5th edn. St. Paul, MN: West Publishing, 1979.

Blackstone William Blackstone, *Commentaries on the Laws of England*, 4 vols. Oxford: Clarendon, 1765.

Bloomfield Morton W. Bloomfield, *Piers Plowman as a Fourteenth-Century Apocalypse*. New Brunswick, NJ: Rutgers University Press, 1962.

Buckland	W. W. Buckland, *A Text-book of Roman Law from Augustus to Justinian*. 3rd edn, rev. by Peter Stein. Cambridge: Cambridge University Press, 1963.
Cam	Helen Cam, *Law-Finders and Law-Makers in Medieval England*. New York: Barnes and Noble, 1963.
Cath. Encyc.	*The Catholic Encyclopedia*, 15 vols. New York: The Encyclopedia Press, 1913 (orig. publ. in 1907).
Cheney	C. R. Cheney, *Episcopal Visitation of Monasteries in the Thirteenth Century*. Manchester: Manchester Univ. Press, 1931.
Chrimes	S. B. Chrimes, *An Introduction to the Administrative History of Mediaeval England*. Oxford: Blackwell, 1966.
Cohen	Herman Cohen, *A History of the English Bar and Attornatus to 1450*. London: Sweet and Maxwell, 1929.
Cotgr.	Randle Cotgrave, *A Dictionarie of the French and English Tongues*. London: Adam Islip, 1611; facs. repr. Columbia, SC: University of South Carolina Press, 1950.
Cowell	John Cowell, *The Interpreter*. London, 1658.
Cyc. Law Dict.	Walter Adams Shumaker, *The Cyclopedic Law Dictionary*. Chicago: Callaghan, 1940.
Denholm-Young	N. Denholm-Young, *Seignorial Administration in England*. London: Oxford Univ. Press, 1937.
De Roover	Raymond A. De Roover, *San Bernardino of Siena and Sant' Antonino of Florence: The Two Great Economic Thinkers of the Middle Ages*. Boston: Baker Library, Harvard Univ. Graduate School of Business Administration, 1967.
Donaldson	E. Talbot Donaldson, *Piers Plowman. The C-Text and Its Poet*. Yale Studies in English 113. New Haven: Yale Univ. Press, 1949.
DuCange	C. D. DuCange, *Glossarium ad Scriptores Mediae et Infimae Latinitatis*. 6 vols. Paris, 1733.
Edler	Florence Edler, *Glossary of Mediaeval Terms of Business. Italian Series 1200–1600*. Cambridge, Mass.: Mediaeval Academy of America, 1934.
Fourquin	Guy Fourquin, *Lordship and Feudalism in the Middle Ages*, trans. Iris and A. L. Lytton Sells. London: Allen and Unwin, 1976.
Ganshof	François Louis Ganshof, *Feudalism*, trans. Philip Grierson. 3rd English edn. New York: Harper and Row, 1964.
Geldart	William M. Geldart, *Elements of English Law*. 5th edn rev. by William Holdsworth. London: Oxford Univ. Press, 1953.
Goebel	Julius Goebel, Jr. *Felony and Misdemeanor: A Study in the History of Criminal Law*. Philadelphia: University of Pennsylvania Press, 1976 (orig. publ. in 1937).

Gray	Nick Gray, 'Langland's Quotations from the Penitential Tradition', *Modern Philology* 84 (1986), 53–60.
Hall, *Antiq.*	Hubert Hall, *The Antiquities and Curiosities of the Exchequer*. London: Stock, 1891.
Hall, *Studies*	Hubert Hall, *Studies in English Official Historical Documents*. Cambridge: The University Press, 1908.
Harding 1966	Alan Harding, *A Social History of English Law*. Harmondsworth: Penguin, 1966.
Harding 1973	Alan Harding, *The Law Courts of Medieval England*. London: George Allen and Unwin, 1973.
Helmholz	R. H. Helmholz, *Marriage Litigation in Medieval England*. Cambridge: Cambridge University Press, 1974.
Holdsworth	William Holdsworth, *A History of English Law*, 14 vols., 7th edn. London: Methuen, 1956.
Hussey	S. S. Hussey, ed., *Piers Plowman: Critical Approaches*. London: Methuen, 1969.
Jowitt	William Allen Jowitt, *The Dictionary of English Law*. London: Sweet and Maxwell, 1959.
Kiralfy	A. K. R. Kiralfy, *The English Legal System*, 3rd edn. London: Sweet and Maxwell, 1960.
LeBras	Gabriel LeBras, 'Canon Law', *The Legacy of the Middle Ages*, ed. C. G. Crump and E. F. Jacob. Oxford: Clarendon, 1926.
Levy-Ullmann	Henri Levy-Ullmann, *The English Legal Tradition: Its Sources and History*, trans. M. Mitchell. London: Macmillan, 1935.
Maitland	F. W. Maitland, *Roman Canon Law in the Church of England*. London: Methuen, 1898.
Maitland, *Forms*	F. W. Maitland, *The Forms of Action at Common Law*, ed. A. H. Chayter and W. J. Whittaker. Cambridge: Cambridge Univ. Press, 1962.
McKisack	May McKisack, *The Fourteenth Century 1307–1399*, Vol. 5 of *The Oxford History of England*, ed. George Clark. Oxford: Clarendon Press, 1959.
MED	*Middle English Dictionary*, ed. Hans Kurath, Sherman Kuhn, John Reidy, Robert Lewis, et al. Ann Arbor: Univ. of Michigan Press, 1952– .
Noonan	John T. Noonan, *The Scholastic Analysis of Usury*. Cambridge: Harvard Univ. Press, 1957.
O'Brien	George A. T. O'Brien, *An Essay on Mediaeval Economic Teaching*. London: Longmans, Green, 1920.
OED	*Oxford English Dictionary*.
Osborn	P. G. Osborn, *A Concise Law Dictionary*. 5th edn. London: Sweet and Maxwell, 1964.
Oxf. Comp.	David M. Walker, *The Oxford Companion to Law*. Oxford: Clarendon Press, 1980.

Pantin	W. A. Pantin, *The English Church in the Fourteenth Century*. Cambridge: Cambridge Univ. Press, 1955.
P&M	Frederick Pollock and Frederic William Maitland, *The History of English Law*, 2nd edn (1898), reissued with a new introduction by S. F. C. Milsom, 2 vols. Cambridge: Cambridge Univ. Press, 1968.
Plucknett	T. F. T. Plucknett, *A Concise History of the Common Law*. 5th edn. Boston: Little, Brown, 1956.
Plucknett, *Statutes*	T. F. T. Plucknett, *Statutes and their Interpretation in the First Half of the Fourteenth Century*. Cambridge: Cambridge Univ. Press, 1922.
Purvis	J. S. Purvis, *An Introduction to Ecclesiastical Records*. London: St. Anthony's Press, 1953.
Rickert	Edith Rickert, *Chaucer's World*. New York: Columbia University Press, 1948, rpt. 1964.
Sheehan	M. M. Sheehan, *The Will in Medieval England*. Toronto: Pontifical Institute of Mediaeval Studies, 1963.
Simpson	A. W. B. Simpson, *An Introduction to the History of the Land Law*. Oxford: Oxford Univ. Press, 1961.
Stokes	Myra Stokes, *Justice and Mercy in Piers Plowman: A Reading of the B Text Visio*. London and Canberra: Croom Helm, 1984.
Stroud	Frederick Stroud, *Judicial Dictionary of Words and Phrases*. 3rd edn. London: Sweet and Maxwell, 1953.
Szittya	Penn R. Szittya, *The Antifraternal Tradition in Medieval Literature*. Princeton: Princeton Univ. Press, 1986.
Ullmann	Walter Ullmann, *Law and Politics in the Middle Ages*. Ithaca, NY: Cornell Univ. Press, 1975.
Woodcock	Brian L. Woodcock, *Medieval Ecclesiastical Courts in the Diocese of Canterbury*. London: Geoffrey Cumberlege, 1952.

A

ABOUGHT THE TIME *Fig.* paid interest on money: B.13.375 And what body borwed of me abouȝte þe tyme (C.6.247). The idea that usury involves the selling of time, though argued by Seneca, Aquinas, et al., is rejected by some canon lawyers, who note that ownership does not pass (Noonan 43, 48–50, 66, 80–81 passim). Nevertheless, Thomas Wilson can still invoke it in the sixteenth century: 'Doth not the sunne shyne upon us freelye? The ayre is open to us all, and wee breathe, thoroughe goddes great mercy: the tyme endureth for our benefite. And wil these idle men sell the sunne, the ayer, and the tyme for their proper gayne?' (288). See USURIE.

ABSOLUCIOUN A document granting remission of sins; an INDULGENCE: A.8.66 Alle libbyng laboureris ... Þat trewely taken, & trewely wynnen ... Hadde þe same absolucioun þat sent was to peris (B.7.64).

ACCEPTOR PERSONARUM See *NE SITIS PERSONARUM ACCEPTORES*

ACCIOUN 'An action is no other thing than a lawful claim of one's right' (*Mirror* 43); cause or grounds for a lawsuit: C.1.94 Kynges and knyghtes sholde ... halden with hem and here þat han trewe accion. Cf. *Jac.Well* 130/34: 'A fals pleyntyf ... feynyth a fals accyoun'; *D&P* 2:156/84: 'Neyþer of hem hat lauful accioun aȝenys hym.' CAUSE.

ACCORDEN **I.** In legal disputes, to arrive at a settlement or compromise; to be reconciled: C.3.392 How þat cliauntes acorde acounteth mede litel; B.17.309 Þe kyng may do no mercy til boþe men acorde (C.19.284); C.3.394; A.5.177 (B.5.328, C.6.386); B.20.353 (C.22.353). Cf. *Jac.Well* 16/7: 'We denouncyn hem acursed þat mede takyn, to lettyn þe pees, þat þe partyes pletyng & stryvyng in þe lawe to-gedere schulde noȝt ben acordyd' (see Lyndwood 55 [De pace & concordia reformanda]). Blackstone 3:15–16: 'AC-CORD is a satisfaction agreed upon between the party injuring and the party injured; which, when performed, is a bar of all actions upon this account.' **II.** To agree; to concur in a judgement or statement of fact: B.4.158 Kynde wit acorded þerwiþ [i.e., with Reason's verdict on Mede]; B.4.91 Wit acordeþ þerwiþ and witnessede þe same (A.4.78, C.4.87); B.3.319 After þe dede þat is doon oon doom shal rewarde Mercy or no mercy as Truthe may acorde (Schmidt B.3.319 moste acorde; C.3.471). Cf. *Lib.Alb.* 508: 'En quele Parlement accorde estoit et assentuz'; Fisher 142/50 ff.: 'Examined vpon þe first article ... he accorded with wawton: in the þridde ... he accorded in his

1

deposicion with wawton and Enderby,' etc. The phrase 'as Truthe may acorde' translates the judicial formula 'according to the degree of one's offence' (secundum quantitatem delicti illius [see TRUTH]); cf. C.8.36 Loke þe tene no tenaunt but treuthe wol assente.

ACCOUNT   A financial record or statement; more generally, any explanation concerning the discharge of responsibilities: C.7.40 Reuthe is to here rekenynge when we shal rede acountes (B.5.427); A.Prol.91; A.7.81 (B.6.89, C.8.98); A.8.172 (B.7.194, C.9.341); C.13.34; B.19.462 (C.21.462). Cf. *K.Counc.* 12: 'E par ceus roules tendi de rendre aconte.' For a selection of formulas used in royal accounts, see Hall 2:91–125. RESONABLE ACCOUNT.

ACCOUNTEN   I. To keep or present an official record or statement (of funds, goods); to render account: C.11.300 Selde falleth þe seruant so depe in arrerage As doth the reue or contrerollor þat rykene moet and acounten.
    II. To receive an account or reckoning: C.7.33 ꝺut kan y nother solfe ne synge... Ac y can ... holden a knyhtes court and acounte with þe reue; B.11.132 Ac reson shal rekene wiþ hym [a reneyed caytif]... And conscience acounte wiþ hym and casten hym in arerage (C.12.65); B.4.11 (C.4.11). REKENEN.

ACCUSEN   To charge (sb.) with an offence; to impugn; to indict: C.Prol.95 Consience cam and cused hem – and þe comune herde it; C.2.245; A.3.161 (B.3.174, C.3.219). The term occurs only in collocation with CONSCIENCE, whose office *in foro conscientiae* is to accuse. ACOUPEN, APPELEN, CHALENGEN, IMPUGNEN.

ACOUPEN   To accuse (sb.) of a crime or sin: B.13.458 Conscience acouped hym þerof in a curteis manere. Cf. *Pr.Consc.* 80/2947: 'He es acouped of felony Byfor kynges iustice.' ACCUSEN, CHALENGEN; see also COUPABLE, COUPE.

ACURSEN   To sentence or condemn (sb.); to excommunicate (sb.): B.Prol. 99 Drede is at þe laste Lest crist in Consistorie acorse ful manye (C.Prol.127); A.3.131 (B.3.142, C.3.178); B.20.263 (C.22.263). Cf. *D&P* 1:256: 'Men of holy chirche schuldyn ben disgradid [for perjury], lewid folc acursid.' CURSEN, CURSING.

AD PRISTINUM STATUM IRE   'To return to the first state,' that is, (1) to a state of grace, in which the penitent has to his credit as much merit as though he had never sinned, or (2) to a state of 'good fame' (cf. INFAMIS) with the restoration of all legal privileges: B.10.325 Ac þer shal come a kyng ... And amende Monyals, Monkes and Chanons, And puten hem to hir penaunce, *Ad pristinum statum ire* (C.5.171). The phrase is a common formula in canonical and penitential writings (see Alford 1984, Gray 1986). On (1) the doctrine of the reviviscence of merit, see *Cath. Encyc.*, 'Penance' (p. 623); the doctrine lies behind Grace-Dieu's assurance to the pilgrim in Lydgate's *Pilgrimage of the*

Life of Man: only repent and be 'Restoryd to thy ffyrste place' (EETS es 83 [1901]: 343/12612). On (2) the restoration of good fame, see *D&P* 1:256: 'Synneris whan þei han don penance for hir synne & ben amendith arn be þe lawe restoryd aȝeyn to her fame so þat þey mon ben witnessis in doom, and her oth owyth ben receyuyd.'

ADVOCAT See VOKETTE

*AIEL Grandfather; ancestor: B.15.323 Allas, lordes and ladies, lewed counseil haue ye To ȝyue from youre heires þat youre Aiels yow lefte. Cf. Fisher 203/4: 'Besechit mekely youre poure liege men . . . that they shold haue here Gylde and alle here libertees and frauncheses that they hadde in the tyme of kyng Harry Aiel of kyng Iohn'; *Moots* 88: 'Si soit aile . . . et le terre descend sur le pere. . . .' For writs of aiel, see *Writs* 91; *K.Counc.* 60ff.; Blackstone 3:186.

ALDERMAN The chief official of a ward, charged among other things with holding the WARDMOTE; a member of the ruling body of a city or borough: C.4.188 *Audiatis alteram partem* amonges aldremen and comeneres. Cf. *The Records of the City of Norwich 1* 115: 'Euery ward shal chese be hem self an ardyrman and iij commoners for ye commone counseill of ye same Cite' (cited in *MED*), and *Cov.Leet* 442 ('the Maire, Aldermen & Comiens'). *Lib.Alb.* 3:95: 'And it is provided, that every Alderman, in his Wardmote, shall diligently enquire as to misdoers resorting to and staying in his Ward; and if any such persons shall be found by presentment and indictment of the good folks of the Ward, let them be forthwith bodily attached. . . . And every Alderman is to hold his Wardmote, in all points as heretofore they have done, that is to say, four times in the year.' The aldermen of London also sat in the Court of Husting, presided over by the mayor (Cam 91). Blackstone 1:76. See SENATOUR.

ALLEGGEN To cite (sth.) in defence against or in support of a charge; to bring forward (sth.) as a legal ground or plea: B.11.96: It is *licitum* for lewed men to legge þe soþe . . . ; ech a lawe it graunteþ, Excepte persons and preestes and prelates of holy chirche. Cf. *Pearl* 703: 'Forþy to corte quen þou schal com Per alle oure causeȝ schal be tryed, Alegge þe ryȝt, þou may be innome.' On *Pearl*'s use of the word, see Dorothy Everett and Naomi Hurnard, 'Legal Phraseology in a Passage in *Pearl*,' *Medium Aevum* 16 (1947), 9–15. *K.Counc.* 13: 'The aforesaid Roger and Henry came to court and alleged [aleggerent] that he wrongfully claimed this debt against them.' ALLEGGEN AND PREVEN, PLEDEN, SPEKEN.

ALLEGGEN AND PREVEN To state the ground of a legal defence or charge and then to support it: B.11.89 [Accused friars] wole aleggen . . . and by þe gospel preuen: *Nolite iudicare quemquam* (C.12.30). Black 68: '*Allegata et probata*. Things alleged and proved. The allegations made by a party to a suit, and the proof adduced in their support.'

3

*ALLOWAUNCE   Credit or reimbursement for expenses (esp. those incurred in the service of another): B.14.110 I wiste neuere renk þat riche was, þat whan he rekene sholde, Whan he droȝ to his deeþ day, þat he ne dredde hym soore, And þat at þe rckenyng in arrerage fel, raþer þan out of dette. Ther þe poore dar plede and preue by pure reson To haue allowaunce of his lord; by þe lawe he it cleymeþ (C.15.288); C.9.271. Cf. *Cov. Leet* 114: 'Wherof thei aske alowans of lvj li. [etc.] of bates & oder discharges . . . Also they aske alowance of xlvj s. ij d. that myght not be leued for pouerte & oder causes. Summa allocacionis lviij li, x s. iij d.' Hall 2:91: 'The normal Account should . . . consist of the following parts or clauses: 1. The Heading . . . 2. The Charge . . . 3. The Discharge . . . 4. The Balance (ascertained by subtracting the 'sum' of the Allowances from the 'sum' of the Charge) proving the Accountant to be quit or indebted or possessed of a surplus as the case may be.' Thus *Cov. Leet* 101: 'Joh. Michell and Joh. Euerdon render accounts for Wildegrise's mayo-ralty. Charge £78. 8s. 9d. Allowance £53. 15s. 6½d. Balance in arrears £24. 13s. 2½d.'; *Writs* 212: 'The auditors of the aforesaid account have unduly oppressed the said A. in respect of the said account, debiting him with receipts which he has not received and not allowing [non allocando] in his favour expenses and reasonable outgoings' (the language repeats that of the statute Westminster II, 13 Edw. I c. 11). See ALLOWEN (I).

ALLOWEN   I. To assign (to sb.) as a right or due; to credit; to reimburse or reward (Fr. *allouer* < Lat. *allocare*): B.12.290 Ne wolde neuere trewe god but trewe truþe were allowed (C.14.212); B.10.439; B.10.441; B.16.233 (C.18.251). Cf. Statute 3 Edw. I c. 19: 'The debt shall be allowed in the exchequer [soit la dette allowe al Escheqer, quoted in *Fleta* II.33 as: allocetur debitum in saccario], so that it shall no more come in the summons [or appear in the records]'; *Cov. Leet* 59: '[It is ordained] þat John Cambirge be alowed for his costis þat he made agaynst the comyng of kyng Henre the Fifte.' ALLOWAUNCE, DISALLOWEN.
    II. To praise or commend (sb.); hence, gen. to sanction or permit (Fr. *alouer* < Lat. *allaudare*): B.15.4 Some lakkede my lif – allowed it fewe; C.3.74. *OED*: 'Between the two primary significations there naturally arose a variety of uses blending them in the general idea of *assign with approval*.' L's usage frequently suggests the blending of reward and praise: C.12.193; C.18.82, etc.

AL MANER OF MEN   A standard phrase in writs, charters, etc. (often com-bined with expressions such as LERED AND LEWED, high and low, rich and poor, etc.) to bar the exclusion of any persons or estates: A.Prol.18 A fair feld ful of folk fand I þere betwene Of alle maner of men, þe mene & þe riche (B.Prol.18, C.Prol.20); B.14.183 Thus . . . Iesu crist seide . . . to riche and to poore . . . to alle maner peple (C.16.34 And lereth lewed and lered, hey and lowe); B.2.56; A.7.21 (B.6.19, C.8.17); A.7.208 (B.6.222, C.8.232); C.13.70; B.17.353 (C.19.328); B.19.185 (C.21.184); B.20.112 (C.22.112). Cf. Statute 14 Edw. III c. 8: coroners shall answer 'a tote manere des gentz'; Fisher 4/2: 'We wyl that ye doo make writtes of proclamacion [that . . .] al maner men that wil bryng vitailles vn to oure tovn of Caen,' etc.; Reynes 117/95: 'Alle maner men schall aknowen vs . . . to be holden and be this present obligacion bounden to Raff Pye.'

AMENDEMENT   Alteration (of a document or judgement): C.22.135 [Cov-eitise] iogged til a iustice. . . And ouertulde al his treuthe with 'Taek this on amendement' (B.20.135). Skeat explains: 'This is a humorous allusion to a sort of mock tournament. Simony runs a tilt at the justice's ear, and by a crafty whisper of a bribe overturns all his ideas of truth and justice. He accompanies his offer of money with the words – "take this [deed, and at the same time this money] on amendment"; meaning, "surely you can amend this".' Cf. *Mirror* 122: 'And now justices . . . can falsify and suppress and lose and amend [amender] and impair writs without discovery or punishment.'

AMENDEN   **I.** To pay for, satisfy, give amends or BOTE (for a wrong or a wrongdoer); *theolog.*, to make satisfaction for one's sins or, through the Crucifixion, to make satisfaction for the sins of others; thus also (in speaking of God or his ministers) to forgive or absolve: B.4.90 And he [Wrong] amendes mowe make lat maynprise hym haue, And be borȝ for his bale and buggen hym boote, Amenden þat mysdede and eueremoore þe bettre (A.4.77, C.4.86); B.1.168 [God] Loked on vs wiþ loue and leet his sone dye Mekely for oure mysdedes to amenden vs alle [i.e., to provide, as satisfaction for our sins, what we are unable to provide ourselves] (A.1.142, C.1.164); B.7.15 Bys-shopes . . . in as muche as þei mowe amenden alle synfulle, Arn peres wiþ þe Apostles; A.1.142 (B.1.168, C.1.164); B.4.96; B.5.601 (C.7.248); A.6.83 (B.5.596, C.7.244); A.11.79 (B.10.126); B.10.446; B.11.138 (C.12.71); B.13.408; B.14.188; B.16.271 (C.18.288); B.17.240 (C.19.201); B.17.317 (C.19.292); B.17.338 (C.19.313); B.18.341 (C.20.389); C.20.389. Cf. *Court Baron* 52: 'Sir . . . ready am I to make amends [prest de amender]. . . . [Judge:] How wilt thou amend this trespass [ceo trespas amender], whereas the king enjoineth on pain of his grievous forfeiture of £10 that none do enter to chase or take beasts.'
   II. To set right, correct or reform (sb. or sth.): A.3.83 A sarmon he made For to amende meiris and men þat kepiþ þe lawis (C.3.122 Salamon þe sage a sarmon he made In amendement of mayres and oþer stywardes, B.3.74 amendes); C.4.182 Withouten mercement or manslauht amende alle reumes; B.10.274; B.9.78; B.10.324 (C.5.170); B.11.381 (C.13.197); B.13.207; B.19.442 (C.21.442).
   In L's usage the two meanings cannot always be distinguished, and several puns are likely; e.g., B.13.257 For may no blessynge doon vs boote but if we wile amende (C.15.228).

AMENDES   Reparation (for an injury or crime), BOTE; compensation (in an unequal bargain): B.18.342 Membre for membre was amendes by þe olde lawe; B.4.103 Pees þanne pitously preyde to þe kynge To haue mercy on þat man þat mysdide hym often . . . 'For Mede haþ maad myne amendes; I may na moore axe' (A.4.90, C.4.97 mendes); B.2.119 Mede is muliere of Amendes

5

engendred (C.2.120); B.5.324 Whoso hadde þe hood sholde han amendes of þe cloke; A.4.75 (B.4.88, C.4.84); B.18.327. Cf. *Mirror* 45: 'If anyone seek . . . compensation for damage [amende des damages] then shall he commence his action by a writ'; *Court Baron* 53: 'And we assess thee a day at the next court to speak of the amends [les amendes].' ASSETH, BOTE, *REDDE QUOD DEBES*, RESTITUCIOUN.

AMERCEN To fine (somebody) 'at the mercy,' i.e., at the discretion, of the court: B.6.39 And þou3 þow mowe amercy hem lat mercy be taxour (C.8.37). Cf. Wyclif: 'To amercy þe cely puple wiþouten any mercy' (*OED*); Reynes 136/344: 'If the baker lakke an vnce in the wyght of a ferthyng loff, he be amercyed at xx d.'; *Writs* 227: 'A. claims to have acquittance of five marks at which he was amerced [amerciatus fuit] before . . . our justices . . . in the aforesaid county.'

AMERCIMENT See MERCIMENT

***AMORTISEN** To alienate (property) in mortmain, that is, to convey property into the 'dead hand' (because it ceases to be a living inheritance) of a corporation, e.g., a monastery: B.15.321 If lewed men knewe þis latyn þei wolde loke whom þei yeue . . . Er þei amortisede to monkes or monyales hir rentes (C.17.54). The practice of 'amortising' property was forbidden by the Statute of Mortmain (1279), but exceptions were often granted by the king. See Hall, *Studies* 329, and a typical letter patent in Hall 1:72. FEFFEN.

ANSWEREN To make a defence in response to a charge or accusation: C.6.347 Thy bischop . . . shal onswerie for the at the hey dome (B.5.292); A.11.298 Whanne 3e ben aposid of princes or of prestis of þe lawe For to answere hem haue 3e no doute. Cf. *CT.Friar* 1589: 'Looke that thou be To-morn bifore the erchedeknes knee, T'answere to the court of certeyn thynges.' *Jac.Well* 25/17: Ordinaries should not be indicted 'to answere in lay-court.'

APERTLY Clearly, plainly; also openly, without secrecy or concealment (in contrast to *privily*, as applied to usurious transactions; see DERNE): B.3.258 In marchaundise is no Mede. . . . It is a permutacion apertly, a penyworþ for anoþer (C.3.313). Cf. *D&P* 2:178: 'Wheþir his symonye be pryue or apert, he is suspendit.'

APEIREN *I. To seize, take possession of (property) (OF *emparer*): B.5.46 Lest þe kyng and his conseil youre comunes apeire And be Styward of youre stede til ye be stewed bettre (A.5.38, C.5.144). Several variant spellings attested by *OED* and *MED*, such as *aparen*, *imparen*, *enparen*, support tracing L's usage here to *emparer* (seize) rather than *empeirer* (harm); the latter does not fit, indeed conflicts with, the context. Cf. B.10.327 Ac þer shal come a kyng. . . And amende Monyals, Monkes and Chanons . . . [and] . . . *Bynymen* that hir barnes claymen.

6

II. To make worse; to damage (something); to harm or injure, as by slander, deprivation, etc. (OF *empeirer*): A.7.204 Any frek þat fortune haþ apeirid Wiþ fuyr or wiþ false men (B.6.218, C.8.229); A.3.117 (B.3.128, C.3.163); A.6.51 (B.5.564, C.7.211); A.7.156 (B.6.171, C.8.167); A.8.50 (B.7.48); C.8.229. Cf. *Jac. Well* 15/17: 'And alle þo arn acursyd þat . . . dyffamyn or slaunderyn ony persone, & apeyryn his name among gode men.'

A POENA ET A CULPA 'From the penalty and the guilt,' a common formula in fourteenth-century indulgences: B.7.3 And purchased hym a pardoun *a poena et a culpa* (A.8.3, C.9.3); B.7.19 (A.8.21, C.9.23); C.9.186; cf. C.9.326–27. Cf. *Jac. Well* 34/20: 'And alle þo arn acursed . . . ȝif þey assoylen ony man "a pena & a culpa" [except] be ony priuylege'; *St. John the Evangelist*: '*A poena et culpa* here I them release' (Farmer 352/8). Discussion in T. P. Dunning, *Piers Plowman: An Interpretation of the A Text*. 2nd edn rev. by T. P. Dolan (Oxford, 1980), 109ff. PARDOUN, INDULGENCE.

APOSTATA One who quits his order after completing the year of his novitiate; a member of a religious order who renounces the same without legal dispensation; hence, one who forsakes his allegiance or troth: A.1.102 And whoso passiþ þat poynt is apostata in his ordre (B.1.104, C.1.98). Cf. *Hist. Poems* no. 65: 'Out of the ordre though I be gone, Apostata ne am I none'; *Abbey of H.G.* 340: 'Ȝe schullen vndurstonden þat þer was a fals tyrant apostata þat hyȝte Satanas . . . þe whiche for his pride ran out of his blysful ordre.' Canon law provided that apostate monks should be sought out and returned forceably to their monastery (Lyndwood III.17.2), and secular law cooperated. See, for example, the 'Petition of the Master of the Order of Sempringham for a vagabond canon to be attached by the secular arm (9 October, 1389)' in Hall 1:87; and the discussion of the writ *De apostata capiendo* in P&M 1:437.

*APPEL I. 'Accusation or Appeal is a lawful Declaration of another man's Crime (which by Bracton must be Felony at the least) before a competent Judge by one that setteth his name to the Declaration, and undertakes to prove it upon the penalty that may ensue of the contrary' (Cowell): B.17.308 For þer þat partie pursueþ þe peel is so huge That þe kyng may do no mercy (C.19.283); C.2.186. Cf. *D&P* 1:255: 'The iuge seyde but he wolde sweryn þat his apel was trewe ellys he schulde ben takyn as conuyct.' *K. Counc.* 54: 'These are the injuries and wrongs done to Thomas Ughtred. . . . First, the said sheriff imprisoned the said Thomas Ughtred without process of law or indictment, or of any manner of appeal [ou dascune manere dappelle] and without warrant contrary to law.'
II. A supplication for mercy, protection, special favour, etc.: C.2.244 Symonye and Syuile senten to Rome And putte hem thorw appeles in þe popes grace.

APPELEN To accuse (sb.), make a formal charge (before a judge): B.11.423 Pryde now and presumpcion, parauenture, wol þee appele. Cf. Kail 46/190:

7

'At domesday do ȝow alle quake Whan ȝoure owen werkis wole ȝow apele';
Jac.Well 256/25: 'Go to þe iuge of god, þat is, to þe preest, and þere appele
þiself.' Fisher 212/16: 'He knowleched diuerse felonies and . . . tresons and be
cam a prouowr and ther of appeled diuerse other men.' ACCUSEN, PLEINEN,
PURSUEN, SUEN.

APPOSEN   To question (someone) in a juridical proceeding: A.12.26 Pilat
aposed god almyȝthi, And asked Iesu . . . '*Quid est ueritas?*'; A.11.298
Whanne ȝe ben aposid of princes or of prestis of þe lawe For to answere hem
haue ȝe no doute; A.3.5 (B.3.5, C.3.5); C.5.10. Cf. *CT.Sec.Nun* 363: 'The
sergeantz . . . hem biforn Almache, the prefect, broghte, Which hem ap-
posed'; *CT.Friar* 1597: 'May I nat . . . answere there [in court] by my procuratour To swich thyng as men wole opposen me?' ARESOUNEN, ASSAIEN.

*****APPRENTIS OF LAWE**   A law student; a barrister-at-law of less than 16 years'
standing (*OED*): B.19.231 Some wyes he [Grace] yaf wit with wordes to
shewe . . . As prechours and preestes and Prentices of lawe (C.21.231). Blackstone 1:23: 'The degrees [at the inns of court] were those of barristers (first
stiled apprentices from *apprendre*, to learn) who answered to our [university]
bachelors; as the state and degree of a serjeant, *servientis ad legem*, did to that
of doctor' (1:23–24); 'Of advocates . . . there are two species or degrees;
barristers, and serjeants. The former are admitted after a considerable period
of study, or at least standing, in the inns of court; and are in our old books stiled
apprentices, *apprenticii ad legem*, being looked upon as merely learners, and
not qualified to execute the full office of an advocate till they were sixteen
years standing; at which time, according to Fortescue [chap. 50], they might
be called to the state and degree of serjeants, or *servientes ad legem*' (3:26–27).
Cf. Levy-Ullmann 83–84, Plucknett 224–25.

*****APPURTENAUNCE**   Something annexed to another thing more worthy as
principal, and which passes in possession with it, as a right of way or other
easement of land; an outhouse, barn, garden, etc. belonging to a house or
messuage: B.2.104 To haue and to holde, and hire heires after, A dwellynge
wiþ þe deuel . . . Wiþ alle þe purtinaunces of Purgatorie into þe pyne of helle
(A.2.68, C.2.108). Cf. Reynes 520–21: 'Habendum et tenendum predictam
peciam terre . . . et pertinentie'; Hall 1:30: 'Habendum et tenendum de nobis
et heredibus nostris . . . ad idem manerium pertinentibus.'

AQUITAUNCE   A document in evidence of a transaction, such as a deed,
release, or letter of indulgence: B.14.190 We sholde take þe Acquitaunce as
quyk and to þe queed shewen it. Cf. *Yrbk. Edw.II* 121: 'You have confessed
the deed *et ne moustrez poynt d'aquitaunce qe vous descharge*'; Hall 1:95:
'Nous vous mandons et chargeons . . . s'il ne monstre aquitance. . . .' To be
able to *show* a sealed release or acquittance was crucial; otherwise the law
regarded a person to be still in debt (Barbour 23–25); e.g., St. Germ. 77: 'Yf a
man . . . taketh no acquytaunce or yf he take one & . . . lese it . . . the payment
avails him nothing.' For a common form of acquittance, see Hall 1:131.

8

ARBITOUR A person chosen to decide a controversy; an arbitrator, referee: C.6.382 There were chapmen ychose this chaffare to preyse, That ho-so hadde the hood sholde nat haue þe cloke, And that the bettere thyng, be arbitreres, bote sholde þe worse. . . . They couthe nat by here consience acorden for treuthe Til Robyn þe ropere aryse they bisouhte And nempned hym for a noumper. Cf. *Cov. Leet* 329: 'Memorandum that Will. Huet on that oon partie and Will. Bedon oon that oþer of our Cite of Couentre be agreed to abyde the ward of . . . the seid arbitours . . . and if in the mean tyme the seid iiij arbitrours can not accorde that the seid Mair to be unpar, and to yeve his decre vpon the seid variance be-fore seid day . . .'; see pp. 91–96 for the record of an arbitrated dispute among the weavers of Coventry. NOUMPERE.

ARCHEDEKEN The chief administrative officer of an archbishop or bishop, who presided over the ecclesiastical court of the diocese, had powers of visitation, inducted candidates into benefices, imposed penance, etc. (*MED*): B.2.174 Erchedekenes and Officials and alle youre Registrers, Lat sadle hem wiþ siluer oure synne to suffre; A.Prol.92; C.5.71; C.12.225. Cf. *CT. Friar* 1302: 'Whilom ther was dwellynge in my contree An erchdeken, a man of heigh degree, That boldely dide execucioun In punysshynge of fornicacioun, Of wicchecraft, and eek of bawderye, Of diffimacioun, and avowtrye, Of chirche reves, and of testamentz, Of contractes and of lakke of sacramentz, Of usure, and of symonye also.' Blackstone 3:64: 'The *archdeacon*'s court is the most inferior court in the whole ecclesiastical polity. It is held in the archdeacon's absence before a judge appointed by himself, and called his official; and its jurisdiction is sometimes in concurrence with, sometimes in exclusion of, the bishop's court of the diocese.' OFFICIAL.

ARCHES In English ecclesiastical law, a court of appeals belonging to the Archbishop of Canterbury and held in the church of Saint Mary-le-Bow (*Sancta Maria de Arcubus*), so named from the steeple, which is raised upon pillars built archwise (Black): B.2.61 Forgoers and vitaillers and vokettes of þe Arches (C.2.61); C.22.136 Into þe Arches in haste he ȝede anoen aftur And turnede syuyle into symonye (B.20.136); C.2.186. Cf. *Jac. Well* 256/22: 'Þerfore, apele fro þise iij. courtys of ryȝtwysnes, of truthe, & of pees, to þe heyȝe archys of mercy be-tymes er þe sentence be ȝouyn aȝens þe.' Full discussion of the Court of Arches may be found in Woodcock 6–14 passim.

ARESOUNEN To berate or rebuke (sb.); to arraign (an offender, a sinner), call to account (*MED* [2]): C.14.184 (Sk.) Then ich aresonede Reson (B.11.373 rebukede, C.13.182 resonede); B.12.218 And so I seye by þee þat sekest after þe whyes And aresonedest Reson, a rebukynge as it were; C.13.128; C.13.193 (B.11.376 arated); C.13.243 (B.11.438 rebuked). Cf. *Pr. Consc.* 5997: 'Of alle þir thynges men sal aresoned be At þe day of dome.' *Lib. Alb.* 1:277: Let wrongdoers be brought before the Mayor and Aldermen 'et soient aresoneez de ceo dount ils sount enditeez'; *Court Baron* 36: 'And when the bailiff heard the fruit being knocked down, he . . . found the boy

9

right high on a costard tree ... and debonairely asked him [bonerement ly aresona] by whose commandment and whose sending he entered the lord's garden.'

ARRERAGE   An unpaid debt, the balance due (on a debt, rent, wages, pension, tax, etc.); the condition of being behind in payments or short in one's accounts: B.11.129, 132 Ac he [a cherl] may renne in arerage and rome fro home. ... And conscience [shal] acounte wiþ hym and casten hym in arerage, And putten hym after in prison in purgatorie to brenne; For hise arerages rewarden hym þere riȝt to þe day of dome (C.12.62); B.5.243; C.9.274; B.10.476 (C.11.299); B.14.108; C.15.286. Cf. *Pr.Consc.* 5913: 'Of alle þir gudes men byhoves Yhelde acounte. ... I drede many in arrirage mon falle, And til perpetuele prison gang'; Kail 34/100: 'Ay more and more rerage we renne, And sodeyn deþ nyl no man kenne. I rede we drede domesday; Be euene wiþ world er ȝe gon henne'; *Jac.Well* 128/13: 'Couert thefte ... is ... whan þou hast keypyng of þi lordys godys as baly, sergeaunt, or reve, þat reknyst lesse þi receytys þan þin expensys so slyly, þat þe lord is in þi dette þere þou schuldyst ben in reragys.' Arrearages were common on English manors (H. S. Bennett 191ff.). According to Denholm-Young, 'When a man went out of office he received, if he was quit, a discharge stating that he had paid all his debts, or containing an agreement by which he would pay them in installments' (151). For a typical record of account, including arrearages, see Hall 2:102–03. One who remained in arrears after his account had been heard by an AUDITOR might be thrown into prison. See *Writs* 212: 'Whereas it has been established by the common counsel of our realm [Statute of Westminster II, c. 11] that, if bailiffs who are bound to render their account to their lords are in arrears [in arreragiis] after the rendering of their account, they shall be attached by their bodies and delivered on the testimony of the auditors of the aforesaid account to our nearest gaol' (e.g., *K.Counc.* 12). A form of complaint for wrongful imprisonment for arrearages is printed in *Nov.Narr.* 285.

ASSAIEN   To examine (a witness, defendant, etc.) for the sake of information (= Lat. *examinare*): A.3.5 I wile assaie hire myself, and soþly apose What man of þis world þat hire were leuist (B.3.5, C.3.5). Cf. *K.Counc.* 33: 'And the said Gilbert, having been sworn and examined [iuratus et examinatus] ... upon his oath declared. ...' On the development of the procedure in the fourteenth century, see *K.Counc.* xlii–xliv. APPOSEN, ARESOUNEN.

ASSELEN   To authenticate (a charter, agreement, etc.) with an official mark or seal: A.2.35 Sire symonye is assent to asele þe chartres; A.2.77 (B.2.113, C.2.114); C.19.6 (B.17.4 enseled); C.19.9 (B.17.7 enseled). ENSELEN, SELEN.

ASSETH   Satisfaction, compensation, AMENDES; *eccles.* restitution: B.17.241 So wol þe fader forȝyue folk of mylde hertes That rufully repenten and restitucion make. ... And if it suffise noȝt for assetȝ, þat in swich a wille deyeþ,

Mercy for his mekenesse wol maken good þe remenaunt (C.19.202). For an entire sermon on the place of 'assetȝ' in the economy of salvation, see Anne Hudson, ed., *English Wycliffite Sermons*, vol. 1 (Oxford: Clarendon, 1983), 497–99; e.g., 'And God may not accepte a persone to forȝyue synne wiþowton asseþ,' 'Pat man þat schulde make asseþ for synne of oure furste fadir mot nedis be God and man' (498), etc. BOTE, RESTITUCIOUN.

ASSISE   See SISE

ASSISOUR   See SISOUR

ASSOILEN   To free (sb.) from excommunication or other ecclesiastical sentence: A.3.133 To be cursid in constorie heo [Mede] countiþ not a risshe; For heo copiþ þe Comissarie and cotiþ hise clerkis Heo is assoilid as sone as hireself likiþ (B.3.144, C.3.180). (To be distinguished from the meaning 'absolve from sin' in A.Prol.67, B.3.40, B.5.186, C.19.160, etc.). *Jac.Well* 16/7: 'We denouncyn hem acursed [excommunicate] þat mede takyn, to lettyn þe pees . . . And þey may noȝt ben a-soyled, tyl þey haue payed aȝen to þe ȝyvere þat þey haue take'; 33/1, 34/12, passim; *Fleta* 1.22: 'Wherefore all those implicated . . . are involved from the outset in a sentence of major excommunication, nor can they be absolved [absolui] therefrom by a simple chaplain' (p. 59). Woodcock's description of the process helps to explain why Lady Mede 'countiþ not a risshe' to be cursed in the consistory court: 'Absolution was granted to suspended and excommunicated persons after they had appeared in court or pleaded legitimate excuse and had paid the fees of their contumacy' (97).

ATTACHEN   To secure (sb. or sth.) for legal jurisdiction and disposal, to take or place under the control of a court; to arrest or seize by authority of a writ of attachment (*OED*): A.2.198 And ek [Mede] wep & wrang whan heo was atachid (B.2.239, C.2.252); B.16.261 It is a precious present . . . ac þe pouke it haþ attached, And me þerwiþ . . . ; may no wed vs quyte (C.18.278); A.2.161 (B.2.200, C.2.211); C.11.308. Cf. *Jac.Well* 25/16 against 'alle þo þat endyȝten ordinaryes wrongfully for extorcyouns, or atachyn, or arestyn, or enprysoun, hem, & make hem to answere in lay-court'; *Cov.Leet* 170: 'They orden that [men . . .] be returned to a Capias, and so attached to Com to onsuere.' For sample writs of attachment, see *Writs* 312ff. *CAPIAS*.

ATTEINTE   Convicted, attainted, esp. for perjury or giving a false verdict: B.20.162 Oon Tomme two-tonge, atteynt at ech a queste (C.22.162). Cf. Brown XV 214/32: 'I make to the acorde Vppon payne off a-taynt; I wyll no more suerly to the be so vnjust butt kepe thy lawes truly.' *Mirror* 115–116: 'If either party say that the jurors in any jury have made false oath, the law will succour the plaintiff by an action of attaint. . . . Challenges may be made against jurors, as against witnesses, in this manner: – "Sir, such an one is not a fit juror, for he . . . has been previously attainted of a false oath, or false witness. . . ."' Fisher 202/13–17 records a suit of attaint. For writs of attaint, see *Writs* 127, 274, passim.

AUDIATIS ALTERAM PARTEM   Roman law maxim ('Hear the other side'), cited repeatedly during the Middle Ages as one of the self-evident propositions of natural law: C.4.188 *Audiatis alteram partem* amonges aldremen and comeneres. Other citations noted by Alford 1975.

AUDITOR   An official who examines and verifies accounts, with the power to disallow improper charges: B.19.461 I holde it riȝt and reson of my Reue to take Al þat myn Auditour or ellis my Styward Counseilleþ me (C.21.461). The office of an auditor of manorial accounts is described in *Fleta* 2.88 (p. 260); see also H. S. Bennett 153–92 and Denholm-Young 131–51. Formula writs for the arrest (or release) of bailiffs found in arrears by a lord's auditors are given in *Writs* (212).

AVAUNCEN   To provide (sb.) with a benefice: C.13.103 The tytle ȝe take ȝoure ordres by telleth ȝe ben avaunsed (B.11.290); C.1.188 Aren none hardore ne hungriore then men of holy chirche, Auerous and euel-willed when þei ben avaunsed (B.1.191); A.3.32 Shal no lewidnesse hym lette, þe lede þat I louye, Þat he ne worþ ferst auauncid (B.3.33, C.3.36); A.1.165 (B.1.191, C.1.188); A.4.116. Cf. Usk 51/47: 'But now the leude for symonye is avaunced, and shendeth al holy churche.' Statute of Provisors (1350): 'And now it is showed to our lord the king . . . that many clerks advanced [avances] in this realm by their true patrons, who have held their advancements [avancementz] for a long time in peace, are suddenly ousted.' The technical meaning of the term is discussed by Carter Revard, '*Title* and *Auaunced* in *Piers Plowman* B.11.290,' *Yearbook of Langland Studies* 1 (1987), 116–21; see also Swanton, cited under TITLE. BENEFISEN, PROVENDREN, VAUNCEN.

AVOUTRIE   Violation of the marriage vows; adultery: B.12.74 Þat was þe lawe of Iewes, That what womman were in auoutrye taken, wher riche or poore, Wiþ stones men sholde hir strike and stone hire to deþe; B.2.175 (Sk.; K-D 2.176 emend to *deuoutrye*). Cf. *CT.Friar* 1306: 'Whilom ther was dwellynge in my contree An erchdeken . . . That boldely dide execucioun In punysshynge of fornicacioun . . . and avowtrye.' DEVOUTRIE.

AYEIN CONSCIENCE   Against law or justice: B.7.22 Þei swere by hir soule . . . Ayein clene Conscience hir catel to selle (A.8.24, C.7.26). *Proc.Chanc.*: 'To oppresse and fynalli to distroye yor seid suppliant, ayens conscience and lawe' (*MED* [3.c]). Cf. B.3.92 ayeins reson, C.3.120 aȝeyne þe lawe. See also CONSCIENCE.

B

BAILLIF   An officer of justice under a sheriff, who executes writs and processes, distrains and arrests: B.2.60 Sherreues and hire clerkes, Bedelles and baillifs (C.2.60); A.3.2 (B.3.2, C.3.2). On the duties of bailiffs, see Blackstone 1:334; on manorial bailiffs, often the same as reeves, see *Fleta* II.73 and H. S. Bennett 155ff. CACCHEPOL, SERGEAUNT.

BANISHEN   To exile or outlaw (sb.): A.3.274 Vnkyndenesse is comaundour, & kyndenesse is banisshit. Cf. *Jac.Well* 26/25: '. . . tyl þei ben owtlawyd or banyssched out of þe reem.' CONGIEN.

BARGAIN   An agreement between two parties setting how much each gives and takes, or what each performs and receives; a compact or business 'deal'; also, the act of bargaining: C.5.96 He . . . ofte hath ychaffared And ay loste and loste, and at þe laste hym happed A bouhte suche a bargayn he was þe bet euere; B.2.88 Al I hem graunte In bargaynes and brocages wiþ þe Burgh of þefte (C.2.92); A.5.186 Bargoynes & beuerechis begonne for to arise (B.5.337, C.6.395). Cf. *CT. Prol.* 282: 'Ther wiste no wight that he was in dette . . . With his bargaynes and with his chevyssaunce.' *Lib.Alb.* 1:210: 'Bargaynes et contractz'; *D&P* 2:186/10: 'Barganyyn & brockyn aboutyn syngynge of þe messe.' The collocation 'bargoynes & beuerechis' in A.5.186 is a particularly happy one; cf. Blanch and Wasserman on *SGGK*: 'Bercilak then calls for a "beuerage" (1112), a ceremonial means of sealing an agreement,' 'Medieval Contracts and Covenants: The Legal Coloring of *Sir Gawain and the Green Knight*,' *Neophilologus* 68 (1984), 603. BROKAGE.

BAROUN   **I.** A judge: B.3.319 (Sk.) Al shal be but one courte and one baroun be iustice (C.3.473). Cf. *Cleanness* 1640: 'Þou schal be baroun vpon benche.' As the citation from *Cleanness* shows, the meaning of the word need not be confined to 'one of the judges of the Court of Exchequer' (*OED, MED*), a definition that conflicts with the notion itself of 'one courte.' BURN, LORD.

    II. A great noble who attends the King's Council or is summoned by writ to Parliament: B.20.129 Coueitise . . . cam to þe kynges counseille as a kene baroun (C.22.129); B.10.326 (C.5.172); cf. A.Prol.96 (B.Prol.217, C.Prol.220); B.3.163; A.3.192 (B.3.205, C.3.261); C.6.123. Blackstone 1:387: 'It may be collected from king John's *magna carta*, that originally all lords of manors, or barons, that held of the king *in capite*, had seats in the great council of parliament. . . . By degrees the title came to be confined to the greater barons, or lords of parliament only; and there were no other barons among the peerage but such as were summoned by writ, in respect of the tenure of their lands or baronies, till Richard the second first made it a mere title of honor, by conferring it on divers persons by his letters patent.' ERLS AND BAROUNS.

13

BARRE   The railing in front of the judge's seat in a court of law, at which the litigants and the barristers stand; the court itself (*MED*): A.Prol.85 Þere houide an hundrit in houuis of silk, Seriauntis it semide þat seruide at þe barre (B.Prol.212, C.Prol.160); B.3.296 (C.3.448); C.4.132; B.4.169; C.9.45. Cf. *Simonie* 342: 'Countours in benche that stondeth at the barre'; *Gamelyn* 179/860: '[Gamelyn] leet fettre the justice and his fals brother And dede hem come to the barre'; *D&P* 2:193/29: 'Þe vykyr drempte þat he stod at þe barre aforn þe souereyn iuge.' *Bor.Cust.* 1:137: The defendant is taxed 'yf the playntyf will axette att the barre.'

BASTARD   A person born out of wedlock; an illegitimate person: C.5.65 For sholde no clerke be crouned but yf he come were Of frankeleynes and fre men and of folke ywedded. Bondemen and bastardus and beggares children, Thyse bylongeth to labory; A.2.95 (B.2.131, C.2.144); C.5.71; B.5.158; B.7.93 (C.9.168, A.8.75 barnes þat bois ben holden); C.10.261. On the definition and legal rights of bastards, see Blackstone 1:443–47, esp. 447: 'The incapacity of a bastard consists principally in this, that he cannot be heir to any one [cf. *Writs* 326]. . . . A bastard was also, in strictness, incapable of holy orders.' The definition of 'bastard' in English law was settled for the Middle Ages by the Statute of Merton (1235), which records the following famous scene: 'Concerning the king's writ of bastardy, whether one born before matrimony should be able to inherit in like manner as one born after matrimony, all the bishops . . . stated that they would consent that persons born before matrimony, as well as those born within matrimony, should be legitimate, with respect to the succession of inheritance, since the church holds such to be legitimate. And all the earls and barons responded with one voice that they would not change the laws of England.' Cf. Bracton 31; St. Germ. 51. For a defence of the English position, see Fortescue, chaps. 39–43. In C.10.237 Langland calls attention to another conflict between the Bible and 'Westminster law.'

BATAILLE   Trial by combat: B.16.164 On cros upon Calvarie Crist took þe bataille Ayeins deeþ and the deuel; ?B.3.323 (C.3.475); B.18.64 (C.20.67). *Fleta* 1.32: 'Battle is single combat between two men to prove the truth in a dispute, and the victor is taken to have proved his case' (p. 83). L's description of the Crucifixion conforms in many respects to wager of battle; for contemporary cases, see *K.Counc.* 47 and *K.Bench* 7:127, 133. An account of the process is given in Rickert, 151–56; see also Holdsworth 1:308–11, Plucknett 116–18, and George Neilson, *Trial by Combat* (Glasgow: Hodge, 1890). FIGHT, JUGGEMENT OF ARMES, JUSTE; see also CHAMPION, HERAUD OF ARMES.

BED AND BORD   In bed and at the table, that is, in all conjugal duties (a formula in the marriage vow): A.2.52 Þanne fauel fettiþ hire forþ & to fals takiþ In foreward þat falshed shal fynde hire for euere, And heo be boun at his bode his bidding to fulfille, At bedde & at boord buxum and hende. Cf. *O&N* 1492: 'Hire lauerd is forwurde, An unorne at bedde & at borde.' *York Manual*

14

16: 'Here I take þe N. to be my wedded wyfe, to hald and to have at bed and at borde, for fayrer for layther, for better for werse . . . til ded us depart.' The phrase is also used to define a legal separation; cf. Blackstone 1:429: 'The civil law [i.e., Roman law] . . . allows many causes of absolute divorce. . . . But with us in England adultery is only a cause of separation from bed and board' [*a mensa et thoro*].

BEDEL   A messenger of justice; a warrant officer; an under-bailiff: A.3.2 Now is mede . . . Wiþ bedelis & baillifs ybrouȝt to þe king (B.3.2, C.3.2); B.2.110 Bette þe Bedel of Bokynghamshire (A.2.74, C.2.111); B.2.60 (C.2.60). The phrase 'bedel and bailiff' is an alliterative commonplace; cf. *Simonie* 437: 'And baillifs and bedeles under the shirreve'; *Jac. Well* 61/10: 'And alle forsterys, bedelys, & baylyes, þat makyn scottalys. . . .' For the duties of a manorial beadle (like Bette) see H. S. Bennett 181f.

BEDEN   To petition for mercy; PREIEN: A.9.96 Þanne shulde þe kyng come & casten hem in presoun, And putten hem þere in penaunce wiþoute pite or grace, But dobest bede for hem abide þere for euere (B.8.106). CRAVEN.

BENCH   The seat where judges sit in court; hence, the place where justice is administered (*OED*); 'the king's bench,' *specif.* one of the three superior courts of common law (the other two being the Exchequer and the Court of Common Pleas): A.Prol.95 Archideknes & denis þat dignites hauen . . . And ben clerkis of þe kinges bench; cf. A.4.32 (B.4.45). Blackstone 3:41: 'The court of king's bench (so called because the king used formerly to sit there in person . . .) is the supreme court of common law in the kingdom. . . . Yet, though the king himself used to sit in this court . . . he did not . . . determine any cause or motion, but by the mouth of his judges, to whom he hath committed his whole judicial authority.' For brief accounts of the court of King's Bench, see Harding 1973, chap. 2 (esp. pp. 77ff.), and Kiralfy 145–46; the most extensive information will be found in the introductions by G. O. Sayles to *K. Bench* 5–7. See also COURT, KINGES BENCH, KINGES COURT.

BENEFICE   An ecclesiastical office or living: C.3.33 And Mede hendeliche behyhte hem . . . 'And purchase ȝow prouendres . . . And bygge ȝow benefices, pluralite to haue'; B.3.314; cf. A.11.195 var. Cf. *Jac. Well* 127/3: 'An-oþer [type of simony] is whan þou ȝeuyst mede, or byest a benefyse, cherche, or prouendre'; *CT. Gen. Prol.* 291: 'Ful thredbare was his overeste courtepy; For he hadde geten hym yet no benefice, Ne was so worldly for to have office.' Addleshaw 10: 'In the second half of the twelfth century when benefice in ordinary feudal terminology was dying out, it was taken over by the new canon law to denote any ecclesiastical office, bishopric, deanery, canonry, as well as that of a parish priest, to which was attached an endowment belonging by right to the holder of the office for the time being.' FINDING, PATRIMOINE, PERSONAGE.

BENEFISEN To endow or invest (sb.) with a benefice: C.3.185 She blesseth [MS F *benefiseth*] this bischopes thow thei ben ny lewede. AVAUNCEN, PROVENDREN.

BILLE *A written petition or complaint (Lat. *libellus*), used to initiate an action at law: A.4.34 Panne com pes into þe parlement & putte vp a bille How wrong aȝen his wil hadde his wyf take (B.4.47, C.4.45). Cf. *Assembly of Ladies* 123/626: 'The gentil wymmen of oure company Put up their billes.' *K.Counc.* xxxv–vi: 'The first step to bring a suit or complaint before the [king's] council was a petition; a bill as it was commonly called in litigation. . . . Customarily the petition consisted of the address, the grievance, and the prayer. The address was to the king, the king and council, the king or lords in parliament . . . with other variations. . . . The grievance was stated usually with brevity, the only elaboration being the horrible nature of the offence and the hardship endured. . . . Finally, the prayer was for remedy. . . . It concluded with a pious exhortation, "for God," "for the love of God and in the way of charity," "we shall pray for you" . . . etc.' Numerous examples of fourteenth-century bills follow. PREIERE, *PRO DEI PIETATE*.

BIQUESTE A testament or will: B.6.85 Forþi I wole er I wende do write my biqueste (C.8.94). As Pearsall notes (150 n.), 'The will itself, disposing in order of soul, body and property, follows the pattern of contemporary wills' (e.g., Holdsworth 3:671). See *Fleta* 2.57 (De Testamentis); Sheehan. RESIDUE AND REMENAUNT, TESTAMENT, WILLE.

BIQUETHEN To assign (property, rights, etc.) by a formal will: B.13.10 Freres folwede folk þat was riche . . . And no corps in hir kirkȝerd . . . was buryed But quik he biqueþe hem auȝt or sholde helpe quyte hir dettes (C.15.12). Cf. *Jac.Well* 18/3: 'Also we schewyn hem acursed þat lettyn . . . þe last wyll of þe dede; namely in swyche thynges as þey mowe lawfully beqwethe, by lawe or by consuetude'; Fisher 181/5: 'bequath and deuised.' BISETTEN.

BISETTEN To bestow in a will; to allot or allocate (an estate): C.6.254 Shal neuere seketoure wel bysette the syluer þat thow hem leuest (B.5.263); B.15.324 Allas, lordes and ladies, lewed counseil haue ye To ȝyue from youre heires þat youre Aiels yow lefte, And bisette to bidde for yow to swiche þat ben riche, And ben founded and feffed to bidde for oþere; B.5.261; B.5.291 (C.6.346). Bennett 169: '*bisett*: "bestow": sc. on chantry masses sung by a (chantry) priest for his soul (and regularly provided for in medieval wills).'

BONDAGE *The class of bondmen and serfs, the unfree (*MED*): A.Prol.96 Barouns and burgeis & bondage also I sauȝ in þat semble (B.Prol.217). No other examples of *bondage* in this sense are cited in *MED*.

BONDE A customary tenant (as distinct from a free-holder); a villager (villain) or farmer (husbandman) holding land under a lord in return for custom-

16

ary services, esp. plowing; a serf or servant (*MED*): C.3.200 Trewe burgeys and bonde she [Mede] bryngeth to nauhte ofte; C.10.261 (adj.); C.15.14. *Court Baron*: 'Then shall the steward make inquest . . . as to how the lord's franchise is maintained. . . . Whether there be any voidance in the tenements of free or bond [de frankes ou de bondes]. . . . Whether any bond [bonde] be insufficient to hold the tenement that he holdeth . . . and the land that he holdeth shall be let out to another bond [un autre bonde]' (102–03). THRAL, BONDEMAN.

BONDEMAN The tenant of a lord, a BONDE: A.7.44 [Piers to the knight:] Loke þou tene no tenaunt but treuþe wile assent . . . And mysbede nouȝt þi bondemen (B.6.45, C.8.42); A.Prol.96 (Sk.; B.Prol.216 [Sk.]); C.Prol.220 (bondemen of thorpes); C.5.65; C.5.70; B.5.193 (C.6.201); A.10.138 (bondemen of tounes). Cf. *Jac.Well* 186/5: 'Þi seruaunt or þi bonde-man is fals & vnkynde to þe, þat wyl noȝt serue þe, but rennyth awey to þi most enemye, & seruyth him.' BONDAGE, CHERL, TENAUNT.

BORGH I. (Of persons) a surety, pledge: A. One who becomes legally responsible for the behaviour of another; a guarantor; a sponsor at baptism: B.4.89 And he amendes mowe make lat maynprise hym haue, And be borȝ for his bale and buggen hym boote (A.4.76, C.4.85); A.1.75 Þou brouȝtest me [Holy Church] borewis my biddyng to werche (B.1.77, C.1.74); A.11.91 (B.10.138); B.16.263 (C.18.280); B.20.13 (C.22.13); B.20.248 (C.22.248). The phrase 'be borȝ . . . and buggen boote' (B.4.89) recalls the Old English formula *borh oððo bote* (Bethurum 272). B. One who guarantees the repayment of a loan: B.7.82 He þat biddeþ borweþ and bryngeþ hymself in dette. For beggeres borwen eueremo and hir borgh is god almyȝty. Cf. *D&P* 1:236/15: 'A Iew lente a cristene man a gret sum of gold into a certeyn day & tok non sekyrnesse of hym but his feyth & Sent Nicholas to borwe.' To offer one's faith or God himself as *borgh* is an ancient custom; cf. P&M 1:191: 'When a man makes a vow to God he will place his faith upon an altar and will find sureties who are to have coercive power over him. But more, when he makes a promise to another man, he will sometimes offer God as his surety.' See also Thomas Wilson on spiritual usury: 'Lay up thy almes in the hande of the poore. . . . The poore man is bounde to paye, and god is his suertie and wyll paye the debte hymselfe, yf the poore man bee decayed.' USURIE (II).
    II. Suretyship; the condition of being protected by a surety: B.14.191 We sholde take þe Acquitaunce . . . and preuen vs vnder borwe. Cf. *Gamelyn* 178/795: 'Whan the justice sitt, we moote be thare; For I am under borwe til that I come And my brother for me to prisoun shall be nome.'

BORWEN I. To become surety for; to obtain the release (of somebody) from prison or punishment: B.4.109 He shal reste in þe stokkes . . . but lowenesse hym borwe. Cf. *Beryn* 490: 'Now wold to God, she were in stokkis til I shuld hir borowe!' MAINPRISEN.
    II. To take (something) with the understanding that it will be returned; to obtain money by pledging something as security: A.4.40 [Wrong] borewide of

me bayard & brouȝte him neuere aȝen (B.4.53, C.4.56); B.13.375 And what body borwed of me abouȝte þe tyme; B.5.422 (C.7.35); B.7.81; B.15.312; B.20.286 (C.22.285). See DETTE.

BOTE   Amends or compensation: **A.** For an injury or wrong-doing: B.4.92 Bettre is þat boote bale adoun brynge Than bale be ybet and boote neuere þe bettre (A.4.79, C.4.88 glossed by Pearsall as: 'It is better that a financial settlement should mitigate the offence than that the offence should be punished and no-one be better off'); B.4.89 (A.4.76, C.4.85); B.12.86; C.20.156. In Anglo-Saxon law, *bot* was a fixed tariff (e.g., *manbot*, *wergild*); the system of monetary compensations was largely replaced in Norman law by punishment. See Goebel, 379–84. **B.** For the worse part of a bargain; something to make up the difference, as in the phrase 'to boot': B.14.269 A maiden . . . þat is maried þoruȝ brocage As by assent of sondry parties and siluer to boote (C.16.109). Cf. *Jac.Well* 127/5 on the exchange of unequal benefices: 'He þat hath þe lesse schal haue bote.' AMENDES, RAUNSOUN.

BOTEN   To compensate in value for (sth.): C.6.382 There were chapmen ychose this chaffare to preyse, That ho-so hadde the hood sholde nat haue þe cloke, And that the bettere thyng, be arbitreres, bote sholde þe worse (cf. B.5.324 Whoso hadde þe hood sholde han amendes of þe cloke). AMENDEN.

*****BOTHE LAWES**   Civil and canon law: A.8.13 Bisshopis þat blissen, & boþe lawes kenne, Loke on þat o lawe, & lere men þat oþer (B.7.14 Bysshopes . . . ben . . . Legistres of boþe lawes). Skeat explains: '*Bothe the lawes*, i.e., our duty towards God, and towards our neighbours.' However, the meaning of the phrase is more technical; it translates the common formula *doctor utriusque juris*, 'doctor of both laws' (canon and civil). Cf. Lydgate, *The Dance of Death*, EETS 181 (1931), 35/225: 'Com forth, doctour of Canon & Cyvile'; *Lud.Cov.* 179/25: 'In grett canon and in Cevyle lawe'; 228/94: 'Both sevyle and Canone.' The two branches of law were conventionally paired, since the study of the civil law (i.e., Roman law) was the normal preparation for a career in canon or ecclesiastical law. Thus Maitland: 'Owing to the rapid development of our own English system of temporal law, the civilian who was only a civilian had never found much to do in this country, and "the civil law" seems to have been chiefly studied as a preparation for the canonist's more lucrative science. The consequence is that we in England are apt to lump the legists and decretists together, and contrast them with "the common lawyers"' (93). Bishops learned in the law were normally *doctores utriusque iuris* – able, as L says, to 'loke on þat o lawe [civil], & lere men þat oþer [canon]' – though Maitland notes that in the fourteenth century some were civilians only, *doctores legum* (93 n.). The distinction between English law and civil-canon law was commonplace knowledge in L's day. In 1381 insurgent villeins on the estates of the abbey of St. Albans 'chased away the doctors of both laws, saying that they would not henceforth submit to the civil or the canon law' (Plucknett 186). The distinction was partly one of native versus

18

foreign ('papal and imperial') laws: as Blackstone puts it, 'The civil and canon laws . . . bind not the subjects of England . . . for the legislature of England doth not, nor ever did, recognize any foreign power, as superior or equal to it in this kingdom' (1:79). See also CIVILE, DECRETISTRE, DOCTOUR, LEGISTRE.

BREF   A letter of authority or credentials; a written authorization; cf. BREVET: B.20.327 The frere . . . cam with his lettre Boldely to þe bisshop and his brief hadde In contrees þer he coome confessions to here (C.22.327). Boniface VIII's bull *Super cathedram* (1300) established that mendicants, in order to hear confession, 'had to be licensed by the bishop of the diocese, who could limit the number of friars confessors and supervise their activity'; see Arnold Williams, 'Chaucer and the Friars,' *Speculum* 28 (1953), 499–513. BREVET, LETTRE.

BREKEN   To make forced entry into (a place, usu. for the purpose of theft): B.18.287 For þow gete hem wiþ gile and his Gardyn breke (C.20.313); B.11.164; C.20.380; B.19.344 (C.21.345). Cf. *Abbey of H.G.*: 'False þeues broken þus þis holy abbeye & beren away here goodys'; *CT.Pars.* 878: 'This is a fouler thefte than for to breke a chirche and stele the chalice.' Fisher 230/11: 'The seide late Shirreves . . . by colour of heer office brak & entrid þe hows of þe seid Gieffrey.'

BREKEN DAI   To fail to keep (one's) promise by an appointed time: B.5.242 I lerned among lumbardes . . . to legge a wed and lese it. Swiche dedes I dide write if he his day breke. Cf. *Treat.10 Com.* 29: 'If þou lene a weed [wed] to a day . . . & he breke þe day, þou takest alle' (*MED* 23[c]); *Impatient Poverty*, in Farmer 321: 'Of my ware he getteth right nought Without a good pledge he lay. . . . If the day be expired and past, Then will I hold it fast'; *CT.Ship.* 275: 'I wolde prey yow . . . to lene me An hundred frankes . . . ; I shal nat faille surely of my day.'

***BREVET**   A written document, an official letter: B.5.640 Quod a pardoner . . . 'I wol go fecche my box wiþ my breuettes & a bulle with bisshopes lettres'; A.Prol.71 A pardoner . . . Brouȝte forþ a bulle wiþ bisshopis selis And . . . bunchide hem wiþ his breuet (B.Prol.74, C.Prol.72); C.13.54 Pe messager . . . bereth but a box, a breuet þerynne. BREF.

***BRIBOUR**   A thief or robber, esp. by fraudulent means; an imposter (OF *bribeor*, beggar; cf. FAITOUR): B.20.262 Kynges and knyghtes . . . Han Officers vnder hem . . . And if þei wage men to werre þei write hem in noumbre . . . ; Alle oþere in bataille ben yholde Brybours, Pylours and Pykeharneys (C.22.262). Cf. Woodcock 49 n.: 'Ricardus Herford de Chylham notatur quod publice dixit in foro publico apud Godmersham: omnes officiarii Consistorii Cant' fuerunt latrones et bribors.'

*BROKAGE   *I. A business transaction, esp. by an agent or third party;
brokerage (citations of the word often imply the influence of favour or bribery
in the process): B.2.88 The Countee of Coueitise and alle þe costes aboute,
That is vsure and Auarice; al I hem graunte In bargaynes and brocages wiþ þe
Burgh of þefte (C.2.92). Cf. *D&P* 2:186/10: It is simony 'to *barganyyn &
brockyn* aboutyn syngynge of þe messe.' *Lib.Alb.* 1:587: 'Ordenaunce qe nul
Correctour face eschaunge ne chevance par voie dusure, ne nul *bargayne* ne
face, avaunt qil amesne lachatour et vendour ensemble; ne preigne pur soun
Brocage autre ce qest ordeigne'; *Law Merch.* 1:45: 'John of Boston complains
of Simon of Lindsey, for that he . . . does not pay him 12d. for brokerage [*de
abrocagio*]; Statute 12 Ric. II c. 2 (1388): No minister of the king shall be
appointed 'for any gift or brokage, favour or affection' [par null manere doun
ne brogage favour naffection]. BARGAIN.

   *II. Mediation between the sexes, employment of a go-between; procur-
ing: B.14.268 A maiden is þat is maried þoruȝ brocage As by assent of sondry
parties and siluer to boote (C.16.108). Cf. *CT.Mil.* 3375: '[Absolon] woweth
hire by meenes and brocage.'

*BROKOUR   *I. A commercial agent or middleman; a retailer of second-
hand goods; a pawnbroker: B.5.245 I haue lent lordes and ladies my chaffare
And ben hire brocour after and bouȝt it myselue; B.5.131 Amonges Burgeises
haue I be, biggyng at Londoun, And gart bakbityng be a brocour to blame
mennes ware (C.6.95); B.2.60 (C.2.60). For regulations governing commercial brokers, see *Lib.Alb.* 1:586–89; for the oath of brokers, 1:315–16.

   *II. A hired match-maker; a marriage agent or procurer: B.2.66 And as a
Brocour brouȝte hire to be wiþ fals enioyned (C.2.66). BROKAGE (II).

BULLE   A lead seal (Lat. *bulla*); hence, any papal or episcopal edict, as of
licence, pardon, excommunication, bearing such a seal: A.Prol.66 A pardoner . . . Brouȝte forþ a bulle wiþ bisshopis selis And seide þat hymself miȝte
assoile hem alle (B.Prol.69, C.Prol.67); A.Prol.70 (B.Prol.73, C.Prol.71);
A.3.137 (B.3.148, C.3.184); B.5.640; B.7.39 (C.9.42); B.7.65 (C.9.61);
A.8.92 (B.7.110, C.9.285); A.8.170 (B.7.192, C.9.339); B.13.249. Pearsall
notes: 'A pardoner carried a papal bull, which was the formal statement of
"indulgence", and to it were affixed the seals of the bishops [cf. A.Prol.66] in
whose dioceses he was licensed to preach' (32 n.).

*BURGAGE   A house or land in a borough; technically, a tenement held by
burgage tenure, that is, held directly of the king or other lord in return for a
fixed annual rent (though it could be bought or sold as an article of commerce): B.3.86 For toke þei on trewely þei tymbred nouȝt so heiȝe, Ne bouþte
none burgages (A.3.75, C.3.85); C.3.105. *Britton* 2:12: 'Bourgage est tenement de cite ou de bourg ou de autre lu privilegie par nous ou par nos prede-
cessours'; *Bor.Cust.* 2:85: 'And we are not wont to do fealty . . . to the lords of
the fee for our tenements, but only to pay our rents issuing from the said
tenements. For we say that we hold our tenements by the service of burgage
[*per servicium burgagii*], so that we have no means between the lord king and

ourselves.' Sayles distinguishes burgage tenure as that 'whereby property was held by a fixed money rent in quittance of all services, was heritable, and could be disposed of easily' (439). It is likened to a chattel; not only can it be disposed of by will, but 'it can be sold like a chattel' (P&M 1:296). See also Blackstone 2:82; Simpson 14.

BURGEIS   **I.** A magistrate or member of the governing body of a town: A.2.130 (Sk.) Lette sompne alle men in cuntre a-boute, To arayen hem redi bothe burgeys and schirreues.
    II. A member of a borough; strictly, one possessing full municipal rights (hence, a freeman): C.14.90 Ne in no cote ne caytyfs hous Crist was ybore But in a burgeis hous, the beste of þe toune (B.12.147); A.Prol.96 (B.Prol.217, C.Prol.220); B.3.163 (C.3.200); B.5.130; A.10.138; B.15.202; B.15.343.

BURN   Nobleman, lord; often equated with BAROUN as a gen. word for judge: C.3.473 Al shal be but a court and o buyrne be iustice (B.3.321). Cf. *RR* 4.69: 'No burne of þe benche [þe conclucion þan constrewe ne couþe]'; *W&W* 314: 'And thies beryns one the bynches ... bene knowen and kydde for clerkes of the beste.'

C

CACCHEPOL   *A minor officer of justice; a petty bailiff (often contemptuously), so named from his pole used to catch or secure offenders: B.18.73 A Cachepol cam forþ and craked boþe hir legges (C.20.76); B.18.46 (C.20.46). Cf. 'The Farmer's Complaint,' Sisam 113/50: 'Nede I mot spene that I spared yore; Ayain thes cachereles come thus I mot care.' *LawMerch.* I:115: 'Thomas Carrier, catchpoll of the said town [cachepollus ville predicte], . . . arrested Edward Welshman to answer . . . in a plea of debt.' L uses the term to translate Lat. *milites* (John 19:32), partly in derogation and partly in explanation of how the thieves' legs were broken (with the pole itself). For illustrations of the instrument, see Dorothy Hartley, *Lost Country Life* (1979), 292.

*CANONISTRE   An expert in canon law: A.8.134 Catoun construiþ it nay & canonistris boþe (B.7.155, C.9.305). *Wycl.Serm.* 1.32: 'þis man of lawe ... was neþir civilian ne canonistre, but he was man of Goddis lawe' (*MED*). DECRETISTRE, DOCTOUR.

CANOUN   **I.** A rule, law, or decree of the Church; ecclesiastical law, as laid down in decrees of the popes and statutes of councils; *specif.*, Gratian's *Concordia discordantium canonum*, also called *Decretum* (c.1140): B.5.421 Ac in Canoun nor in decretals I kan noȝt rede a lyne; C.15.85 This doctour and dyvynour . . . and decretistre of canoen. Cf. *Lud.Cov.* 179/25: 'In grett canon and in Cevyle lawe.' Though *canoun* refers to the whole body of ecclesiastical law, L's wording in B.5.421 may suggest a more precise distinction between the canons compiled by Gratian, never adopted as official law (*pace* Bennett 179), and the authentic decretals of the Church. The official body of decretals or canon law, known as the *Corpus Iuris Canonici* (*CIC*), consists of the following: the *Decretals* of Gregory IX (1234), the *Novellae* of Innocent IV (c.1254) and Gregory X (c.1275), the *Liber Sextus* of Boniface VIII (1298), and the *Constitutiones Clementinae* of John XXII (1317). See 'Canon Law,' *Oxf. Comp.*; Ullmann, 119–89; and Maitland. BOTHE LAWES, CANONISTRE, DECREE, DECRETAL, DECRETISTRE, DOCTOUR, LAWE.

II. A. A clergyman serving in a church or cathedral but not living under a rule; a canon secular: A.11.33 For ȝif harlotrie ne halpe hem betere . . . Wolde neuere king, ne kniȝt, ne canoun of seint poulis ȝiue hem to here ȝerisȝiue þe value of a grote (B.10.47). **B.** A clergyman living with others, usu. in the close of a cathedral or collegiate church, under a rule (*regula*); a canon regular: C.5.156 Bothe monkes and chanons Haen ryde out of aray, here reule euele yholde; B.10.324 (C.5.170).

CAPIAS ET SALVO CUSTODIAS 'Take and guard securely'; the standard formula in writs of attachment, addressed to the sheriff and served by his clerk: C.4.164–65 A shyreues clerk cryede, 'A! *capias* Mede *Et saluo custodias set non cum carceratis*.' *Writs* 224: 'The king to the sheriff, greeting . . .; we command you to take the body of the aforesaid B . . . and cause him to be safely kept in our prison [capias et in prisona nostra saluo custodiri facias].' A precedent for L's addition, *set non cum carceratis*, has not been found.

*CARISTIA Dearth, scarcity, dearness (Black): B.14.73 If men lyuede as mesure wolde sholde neuere moore be defaute…Ac vnkyndenesse *caristiam* makeþ amonges cristen peple. *Caristia* is a common word in writs and ordinances, esp. those directed against victuallers who in order to drive up prices created artificial scarcities; e.g., *Lib. Alb.* 1:631: 'Breve ne Ingrossatores seu Regratores faciant caristiam victualium.' L's statement is a topos of medieval economic theory (see DeRoover 12f., J. W. Baldwin, 17), still viable in the sixteenth century: 'For nothinge causeth dearth of al things so muche as usurye. . . . [T]he usurer . . . bringeth a dearthe also of all thynges through hys excessive dealing' (Wilson 258, 284).

CAS   *A suit or cause in a court of law: C.3.388 Such inparfit peple repreueth alle resoun And . . . reccheth thei neuere Of the cours of case so thei cache suluer (with a pun on grammatical case); A.8.51 He þat spendiþ his speche & spekiþ for þe pore Þat is Innocent & nedy . . . Counfortiþ hym in þat cas (B.7.49, C.9.48); C.3.432. Cf. *Assembly of Ladies* 594: 'In this case sue until hir presence, As reason wold, to have recompense'; *CT. ML* 36: 'Sire man of lawe . . . Ye been submytted . . . To stonden in this cas at my iuggement.' Like the example from Chaucer, A.8.51 probably involves a pun on *cas* as 'legal cause' and 'situation.' ACCIOUN, CAUSE.

CATEL   An article of personal property, as opposed to real property (Black); movable goods; money, often in combination as 'goods and chattels': C.3.322 Here ayres hardy to claymen That kyng oþer kayser hem gaf catel oþer rente; C.12.60 For may no cherl chartre make ne his chatel sulle Withouten leue of þe lord (B.11.127); B.3.68 (C.3.72); A.4.69 (B.4.82, C.4.78); B.5.266 (C.6.288); A.7.84 (B.6.92, C.8.101). Cf. Hall: 'Catalla Felonum et Fugitivorum' (1:103), 'pro bonis et catallis' (104), 'cum omnibus bonis et catallis' (171). MOEBLES.

*CATELES   Property-less; indigent: A.10.68 ȝif þei ben pore & cateles . . . Þanne is holichirche owyng to helpe hem.

CAUCIOUN   Security given for the performance of some engagement; a guarantee or pledge (Lat. *cautio*; cf. Edler, *cauzione*): B.5.143 (MS Bodley 851, ed. Rigg and Brewer) Caucyon, ant Y couthe, *caute* wold Y make, That Y ne begged ne borwed ne in despeyr deyde. The term translates Luke 16:6 *Accipe cautionem tuam*. The pun on *caute* (prudently) is the author's own. Rigg and Brewer render the passage: 'If I could, I would prudently make a down payment, in order not to beg or borrow or die in despair.' Cf. *Writs* 134 (writ of procuration): '. . . promitto et caucionem expono'; *Cov. Leet* 544: Any public official charged with a wrong should be 'eloyned from all worship & goode companye till he fynde sufficient and suer caucion or suertie of amendement.'

CAUSE   A legal suit or ACCIOUN; any question in litigation before a court of justice; also, a ground or reason. Langland seems to be playing on the word in a few passages, e.g., B.11.174 Lawe wiþouten loue . . . ley þer a bene! Or any Science vnder sonne . . . But þei ben lerned for oure lordes loue, lost is al þe tyme, For no cause to cacche siluer þerby, ne to be called a maister, But al for loue of oure lord . . .; B.13.126 For oon Piers þe Plowman haþ impugned vs alle . . . And no text ne takeþ to mayntene his cause But *Dilige Deum*. Cf. *RR* 3.318: 'Chyders of Chester were chose many daies To ben of conceill ffor causis that in the court hangid'; *Jac. Well* 256/15: 'In þo thre courtys þou schuldyst be conuicte in þi cause, for þou art gylty in wrong.'

CHALENGEN   I. To accuse (sb.), bring charges against: B.5.87 Of chidynge and chalangynge was his [Envy's] chief liflode, Wiþ bakbitynge and bismere and berynge of fals witnesse (C.6.68). Cf. *Bor. Cust.* 1:97: The arrested person 'to come to the barre and answer to the party playntif, if the party playntif will him chalange.' Envy's false *chalangynge* is normally associated in penitential treatises with the sin of Avarice; e.g., *Vices and Virtues* 35: 'Þe ferþe braunche of auerice is chalengyng; þat is to seye, renne on a-noþer man wiþ wrong. To þis synne longeþ al baret, conteke, bigilenges, and alle falsenesses þat fallen among men bi cause of plee'; *Jac. Well* 130/32: 'Þe ferthe fote brede of wose in coueytise is fals chalange.'
    II. To claim (sth.) as one's right, due, privilege, or property: B.Prol.93 Somme seruen þe kyng and his siluer tellen, In Cheker and in Chauncelrie

23

chalangen hise dettes (C.Prol.91); B.15.31 (C.16.190); B.15.165; B.15.345. Cf. *Abbey of H.G.*: 341: The heirs of Adam and Eve have 'no riȝt to chalenge þe lordschip of þis world ne þe blisse of heuene'; *Bor. Cust.* 1:58: 'Si un home chalenge une chose de un autre cum perdue'; Fisher 105/4: 'Alle manere men that haue any . . . land with ynne oure toun . . . shal . . . comme and chalenge eche man his owen grond.' CLAIMEN, CRAVEN, SUEN.

*III. To object or take exception to (a person, e.g., as a candidate for a jury or office): C.6.136 Prioresse worth she neuere; For she hadde childe in the chapun-cote she worth chalenged at þe eleccioun.

*CHALENGEABLE   Contestable (as a deed or charter); open to criticism or objection; revocable: B.11.303 A chartre is chalangeable bifore a chief Iustice; If fals latyn be in þat lettre þe lawe it impugneþ (C.13.116 chaleniable). Cf. *Yrbk.Edw.II*, 70: 'Miggele challenged the deed because of an interlineation [chalenges le fet pur entrelinarie]'; *Mirror* 148: 'And if anyone knowingly receives a felon into his fraunchise, it is challengeable [chalengeable] on that account. PARENTRELINARIE.

CHALENIABLE   See CHALENGEABLE

CHAMPION   One who does battle for another in 'wager of battle': B.18.99 Youre champion chiualer [Longinus] . . . ȝilt hym recreaunt remyng, riȝt at Iesus wille. For þe þis derknesse ydo deeþ worþ yvenquisshed; And ye, lurdaynes, han ylost for lif shal haue þe maistrye; And youre fraunchise þat fre was fallen in þraldom (C.20.103). Cf. A.9.41 (B.8.45); B.15.164; B.15.216; C.15.277. Here L treats the Crucifixion under the figure of a judicial combat, with Christ and Longinus as the champions respectively of Life and Death. Of the three cases in which such trials were held – in the court-martial, in an appeal of felony, and in a writ of right – L clearly had in mind the third. Thus Blackstone 3:338–40: '[T]he tenant in a writ of right pleads the general issue, viz. that he hath more right to hold, than the demandant hath to recover; and offers to prove it by the body of his champion. . . . and, if the champion of the tenant can defend himself till the stars appear, the tenant shall prevail in his cause. . . . Or victory is obtained, if either champion proves *recreant* . . . [thus] forfeiting the land of his principal.' For a brief discussion, see Plucknett, who offers evidence of 'a professional band of champions who undertook business all over the country' (117). See also *Writs* 230, and for a description of the process in a writ of right, *Moots* 95–96. The oath of a champion is given in Statute 3 Edw. I c. 41, and *Court Baron* 77. BATAILLE, CREAUNT.

CHAPITLE   See CHAPITRE

CHAPITRE   I. An assembly of the members of a religious house, acting as a disciplinary court: C.3.472 Kynges court and comune court, constorie and chapitre Al shal be but a court and o buyrne be iustice (B.3.320 chapitle); cf. B.5.174 (C.6.156). Cf. *Jac.Well* 129: 'Offycyallys & denys þat oftyn settyn chapetlys . . . haue more affeccyoun to gadere syluer þan to don correccyoun.'

24

Court Baron 102: 'Then shall the steward make inquest. . . . Whether any bond man's unmarried daughter hath committed fornication and been convened in chapter [conu en chapitre], and what hath she given to the dean for her correction, etc.' Blackstone 1:370–71. CONSISTORIE, COURT.

II. The body of members of a religious order: B.5.161 She hadde child in chirietyme; al oure Chapitre it wiste.

CHAPITREHOUS A room (or attached building) in a religious house where members assemble for judgement and correction, business, episcopal visitations, and so forth: B.5.174 And if I telle any tales . . . am chalanged in þe Chapitrehous as I a child were And baleised on þe bare ers (C.6.156). Cf. *Brut* 1447: 'Roger Norman . . . was . . . brought before the Bisshop of London and tofore the clergie in the Chapitre hous of Seint Paules, and there . . . conuicte in heresye' (*MED*).

CHARGE An accusation: A.10.73 Iche wiȝt . . . Is chief souereyn ouer hymself his soule to ȝeme, And cheuisshen hym for any charge whan he childhod passiþ.

CHARGEN **I.* (Accounting) To encumber or to reckon (something) an encumbrance: B.14.315 And þouȝ he [poverty] chaffareþ he chargeþ no losse, mowe he charite wynne: *Negocium sine dampno* (C.16.148). A normal record of account consisted of the 'charge' (the sum of the arrears, receipts, imprests, etc. to be accounted for), the 'discharge' (the sum of authorized disbursements, expenses incurred, and other 'allowances'), and the 'balance,' ascertained by subtracting the discharges from the charges (Hall 2:91). See, e.g., the wardens' accounts in *Cov. Leet*: 'Atte whiche accounte thei were charged withe iiij iij li. xvj s. j d. ob. Summa oneracionis iiij iij li, xvj s. j d. ob. Whererof thei aske alowans of lvj li, iiij s. ij d. of bates & oder discharges. . . . And so thei abyden in arrerage & clere dete xxv li. v s. ix d. ob.' (114 and passim). L's point is that patient poverty does not 'charge' a loss to his account but 'allows' what is owed if thereby he 'wins' or earns charity; cf. C.16.288–91 Charite . . . chargeth naught [but . . .] I knewe neuere . . . clerk noþer lewed That he ne askede aftur his. See also ALLOWAUNCE, ALLOWEN, DISCHARGEN.

II. To entrust (somebody) with an office or duty: C.Prol.87 Bischopes and bachelers . . . That han cure vnder Crist . . . And ben charged with holy chirche charite to tylie; C.22.237 Late hem chewe as thei chose and charge hem with no cure! (B.20.237); A.10.23.

III. To levy a tax or rent upon (a tenant): C.9.73 Pore folk in cotes, Charged with childrene and chief lordes rente. Here L plays on the meaning of *chargen* as both 'to burden' and 'to impose a rent.' The collocation 'charge . . . rent' is common; see *MED* 'chargen' (8) and 'charge' (10).

CHARTRE A written document, signed and sealed, which grants certain rights and privileges, or conveys landed property (as a deed): B.2.79 Fauel wiþ his fikel speche feffeþ by þis chartre; B.11.127 For may no cherl chartre

25

make ne his chatel selle Wiþouten leue of his lord; no lawe wol it graunte (C.12.60) (see CHERL); B.11.303 A chartre is chalangeable bifore a chief Iustice (C.13.115) (see CHALENGEABLE); C.5.166 Religious þat haen no reuthe ... Of þe pore haueth thei no pite and þat is here puyre chartre (B.10.320); A.2.35; B.2.69 (C.2.69); B.11.306 (C.13.119); C.16.36. Pearsall glosses C.5.166 as follows: ' "That is the simple way in which they interpret their legal responsibility" (i.e., as a charter of freedom).' For a selection of charters, see Hall 1:24–40. L's parody of a charter of enfeoffment in A.2.57–71 (B.2.74–114, C.2.78–115) was a conventional device; other examples are *The Charter of the Abbey of the Holy Ghost* (Horstman 1:337–62); the various *Middle English Charters of Christ*, ed. Spalding; and *The Devil's Charter*, ed. R. B. McKerrow (1904). For a related genre, see Perrow, cited under TESTAMENT.

CHATTEL See CATEL

CHAUNCELER The Lord Chancellor of England: C.4.185 Forthy, Resoun, redyly thow shalt nat ryden hennes But be my cheef chaunceller in cheker and in parlement. Cf. Nicholas Love, *Mirror*, ed. L. F. Powell (1908): 'Souereyn wisdom wroot the sentence and the dome ... and toke it to his Chauncelere, Resoun, to rede it in his name' (17). The *MED* takes C.4.185 as referring to the chancellor of the Exchequer, but L's use of the phrase 'cheef chaunceller' suggests rather the Lord Chancellor, to whom the chancellor of the Exchequer was deputy (see Hall, *Antiquities* 83); moreover, Reason's responsibilities are broader than those of the chancellor of the Exchequer. The king says that Reason 'shal rule my Reaume' (B.4.9), takes him for his principal counselor (B.4.190, etc.), and 'sette hym on benche' between himself and his son (B.4.45).

*****CHAUNCELRIE** The office of the Chancellor; also, the chancery court: B.Prol.93 Somme seruen þe kyng and his siluer tellen, In Cheker and in Chauncelrie chalangen his dettes Of wardes and of wardemotes (C.Prol.91); A.4.26 (B.4.29). The chancery in late fourteenth-century England was both a secretariat and a court. Historians refer to its two functions as 'the Latin side' of chancery, the office which produced all original writs for actions at common law, and 'the English side' of chancery, a court of equity which served to correct the injustices of common law in individual cases. The chancery had just begun to emerge as a separate court in L's day; and it is by no means clear that B.Prol.93 refers to its equitable jurisdiction. For a collection of chancery documents in English, see Fisher.

CHEKER The fiscal department of the Crown, including the treasury and the court of accounts; the Court of Exchequer (concerned mainly with revenue cases): B.Prol.93 Somme [i.e., clerics] seruen þe kyng and his siluer tellen, In Cheker and in Chauncelrie chalangen hise dettes Of wardes and of war- demotes (C.Prol.91); A.4.26 (B.4.29); C.4.185. Cf. 'Verses on the Ex- chequer in the Fifteenth Century,' ed. by Charles Haskins and M. Dorothy

George, which describes all the stages through which an account passes (*English Historical Review* 36 [1921], 58–57). For an introduction to the Exchequer and its records, see Hall, *Antiquities*, who notes that exchequer personnel were 'for the most part ecclesiastics' (114).

CHERL   A bondman or *villanus*; an unfree tenant: B.11.127 For may no cherl chartre make ne his chatel selle Wiþouten leue of his lord; no lawe wol it graunte (C.12.60); B.19.35 The Iewes þat were gentil men, Iesu þei despised, Boþe his loore and his lawe; now are þei lowe cherles (C.21.35); B.20.146 And [he] leet leautee a cherl and lyere a fre man (C.22.146); B.1.33 (C.1.29); B.6.48 (C.8.45); B.11.127 (C.12.60); B.16.121; B.18.104 (C.20.108); B.19.37 (C.21.37); B.19.55 (C.21.55). Cf. *Vices* 14/29: 'Euery man and womman þat synneþ dedly . . . makeþ omage to þe deuel and bicomeþ his cherl.' Fisher 163/118: 'We be fre tenentz and fre lond holderes. . . . Neuertheles the forsaide Priour and Chanons of Bernewell han [forced . . .] vs to ben her bonde cherles.' On B.11.127, see *Court Baron* 102: 'Then shall the steward make inquest . . . as to how the lord's franchise is maintained. . . . Whether any bond man [bonde] demiseth his land or part of it . . . without licence [sanz congee].' BONDE, BONDEMAN, THRAL.

CHETE   See ESCHETE

CHEVISAUNCE   Trading in money or goods for profit, esp. by devious means to circumvent the law (e.g., laws against usury): B.5.246 I haue lent lordes and ladies my chaffare And ben hire brocour after and bouȝt it myselue. Eschaunges and cheuysaunces, wiþ swich chaffare I dele, And lene folk þat lese wole a lippe at euery noble; C.6.252; cf. B.20.16 (C.22.16). Cf. *CT. Prol.* 282: 'Ther wiste no wight that he was in dette . . . With his bargaynes and with his chevyssaunce.' The *Liber Albus* contains a declaration by the Mayor and Aldermen (1390) concerning 'in especial what is usury or unlawful chevisance': 'If any person shall lend or put into the hands of any person gold or silver, to receive gain thereby, or a promise for certain without risk, let such person have the punishment for usurers. . . . And if any man . . . shall sell any merchandize and retain the same in his possession, or forthwith upon such sale shall buy back the same merchandise, to the loss of the buyer. . . . And if any partners in trade, by covin before made, shall sell goods for the purposes of chevisance, and one of them shall sell the same goods, and the other of them, forthwith upon the sale, shall buy them of him who is so practised upon, for a less price than that at which they were at first sold, let them have the same punishment' (1:399–401, trans. 3:161–63). ESCHAUNGE, USURIE.

CHEVISHEN   To defend (oneself) against a charge: A.10.73 Iche wiȝt . . . þat haþ wys vndirstonding Is chief souereyn ouer hymself his soule to ȝeme, And cheuisshen hym for any charge whan he childhod passiþ. Cf. Hoccleve, *Cupid* 325: 'O womman, how shalt thow thy self cheuyce, Syn men of thee so mochil harm witnesse?' (*MED*).

CHIEF JUSTICE   Strictly, the highest-ranking judge in the courts either of King's Bench or Common Pleas: C.13.116 A chartre is chaleniable byfore a chief iustice (B.11.303). On the duties and jurisdiction of the chief justices, see *Mirror* 124. BAROUN, JUGGE, LORD.

CHIEF LORD   The immediate lord of the fee, to whom the tenants were directly and personally responsible (Black): C.9.73 Most neden aren oure neyhebores . . . pore folk in cotes, Charged with childrene and chief lordes rente. Cf. *Abbey of H.G.* 340, which describes God, in his relation to Adam and Eve, as 'þe chef lord of þe fee.' Statute 18 Edw. I c. 2: 'And if anyone sell any part of such lands or tenements, the feoffee shall immediately hold it of the chief lord [immediate de Capitali domino], and shall be charged [oneratur] with the services, for as much as pertain or ought to pertain to the said chief lord for the same parcel.'

*CIVILE   Civil (i.e., Roman) law or its study (here personified): B.2.63 Ac Symonie and Cyuylle and Sisours of courtes (C.2.63); B.2.67 (C.2.67); B.2.72 (A.2.54, C.2.72); B.2.142 (A.2.106, C.2.155) passim; B.20.137 (C.22.137). See Beverly Brian Gilbert, ' "Civil" and the Notaries in *Piers Plowman*,' *Medium Aevum* 50 (1981), 49–63; Alexandra Barratt, 'Civil and Theology in *Piers Plowman*,' *Traditio* 38 (1982). BOTHE LAWES, CANOUN.

CLAIME   An assertion of a legal right, a demand for something due: C.4.98 Mede hath made my mendes, y may no more asken, So alle my claymes ben quyt. QUITEN.

CLAIMEN   To demand (something) by virtue of a right or title; to affirm a right or possession: B.14.110 Ther þe poore dar plede and preue by pure reson To haue allowaunce of his lord; by þe lawe he it cleymeþ (C.15.288); C.10.210 Men þat ben bygeten Out of matrimonye . . . mowen nat haue þe grace That lele legityme by þe lawe may claymen; B.10.327 Ac þer shal come a kyng . . . And amende Monyals, Monkes and Chanons . . . [and] . . . Bynymen that hir barnes claymen; B.18.343 Membre for membre was amendes by þe olde lawe . . . and by þat lawe I clayme Adam and al his issue at my wille herafter; C.3.321; C.3.377; A.8.139 (B.7.161); B.10.348; B.11.123 (C.12.56); B.14.142; B.14.260 (C.16.100); C.17.57; C.17.70; B.16.191 (C.18.201); B.18.20 (C.20.18); B.18.329 (C.20.372); B.20.96 (C.22.96); cf. B.1.93; B.10.327; B.19.443. *Writs* 96: 'Command W. and B., his wife, that . . . they render to A. . . . so much land with appurtenances in N. which he claims [clamat] to be his right and his inheritance'; *Court Baron* 62: '. . . a hide of land with the appurtenances in N. which W. Chapman claimeth as his right [cleime cum son dreit] against R. of C.'

CLAMAT COTIDIE   'Cries out daily'; a formula sometimes used to initiate criminal proceedings against a public enemy; B.19.416 The comune *clamat cotidie*, ech a man til ooþer, 'The contree is þe corseder þat Cardinals comme Inne' (C.21.416). Cf. *Mirror* 81: '*Of summonses.* . . . A general summons every one of the people can make by a public cry [par commone criee].' On the

28

technical meaning of the phrase see Gabrielle Lambrick, 'The Impeachment of the Abbot of Abingdon in 1368,' *English Historical Review* 82 (1967), 250–76; and Alford 1984, 283.

CLAUSE   A written message, letter, legal document; also, a part or subdivision thereof: A.8.44 Þanne were marchauntis merye . . . And ȝaf wille for his writyng wollene cloþis; For he copiede þus here clause þei couden hym gret mede; A.3.264 (Sk.); A.4.133; A.8.90 (B.7.108). To call Truth's letter to the merchants a 'clause' is particularly apt, since it is a 'letter close' (*litera clausa*) sent 'vndir his secre sel' (see Blackstone 2:346).

CLEMENCIA NON CONSTRINGIT   'Mercy is not restricted': C.5.60a. Cf. 'The quality of mercy is not strained' (*Merchant of Venice* IV.i.179). Probably a legal maxim, though no source has been found.

CLERK   The general name given to virtually any officer in the judicial system, lay or cleric, whose duties required or involved a certain level of literacy; *specif.* a secretary or recorder; a keeper of official records and accounts; one who writes writs (in the chancery); a court officer responsible for serving writs, arranging the schedule of the court, arraigning prisoners, etc.; an undersheriff; an advocate; a lord spiritual: B.3.3 The kyng called a clerk . . . To take Mede þe maide and maken hire at ese (A.3.3, C.3.3); B.10.452 Thouȝ ye come bifore kynges and clerkes of þe lawe, Beþ noȝt afered of þat folk (translates Mk. 13:9, 'Dum steteritis ante reges et presides,' etc.); B.3.115 Thanne was Conscience called to come and appere Bifore þe kyng and his conseil, clerkes and oþere (cf. A.3.104, B.3.115, C.3.150); C.4.164 A shyreues clerk cryede, 'A! *capias* Mede' (B.4.168; cf. B.2.58–59, C.2.59); A.3.9, 25, 33, 41 (B.3.9, C.3.9 etc.); A.3.132 (B.3.143, C.3.179); C.3.210; B.4.189; B.5.311; C.12.225; B.13.247; B.15.32 (C.16.191). Cf. *Court Baron* 96 ('On the manner of holding courts'): 'And of those matters which are against the crown, inquire among yourselves and if ye wish for a clerk ye shall have one.' Bennett identifies the clerk of B.3.3 as 'the permanent salaried secretary of the King's Council' (135), the clerks of B.3.115 as 'presumably . . . the lords spiritual' (137).

CLERK OF ACCOUNTS   An accountant; an official in charge of accounts: A.Prol.91 I sauȝ bisshopis bolde & bacheleris of deuyn Become clerkis of acountis þe king for to serue.

*CLIENT   One who employs a lawyer: C.3.392 Reccheth thei neuere Of the cours of case so thei cache suluer. . . . How þat cliauntes acorde acounteth mede litel. Cf. *Jac. Well* 131/20: 'A fals atourne . . . wyl be of assent to letyn his maysterys cause falle, & so he is a tretour to his clyent.' *Lib. Alb.* 1:473: 'Item, qe lez attournez . . . bien et loialment suyrount lez bosoignes de lour clyens, sanz fraude ou deceit faire a la Court ou a eux.' On clients and their lawyers in ecclesiastical courts, see Woodcock 43–44. The client of an attorney is often referred to as his 'master' (as above) or 'lord' (*Writs* 44, 123, 233; Woodcock 52).

CLOUDES AND CUSTUMES   (The study of) natural science and law: C.14.73 Kynde-wittede men han a clergie by hemsulue; Of cloudes and of costumes they contreuede mony thynges ... And of the selcouthes þat þei sye, here sones þerof þei tauhten For they helden hit for an hey science here sotiltees to knowe ... Of briddes and of bestes, of blisse and of sorwe. Natural science and customary (or secular) law were studies forbidden to the clergy. Thorsby's Constitutions (1363) count it a grave irregularity 'when archdeacons, deans, plebans, provosts, chanters, and other clergymen that have parsonages, and priests, study law or physic [legem vel physicam], unless within two months' space they wholly desist' (*Engl. Canons* 2:435).

COLLATERAL   *Attendant or additional; in legal usage, 'something distinct from but existing alongside or contemporaneous with another principal subject' (*Oxf. Comp.*); 'collateral comfort,' collateral aid or assurance, something given in addition to the principal subject for the purpose of securing its validity or effect: B.14.300 Pouerte ... is a fortune þat florissheþ þe soule Wiþ sobretee fram alle synne and also ʒit moore; It afaiteþ þe flessh fram folies ful manye, A collateral confort, cristes owene ʒifte: *Donum dei* (C.16.135). L may have had in mind the notion of collateral warranty (e.g., *Moots* 86, 'collaterall garrantie'), an important element in fourteenth-century land law (Blackstone 2:300–03, Simpson 118–121); and possibly his use of the phrase was inspired by the words *donum dei*, as the doctrine of collateral warranties itself grew out of the statute *De donis* (i.e., Westminster II, 13 Edw. I c. 1). COMFORT.

COLOUR   A specious argument, ruse, pretext: B.19.351 'Conscience shal noʒt knowe who is cristene or heþene, Ne no manere marchaunt þat wiþ moneye deleþ Wheiþer he wynne wiþ right, wiþ wrong or wiþ vsure.' Wiþ swiche colours and queyntise comeþ pride yarmed (C.21.352). Cf. *Wisdom* 547: 'Thus by colours and false gynne Many a soule to hell I wyn.' *Lib. Alb.* 368: 'Certain persons ... do daily exert themselves, to maintain the false and abominable contract of usury, under cover and colour [desouz le coverture et colour] of good and lawful trading'; *Bor. Cust.* 1:60: 'None inhabitant ... by no frawd nor collour shall buy no goods nor cattells of no suspect persons within nor without the same town.'

*COLOUREN   To misrepresent (sth.) under COLOUR or pretence of a lawful or higher motive: B.19.458 Ech man subtileþ a sleiʒte synne to hide And coloureþ it for a konnynge and a clene lyuynge (C.21.458); B.19.347 (C.21.348). Cf. *Jac. Well* 131/14: 'He colouryth it so in þe lawe, þat þe falshed may noʒt be knowyn.'

COMEN   To appear in court: C.Prol.95 Consience cam and cused hem; C.3.149 Thenne was Consience ykald to come and apere Byfore þe kyng and his consayl; A.3.103 (B.3.114); C.13.84. Cf. *D&P* 2:237/28: 'Witnessis in doom schuldyn nout ben hard aʒenys hym þat is absent but he were obstinat and wolde nout comyn.' *Nov. Narr*. 340: 'Afterwards at that day Robert and William came [venerunt], and the aforesaid John did not come [non venit].' COMEN AND CLAIMEN.

COMEN AND CLAIMEN   To come into court and put forth a claim: B.11.123 Thanne may alle cristene come . . . and cleyme þere entree By þe blood þat he bouȝte vs wiþ (C.12.56). Cf. *Nov. Narr*. 311: 'There came one W., clerk, and claimed this church' [vint . . . et clama]; *Court Baron* 144: 'Roger King of Wells and Adam Bateman . . . came here into court and claimed two third parts of a boat' [venerunt . . . et calumpniaverunt]; Fisher 105/4: 'We wol and charge . . . that alle manere men . . . comme and chalenge eche man his owen grond.' See ENTRE.

COMFORT   Assistance or support; abetment (in MAINTENAUNCE): B.4.151 For þe kynges profit, Ac noȝt for confort of þe commune (C.16.135); B.20.91 The lord þat lyued after lust þo aloud cryde After Confort a knyght to come and bere his baner (C.22.91); C.5.75; B.12.83; B.14.300. Cf. Fisher 202/18: 'After whiche tyme Thomas Stamford . . . by comfort of other vntrue persones . . . feyned diuers vntrue accions of trespases.' See COLLATERAL.

COMFORTEN   To aid or support (sb., e.g., legally, materially, etc.): B.7.49 Ac he þat spendeþ his speche and spekeþ for þe pouere That is Innocent . . . Conforteþ hym in þat caas (A.8.51, C.9.48); C.9.97 These are almusse, to helpe þat han suche charges And to conforte such coterelles and crokede men and blynde; B.6.220 (C.8.230); B.7.152; B.12.81; B.14.175, 179, 180; C.17.50; B.20.67 (C.22.67).

*COMMISSARIE   An officer exercising spiritual or ecclesiastical jurisdiction as the representative of the bishop in parts (esp. the more distant parts) of his diocese; or one entrusted with the performance of an absent bishop's duties (*OED*): B.15.239 In þe Consistorie bifore þe Commissarie he comeþ noȝt ful ofte For hir lawe dureþ ouerlonge but if þei lacchen siluer (C.16.361); A.2.141 (B.2.180, C.2.190); A.3.132 (B.3.143, C.3.179). *K. Counc*. 30: 'Ye are . . . to appear before the . . . official of the lord the archdeacon of Norfolk or his commissary . . . in a cause of matrimony and divorce'; *Writs* 137 (item 121). Discussion in Woodcock 26ff. and 37ff.

COMMUNE   ***I.** ?An organized body of the freemen of shires or towns, here meeting in the court of the *communitas*, that is, the County Court (Donaldson 104): C.16.359 In kynges court a [Charity] cometh. . . . Amonges þe comune in court a cometh bote selde (B.15.237). The difficulty of getting justice in the county court is a common theme; e.g., *Fleta* 2.66: 'It is still perilous, however, to plead, if one must, in the county court [in comitatu], for these stewards often influence the judgements of the court . . .' (225).
II. The common people; the lower order of society, as distinguished from those of noble or knightly or gentle rank: C.8.84 Consayle nat so þe comune þe kyng to desplese; B.3.316 (C.3.468); B.10.29; C.15.11; B.15.553 (C.17.216); C.17.310.

III. The common body of the people; the community or commonalty; sometimes, the commonwealth or state, as a collective entity: B.Prol.113 Thanne kam þer a kyng; knyȝthod hym ladde; Might of þe communes made hym to regne; C.5.75 Knyhtes ... For the ryhte of this reume ryden aȝeyn oure enemyes In confort of the comune; B.Prol.143; B.Prol.187 (C.Prol.201); C.3.206; C.3.374 passim; B.4.182 (C.4.176); B.5.48 (C.5.180); C.5.186; C.9.10; B.12.296; C.17.291; B.19.155 (C.21.155); B.19.214 (C.21.214); B.19.416 (C.21.416); B.19.466 (C.21.466) passim. *K.Counc.* 71: '... tresgrant oeure de charite pour les communes.'

Donaldson 85–120 analyses in great detail the many uses of this word in the B and C versions; as applied to groups of persons, according to his count, there are 33 occurrences in B, 38 in C. See also Bennett 98. COMUNER, COM-UNES.

*COMMUNE COURT   The Court of Common Pleas; also, the county court: B.3.320 Kynges Court and commune Court, Consistorie and Chapitle, Al shal be but oon court, and oon burn be Iustice (C.3.472); C.2.22 In kynges court, in comune court [Mede] contrarieth my techynge; cf. B.15.237 (C.16.359). Held at Westminster, the Court of Common Pleas had jurisdiction over civil actions brought by one subject against another, all real actions, and the decisions of local and manorial courts; it was inferior to the Court of King's Bench, since error lay from it to that court (*Oxf. Comp.* 254). Donaldson interprets as a county court, the court of the *communitas* (104). COM-MUNE (I), COURT.

COMMUNE LAWE   The law of the land: B.18.72 Two þeues þat tyme þoled deeþ also Vpon a croos bisides crist; so was þe comune lawe (C.20.75). *K.Counc.* 69: 'Forestalling ... punished by the common law of the land [le commune ley de la terre].'

COMMUNE PROFIT   The common good; Lat. *res publica*: B.Prol.148 Mo þan a þousand Comen to a counseil for þe commune profit (C.Prol.167); B.Prol.119 For profit of al þe peple (= *pro bono publico*); B.4.150–51 Clerkes [construed ...] þis clause for þe kynges profit, Ac noȝt for confort of þe commune; B.Prol.169 (C.Prol.184); B.Prol.187 (C.Prol.201); B.4.123 (C.4.119). Cf. *D&P* 2:160: 'Alwey þe comon profyth owyth to be chargyd mor þan þe profyt of on persone.' The phrase is a standard opening in a variety of writs, e.g., 'Whereas to the common benefit [ad communem vtilitatem] of the people of our realm, it is enacted,' etc. (*Writs* 254), and a regular feature of oaths taken by public officials, e.g., *Lib.Alb.* 1:318–19. The complaint in B.4.150 occurs also in the *Mirror*: 'And whereas ordinances ought to be made by the common assent of the king and his earls, they are now made by the king and ... others who dare not oppose the king but desire to please him and to counsel him for his profit [a son proffit], albeit their counsel is not for the good of the community of the people [covenable al comun del people]' (156). For a discussion of the background that gave rise to the currency of the phrase, see Cam, chaps. 8 and 9; for L's understanding of the phrase, Elizabeth Orsten, 'The Ambiguities in Langland's Rat Parliament,' *Medieval Studies* 23 (1961), 216–39.

COMMUNER   **I.** A burgess or citizen; *specif.* a member of the general body of a town council: C.4.188 *Audiatis alteram partem* amonges aldremen and comeneres. *Lib.Alb.* 371: 'There shall be chosen two Aldermen and four Commoners [deux Aldermans et quatre Comuners] . . . before whom . . . all such complaints shall be heard and determined.'
   II. One of the common people; a member of the commonalty: C.5.183 Y rede ȝow ryche And comuners to acorde in alle kyn treuthe; B.15.332.

COMMUNES   ***I.** Property held in common by members of a religious house (Lat. *communa, -ia*; see DuCange): A.5.38 And siþþe he redde religioun here rewele to holde 'Lest þe king & his counseil ȝour comunes apeire' (B.5.46, C.5.144). See the charter of Henry III to the canons of Salisbury, *Lib.Cust.* 34: 'Sciatis me concessisse, et praesenti Charta confirmasse . . . ad communam Canonicorum Sarum ecclesiae, omnes decimas de Nova Foresta.'
   *II. Sustenance: B.Prol.117 The kyng and knyȝthod and clergie boþe Casten þat þe commune sholde hire communes fynde (C.Prol.143); B.19.407 (C.21.407); B.19.414 (C.21.414).

COMPAIGNIE   Accomplices, band of conspirators; a gang: B.13.160 Myȝte neuere . . . Coold ne care ne compaignye of þeues . . . Tene þee any tyme; B.19.155 The Iewes . . . preide þe knyghtes Telle þe comune þat þer cam a compaignie of his Apostles . . . and awey stolen it (C.21.155). Cf. *Court Baron*: 'Now name some of thy fellows, for it cannot be but that thou hadst fellowship [compaingnie] in thy evil deeds' (63); 'And when he had done this felony . . . he straightway fled to a fellowship [une compaingnie] . . . where he was right gladly received and harboured' (65). FELAWSHIP.

COMPLEINT   See PLEINT

CONFERMEN   To ratify, approve or confirm, usually in the form of a deed, charter, or some other written instrument: C.14.39 Lawe of loue oure lorde wroet long ar Crist were, And Crist cam and confermede . . . And in soend a signe wroet; B.10.358 Crist for cristene men deide, and confermed þe lawe; cf. B.13.213, B.15.457 (the sacrament of confirmation). Cf. *Abbey of H.G.* 338: 'Wetiþ ȝe . . . þat almiȝti god . . . haþ ȝouen & graunted & wiþ his owne word confermed . . .'; *Cov.Leet* 106: 'Thomas Grene of Couentre enfeffed hym & . . . confermed the astate of the seyd Hugh to hym & to his heires be a ded there shued.' In the Middle English 'charters of Christ,' the crucified body of Christ is treated as the deed that confirms his promise of an eternal inheritance (Spalding). Hall prints a number of charters of confirmation (1:41–50).

CONGIEN To banish or exile (sb.): A.3.161 Consience acusiþ þe to cunge þe for euere (B.3.174, C.3.219); A.4.4 (B.4.4, C.4.4); C.16.366. BANISHEN, FOR EVER.

CONSCIENCE The faculty or principle which pronounces upon the moral quality of one's actions or motives, approving the right and condemning the wrong (*OED*); that faculty which applies the general principles of moral reason to specific circumstances; as a legal personification, an accuser or witness, esp. in the internal forum of the mind (*in foro conscientiae*): C.Prol.95 Consience cam and cused hem; C.2.245 Consience to þe kyng accused hem bothe; B.15.32 Whan I chalange or chalange noȝt . . . Thanne am I Conscience ycalled (C.16.191); A.3.161 (B.3.174, C.3.219), etc. Cf. *Pr.Consc.* 5440: 'First sal þair awen conscience Accuse þam þan in Cristes presence'; *D&P* 2:238/7–12: 'Þer is a witnesse withynnyn us þat is our conscience . . . And þer is a witnesse withoutyn us þat is our neyhebore & alle creaturys whiche schul beryn witnesse aȝenys us at þe doom aforn þe heye iuge.' The legal image of conscience as a witness or accuser goes back to the Bible, e.g., Rom. 2:15, 2 Cor. 1:12. On the 'court of conscience,' originally a canonistic idea (cf. Aquinas, *S.T.* 1–2.96.4; *Engl.Canons* 2:343, 371), see Levy-Ullmann 287–313; and on the relation of reason and conscience as juristic concepts: St. German's *Doctor and Student*; Baldwin 42 passim. See also AYEIN CONSCIENCE.

CONSENCIENTES & AGENTES PARI PENA PUNIETUR 'Those who consent to a deed and those who do it are to be punished equally,' a maxim of canon law: B.13.426a (C.7.87a). Cf. *D&P* 1:238; *Hand.Synne* 242; and for additional examples, Alford 1975.

CONSENTEN To grant, concede (something): C.2.90 The counte of coueytise he consenteth to hem bothe (B.2.87 al I hem graunte).

CONSISTORIE The court of a diocese for adjudication under canon law, bishop's court; *gen.* any court of law; *fig.* the court of God at the Last Judgement: A.3.131 To be cursid in constorie heo [Mede] countiþ not a risshe (B.3.142, C.3.178); B.Prol.99 Drede is at þe laste Lest crist in Consistorie acorse ful manye (C.Prol.127); A.2.139 (B.2.178); A.3.30 (B.3.31, C.3.34); B.3.320 (C.3.472); B.15.239 (C.16.361). Cf. Wright 155–59, 'A satyre on the consistory courts'; *Mirror* 37: 'Those primitive assemblies were the origin of the consistories which we now call courts. And these exist in various places, and are of various kinds.' Kiralfy 174; Holdsworth 1:599; Woodcock passim. CHAPITRE, COURT.

*CONSPIREN To plot (someone's injury, death, etc.); to enter into a confederacy for the purpose of maintaining false legal causes: B.10.429 Who dide worse þan Dauid þat vries deeþ conspired; A.11.19 Þat can construe deseites, & conspire wrongis . . . to counseil ben yclepid (B.10.19); C.11.80. Cf. *Jac. Well* 34/31: 'And alle þo arn acursed þat . . . falsly conspyrin, confederyn, comettyn, ymagyn, or castyn, ony fals cause.' The Eyre article 'de mutuis sacramentis' defines conspirators as 'those who bind themselves reciprocally by mutual oaths to sustain the causes of their friends and well wishers in their pleas, whereby truth and justice are suppressed' (*Eyre* 48). A formula count of conspiracy appears in *Nov.Narr*. 328–29, and the record of a conspiracy trial is printed in *Eyre* 43ff. IMAGINEN, MAINTENEN.

CONSTABLE   I. An officer of the king's peace (as of a county, hundred, or town); a justice of the peace: B.2.209 Þe kyng comaunded Constables and sergeauntȝ Falsnesse and his felawship to fettren and to bynden; A.2.160 (B.2.199, C.2.210); B.3.315 (C.3.467); A.4.72 (B.4.85, C.4.81). Cf. Reynes 154: 'Charge to the Constabelis. ȝe schul first pryncypaly take hede þat þe pees be kepte in ȝour towne, etc.' Blackstone 1:343–45 distinguishes the various ranks of constable.

II. A governor or warden of a castle, stronghold, or domain: A.10.16 Þe cunstable of þe castel ... Is a wys kniȝt (B.9.17, C.10.142); B.20.214 (C.22.214). See *Bor.Cust.* 2:164–66; *Writs* 167.

III. The chief officer of a ruler's household or court (*MED*): C.3.255 Sholde neuere Consience be my constable were y a kyng ... Ne be marschal ouer my men there y moste fyhte.

*CONSTRUEN   *I. To construct or fabricate (sth.) (cf. Lat. *construo*, to heap, make by piling up, construct): A.11.19 Þat can construe deseites, & conspire wrongis, And lede forþ a loueday to lette þe treuþe, þat suche craftis conne to counseil ben yclepid (B.10.19). Cf. *RR* 3.327: 'They constrewed quarellis [legal suits] to quenche the peple, And pletid with pollaxis and poyntis of swerdis.' L's usage may also suggest the nature of the 'deseites' – perverse interpretations of the law or 'false constructions' (see II below). The paired elements 'construe deseites & conspire wrongis' are restated in C.11.22: He is reuerensed and yrobed þat can robbe þe peple Thorw *fallas and fals questes* (see FALLAS, CONSPIREN). The use of ingenious constructions for fraudulent purposes is a legal topos. Cf. *Moots* 19: 'To construe [construer] *proponant* to mean *primo ponant* is nothing but a sophistical construction, etc.' Plucknett, *Statutes* 164: 'And every man ... shall keep and observe the aforesaid ordinances and statutes ... without addition, or fraud, by covin, evasion, art, or contrivance or by interpretation of words [*ou par interpretation des paroles*].' The statutes themselves are full of warnings against 'malveis interpretation' (e.g., 31 Edw. III c. 10, 36 Edw. III (2), 1 Ric. II c. 6). CONTREVEN.

*II. To gloss, translate or explain (a clause, text, etc.): B.4.150 Clerkes þat were Confessours coupled hem togideres Al to construe þis clause for þe kinges profit (A.4.133, C.4.147); B.7.108 Þi pardon moste I rede, For I shal construe ech clause and kenne it þee on englissh (A.8.90, C.9.283); A.Prol.58 (B.Prol.61); B.Prol.144; B.2.36; A.4.128 (B.4.145, C.4.142); B.5.278; B.5.419; B.14.277 (C.16.117); cf. B.15.375 (C.17.110).

CONTREE   I. A jury consisting of inhabitants of a judicial district (*MED*): C.2.63 Simonye and Syuile and sysores of contrees Were most pryue with Mede. Blackstone 3:349, '... trial *by jury*; called also the trial *per pais*, or *by the country.*' Cf. *Bor. Cust.* 1:175: 'The issue shall be tried by a jury [trie par pais]'; *LawMerch.* 2:4: 'And Roger . . . puts himself on a jury of the country [super juratam patrie]'; *Writs* 194: 'If A. . . . wishes to put himself upon the country [super patriam] for good and ill in this matter. . . .'

II. A geographical district; *specif.* a shire: A.2.129 (Sk.) Lette sompne alle men in cuntre a-boute . . . to witnesse the deede (Kane A.2.123 Let somoune alle þe segges in shires abouten; B.2.159 shires aboute); A.2.43 Kniȝtes of cuntre. Knights of the shire were elected to represent the shire in Parliament, as burgesses were elected to represent the borough. Nobility was not a requirement. Cf. Chaucer's Franklin, 'Ful ofte tyme he was knyght of the shire' (*CT. Prol.* 356).

CONTREVEN (CONTROVEN)   To contrive or plot (harm); also, to fabricate (a deceit or lie) (OF *controver*): B.10.19 (Sk.) Who-so can contreue deceytes and conspire wronges . . . to conseille is clepid (C.11.16 contreue to disseyue); B.16.137. Cf. Gower *CA* 2.1708: 'That was afterward wel proved In him which hath the deth controved.' Possibly in B.10.19 the two meanings of the word merge. Black 298: 'Controver. In old English law, an inventor or deviser of false news'; e.g., Statute 3 Edw. I c. 34 (controveures); Statute 2 Ric. II c. 6: 'It is strictly forbidden upon grievous pain . . . that from henceforth anyone should be so bold as to devise [controver], speak, or tell any false news, lies, or other such false things [ascune fauxe novelle mensonge ou autre tiel fauxe chose] of prelates, lords, or of other aforesaid persons'; *Lib. Alb.* 601: 'Jugement de prisoun par un an et un jour . . . pur mensonges controeves.' CONSTRUEN, COUNTREFETEN, DECEIT.

*CONTUMAX   'Contumacious,' in both English and canon law a pronouncement made upon persons for contempt of court, esp. those who fail to answer a summons; 'Contumax est, qui trinis edictis, vel uno peremptorio citatus, non venit, vel venit, sed non obedit; seu illicentiatus recedit' (Durandus I:448): C.13.84 Þe lawe ȝeueth leue such low folk to be excused . . . Ne in none enquestes to come ne contuimax thogh he worche Haly day or holy euene his mete to discerue. Cf. *K. Counc.* 30: 'The said official because the said countess did not appear before him on the day aforesaid deemed her the countess to be contumacious [contumacem].' Under English law, repeated contumacy might result in forfeiture of an appellee's property and/or outlawry (P&M 2:581). Thus *Fleta* 2.220: 'If . . . the defendant does not appear . . . the sheriff will be ordered to distrain the contumacious party by all the lands and chattels he has within his bailiwick . . . And if the defendant does not then appear, thereupon he shall lose the issues of his property, etc.' Cf. *Chateau d'Amour*, 'Defaute apres defaute e fine, Fet par dreit perdre seisine' (Alford 1977, 943). Part of L's point is that the poor have nothing to forfeit. Durandus addresses this very point: 'Quid si accusatus ante litem contestatem sit contumax, nec habet bona, que possint annotari?' (III.6.11). The concept of contumacy was fully developed in Roman law (see Buckland, 666), whence canon law derived much of its doctrine. Durandus (Lib. II, Partic. I, 'De Contumacia,' pp. 448–57) provides an excellent survey and commentary.

*COPIEN   To copy or put in writing (a legal document): A.8.44 Þanne were marchauntis merye . . . And ʒaf wille for his writyng wollene cloþis; For he copiede þus here clause þei couden hym gret mede. The importance attached by the merchants to having a copy of their pardon reflects the medieval emphasis on written evidences. See *Fleta* 1.28: 'Those who are inlawed needs must always carry these charters [of pardon] with them wherever they go, lest any who do not know that they have received the grace of pardon should slay them as outlaws'; *Mirror* 169: 'Wolfston . . . judged Hubert to death at the king's suit for a deed which Hubert had confessed, whereas the king had pardoned his suit; but Hubert had no charter of pardon, but vouched the king to warranty'; B.14.190 We sholde take þe Acquitaunce as quyk and to þe queed *shewen* it. See also AQUITAUNCE, CAUSE.

*CORRECTOUR   A clergyman authorized to administer justice or prescribe penance: B.10.289 Forþi, ye Correctours . . . correcteþ first yowselue. One of the main purposes of the ecclesiastical courts was to provide 'correction.' Persons convicted were given 'letters of correction,' and their names entered in the *Liber Correctionum* (Woodcock 27, 31). Canonical visitations (see VISITING) also existed 'in order to correct what required correction' (Lynch 181; *Engl. Canons* 2:234). The penance meted out by the parish priest was, at the lowest level, part of the same judicial process.

*COTER   A peasant who holds a cottage and sometimes a small piece of land by service of labour (OF *cotier*; ML *cotarius*): C.10.97 (Sk.) These were almes . . . to comfortie such cotyers and crokede men and blynde (Pearsall C.9.97 coterelles); C.10.193 (Sk.). Cotgr. on *cotterie*: 'A base, ignoble, and servile tenure, or tenement, not held in fee, and yeelding only rent.' The *Court Baron* lists *cotarii* at the bottom of a lord's tenants: 'holders of full-lands, half-lands, six-acre tenements and cottage tenements' (143); for a cottage 11 feet long and 24 feet wide, 'Geoffrey Whitring and Mabel his wife . . . give to the lord 2 s. 6 d. for entry' (142).

*COTEREL   A lesser *coter* or a subtenant (Lat. *coterellus*): C.9.193 Thise lollares, lache-draweres, lewede ermytes . . . as coterelles they libbeth; C.9.97. Black: 'In feudal law, a cottager; a servile tenant, who held in mere villenage; his person, issue, and goods were disposable at the lord's pleasure. A coterellus, therefore, occupied a less favorable position than a cotarius [COTER], for the latter held by socage tenure.' See the formula for agrarian surveys in Hall 2:14: 'Item, inquirendum est de coterellis, que cotagia et curtulagia teneant, per quod servicium et quantum reddant per annum pro predictis cotagiis et curtulagiis.' The association of lollares and lache-draweres with coterels may be explained by the Lat. plural *coterelli*, 'anciently, a kind of peasantry who were outlaws; robbers' (Black).

COUNSEIL   I. In phrases like the king's council, the KING AND HIS COUNSEIL, etc., the permanent body of advisers to the king on matters of state; the Privy Council; also Parliament: C.3.150 Thenne was Consience ykald to come

37

and apere Byfore þe kyng and his consayl, as clerkes and oþere (A.3.104, B.3.115); A.7.298 But he be heiȝliche hirid ellis wile he chide . . . and þanne curse þe king & alle þe counseil aftir Suche lawis to loke (B.7.317); B.Prol.144; A.3.90 (B.3.101, C.3.127); C.4.166; A.5.38 (B.5.46, C.5.144); B.20.68 (C.22.68); B.20.129 (C.22.129). As the quotations above indicate, the king's council functioned as both a court (Baldwin 40–41) and a legislative body (Donaldson 99). The standard history is J. F. Baldwin, *The King's Council in England during the Middle Ages* (1913; rpt. 1969). For records of judicial proceedings before the Council, see *K.Counc.* (*Select Cases before the King's Council*). In writs, the word often refers to Parliament (as it may in A.7.298 above); see *Writs* 254: 'It is enacted by the common counsel [communi consilio] of the said realm. . . .' The oath of those of the King's Council appears in *Statutes* 1:248. PARLEMENT.

II. An adviser in matters of law; also advice or legal counsel: A.11.21 Þat can construe deseites, & conspire wrongis, And lede forþ a loueday to lette þe treuþe, þat suche craftis conne to counseil ben yclepid (B.10.21, C.11.18); A.2.103 (B.2.139, C.2.152); B.4.123 (C.4.119); B.20.30 (C.22.30). Cf. *RR* 3:318: 'Chyders of Chester were chose . . . To ben of conceill ffor causis that in the court hangid'; Gower, *CA* 2.3415: 'That dai [Doomsday] mai no consail availe, The pledour and the plee schal faile'; Brown XIV 97/27: 'May no falas help in þis case, ne cownsel getes þou noght.' The main argument for not identifying A.11.21 (B.10.21, C.11.18) with the king's council or parliament is that L everywhere else regards these positively as the agents of reform and seems scrupulously to have avoided any criticism. On the etymological relation between 'counsel' and 'council' see Plucknett 221.

COUNTREFETEN   To contrive (deceit, murder, treason) (*MED*): A.11.19 (Sk.) That conterfeteth disseites and conspiret wronges . . . to counseil beoth i-clept. CONSTRUEN, CONTREVEN.

*COUNTREPLEDEN   To plead in opposition to (a demand); to argue against, contradict: C.8.88 Maystres, as þe mayres ben, and grete menne, senatours, What þei comaunde as by þe kyng countreplede hit neuere; C.Prol.138; C.8.53; B.12.98; B.20.384 (C.22.384); cf. C.11.225 countresegge. Cf. Statute 5 Edw. III c. 7 (Ruffhead): 'Ordinaries and their clerks . . . were not received to show nor defend their right in this behalf, nor to counterplead [contrepleder] the king's right so claimed, which is not reasonable'; 13 Ric. II c. 17: '. . . as well where the receipt is counterpleaded, as where it is granted'; *Moots* 70: 'If . . . the plaintiff counterpleads [counterplede] . . .' (73, 79, 129, passim).

*COUNTROLLOUR   One who keeps a counter-roll so as to check a treasurer or person in charge of accounts (*OED*); a steward: C.11.300 Selde falleth þe seruant so depe in arrerage As doth the reue or contrerollor þat rykene moet and acounten Of al þat they haen had of hym þat is here maister.

COUPABLE Guilty; also, a plea or finding of guilty: C.19.281 Coupable bifore a kynges iustice (B.17.306); B.12.88. Cf. *Writs* 174: 'Omnes illos quos per inquisicionem illam inde culpabiles inueneris . . .'; *Bor.Cust.* 1:18: 'And yf distourbance of the peas be made . . . they will take an enquest . . . to enquere and wite who ys coupable'; Hall 2:175: Offenders against the Statute of Labourers shall be punished 's'ils soient trovez coupables.' GILTI.

*COUPE Guilt, sin, fault (Fr. *coupe* < Lat. *culpa*): A.5.59 Enuye wiþ heuy herte askide aftir shrift, And carfulliche his cope comsiþ he to shewe (B.5.76); B.5.297 (C.6.351); A.5.247 (B.5.473, C.6.328). Cf. *mea culpa*, part of the formula of confession (quoted at C.6.64). The word had a precise meaning in civil law (neglect, negligence) but was broadened in canon law to include both venial and mortal sins of every kind. DEFAUTE, GILT.

COURT I. A court of law under royal administration: **A.** The Court of King's Bench: A.Prol.95 Clerkis of þe kinges bench; ?B.3.320 Kynges Court and commune Court, Consistorie and Chapitle, Al shal be but oon court (C.3.472); C.Prol.158; C.2.22. BENCHE, KINGES BENCH, KINGES COURT. **B.** ?The Court of Common Pleas: C.2.22 In kynges court, in comune court; B.3.320 (quoted above). COMMUNE COURT. **C.** The Exchequer: C.4.185. CHEKER. **D.** Any royal court: C.4.186 Y wolde . . . Consience in alle my courtes be a kynges iustice; B.15.235 In kynges court he [charite] comeþ ofte þer þe counseil is trewe (C.16.357). See also CHAUNCELRIE, COUNSEIL, PARLEMENT, WESTMINSTRE.
　　II. ?The shire or county court: B.15.237 In court amonges þe commune he [charite] comeþ but selde (C.16.359); B.3.320 (C.3.472). Cf. Wright 157: 'Nou wol uch fol clerc . . . Come to countene court couren in a cope.' See Donaldson 104. COMMUNE COURT.
　　III. A manorial court, the Court Baron: C.7.33 Ac y can . . . holden a knyhtes court and acounte with þe reue. See *The Court Baron.* KNIGHTES COURT.
　　IV. An ecclesiastical court: **A.** CONSISTORIE: B.3.31 And in Consistorie at court callen hire names (A.3.30, C.3.34); B.3.320 (C.3.472). **B.** The Court of ARCHES: B.2.61 (C.2.61); C.2.186; B.20.136 (C.22.136). **C.** CHAPITRE: B.3.320 (C.3.472).
　　V. Any court of law: B.3.316 Shal neiþer kyng ne knyght, Constable ne Meire Ouercarke þe commune ne to þe Court sompne (C.3.468); B.2.63; B.15.237 (C.16.359); B.19.304 (C.21.305); B.18.39 (C.20.38).
　　For a survey of the courts of England, see Blackstone 3:30–85; Kiralfy 140–53; and, with illustrative documents from each, Alan Harding, *The Law Courts of Medieval England.*

COVENAUNT An agreement between parties binding them to certain provisions; a contract or promise: B.6.160 Thanne Piers þe Plowman pleyned hym to þe knyȝte To kepen hym as couenaunt was fro cursede sherewes (A.7.147, C.8.157); A.5.181 (B.5.332, C.6.390); A.7.29 (B.6.27, C.8.26); B.14.151; C.14.216; B.18.417 (C.20.463); B.19.186 (C.21.186). For a discussion of covenant in equity law, see Barbour. CURTESIE, FOREWARD.

CRAVEN   To claim (something) as one's due; demand (rent, tithes, wages, inheritance, etc.); to petition for mercy, judgement, etc.: A.7.84 Of my corn & my catel he crauide þe tiþe (B.6.92, C.8.101); B.14.214 Ther þe poore preesseþ bifore . . . and boldeliche he craueþ For his pouerte and pacience a perpetuel blisse (C.16.56); B.15.165 Charite . . . ne chaffareþ noȝt, ne chalangeþ, ne craueþ; A.3.209 (B.3.222, C.3.276); A.3.212 (B.3.225, C.3.279); B.13.164; B.14.187; B.19.476 (C.21.476). Cf. *Castle of Love* 363: 'Þeuwe and þral may not crave Þorw riht non heritage to have.' The word translates Latin *petere*: e.g., *Court Baron* 84: 'petit diem amoris' [he craveth a love-day]; *Fleta* 2.63: 'poterit peti iudicium' [judgement can be craved]; etc. A formal petition for ALLOWAUNCE is called a 'craving' (Hall 2:96). BEDEN, CHALENGEN (II), CLAIMEN, PREIEN.

CREAUNT   Defeated, vanquished; 'to yield (oneself) creaunt,' to acknowledge (oneself) vanquished; a formula in trial by battle (see CHAMPION): B.12.193 The þef þat hadde grace of god on good fryday . . . yald hym creaunt to crist & knewliched hym gilty (C.14.132); B.12.214 (C.14.153); B.18.100 (C.20.104 recreaunt). Possibly L plays on the word in B.12.193: the thief on the cross yields himself to Christ as 'vanquished' and as 'believing' (Skeat 2:184).

CRIEN MERCI   To plead for pardon (usually on one's knees): B.18.87 Thanne fil þe knyȝt vpon knees and cryde Iesu mercy (C.20.90); C.6.338 Of alle manere men þat with goode wille confessen hem And cryen hym mercy, shal neuere come in helle; B.11.135f. (C.12.68f.); C.13.12; B.14.334; B.17.245 (C.19.206); cf. B.1.79; A.2.1 (B.2.1., C.2.1); B.10.147; B.17.301. Cf. *K.Counc*. 80: 'It behooved [one William Beaumont, sworn and examined before the king and his council] to kneel and cry "mercy" [janoiller et crier merci].'

CURA ANIMARUM   'The CURE of souls,' technically defined as 'the exercise of a clerical office involving the instruction, by sermons and admonitions, and the sanctification, through the sacraments, of the faithful in a determined district, by a person legitimately appointed for the purpose,' *Cath. Encyc*. 4:572: B.14.286 Riȝt as contricion is confortable þyng, conscience woot wel, And a sorwe of hymself and solace to þe soule, So pouerte propreliche penaunce is to þe body, And Ioye to pacient pouere, pure spiritual helþe, And Contricion confort and *cura animarum*. The entire passage seems to have been generated out of the various meanings of *cura*, on which L plays: attention, care, sorrow, solace, cure (med.).

*CURATOUR   A curate, one having the CURE OF SOULES: B.20.282 Persons and parissh preestes þat sholde þe peple shryue Ben Curatours called (C.22.281); A.1.169 (B.1.195); B.10.415 (C.11.249); B.13.13 (C.15.16); B.15.90; B.15.136 (C.16.279); C.16.273; B.15.530 (C.17.280); C.17.291; B.19.222 (C.21.222); B.19.410 (C.21.410); B.19.451 (C.21.451); B.20.326 (C.22.326). Purvis 18: '"Curate" and "Vicar" or even "Rector," are often synonymous. This is in accordance with the statement of Lyndwood – "Persona dicitur quandocumque curator alicuius ecclesie parchialis." '

CURE The government of souls (*cura animarum*); hence also the living or benefice, esp. a parish, supporting its exercise: C.22.237 Late hem [friars] chewe as thei chose and charge hem with no cure! (B.20.237); B.Prol.87 Boþe maistres and doctours, That han cure vnder crist (C.Prol.85); C.22.233 Freres . . . cam for couetyse to haue cure of soules (B.20.233). Cf. *Jac.Well* 18/11: 'And alle þey bene acursed þat receyvin & holdyn pluralyte of cherchys, hauyng cure of soule, but ȝif it be by dyspensacyoun.' Purvis 15: 'Of the documents found in an Archbishop's or a Bishop's Register, the commonest of all are those used at the appointment of an incumbent to the charge of a parish, or "cure of souls." '

CUREN To have the CURE OF SOULES; *specif.* to hear confession: C.14.70 For clergy is Cristes vycary to conforte and to cure; C.22.325 The frere . . . hyede faste To a lord for a lettre, leue to haue to curen As a curatour a were (B.20.326).

CURSED TIME A period of time during which sexual intercourse is forbidden by the church: B.9.123 Wastours and wrecches out of wedlock . . . Conceyued ben in cursed tyme as Caym was on Eue. See UNTIME.

CURSEN To pronounce or impose an ecclesiastical curse upon (somebody); excommunicate, anathematize, interdict: B.Prol.99 Drede is at þe laste Lest crist in Consistorie acorse ful manye (C.Prol.127); A.3.131 (B.3.142, C.3.178).

CURSING The formal pronouncement of an ecclesiastical curse; excommunication (*MED*): C.8.159 This wastors . . . acounteth nat of corsynges ne holy kyrke nat dredeth.

CURTESIE *I. A sum of money (or other recompense) given above the stated terms of a contract or agreement: C.14.216 And þat is loue and large huyre, yf þe lord be trewe, And a cortesye more þen couenant was; cf. B.14.151 And as an hyne . . . whan he haþ doon his devoir wel men dooþ hym ooþer bountee, ȝueþ hym a cote aboue his couenaunt, riȝt so crist ȝueþ heuene. Cf. *Lib.Alb.* 266: 'It is provided . . . that no baker of the town shall give unto the regratresses . . . the three pence on Friday for curtesy-money [pur curtasie].'
II. Favour or GRACE, as distinguished from inherent legal right, esp. in the formulaic phrase 'of his courtesy': B.12.77 A womman . . . was gilty of þat dede [adultery], Ac crist of his curteisie þoruȝ clergie hir saued; C.19.206 So wol Crist of his cortesye, and men crien hym mercy, Bothe forȝeue and forȝete (B.17.245); B.1.20 (C.1.20); C.3.314; C.14.216; B.14.147; B.15.557 (C.17.220); B.19.449 (C.21.449); B.20.106 (C.22.106). *K.Counc.* 51: 'The same king out of his courtesy [de curialitate] granted the writ aforesaid.'

41

CUSTUME   A common usage having the force or validity of law: C.3.373 Ac relacoun rect is a ryhtful custume, As a kyng to clayme the comune at his wille To folowe and to fynde hym and fecche at hem his consayl; C.3.206; B.12.97; C.14.73 (?). On custom as a branch of unwritten law, see Blackstone 1:74–79; Plucknett 307–14. CLOUDES AND CUSTUMES, LAWE AND CUSTUME.

*****CUTTEPURS**   A pickpocket, thief, robber: A.6.115 'Be crist,' quaþ a cuttepurs, 'I haue no þere' (B.5.630, C.7.283). The standard punishments were, for a trivial amount, the pillory (*Lib.Alb.* 602: 'Judicium Pillorii pro quodam burso cisso'), for six to twelve pence, the loss of an ear (*Fleta* 1.36, *Mirror* 146), and for greater amounts or repeated offences, banishment and even death. PIKEPORSE, ROBBER, THEF.

D

DAMPNEN   **I.** To declare (somebody) guilty; to convict, condemn to death: B.17.307 Ac it is but selden yseiʒe . . . Any creature be coupable afore a kynges Iustice Be raunsoned for his repentaunce þer alle reson hym dampneþ (C.19.282); B.15.550 (C.17.213). *Fleta* 1.28: 'A judge . . . slays in justice when he lawfully condemns [iuste dampnat].' JUGGEN.
   II. *Fig.* to condemn (sb.) to purgatory or hell: B.18.294 [Gobelyn to Satan:] We haue no trewe title to hem, for þoruʒ treson were þei dampned; B.2.103; A.5.244 (B.5.470, C.6.325); C.7.147; C.9.158; B.11.142 (C.12.75); B.12.91; C.12.242; C.17.137; B.17.268 (C.19.229); C.19.238; C.20.308; B.18.385 (C.20.427).

DECLAREN   'To declare (law or truth),' to serve as an advocate (or judge); to handle a legal cause: C.9.49 He þat . . . speketh for þe pore . . . And for þe loue of oure lord lawe for hem declareth Shal haue grace of a good ende; C.16.123 Selde syt pouerte þe sothe to declare, Or a iustice to iuge men (B.14.288). SHEWEN.

DECREE   A law or edict; *pl.* the body of canon law, the *Corpus iuris canonici*: A.11.241 For cristene han a degre . . . *Dilige deum &c, Et proximum tuum sicut teipsum*; B.15.380 Doctours of decrees and of diuinite maistres . . . sholde konne and knowe alle kynnes clergie (C.17.113). Kiralfy 175: 'The judgment [of an ecclesiastical court] was called a decree.' DECRETAL, CANOUN.

DECRETAL A papal decree; *pl.* the collection of such decrees, forming a part of the canon law (e.g., *Decretales Gregorii IX*): B.5.421 In Canoun nor in decretals I kan noȝt rede a lyne. CANOUN.

DEGRE See DECREE

*****DECRETISTRE** One versed in the *Decretum* or the decretals, a canon lawyer: C.15.85 This doctour and dyvynour . . . and decretistre of canoen . . . Hath no pyte on vs pore. In technical usage, a 'decretist' was an expert in Gratian's *Decretum* or, as it is properly called, *Concordia discordantium canonum*; a 'decretalist' was an expert in the decretals, compiled later under Gregory IX and his successors and properly regarded as the *Corpus iuris canonici*; see Ullmann 176ff. CANONISTRE, DOCTOUR, LAWIER, LEGISTRE; see also BOTHE LAWES.

DEDE A written evidence of a legal transaction, as a charter, deed, promissory note: B.2.113 In þe date of þe deuel þe dede is asseled (A.2.77, C.2.114); B.18.187 'Lo! here þe patente,' quod Pees, '*In pace in idipsum*, And þat þis dede shal dure *dormiam & requiescam*' (C.20.192); A.2.125 (B.2.161); B.5.242; A.12.87. Fisher 205/15: 'By Evydence of his dedys . . . the forseyd Rauf was wrongfully put from his Right'; *Nov.Narr.* 301: 'By this deed [fait] which they put forward they had an estate only for the term of eight years and . . . the feoffment was made in assurance of their term.' CHARTRE, WRIT, FEFFEMENT; see also CONFERMEN.

DEFAMEN To accuse (sb., as in court); also, to slander, speak against (sb.): A.2.138 (Sk.) The feith [the true party] is defouled and falsly defamed; B.Prol.190; A.11.64. Cf. *Jac.Well* 15/16: 'And alle þo arn acursyd þat for malyce, or wynnyng, or fauour, or for ony oþer cause, dyffamyn or slaunderyn ony persone, & apeyryn his name among gode men and worschipfull.' To defame another person for the sake of 'wynnyng' was a common form of legal theft. See, for example, BROKOUR (I) and the documents in a defamation suit reproduced by Woodcock (134–35). DEPRAVEN, FAMEN.

DEFAUTE An offence, a crime, sin; 'to find in default,' to judge guilty of an offence: B.2.140 If he [Conscience] fynde yow in defaute . . . It shal bisitte youre soules wel soure at þe laste (A.2.104, C.2.153); B.11.215; B.12.95. *Lib.Alb.* 521: 'Quant un homme est arrestuz pur trespas ou autre accioun personele, et troeve en defaute'; *K.Counc.* 81: 'If any default [si ascune defaute] on his part should be found. . . .' Cf. B.5.146 Thise possessioners preche and depraue freres; And freres fyndeþ hem in defaute (i.e., find fault with, blame or accuse). COUPE.

DEFENCE A law or commandment that forbids: B.18.195 Adam afterward, ayeins his [God's] defence, Freet of þat fruyt (C.20.200). Cf. Gower *CA* 5.1710: 'Adam ek in Paradis . . . Ayein the god brak his defence.' The phrase *ayeins his defence* reflects the legal formula *contra defensionem*, e.g.,

43

Lib.Alb. 489: 'Qui quidem Andreas postmodum maritavit praefatam Aliciam . . . contra defensionem Majoris et Aldermannorum, in contemptum Domini Regis et Curiae praedictae,' etc.

DEFENDEN   **I.** To forbid, prohibit (sth.): A.8.40 Vsure, & auarice, & oþes I defende; C.20.111 [The life of usury] is lif þat oure lord in all lawes defendeth; A.3.53 (B.3.64, C.3.68); A.12.19; C.14.6.

II. To provide legal defence for (sb.): C.16.37 (*fig.*) These thre þat y spak of [contrition, confession, satisfaction] at domesday vs defende; C.19.265. KEPEN AND DEFENDEN.

DEFIEN   To repudiate (sth.); *specif.* in feudal law to renounce one's faith to (a lord), to break a tie of fealty (OF *desfier*): B.20.66 Mylde men . . . Defyed alle falsnesse and folk þat it vsede (C.22.66). Although L here uses the term in its general sense, he may be punning at the same time on its technical meaning: Mylde men were 'false to falseness.' Cf. *Mirror* 176: '. . . in case the right heirs defy [defoient] their lords or cannot or will not do homage'; Ganshof, *Feudalism* 98. RENEIEN.

*DEFRAUDEN   To cheat (somebody), commit fraud against: A.8.70 He þat beggiþ or bit, but he haue nede . . . defraudiþ þe nedy (B.7.68, C.9.64).

DELIVEREN   To release (somebody) from custody or prison: B.15.346 For charite wiþouten chalangynge vnchargeþ þe soule, And many a prison fram purgatorie þoru3 hise preieres deliuereþ; B.16.266 (C.18.283); C.13.40. Cf. *Gamelyn* 752: 'Let deliver him anon.' *Bor.Cust.* 1:19: 'It is our wont . . . that the trespasser be attached and put in prison without any release [sanz nule deliverance]'; *Writs* 204: '. . . our justices assigned to deliver the gaol [ad gaolam deliberandam] at N' (i.e., 'to try the prisoners': see Plucknett 104).

DEMEN   To preside over a court (e.g., as a steward); to serve as a DOMESMAN; to judge: B.Prol.96 And somme seruen as seruaunt3 lordes and ladies, And in stede of Stywardes sitten and demen (C.Prol.94); B.19.305 Counteþ he no kynges wraþe whan he in Court sitteþ; To demen as a domesman (C.21.306); B.3.307 (C.3.459); B.4.178 (C.4.171); B.4.181 (C.4.175); A.7.73 (B.6.81, C.8.83); C.9.21; B.15.27 (C.16.186); B.15.552; B.19.196 (C.21.196); C.12.78; B.18.37 (C.20.36); B.19.174 (C.21.174). DAMPNEN, JUGGEN, JUSTIFIEN, TERMINEN.

DENE   **I.** A church official invested with jurisdiction over a subdivision of an archdeaconry: A.Prol.92 Archideknes & denis þat dignites hauen . . . Ben ylope to lundoun . . . And ben clerkis of þe kinges bench; B.2.173. Blackstone 1:370–71; Holdsworth 1:600 n.: 'It was the duty of Rural Deans to report on the manners of the clergy and laity; this rendered them necessary attendants at the episcopal visitation [see VISITING], and gave them at one time a small jurisdiction.' A particular corruption to which rural deans were subject (perhaps the reason for their inclusion among Mede's followers in B.2.173) is condemned in Peckham's Constitutions: 'Some rural deans ... sell certificates for money to fraudulent men, when no notice of the citation is given to the party concerned' (Lyndwood lib. 2 tit. 1; *Engl. Canons* 289). See CHAPITRE.

II. The head of the chapter of canons of a collegiate or cathedral church: B.13.65 þis freke, bifore þe deen of Poules, Preched of penaunces. CANOUN (II).

DEPARTEN   To separate (a married couple), as in the marriage vow 'til death us depart': C.11.271 (Sk.) Thei lyue here lif vnlouely til deth hem departe. Cf. B.20.139 [Coveitise] made lele matrymoyne Departen er deeþ cam and deuors shapte (C.22.139) – a further play on the meaning of *departen* as 'to divorce' (*MED* 2b[e]). Cf. *D&P* 2:76: 'Only deth departyth þe bond of wedlac.'

DEPOSEN   To remove (sb.) from office; to degrade (an ecclesiastic): B.15.552 [Reason and justice shall] demen *dos ecclesie*, and depose yow for youre pride (C.17.215). Cf. *D&P* 2:178: 'Ȝif a clerc be symoniac in takyng of his ordre ... And ȝif he be conuyct aforn hys iuge he shal ben deposyd & vnablyd to euery worchep'; 2:239 'deposyd & degradyd.'

*DEPRAVEN   To defame, vilify, exhibit contempt for (sb.): B.3.179 I kam noȝt to chide, Ne to depraue þi persone (A.3.166, C.3.224); B.5.145. Black: 'In England it was a criminal offense to "deprave" the Lord's Supper or the Book of Common Prayer.' DEFAMEN, FAMEN.

DERNE   Of actions: secret or concealed, deceptive: B.2.176 Lat sadle hem wiþ siluer oure synne to suffre, As deuoutrye and diuorses and derne vsurie; cf. 'doings' that are 'derne oþer elles' (C.3.291); confession that is either 'derne' or open (B.13.55), and so forth. The law distinguishes between usury that is *apert* and *derne*, or 'plain' and 'coloured' (see R. H. Tawney in Wilson 129): 'derne vsurie' is usury hidden within an apparently legal agreement (cf. CHEVISAUNCE).

DESPOILEN   To rob (sb.) or plunder: C.13.57 Robbares and reuares þat ryche men despoilen. PILEN, RAVISHEN, RIFLEN, ROBBEN, STELEN.

DETERMINEN   See TERMINEN

DETTE   **I.** That which is owed or due; anything (as money, goods, service) which one person is under obligation to pay or render to another; the condition of being under such obligation, as in 'to be or bring in debt': A.7.90 Þeiȝ I deiȝe today my dettis ben quyt (B.6.98, C.8.107); B.7.81 He þat biddeþ borweþ and bryngeþ hymself in dette; C.3.304; C.13.37; B.13.10 (C.15.12); B.14.108; B.20.10 (C.22.10); B.20.293 (C.22.293). To die 'quit' of one's debts was a central concern of testators; their legacies could not be distributed until all debts had been paid (see BIQUESTE). Nevertheless, as Woodcock notes of the province of Canterbury, 'The majority of cases labelled *testamen-taria* are cases of debt' (85). Medieval law regarded debt as a *grant*; in actions of debt, the defendant 'was conceived to withhold something from the plain-tiff, which it was his duty to surrender' (Barbour 34). On forms of action to recover debts, see Barbour 25–40. LONE, *REDDE QUOD DEBES*, SUM CER-TEIN.

II. *Fig.* a debt incurred through sinful behaviour, payable to God in the form of love and penance: C.6.301 Þe prest þat thy tythe toek . . . Shal parte with the in purgatorye and helpe paye thy dette; C.22.321 Peres the plouhman . . . indulgence may do, but yf dette lette hit (B.20.321); A.5.145 (B.5.229); B.19.190 (C.21.190). L develops the notion of spiritual debt most fully in the recurring formula *Redde quod debes* (q.v.). On the important role of debt in L's thinking, see Stokes chap. 1; and Yunck, in Alford 1988, 149–52.

*DEVOUTOUR   An adulterer [altered form of *avouter*] (*MED*): C.2.184 Syuyle, and Symonye my felawe Wol ryde vppon *rectores* and ryche men deuoutours, And notaries on persones þat permuten ofte And on pore proui-sores and on appeles in þe Arches. The definition given by the *MED*, based on the word's similarity to *avouter*, is not entirely satisfactory. Neither Syuyle nor Simony has any obvious connection with the prosecution of adultery (a sin explicitly mentioned seven lines later in connection with Commissaries); their presence, along with the mention of *rectores*, notaries, persones, permuten, prouisores, and appeles in þe Arches, suggests that *devoutours* have some-thing to do with the corrupt practice of trading in benefices. Since the word *devoutour* occurs only in *Piers Plowman*, it may be L's own coinage to signify one who misuses or interferes with the 'advowson' to an office (possibly influenced by Lat. *devotare*; see DuCange, 'Devotare: Fraudare votum'; *Catholicon Anglicum* 'to breke Vowe; *deuotare, deuouere*').

*DEVOUTRIE   Adultery (according to the *MED*, an altered form of AVOU-TRIE, but see above): B.2.176 Erchedekenes and Officials and alle youre Registrers, Lat sadle hem wiþ siluer oure synne to suffre, As deuoutrye and diuorses and derne vsurie.

DEWID   Endowed or having a benefice: A.11.199, 201 Dobet doþ ful wel, & dewid he is also, And haþ possessions & pluralites for pore menis sake; For mendynauntȝ at meschief þo men were dewid. AVAUNCEN, DOWEN.

DIES IUDICII   Judgement Day, DOMESDAY: C.15.119 Dowel wol endite ȝow *in die iudicii*; C.15.22.

DIGNITE   A high OFFICE, title, or benefice; also, the honour or duty at-tached thereto: A.Prol.92 Archidekues & denis þat dignites hauen To preche þe peple & pore men to fede. See Barraclough 139, 'Processus de dignitate vacante'; *K.Counc.* 24: 'Pope Boniface VIII . . . deprived John de Colonna . . . of the said treasurership and canonries, prebends, dignities [dignitatibus], personatus and other ecclesiastical benefices'; *Mirror* 105–06: 'He may say that the writ is vicious because of . . . the omission of titles of dignity. Thus if a bishop, abbot, prior, or other prelate be disseised in right of his dignity [del droit de sa dignetie] and complains simply of a trespass done to his person and not to his church or dignity, and speaks thus: "A. complains to you," whereas in this case he should have said "A., Bishop of London, complains to you." '

DIGNUS EST OPERARIUS   'The worker is worthy [of his hire],' Luke 10:7: B.2.123 God graunted to gyue Mede to truþe, And þow hast gyuen hire to a gilour. . . . The text telleþ þee noȝt so . . . For *Dignus est operarius* his hire to haue (A.2.86a). The text was 'traditionally used by canonists and legists to justify the acceptance by lawyers of moderate fees from those who could afford to pay' (Beverly Brian Gilbert, *Medium Aevum* 50 [1981], 56).

DIME   The tithe due by law to ecclesiastics as an incorporeal hereditament (see TITHE): C.17.227 Taketh here [prelates'] londe, ȝe lordes, and lat hem lyue by dymes (B.15.564). Blackstone 1:274–75.

*DISALLOWEN   **I.** To refuse credit to (somebody, or for something) in an account: B.14.131 Som riche . . . han hir hire heer . . . And whan he dyeþ ben disalowed; C.16.7 Thenne may men wyte what he is worth and what he hath deserued, Ac nat to fonge byfore for drede of dessallouwynge (B.14.139). *Rot.Parl.* 4.478a: 'The seid Auditours that shall be chosen . . . to here the accounte of the seid Balliffs . . . to allowe or disallowe hem aftir the fourme of accounte' (*MED*). See ALLOWEN.
   II. To annul, cancel, invalidate: C.3.319 Thow the kyng . . . cayser or pope, ȝeue lond or lordschipe . . . Bothe . . . May desalowe that thei dede and dowe þerwith another. DISAVOWEN.

*DISAVOWEN   To annul, disclaim, or repudiate (an action): C.4.322 (Sk.) Bothe kyng and kayser and the coroned pope May desauowe that they dude and douwe ther-with other. DISALLOWEN (II).

DISCHARGEN   **I.** To release (sb.) from debt or other legal action or liability: B.4.29 Oon waryn wisdom and witty his feere Folwed hem faste for þei hadde to doone In cheker and in Chauncerye, to ben descharged of þynges (A.4.26). *Fleta* 2.33 (on the exchequer, quoting Statute 3 Edw. I c. 19): 'In cases where anyone can prove that he has paid, let him be discharged, whether the receiver is alive or dead'; Fisher 26/4: 'We sende to yow closed wiþynne þees oure lettres a supplicacion . . . makyng mencion how þat þe barons of oure Eschequer at Westminstre wol not discharge hem of certeine sommes of moneye rennyng on hem at oure saide Eschequer [and . . .] we wol þat . . . ye doo ordeine and see þat þai be discharged of þe saide dymes and quinzimes after þeffect of oure saide lettres patentes.' On 'discharges' in the exchequer, see Hall 2:91ff., and his *Antiquities*, chap. 5.
   II. To purge (of a harmful substance); *fig.* disendow, dispossess: C.17.231 If possession be poysen . . . Hit were charite to deschargen hem [corrupt

clergy] for holy churche sake And purge hem of þe olde poysen (B.15.566). Pearsall 288: 'L shows in this passage how close he is in spirit to many of Wyclif's ideas and to Lollardy . . . for whom the disendowment of the Church was an essential requisite of reform.'

DISCLAUNDRE   Public disgrace or opprobrium; infamy: A.5.75 (Sk.) I haue anuyȝed him ofte, Ablamed him be-hynde his bak to bringe him in disclaundre (Kane A.5.74: *in fame*). Fisher 161/29: 'And we ben openlich disclaundred, holden vntrewe & traitours to owre kyng.' FAME, SCLAUNDRE.

DIVINOUR   *A theologian; an expert in canon law: C.15.85 This doctour and dyvynour . . . and decretistre of canoen . . . Hath no pyte on vs pore; A.11.302 (B.10.458); B.7.141; B.13.115 (C.15.123).

*__DIVORCE__   In medieval usage, an annulment or a declaration that a marriage had been invalid *ab initio* (Helmholz 74): B.20.139 [Coveitise] made lele matrymoyne Departen er deeþ cam and deuors shapte (C.22.139); B.2.176. Cf. *Jac. Well* 53/8: 'In alle þise degrees forsayde . . . contract of matrymonye is forfendyd . . . [and] . . . þer owyth be lawe to be made a deuorce.' How divorces were made, with the help of meed and a few false witnesses, is told in *The Simonie* 332/199–203: 'If a man have a wif, and he ne love hire noht, Bringe hire to the constorie ther treuthe sholde be souht, And bringge tweye falsse wid him and him self the thridde, And he shal ben to-parted so faire as he wole bidde from his wif.' On suits for divorce in medieval England, see Helmholz 74–111.

DOCTOUR   A doctor of canon law: B.Prol.87 Boþe maistres and doctours, That han cure vnder crist (C.Prol.85); B.15.380 Doctours of decrees and of diuinite maistres . . . sholde konne and knowe alle kynnes clergie And answere to Argumentȝ and assoile a *Quodlibet* (C.17.113); B.13.61 (C.15.66 passim); B.15.243. Cf. Statute 5 Ric. II St. 2 c. 5: 'Prelatz & Maistres de Divinite & Doctours de Canoun & de Civile'; *Abbey of H.G.* 353: 'Marie & Ioseph . . . founden hym sittande in þe temple among þe doctoures of þe lawe.' BOTHE LAWES, CANONISTRE, CANOUN, CIVILE, DECRETISTRE, LEGISTRE.

DOM   I. A judicial decision; a sentence at law: B.3.318 After þe dede þat is doon oon doom shal rewarde Mercy or no mercy as Truthe may acorde (C.3.470); B.2.208; B.18.191 (C.20.196); B.18.385 (C.20.427). JEWISE.
  II. The administering of justice; the act of judging: B.15.550 Reson and rightful doom þo Religiouse dampnede (C.17.213; cf. B.15.27); B.11.145 (C.12.78 lawes demynge); C.12.87.
  III. The Last Judgement, DOMESDAI: B.7.193 At þe dredful dome, whan dede shulle rise (A.8.171, C.9.340); B.5.275 (C.6.299); B.5.292 (C.6.347); A.8.19 (B.7.17, C.9.21 domesday); A.8.155 (B.7.177, C.9.323); B.10.364; B.11.134 (C.12.67); B.12.91.

DOMESDAI The day of the Last Judgement: C.5.122 That dedly synne ar domesday shal fordon hem alle (A.5.20, B.5.20); A.5.244 (B.5.470, C.6.325); C.9.21; B.10.417 (C.11.252); B.11.134 (C.12.67); C.16.37; B.19.196 (C.21.196); B.20.293 (C.22.293). DOM (III).

DOMESMAN The chief officer of a law court; a judge or magistrate: B.19.305 He in Courte sitteþ To demen as a domesman (C.21.306). Fisher 161/54: 'Goddes lawe & al resoun wole that no domesman stonde togidre Iuge & partye.' The word has a complex history. Plucknett notes that the early county courts were composed 'not of judges but suitors who sometimes bear the significant name of "Doomsmen." They were not lawyers, nor even officials, but merely lay persons who by custom were bound to attend' (91). STIW-ARD.

DOMINUS In feudal and ecclesiastical law, a lord or feudal superior (Black): B.10.336 Dominus and knyȝthode ... Kynghod and knyȝthod. Fourquin defines as 'the superior person in homage' (115); thus also P&M 1:412: 'If the serf has a *dominus*, the palantine earl, nay, the king of England, so long as he is duke of Aquitane, has a *dominus* also.'

DOMINUS PARS HAEREDITATIS MEAE 'The Lord is the portion of my inheritance,' Psalm 15:5, quoted in the ceremony of tonsuring new clerks; hence, the cleric's motto (cf. *Engl. Canons* 2:449): C.14.128 *Dominus pars hereditatis* is a merye verset, Hit hath take fro Tybourne twenty stronge theues (B.12.189); C.5.60a. Though not a neck-verse (*pace* Skeat 2:184), the quotation of Ps. 15:5 above is clearly meant to allude to 'the custom of pleading "benefit of clergy," whereby condemned criminals could claim to be beyond the jurisdiction of lay courts by proving their literacy (equivalent to clerical status), usually by reading a passage from Psalms in the Latin (the "neck-verse"). Ps. 50 was the usual choice' (Pearsall 241 n., 100 n.). The process is described in *Fleta* 1.28.

DOWEN To endow; provide (somebody) with privileges, property, tenure, etc.: B.15.557 Costantyn of curteisie holy kirke dowed Wiþ londes and ledes, lordshipes and rentes (C.17.220); C.3.319; A.11.199. Cf. Statute 3 Ric. II c. 3: 'Our lord the king has perceived ... how the churches ... abbeys, priories and other benefices of his realm, which were lately founded, and richly endowed [dowez] by his noble progenitors. ...' BENEFISEN, DEWEN, FINDEN, FOUN-DEN, MAKEN, MARIEN, RENTEN, SETTEN.

DUE Of a DETTE, owed, payable: C.3.304 Þat is no mede but a mercede, a manere dewe dette. Cf. *Jac. Well* 20/30 against lords who 'takyn to hem þe godys of here tenauntys þat dyen untestate, ouer þe dette dewe to hem'; *Lib. Cust.* 187: 'Les dettes qe sunt deues par contract et covenaunt.'

E

ELECCIOUN   The holding of a vote, in accordance with established procedures, by which a body of electors chooses a person for some office (*MED*); also the right or duty to elect: C.6.136 Prioresse worth she neuere; For . . . she worth chalenged at þe eleccioun; B.Prol.110 (C.Prol.137). Cf. *Jac.Well* 127/8: 'Eleccyoun of prelacye or dygnite . . . whan a college or a couent schal chesyn here prelate. . . .' See the petition of the Convent of Barking (1393) for licence to elect an abbess (licencia aliam eligendi in nostri monasterii abbatissam) in Hall 1:88; and the standard licence itself in *Writs* 100.

ENDE, MAKEN   To 'determine' (see TERMINEN) or conclude a legal case; to give a judgement: B.3.161 Lawe is so lordlich and looþ to maken ende (C.3.198); A.3.259 (B.3.281, C.3.433). There is a pun on the expression in C.9.50: lawyers who defend the poor shall themselves 'haue grace of a good ende.' Cf. B.18.161 (C.20.164). Fisher 93/3: 'Bothe parties [are ordered] to bee before vs or oure conseil for to haue had knowlache of the matere þat þay stande in debat fore and for to haue made an ende þerof.' The complaint that law is 'looþ to maken ende' is conventional; the poet of 'Sir Penny' notes that unless domesmen are bribed, 'forto gif dome þam es ful lath' (Robbins 52/43–48). The theme is treated in full by J. A. Yunck, *The Lineage of Lady Meed: The Development of Medieval Venality Satire*. Notre Dame: Univ. of Notre Dame Press, 1963.

ENDITEN   To bring formal accusation against (someone), indict, charge with a crime: C.15.119 Dowel wol endite ȝow *in die iudicii*; B.11.316 Eiþer is endited, and that of '*Ignorancia Non excusat episcopos nec* ydiotes preestes.' *W&W* 313: 'For thayre dede [they] were endityde with twelue.' *Writs* 206: 'A., recently indicted [indictatus] before our justices . . ., as soon as he knew that he was indicted [in dictamento] he gave himself up of his own free will.'

ENDOWEN   See DOWEN

ENFEFFEN   See FEFFEN

ENQUESTE   A trial by jury (the jurors acting more as character witnesses than as fact finders); an investigation conducted by the bailiff or the mayor in the presence and with the assistance of representatives chosen from the community or summoned for that purpose (*MED*): C.22.162 Here syre was a sysour þat neuere swoer treuthe, Oen Tomme Two-tonge, ateynt at vch enqueste (B.20.162 queste); C.11.22 He is reuerensed and yrobed þat can robbe þe peple Thorw fallas and fals questes; C.5.57 Clerkes ycrouned . . . Sholde nother swynke ne swete ne swerien at enquestes; C.2.110; C.13.84. On L's point that tonsured clerks should not participate in inquests, see *Writs* 251: 'Men of religion shall not be bound to come to the view of frankpledge unless their presence is specially required for some purpose'; *Mirror* 38: 'King

50

Henry the Third . . . declared that archbishops, abbots, priors, earls, barons, men of religion and sick folk . . . need not come in their own presence [to sheriffs' inquests or 'turns']; Constitutions of Othobon, tit. 7 (Lyndwood 91–92): 'We forbid any clerk to be judge, or associate in any trial touching life or member.' SISE.

ENSELEN To authenticate (a letter patent, an agreement, etc.) with an official mark or seal: B.17.4 'Is it enseled?' I seide. 'May men see þi lettres?' (C.19.6 asseled). *K.Counc.* 17: 'The said John had good acquittances ensealed [enselees] with the seal of the said Sir Adam.' ASSELEN, SELEN.

ENTRE *The act of taking possession of lands or tenements by entering the same; also, the legal right to do so: C.12.56 Thenne may alle cristene come and clayme þerto entre By þat bloed he bouhte vs with and bapteme as he tauhte (B.11.123). The previous quotation *venite ad aquas* is here expanded in language that is resonant with legal implications – come, clayme, entre, bouhte. Cf. *MED* entren (3a): 'Yf my brothir . . . wil cleyme or entre into ye same maner of Mekilfeld' (1439). Statute 5 Ric. II c. 7: 'And the King defendeth, that none from henceforth make any entry [face entree] into any lands and tenements but in case where entry is given by the law'; *K.Counc.* 14: 'Hereupon our lord the king by his charter granted entry [la entree] to the aforesaid abbot, and the abbot took possession.' Blackstone 2:144. See also the citations under COTER, COMEN AND CLAIMEN.

ENTREN To assume possession of property or title; *fig.* to reap the benefit (*MED* 3b): B.15.138 Curatours of holy kirke, as clerkes þat ben auarouse . . . endeþ intestate and þanne entreþ þe bisshop And makeþ murþe þerwiþ and hise meyne boþe. Cf. Fisher 164/9: 'The forseyd Rauf be wey of Ryght entryd and took p[ossessyon of the] tenement affter decesse of his modor.' By law the bishop was executor of the goods of all those who died intestate within his diocese. *Writs* 229: 'Command R., bishop of Durham, into whose hands have come the goods and chattels of B., who died intestate. . . .' The misadministration of a deceased clerk's goods was a common complaint; e.g., Stratford's Constitutions (1343), tit. 8: 'Improbity hath so blinded the interior sight of some ecclesiastical judges [i.e., bishops] of our province of Canterbury, that they do not permit the executors of beneficed clerks . . . to dispose of their goods according to the direction of the testators . . . and they usurp the movables of testators, and of intestates that have movables . . . so as sometimes to distribute them at pleasure' (*Engl. Canons* 391).

EQUITE Justice; that which is just, right, fair: 'the correction of that, wherein the law (by reason of its universality) is deficient' (Blackstone 1:61, quoting Grotius); 'Equytye is a ryghtwysenes that consideryth all the pertyculer cyrcumstaunces of the dede the whiche also is temperyd with the swetnes of mercye' (St. Germ. 95): B.17.310 Þe kyng may do no mercy til boþe men acorde And eyþer haue equyte (C.19.285); C.21.309 *Spiritus iusticie* spareth nat to spille hem þat ben gulty . . . For counteth he no kynges wreth . . . presente . . . preyere or eny prinses lettres; He dede equite to alle euene-forth his knowyng (B.19.308). Cf. *Jac.Well* 95/27: 'He sparyd no persone for loue, ne dreed, ne for wreth, but þat in his demyng he dyde equite.' The distinction between equity and the justice of the common law is given interpretative value by William J. Birnes, 'Christ as Advocate: The Legal Metaphor of *Piers Plowman*,' *Annuale Mediaevale* 16 (1975): 71–93. GOOD FEITH, JUSTICE (II), RIGHT.

ERITAGE   See HERITAGE

ERLDOM   *Fig.* the territory or manorial estates of an earl: A.2.60 I, fauel, feffe falsnesse to mede . . . Wiþ þe Erldom of enuye for euere to laste (B.2.84, C.2.88).

ERLS AND BAROUNS   The lords temporal, *comites et barones*: B.10.326 Per shal come a kyng . . . And amende Monyals, Monkes and Chanons . . . And Barons wiþ Erles beten hem . . . Bynymen that hir barnes claymen, and blame yow foule. *Fleta* 1.17: 'In the governance of the people [the king] has superiors, namely the law, by which he is constituted king, and his court, that is to say the earls and barons' (p. 36); *Writs* 205: 'In the ordinances lately made by the prelates, earls and barons [comites et barones] of our realm. . . .' See *Oxf.Comp.* 'House of Lords.'

*ESCHAUNGE   A conversion of one kind or denomination of money into another for profit; also, exchange of goods for profit: C.6.280 Y sente ouer see my seruauntes . . . To marchaunde with my moneye and maken here eschaunges (B.13.393); B.5.246 Eschaunges and cheuysaunces, wiþ swich chaffare I dele. 'To marchaunde with . . . moneye' required Letters of Exchange, many of which survive in a series of Exchange Rolls (Hall 1:80ff.). Statute 5 Ric. II c. 2 confirms earlier policy on merchant exchanges. On the connection between 'eschaunges' and 'cheuysaunces,' see *Lib.Alb.* concerning usurious contracts: 'The which kind of contract, the more subtly to deceive folks, they call "exchange" or "chevisance" [eschange ou chevisance]; whereas it might more truly be called "wickedness" [mescheaunce], seeing that it ruins the honour and the soul of the agent' (368); 'Many merchants . . . colourably and subtly have made . . . divers exchanges of money [eschaunges de moneye] and of other things that do not concern the dealings of lawful merchandize' (371). On the gradual development of the idea that money-exhange (cambium) was a form of lawful merchandise (permutatio), see De Roover. As late as the 16th century, popular sentiment lumped exchange and usury together; see R. H. Tawney's introduction to Wilson, *Discourse on Usury* 134ff., 148, etc. CHEVISAUNCE, PERMUTACIOUN.

ESCHETE   Reversion of land or its appurtenances to the king or the lord of a fee, upon failure of heirs to a tenant in fee simple; also, forfeiture of the lands and goods of a FELOUN to the king; thus, any property or goods falling by escheat to the lord or king: C.4.169 Thorw ȝoure lawe . . . y [the king] lese many chetes (B.4.175). *Bor.Cust.* 1:161: 'The mayor and citizens say that all the escheats [*escaete*] within the liberty of the city of London are the king's, no matter of whom the lands are held, whether they are escheat by felony or otherwise. . . . And the king has escheat in these cases: that is, when anyone is convicted of usury, his tenement ought to be the king's escheat, and similarly the lands of those who are convicted of felony,' etc. See for a good discussion of 'escheat and forfeiture,' Simpson 19–23; for a sample 'form of inquisition for escheators,' Hall 2:70–71; and for various writs of escheat, *Writs* 286. L refers to the doctrine of escheat in C.10.237–39: according to 'Westminstre lawe,' he says, 'Thogh þe fader be a frankeleyn and for a felon be hanged The eritage þat þe eyer sholde haue is at þe kynges wille.'

EVENE Justly, equitably: A.4.147 Ac it wel hard . . . herto to bringe it, And alle my lige ledis to lede þus euene (B.4.184, C.4.178); B.19.298 (C.21.299). Cf. *Jac.Well* 131/26: 'A fals iuge doth more wrong þan evynhed in iugement'; Fisher 161/32: 'an even Iuge.'

EXCEPT Excepting, excluding (OF *excepte*; Lat. *exceptus*): B.11.98 It is *licitum* for lewed men to legge þe soþe . . .; ech a lawe it graunteþ, Excepte persons and preestes and prelates of holy chirche; B.9.144 [God to Noah:] Alle shul deye for hise dedes . . . Excepte oonliche of ech kynde a couple (A.10.175 Alle shuln deiȝe for his dedis . . . Outtake þe eiȝte soulis, & of iche beste a couple; C.10.230); B.15.53 (C.16.214); B.15.279 (C.17.9). *Piers* offers the first record in English of this word, common in contemporary legal usage; cf. *Lib.Alb.*: Let no regrators be allowed to sell before prime 'exceptis emptoribus Regis' (252); Prisoners in certain cases not to go to Newgate or Ludgate 'felonie et tresoun exceptes' (523); Hall: 'Volumus eciam quod idem Hugo interim sit quietus de omnibus placitis et querelis, exceptis placitis, etc.' (1:71).

EXCHEQUER See CHEKER

EXCUSEN To clear or acquit (oneself or another) of a charge; to exonerate or free of blame; to pardon: A.3.160 Excuse þe ȝif þou canst . . . For consience acusiþ þe to cunge þe for euere (B.3.173, C.3.218); C.9.239; C.13.82; B.17.93 (C.19.81). Fisher 161/68: 'Also we biseche vnto yowre gracious lordeshipe . . . that we mowe come in answer to excuse vs'; *D&P* 2:235: 'Þer may no man ben iuge & witnesse & acusour togedere in þe same cause, but in caas þe iuge may ben witnesse of trewþe to excusyn.'

EXECUTOUR A person appointed by a testator to execute or carry out his WILLE after his decease: B.12.260 Executours, false frendes, þat fulfille noȝt his wille That was writen, and þei witnesse to werche as it wolde; B.5.263 (C.6.254 seketoure); B.15.132 (C.16.277); B.15.248; B.20.291 (C.22.290). The greed of executors who fail to carry out the testator's will is a literary commonplace; cf. Kail 22; *Jac.Well* 129/11; Brown XIV 97, 195; *Gamelyn* 158ff.; *Castle of Perseverance* (EETS 262) 1660ff., 2606ff.; additional exs. of the topos in Sheehan 219 n. For a full account of the executor's duties, see Sheehan 195–230.

F

FAITOUR An imposter or cheat; esp., a beggar who feigns injury or disease (AF *faitour* < Lat. *factor*): A.7.113 Þanne were faitours aferd & feynide hem blynde (B.6.121, C.8.128); A.2.144 (B.2.183, C.2.193); B.6.72 (C.8.73); A.7.171 (B.6.183, C.8.179); C.9.64; B.9.196 (C.10.295); B.15.215; B.20.5 (C.22.5). Cf. *Jac. Well* 134/13: 'Faytours ... getyn mete & monye of pyteous folk, wyth wyles, as to makyn hem seme crokyd, blynde, syke, or mysellys, & are noȝt so.' 'Faitours' were the object of several statutes passed in L's day, most notably the statute of labourers 1349 (Chap. 7: 'No person shall give any thing to a beggar that is able to labour'), 7 Ric. II c. 5 (1383): 'Item ordeignez est & assentuz ... par restreindre la malice des diverses gentz faitours & vagerantz de lieu en lieu currantz de present par paiis pluis habundantement ...,' etc. See also *faiten* C.Prol.43, A.8.77 (B.7.95, C.9.170), C.9.100, C.9.208, B.15.214, etc., and **faiterie* C.8.138, B.11.92 (C.12.32).

FALLAS A legal strategem intended to deceive; fraud: C.11.22 He is reuerensed and yrobed þat can robbe þe peple Thorw fallas and fals questes; C.16.231. Cf. Brown XIV 97/27: 'May no falas help in þis case, no cownsel getes þou noght.' See CONSTRUEN, STOPPEN.

FALS AND FEITHLES A formula in actions of slander: A.10.139 Fals folk & feiþles, þeuis & leiȝeris, Ben conseyuid in cursid tyme (B.9.121); B.10.198 And so shaltow fals folk and feiþlees bigile. Cf. *Law Merch.*: 'The said William in full court insulted the twelve jurors ... calling them false and faithless knaves [falsos et infideles]' (1:61); 'The said Robert .. .assaulted him with vile words, calling him faithless and false merchant [infidelem et falsum mercatorem]' (1:57). Numerous other instances of the phrase will be found in Helmholz, *Defamation* (passim).

FALS DOM False judgement: B.18.28 Þe fend and fals doom [to joust with Christ] (C.20.27). Cf. *O&N* 210: 'Ne schaltu neure so him queme Þat he for þe fals dom deme' (see Stanley's intro., p. 29); *D&P* 1:253: '[Perjurers] deseyuyn þe juge & don hym ȝeuyn a fals dom.' The joust between Christ and *fals doom* is illuminated by French practice: 'In old French law, the defeated party in a suit had the privilege of accusing the judges of pronouncing a false or corrupt judgment [viz. Christ's trial], whereupon the issue was determined by his challenging them to the combat or *duellum*' (Black, 'false judgment'). BATAILLE, CHAMPION.

FALSLICHE AND FELOUNLICHE With deceit and criminal intent: B.18.351 [Christ to Satan:] Thow fettest myne in my place maugree alle resoun, Falsliche and felonliche; cf. C.12.237 Fals folk fecche awaye felonliche his godes. Froissart 2.94.281 (Berners trans. 1525): 'They said it was falsely and feloniously done' (*OED*). Cf. FELOUNLICHE.

FALS MESURE An inaccurate instrument for measuring length or quantity, esp. one that has not been checked and sealed by the proper city authorities: B.13.358 Þe gome . . . ymagynede how he it myȝte haue Thoruȝ false mesures (C.6.258); B.14.295 vnseled mesures (C.16.129). The view of frankpledge included the question: 'Whether there be among you any ale-wives or regratresses who brew and sell contrary to the assize, and that by false measures' (*Court Baron* 94); similarly, *Lib.Alb.* 259: 'Item, si ascun taverner, braceresse, hostiller . . . vendent saunz mesure ensele ou encountre lassise . . .' (cf. LAWE [V.C]). To buy by one measure (or weight) and sell by another was explicitly forbidden by statute (e.g., 51 Hen. III [6] para. 3). See SELEN, UNSELED.

FALS WIGHTE An inaccurate weight: B.14.295 Wynneþ he noȝt wiþ wiȝtes false ne wiþ vnseled mesures (C.16.129); cf. A.5.118 (B.5.202, C.6.210); B.5.215; A.5.143 (B.5.227). The practice of buying and selling by different weights is described in B.5.215: My wif was a wynnestere and wollen cloþ made . . . The pound þat she paied by peised a quartron moore Than myn owene Auncer whan I weyed truþe. The standard weights and measures were kept in the exchequer, as required by statute (e.g., 9 Hen. III c. 25, 14 Edw. III c. 12, 16 Ric. II c. 3), and all other weights and measures were supposed to conform to these. Cf. *Cov.Leet* 133: 'Hit is to haue in mynd, for-also-moche as hit is ordenyd þat ther shuld be but one Weyght & one mesure thorout this Realme, the said maiour sent to London for to haue the weightes acordyng to the weightes of thexechecour and thens brought xiiij li., vij li., ij li., j li., in brass.'

FALS WITNESS False testimony, esp. by one who initiates a false suit and then agrees to drop it in return for a 'settlement' (MAINTENAUNCE); also, a juror paid by one of the parties to a suit to give false testimony: B.13.358 Moore to good þan to god þe gome his loue caste, And ymagynede how he it myȝte haue . . . wiþ fals witnesse; A.2.111 Fauel . . . bad gile go gyue gold al aboute . . . And feffe false wytnesse wiþ floreynes ynowe (B.2.147, C.2.160); B.5.580 Bere-no-fals-witnesse . . . is fryþed In wiþ floryns and oþere fees manye (A.6.67, C.7.227); B.15.238 (C.16.360). JUROUR, QUESTMONGERE, WITNESS; see also ATTEINTE, CONSPIREN, FORSWEREN, SCLAUNDRE.

FAME Bad reputation: A.5.74 I haue noiȝed hym often, And blamide hym behynde his bak to bringe him in fame (B.5.94). Cf. *Hand.Synne* 1519: 'Bakbyters . . . a-peyryn many mannes lyfe. ȝif þou bryng a man yn fame . . . þou hym slos.' *LawMerch.* 1:57: 'Robert Woodfool . . . assaulted him with vile words, calling him faithless and false merchant, by which defamation [*per quam famam*] he lost credit with a certain Robert of St. Neots for three quarters of wheat.' In canon law, defamation is a technical term, 'signifying that evil reputation which is sufficiently notorious to put a man on his trial. Mere rumour is not sufficient' (Plucknett 484); see Lyndwood lib. 5 tit. 14 (Item licet). L alludes to the doctrine of notoriety in B.11.101: 'Þyng þat al þe world woot, wherfore sholdestow spare To reden it it Retorik to arate dedly synne?' DISCLAUNDRE, SCLAUNDRE; see also *INFAMIS*.

FAMEN To defame or slander (sb.): A.3.173 Þou hast famid me foule before þe king here, For kilde I neuere no king ne counseilide þeraftir (B.3.186, C.3.231). For numerous cases of slander, see Helmholz, *Defamation*. DE-FAMEN, DEPRAVEN, SCLAUNDREN.

FAUTOR A favourer or supporter of others; an abettor; one who encourages resistance to the execution of process (Black): B.15.215 Charite . . . lyueþ noȝt in lolleris ne in londleperis heremytes. . . . Fy on faitours and *in fautores suos*! Cf. *D&P* 1:159: 'Wychys schuldyn ben hefdyd or ellys brend and here fautourys exylyd.' *Mirror* 26: 'Into the sin of larceny fall those who take purses or bags . . . and all their abettors [fautours].' The context closest to L's is Statute 5 Rich. II st. 2 c. 5 against wandering preachers (Lollards) and their abettors: 'Plusours malurees persones . . . alantz de Countee en Countee & de ville a ville en certains habitz souz dissimulacion de grant saintee, & sanz licence . . . & lours fautours maintenours & abettours.' FELAWE, MAINTEN-OUR.

FECCHEN (also FETTEN) *I. To steal (sth.): B.4.51 Boþe my gees and my grys hise gadelynges feccheþ (A.4.38); C.12.237 Ful ofte hath he drede That fals folk fecche awaye felonliche his godes; B.13.372 If I yede to þe Plowȝ I pynched so narwe That a foot lond or a forow fecchen I wolde Of my nexte Neghebore, nymen of his erþe (C.6.268); A.7.145 (B.6.157, C.8.154); B.16.49 (C.18.49); B.18.295 (C.20.325); B.18.348 (C.20.393); B.19.145 (C.21.145). Normal usage calls for an object that is movable; the use of the word in B.13.372 to describe the appropriation of *land*, coupled with the amount 'a foot,' may owe something to the custom known as 'fetch and have' by which a person extended the boundary of his land in a dispute: 'The claimant . . . shall set his right foot so that the big toe reaches to the edge of the land which he claims . . . and say . . . "All the land which I measure with my foot . . . is mine, so help me the Holy of Holies." And this custom is called "Fetch and have" [Et vocatur ista consuetudo *Fetche and have*]' (*Bor.Cust.* 1:250). The 'pinching' of land in plowing was a common charge. See *Court Baron* 98: 'Also they say that James Day hath ploughed with his plough and appropriated to himself [apprporians sibi] three furrows from the King's highway.' PILEN, STELEN.

II. To recover (what is rightfully one's own): B.19.247 [Grace taught] some to ryde and to recouere þat vnriȝtfully was wonne . . . And fecchen it fro false men wiþ Foluyles lawes (C.21.247); B.18.20 [Jesus will] fecche þat þe fend claymeþ, Piers fruyt þe Plowman (C.20.18); B.18.33 (C.20.32); B.19.464 (C.21.464). RECOVEREN.

III. To recover (someone) through ransom: B.16.264 Out of the poukes pondfold no maynprise may vs fecche (C.18.281); B.16.269 (C.18.286). RAUNSOUNEN, MAINPRISEN.

FEE See KNIGHTES FEE

FEFFEMENT   The investing of a person with an estate in land, tenements, rents, etc.; also, the written instrument (DEDE, CHARTRE, etc.) by which such conveyance was made: B.2.73 [Simony and Civil] vnfoldeþ þe feffement that Fals hath ymaked (A.2.55, C.2.73). *K.Counc*. 71: 'William Clopton by virtue of the aforesaid enfeoffment [feoffamenti] and quit-claim had been in peaceful possession and seizin of the said manor.'

FEFFEN   **I.** To put (sb.) in legal possession: **A.** Of lands, rents, etc. B.15.325 Allas, lordes and ladies . . . To ȝyue from youre heires . . . to swiche þat ben riche, And ben founded and feffed ek to bidde for oþere (C.17.56); B.2.79 (C.2.83); C.3.369. Cf. Reynes 522: 'Sciant presentes et futuri quod ego Robertus Reynes de Acle tradidi, dimisi, feofaui . . .'; *Writs* 309: 'We permit J. de C. to enfeoff [feoffare] R. Tuk and John his son of fifteen acres of land.' **B.** Of anything by way of gift: B.2.147 (C.2.160) Fauel . . . bad gile . . . feffe fals witnesse wiþ floryns. AMORTISEN, GIVEN AND GRAUNTEN, GRAUNTEN, SEISEN.
   II. *To join (one person to or with another) in a marriage contract; to affiance: C.2.137 Mede may be wedded to no man bot Treuthe; And thow hast feffed here with Fals; A.2.37; A.2.58; A.2.92 (Sk.).

FEITH   Good faith: B.3.157 Wiþ hire Ieweles youre Iustices she [Mede] shendeþ And liþ ayein þe lawe and letteþ hym þe gate That feiþ may noȝt haue his forþ, hire floryns go so þikke (C.3.194); B.20.131 (C.22.131). The concept was associated primarily with equitable jurisdiction, and petitions before courts of equity routinely complained of *laesio fidei* or 'breach of faith' (Barbour 163). GOOD FEITH.

FELAWE   An associate in crime, an accomplice or accessory (Lat. *socius*); MAINTENOUR: B.9.87 Iewes, þat we Iugge Iudas felawes, Eyþer of hem helpeþ ooþer; B.2.209 (Sk.) Thanne Drede . . . warned the Fals, And bad hym flee for fere and his felawes alle; B.15.379 Go now to any degree, and but if gile be maister, And . . . Flatere his felawe, ferly me þynkeþ. *Court Baron* 76: 'Hear this sir steward N. etc. that I, N. will not be a thief nor the fellow of a thief [socius latronis].'

FELAWSHIP   A band of fellows, a COMPAIGNIE; MAINTENAUNCE: B.2.210 Þe kyng comaunded Constables and sergeauntȝ Falsnesse and his felawship to fettren and to bynden. *RR* 1.61: 'Men myȝtten as well haue huntyd an hare with a tabre, As aske ony mendis . . . ffor all was ffelawis and ffelawschepe that ȝe with fferde, And no soule persone to punnyshe the wrongis.' *Court Baron* 91: 'One F . . . is appealed by an approver for fellowship [societate, i.e., association with criminals] and receipt' [see RECETTEN].

FELOUN   A criminal, *specif.* one who has committed a felony (treason, murder, rape, theft, etc.): C.10.238 [By] Westminstre lawe . . . thogh þe fader be a frankeleyn and for a felon be hanged The eritage þat þe eyer sholde haue is at þe kynges wille; C.20.421 Hit is nat vsed on erthe to hangen eny felones

Oftur then ones, thogh they were tretours (B.18.379); A.5.245 (B.5.471, C.6.326); A.11.279 (B.10.420, C.11.255); B.12.202 (C.14.141); B.17.113; B.18.382. The word *felon* was not used with great precision in the Middle Ages. Felony and 'breach of the peace' are often paired (see the citations under FELOUNLICHE), but the two are not convertible. Although a felony was an action committed 'against the king's peace' (Baldwin 43), not every breach of the peace was counted a felony; see the discussion in Harding 61–67. By 'Westminstre lawe,' the property of a convicted felon escheated to his lord or to the crown; see *Writs* 286, Simpson 19, Bellamy 188–89 passim, ESCHETE. In contrast to English law, St. German observes, 'There is no suche lawe of forfeyture of goodes by outlagarye in the spyrytuell lawe' (45).

FELOUNLICHE   Criminally; with criminal intent or against the king's peace: C.12.237 Fol ofte hath he [the rich man] drede That fals folk fecche awaye felonliche his godes; B.18.351. *Court Baron* 27: 'He might ... carry off their goods ... feloniously [felonousement] as a felon'; *K.Counc.* 107: 'The said misdoers felonousely as riottours breking the same dore made assaute to the wif of the said Thomas ... felonousely and ayenst oure pees'; *Writs* 191: A. killed B. 'in self-defence ... and not feloniously [per feloniam] or with malice aforethought.' FALSLICHE AND FELOUNLICHE.

FERME   A lease; a fixed yearly amount (Lat. *firma*) payable as rent, tax, or the like (as opposed to a rent, tax, etc. of variable amount (*OED*); 'haven to ferme' [*ad firmam*], to have the use or revenues of (something) in return for a fixed payment: B.16.16 *Liberum arbitrium* haþ þe lond to ferme, Vnder Piers þe Plowman to piken it and weden it. Simpson: 'In the earlier Middle Ages one who took land in return for an agreed money rent was called a *firmarius* or *farmer*, the rent payable being the *firma*, and the transaction was described by saying that the lands were *ad firmam*' (12 n., cf. 73–74). Thus *Bor.Cust.* 1:312–13: '*De fermariis*. If a man or woman has let to another a house or piece of land or a garden under culture for a term of years, and it chances that he who has leased the same to farm [a ferme] comes forward. ...' See also Harding 32.

FETTEN   To take (something) against another's will; to steal (cf. FECCHEN): B.18.350 [Christ to the devil:] Thow fettest myne in my place maugree alle resoun; B.18.267 Swich a light, ayeins oure leue laȝar it fette (C.20.275); B.18.336 (C.20.379).

FIGHT   Judicial battle: B.15.164 Charite is noȝt chaumpions fight ne chaffare. Cf. *Jac.Well* 134/29: 'Champyouns dwellynge wyth lordys, feyȝtynge in here querels, and getynge here lordys þe maystrye in wrong aȝens þe ryȝt ...'; *D&P* 1:255: 'Whan þei schuldyn fyȝtyn aforn a iuge in here cause, þe iuge, as þe maner is, putte hem boþin to her oth.' See Neilson, *Trial by Combat*. BATAILLE, JUGGEMENT OF ARMES, JUSTE.

FIN   *A final agreement or settlement (*finalis concordia*) relating to the alienation of property or property rights; also the legal process by which lands could be vested in a buyer, heir, feoffee, etc., especially in cases where ordinary modes of conveyance would be impracticable or less efficacious (cf. *MED* [5a]): A.2.36 Sire symonye is assent to asele þe chartres Þat fals & fauel be any fyn halden, And feffe mede þermyd in mariage for euere; A.2.48 Alle to wytnesse wel what þe writ wolde, In what maner þat mede in mariage was feffid; To be fastnid wiþ fals þe fyn is arerid. The technical meaning of the word here is missed by both Skeat ('fine, fee') and the *MED* ('an agreement or contract, esp. a marriage contract'). The essential character of a fine partly explains why L chose to associate this form of conveyancing with Fals; though entirely legal, fines were based on a deception agreed to by both parties, namely the pretence of a quarrel requiring some sort of material settlement. As Simpson explains, 'Such a conveyance took the form of a compromised fictitious personal action [as opposed to a 'real' action]. . . . The main varieties of fine differ in the grounds upon which the grantor . . . pretends he has had to compromise' (115–16). The whole process is described in the formula 'the fine is levied' ('þe fyn is arerid'). Cf. *K.Counc.* 50: 'Gill says that a certain fine was formerly levied [quidam finis quondam leuauit] . . . and for this acknowledgement, fine and concord [recognicione fine et concordia] the same Robert granted to the aforesaid John and Gill the aforesaid manor. . . . And he produces here the part of the fine [partem finis] which is evidence of this.' The use of fines, 'the most secure of all medieval conveyances' (Simpson 116), was extremely common in the fourteenth century. For further information, see the Statute of Fines ('De Finibus levatis') 27 Edw. I c. 1 (1299); the relevant writs (*Writs* 115, 236 passim); the *Readings and Moots at the Inns of Court* (*Moots* 95, 199, 202 passim); and the discussion in P&M 2:94–105.

FINDEN   I. To determine and declare (a person) guilty or innocent (*OED*): B.2.140 And if he [Conscience] fynde yow in defaute, and with fals holde, It shal bisitte youre soules wel soure at þe laste (A.2.104, C.2.153); B.5.146 Thise possessioners preche and depraue freres; And freres fyndeþ hem in defaute. Hall 2:175: Offenders against the Statute of Labourers to be punished 's'ils soient trovez coupables'; *Writs* 174: 'All those whom you find guilty [culpabiles inueneris] by that inquisition to be before our justices at Westminster. . . .'
    II. 'Finden witnesse,' to furnish proof: B.9.75 Of þis matere I myȝte make a long tale And fynde fele witnesses among þe foure doctours. Cf. *CT.Phys.* 169: 'I wol it preue and fynde good witnesse, That sooth is that my bille wol expresse.'
    III. To support or maintain (someone) with a benefice, endowment, salary, etc.: B.15.307 Religiouses rightfulle men sholde fynde (C.17.34); C.5.36 My fader and my frendes foende me to scole; C.9.35 Fynde . . . fauntkynes to scole; C.5.76; B.19.445 (C.21.445); B.20.295 (C.22.295). Cf. *Jac.Well* 128/28: 'ȝif his freendys fynden him to scole, & he mysspende his tyme in ryott . . . he is a theef'; Fisher 219/13: 'The seid Thomas . . . hath preyed . . . the seid Robert to putt and to fynde hym to scole . . . after the effecte of the seid

couenaunt' (also quoted in Barbour 208f.); Fisher 224/16: 'He and his successors shall fynde twey prestes ... to pray for þe gode estate of our souerain lord the kyng'; Hall 1:72: letter patent assigning certain lands to Dore Abbey 'ad inveniendum tres monachos' (to pray for the souls of the donors); *Nov.Narr.* 245: 'The aforesaid David has ceased providing [trouant] the said chantry.' DOWEN, SETTEN.

IV. To sustain (someone) with the necessities of life: B.7.31 Treuþe ... bad hem [i.e., merchants] ... Fynden swiche [prisons in stokkes] hir foode (A.8.33, C.9.35); A.2.50; C.3.41; C.5.27, 49, 88; C.7.259; A.7.63 (B.6.69, C.8.70); B.7.135; B.9.70 (A.10.70); B.10.94; C.10.181; B.15.178 (C.16.316); B.13.243 (C.15.217). The Statute of Merchants (1285) provides that where a merchant has caused a debtor to be put in prison, 'le marchaunt luy truisse [should find] pain e ewe'; cf. the resulting writ 'De pane et aqua inueniendis debitoribus in prisona commorantibus' (*Writs* 225); *Lib.Alb.* 282 on fugitives having 'amys qi eux troevent.'

FINDING *That which is provided for sustenance and support, such as a salary, grant, endowment, etc.; a BENEFICE: B.20.383 And þat freres hadde a fyndyng þat for nede flateren (C.22.383); C.6.294. On the debate concerning *fyndyngs* for friars, see Szittya 286–87 passim.

***FOLVILE'S LAWES** Extralegal justice, lynch law (*MED*): B.19.247 [Grace taught] some to ryde and to recouere þat vnriȝtfully was wonne: He wissed hem wynne it ayein þoruȝ wightnesse of handes And fecchen it fro false men wiþ Foluyles lawes (C.21.247). The term has been traced to the Folville brothers, a notorious gang in Lincolnshire during the 1330s; see E. L. G. Stones in *Transactions of the Royal Historical Society*, 5th ser. 7 (1957), 117–36; and R. H. Bowers, *Notes and Queries* ns 8 (1961), 327–28.

FOREGOER A purveyor; one who goes ahead to prepare the way for another, esp. an officer who precedes a king in order to arrange for lodging and provisions (*MED*): B.2.61 Bedelles and baillifs and Brocours of chaffare, Forgoers and vitaillers and vokettes of þe Arches (C.2.61). Pearsall 57 n.: ' "Foregoers" or purveyors were men who travelled in advance of a great lord to commandeer provisions and accommodations. ... The practice was much abused ... and frequent attempts were made to restrict purveying (e.g., Statutes of 1360–62).' See citations under TAILLE.

***FORESTALLEN** To intercept or buy up goods before they reach the market, usually for the purpose of resale at a higher price; to sell before legal business hours: B.4.56 (Wrong) Forstalleþ my feires, fiȝteþ in my Chepyng (A.4.43, C.4.59). Forestalling was repeatedly condemned by Parliament (e.g., Statutes 35 Edw. III and 5 Richard II) as an offence against the common good. *Fleta* explains why: 'Inquiry must be made ... regarding forestallers [forstallariis] who divert foodstuffs from the market and thereby raise prices' (p. 122); so also the *Mirror*: 'Forestallers [forstallours] are those who within an enfranchised town purchase to regrate or to sell dearer unlawfully' (28).

Another motive for forestalling must have been to avoid paying customs. See *Lib.Alb.* (De Forstallatoribus): 'No one shall put up his wares for sale, that owe custom, until he has paid custom thereon' (263). R. H. Britnell, '*Forstall, Forestalling and the Statute of Forestallers,*' *English Historical Review* 102 (1987), 89–102.

FORESTER   A sworn officer of the forest, appointed by the king's letters patent to walk the forest, watching both the vert and the venison, attaching and presenting all trespassers against them within their own bailiwick or walk (Black): B.17.115 And þanne shal Feiþ be forster here and in þis Fryth walke, And kennen outcomen men þat knowen noȝt þe contree. Cf. *CT.Prol.* 117: 'A Yeman . . . clad in cote and hood of grene . . . And in his hand . . . a myghty bowe . . . A forster was he,' etc.; *Jac.Well* 61/10: Cursed are 'alle forsterys, bedelys, & baylyes, þat makyn scottalys, or gaderyn schevys.' Formulas relating to the duties of a forester are printed in Hall 2:83–86; relevant statutes include 9 Hen. III (Charta Forestae), 21 Edw. I, 7 Ric. II c. 4.

FOR EVER   **A.** In grants of land, 'for ever' ('ay,' 'without end,' etc.) is associated with unconditional possession (i.e., fee simple): B.2.103 Fauel . . . feffeþ by þis chartre . . . And þei to haue and to holde, and hire heires after, A dwellynge wiþ þe deuel and dampned be for euere (C.2.106 day withouten ende); B.9.49 [God] graunted hym blisse, Lif þat ay shal laste, and al his lynage after; B.16.240 (C.18.257). The gift of an estate in fee simple, 'the highest and largest estate that a subject is capable of enjoying' (Blackstone 2:164), normally includes the words 'to him and his heirs for ever.' Cf. *K.Counc.* 74: 'He drew up a charter of enfeoffment in fee simple . . . granting to Master William Clopton the manor of Newland . . . for himself and his heirs to hold forever [a touz jours].' On the kinds of estate defined by the words for ever, heirs, assigns, etc. (or their absence), see *Moots* 176–80 and Blackstone 2:164. See HEIR, HEIRS FOR EVER. **B.** Certain punishments, such as imprisonment and exile, were for a term of years or forever: A.3.161 Consience acusiþ þe to cunge þe for euere (B.3.174, C.3.219); C.20.375 [Christ speaking to Lucifer concerning the souls in limbo:] Y bihihte hem nat here helle for euere (B.18.332); A.3.257 (B.3.279, C.3.431); A.9.96 (B.8.106); B.15.555 (C.17.218). Cf. *Fleta* 2.1: 'There are certain wrongs that entail imprisonment for three years with perpetual banishment [cum exilio perpetuo] when the wrongdoers have no sureties' (p. 106); *Mirror* 103: 'On the king's death . . . those who have abjured or been banished from the realm, return, save those who have been exiled or banished for ever'; *Mirror* 125: '[Outlaws] forfeit . . . every kind of right that they ever had . . . not only for themselves but for their heirs for ever.'

FOREWARD   An agreement, a contract: B.6.35 By my power, Piers, I pliȝte þee my trouþe To fulfille þis forward þouȝ I fiȝte sholde (A.7.37); A.2.50; A.4.13 (B.4.13, C.4.13); B.11.64. Cf. *SGGK* 1105: ' "Ȝet firre," quoþ þe freke, "a forwarde we make: Quat-so-euer I wynne in þe wod hit worþez to yourez, And quat chek so ȝe acheue chaunge me þerforne." ' COVEN-AUNT.

FORFETEN   To overstep the bounds, transgress or offend: B.20.25 For *Spiritus fortitudinis* forfeteþ wel ofte; He shal do moore þan mesure many tyme and often, And bete men ouer bittre (C.22.25). Cf. *D&P* 2:85: 'Crist seyth in þe gospel, hoso loke on a woman in wil to don omys with hyr . . . forfetyth aȝenys þis comandement: Non mechaberis.' See MESURE.

FORFETURE   Loss of life or property as punishment for crime; 'up forfeture,' on pain of losing: A.4.114 Rome renneris . . . Bere no siluer ouer se . . . Vpe forfaiture of þat fe, who fynt hym at douere, But it be marchaunt . . . Oþer prouisour, or prest þat þe pope auaunciþ (B.4.131, C.4.128). Cf. Statute 9 Edw. III st. 2 c. 1: 'First, it is provided that from henceforth no religious man, nor other, shall carry any sterling out of the realm of England, nor silver in plate, nor vessel of gold, nor of silver, upon pain of forfeiture [sur forfaiture] of the money, plate, or vessel that he shall so carry without our especial licence.' The prohibition was revised and restated in subsequent statutes (e.g., 27 Edw. III st. 2 c. 2, 5 Ric. II c. 2). The Statute of Provisors (25 Edw. III st. 4) cites specifically the purchasers of benefices from Rome, by whom 'a great part of the treasure of the said realm is carried away and dispended out of the realm.'

FORLIEN   To rape (sb.): C.4.46 Wrong wilfully hadde his wyf [Peace's wife] forleyn. Cf. *Ayenbite* 230: 'Yef a mayde were uorlaye be strengþe and a-ye wyl: hi ne ssolde naȝt þeruore lyese hare maydenhod.' RAVISHEN.

*****FORNICATOUR**   One who commits fornication or adultery: A.2.142 Let cartesadil þe Comissare, oure carte shal he drawe, And fetten oure vitailes of fornicatouris (B.2.181, C.2.191 at *fornicatores*). One of the main concerns of the ecclesiastical courts was the punishment of fornicators (a jurisdiction recognized by the statute *Circumspecte agatis* [1285]). The taking of bribes by church officials in such cases is a common theme. Cf. *Mirror* 134: 'Those are infamous who . . . take reward for suffering fornication'; Chaucer's Summoner, *Gen. Prol.* 649–51: 'He wolde suffre for a quart of wyn A good felawe to have his concubyn A twelf month, and excuse hym atte fulle'; *Simonie* 49–52: 'And thise ersedeknes that ben set to visite holi churche . . . wole take mede of that on and that other, And late the parsoun have a wyf, and the prest another, at wille; Coveytise shal stoppen here mouth, and make hem al stille.' Bennett's interpretation (131) is confused. DEVOUTOUR; see also AVOUTRIE, DEVOUTRIE.

FORSWEREN   To lie under oath; commit perjury: B.19.369 A sisour and a somonour þat were forsworen ofte; Witynge and wilfully wiþ þe false helden, And for siluer were forswore (C.21.370); A.10.196 (B.9.175, C.10.275). *Jac. Well* 152–54 identifies seven kinds of forswearing, including perjury ('whanne men sweryn fals wytingly, & beryn fals wyttnessse') and breach of promise ('when a man, be his owyn wyl, brekyth his trewthe'). See ATTEINTE, CONSPIREN, FALS WITNESSE.

FORYEVEN To pardon (sb. of a crime or offence): B.3.108 [The king to Mede:] But I forgyue þee þe gilt and graunte þee my grace (A.3.97, C.3.138); A.3.8 (B.3.8, C.3.8); B.17.246 (C.19.207); B.17.292 (C.19.268); B.17.337 (C.19.312); B.18.184 (C.20.187); B.19.185 (C.21.184). See PARDOUN (II).

FORYEVENESSE Cancellation of a debt: B.20.287 Shame makeþ hem wende And fleen to þe freres, as fals folk to westmynstre That borweþ and bereþ it þider and þanne biddeþ frendes Yerne of forȝifnesse or lenger yeres loone (C.22.286). The comparison is between sinners who confess to friars, and debtors who abuse the sanctuary offered them by Westminster Abbey. Both are trying to avoid paying what they owe. See WESTMINSTRE.

FOUNDEN To establish or endow (a church, monastery, etc.): B.15.325 Lewed counseil haue ye To ȝyue from youre heires . . . to swiche þat ben riche, And ben founded and feffed ek to bidde for oþere (C.17.56); B.15.289. Cf. 'founded and endowed' in Statute 3 Ric. II c. 3: 'Abbeies Priories & autres benefices de son Roialme, qe furent jadis founduz & richement dowez. . . .' DOWEN, MAKEN.

FOUNDOUR One who endows a church, monastery, etc.; a patron, benefactor, esp. one who leaves a bequest in return for prayers ('memories'): A.11.216 Godis flessh, & his fet, & hise fyue woundis Arn more in his mynde [Dobet's] þan þe memorie of his foundours. Cf. Statute 25 Edw. III 6: 'Churches were founded for the souls of the founders [pur les almes de foundours], their heirs, and all Christians. . . .'

FRANKELEIN A landowner; a freeman: C.5.64 For sholde no clerke be crouned but yf he come were Of frankeleynes and fre men and of folke ywedded; B.19.39 And þo þat bicome cristene by counseil of þe baptiste Aren frankeleyns, free men þoruȝ fullynge þat þei toke (C.21.39); C.10.238. L's explanation of baptism as enfranchisement is historically based; cf. *Mirror* 78: 'Serfs become free in divers manners: some by baptism, as are those Saracens who are captured by Christians . . . and held as their slaves.' The meaning of the term *franklin* in 14th cen. England is analyzed by Henrik Specht, *Chaucer's Franklin in the Canterbury Tales: The Social and Literary Background of a Chaucerian Character* (Copenhagen, 1981); esp. chap. 4, 'The Legal and Manorial Background.'

FRAUNCHISE Freedom (as opposed to servitude); the social status of a freeman: B.18.103 Youre fraunchise þat fre was fallen is in þraldom; And ye, cherles, and youre children cheue shulle ye neuere, Ne haue lordshipe in londe (C.20.107). L explains the history of the Jews in terms of the judgement given against the losing side in a trial by battle (see BATAILLE, CHAMPION); cf. *Fleta* 1.32: 'If the appellee is conquered, he shall suffer capital punishment, together with the disherison of his heirs and the loss of his goods' (p. 85).

*Fraunchisen   To make (someone) a freeman of a city or town: C.3.114
Forthy mayres þat maketh fre men, me thynketh þat ȝe ouhten For to spyre
and to aspye . . . What maner muster oþer marchandise he vsed Ar he were
vnderfonge fre and felawe in ȝoure rolles. Hit is nat seemely for sothe in citee
or in borw-toun That vsurers oþer regraters, for enys-kynes ȝeftes, Be
yfranchised for a fre man. Cf. Articles of the Cordwainers 1375 (in Rickert
193–94): 'To the mayor and aldermen of the city of London . . . that no one of
the trade shall keep house within the franchise if he be not free of the city and
one knowing his trade, and that no one shall be admitted to the freedom
without the presence of the wardens of the trade bearing witness to this
standing'; *Eyre* 68: 'John of Gisors, then Mayor of London, after the felony
had been committed [by one Henry of Braundeston], had the name of the
aforesaid Henry put on their register among the names of the freemen [francz]
of the town . . . and by colour of his Mayoralty wrongly used that liberty
[franchise].'

Fre   **I.** Having membership in the 'franchise' or corporation of a city or
town, possessing the rights and privileges of a citizen (see **Fraunchisen**):
C.3.108 Mayres þat maketh fre men, me thynketh þat ȝe ouhten For to spyre
and to aspye . . . What maner muster oþer marchandise he vsed Ar he were
vnderfonge fre and felawe in ȝoure rolles; C.1.73 (*fig.*) Holy churche y am . . .
Y undirfenge þe formeste and fre man the made; C.3.114. Cf. Fisher 161/5:
'The eleccion of Mairaltee is to be to the fre men of the Citee.'
   II. Free from servitude or imprisonment; *fig.* having the social status of a
freeman: C.21.59 His herte bloed he shedde To make alle folk fre þat folweth
his lawe (B.19.59); C.Prol.106; C.5.64; B.18.103 (C.20.107); B.19.39
(C.21.39); B.19.59 (C.21.59); B.20.146 (C.22.146).

G

Gaioler   Jailer, jail-keeper (Lat. *custos*, *custos gaole*): B.3.138 [Mede]
gyueþ þe Gailers gold and grotes togidres To vnfettre þe fals, fle where hym
likeþ (A.3.133, C.3.174). The position of jailer was potentially lucrative; in
addition to the usual fees (cf. Fisher 225/12), prisoners of means were expected to pay for their own upkeep, and many apparently paid more besides,
as bribes, to ameliorate their condition. Fetters were an added punishment.
Cf. *Fleta* 1.32: 'If the appeal is of breach of the peace and imprisonment, then
it shall be stated whether this was in prison or a mere detaining, in fetters or
without, in irons or in wood or both' (cf. A.2.162 [B.2.201, C.2.212]; B.2.210;
A.4.72 [B.4.85, C.4.81]; B.5.405 [C.7.21]; B.8.101 [Sk.]; B.17.113; B.19.57
[C.21.57]). According to the *Mirror*, 'It is lawful for gaolers to put fetters upon
those whom they suspect of trying to escape' (52). It would seem, in the
passage quoted above, that what Mede bribes jailers to do is not to release
prisoners but to facilitate their escape.

GENTILMAN   The highest rank of free persons below the nobility: B.19.34 The Iewes þat were gentil men . . . now are þei lowe cherles (C.21.34); B.19.40 þo þat bicome cristene . . . Aren frankeleyns, free men . . . And gentil men wiþ Iesu (C.21.40). Cf. *D&P* 1:118: 'God . . . hatȝ power and fredam of a page to makyn a ȝeman, of a ȝeman a gentylman, of a gentylman a knyȝt'; *Moots* 231: 'A was summoned to reply to B, formerly gentleman [nuper gent] and now knight [chivaler].' In wills, charters, etc., the designation affirms the necessary free status of the maker, e.g., Reynes 325; cf. B.11.127 (C.12.60) May no cherl chartre make. See YEMAN.

GILT   A crime, sin, transgression; the state or fact of being guilty: C.3.138 Wors wrouhtestou neuere then now, tho thow Fals toke. Ȝut y forgyue the þis gult (A.3.97, B.3.108); A.4.65 Wiþoute gilt, god wot, gat I þis skaþe (B.4.79, C.4.75); B.5.481 (Sk.): [Robert the Robber] knowleched his gult to Cryst (A.5.256 [Sk.]); A.3.8 (B.3.8, C.3.8); C.3.103; A.5.219 (B.5.477, C.7.62); C.6.176; B.9.146 (C.10.232); B.10.80 (C.11.62); C.10.55; B.10.286; B.13.386 (C.6.275); B.19.303 (C.21.304). The phrase 'wiþoute gilt,' meaning without provocation or desert, figures in complaints of battery or trespass; e.g., *Court Baron* 27: 'This Stephen Carter . . . assailed him with villain words which were undeserved [saunz desert] . . . and snatched his staff . . . and gave it him about his head and across his shoulders.' COUPE, DEFAUTE.

GILTI   Blameworthy, having committed a crime or sin; COUPABLE: B.12.76 A womman . . . was gilty of þat dede, Ac crist of his curteisie þoruȝ clergie hir saued; C.21.303 *Spiritus iusticie* spareth nat to spille hem þat ben gulty (B.19.302); B.12.79; cf. C.6.176; B.5.367 (C.6.425); B.10.264; B.12.193.

GIVEN AND GRAUNTEN   A conventional formula in deeds, charters, etc.: C.3.330 And ryhte so sothly may kyng and pope Bothe gyue and graunte there his grace lyketh; B.19.183 (C.21.183); cf. B.18.184 God haþ forgyuen and graunted me, pees, & mercy To be mannes meynpernour (C.20.187). See also C.2.70; B.19.104 (C.21.104). Cf. *Abbey of H.G.* 338: '*Sciant presentes & futuri &c.* . . . þat almiȝti god . . . haþ ȝouen & graunted . . . to Adam, etc.'; *Writs* 132: 'The king to all, etc. Know that we have given and granted [dedimus et concessimus] to our beloved clerk T. the prebend of W.' Blackstone 2:53: 'The manner of the [feudal] grant was by words of gratuitous and pure donation, *dedi et concessi*; which are still the operative words in our modern infeodations or deeds of feoffment.' FEFFEN, GRAUNTEN.

GLOSEN   *To explain or interpret (a writing); *specif.* to adapt a standard form (e.g., a writ or charter) to individual circumstances, as by including the phrases appropriate to the situation, filling in the names, dates, conditions, etc. B.11.306 If fals latyn be in þat lettre þe lawe it impugneþ, Or peynted parentrelynarie, parcelles ouerskipped. The gome þat gloseþ so chartres for a goky is holden (C.13.119); cf. B.17.12 (C.19.13). See also the gloss described in Truth's pardon: B.7.18 Marchauntȝ *in þe margyne* hadde manye yeres (A.8.20, C.9.22).

GOOD FEITH Fidelity; honesty or *bona fides*, sincerity, good intent; equity: C.4.37 Þat coueytise seruen…gyue nat of good fayth (B.4.37); B.19.300 Gile gooþ so pryuely þat good feiþ ouþer while Shal nouȝt ben espied þoruȝ *Spiritus Iusticie* (C.21.301); B.20.131 [Coveitise] knokked Conscience in Court afore hem alle; And garte good feiþ flee and fals to abide (C.22.131); B.5.265 (C.6.287); C.6.341; B.18.347; B.20.28 (C.22.28). Cf. Sisam 349/38: 'Mennes hertes been chaungable, . . . to falshed they been most able: For with good faith wil we not fare.' *Nov.Narr.* 301: 'R. and M. said that the feoffment was made in good faith [en bone foi] and not by collusion.' Stroud, *Judicial Dictionary*: 'The correct province of this phrase is . . . to qualify things or actions that have relation to the mind or motive of the individual. . . . A fact completely within physical apprehension can neither be bona, nor mala, fide: a mental fact may be either.' The doctrine of good faith originated in Roman jurisprudence (see Buckland 210, 224, passim) and reached its highest development in medieval canon law (Le Bras 351ff.); see the gloss by Vacarius, *The Liber Pauperum of Vacarius*, ed. F. de Zulueta, Selden Society 44 (1927), 113. FEITH.

GRACE A favour or indulgence as distinguished from a right (Black); pardon, mercy; also the power to pardon or show mercy: **A.** 'To grant grace': B.3.108 [King to Mede:] But I forgyue þee þe gilt and graunte þee my grace (A.3.97); C.5.192 [Reason] preyede þe pope . . . no grace ne graunte til good loue were Amonges alle kyne kynges ouer cristene peple; A.3.97 (B.3.108, C.3.134); A.4.124 (B.4.141, C.4.138); A.9.95; B.11.149; B.17.225 (C.19.186). **B.** 'To be or lie in (the king's, the pope's, etc.) grace': B.4.73 Boþe þi lif and þi lond lyþ in his grace (A.4.59); B.18.386 It liþ in my grace Wheiþer þei deye or deye noȝt for þat þei diden ille (C.20.428); C.2.244; B.18.90 (C.20.93). See *Lib. Alb.* 517: 'Johan Sampsone et ses ditz compaignons eux submistrent a la mercie et grace de nostre dit Seignour le Roy.' **C.** 'Of his grace': B.9.48 God . . . of his grete grace graunted hym blisse . . . and al his lynage after; B.3.232; B.19.116 (C.21.116). Cf. 'of his CURTESIE.' **D.** 'Without grace': B.8.105 Thanne sholde þe kyng come and casten hem in prison, And putten hem þer in penaunce wiþoute pite or grace. Cf. *Lib.Alb.* 361: attainted aleconners face imprisonment 'sanz redempcioun ou grace faire du Mair.'

GRAUNTEN To make conveyance of (land, property) or to bestow on (someone a privilege, indulgence, etc.); gen., to give, permit, allow: B.2.87 The Countee of Coueitise and alle þe costes aboute, . . . al I hem graunte (C.2.88); B.9.48 God . . . of his grete grace graunted hym blisse . . . and al his lynage after (A.10.36); B.11.128 May no cherl chartre make ne his chatel selle Wiþouten leue of his lord; no lawe wol it graunte (C.12.61); A.1.147 (B.1.173, C.1.169); A.8.8 (B.7.8, C.9.8); C.9.19; A.8.21 (B.7.19, C.9.23); A.8.87 (B.7.105, C.9.184); A.10.206; B.11.97; B.16.241; B.17.225 (C.19.186); B.18.338; C.19.284; B.19.183 (C.21.183). FEFFEN, GIVEN AND GRAUNTEN.

GRETE MEN   Magnates or lords; high officials (as members of a town council or parliament): C.8.87 Maystres, as þe mayres ben, and grete menne, sena-tours, What þei comaunde as by þe kyng countreplede hit neuere; B.4.159 Þe mooste peple in þe moot halle and manye of þe grete ... leten ... Mede a mansed sherewe. Cf. 14 Edw. III st. 2 c. 1: 'By the common assent of the prelates, earls, barons, and other great men [et autres grantz], and commons of our said realm of England ... in Parliament ...'; 27 Edw. III: 'Nostre Seignur le Roi de lassent & a la priere des Grauntz & de la communalte de son Roialme,' etc.; *K. Counc.* 49: 'Which petition having been heard in parlia-ment, it was said by the magnates and others [Magnatos et alios] of the king's council. ...'

H

HAIWARD   An officer of a manor, village, or religious establishment, charged with maintaining hedges and enclosures, with keeping cattle on the common, with protecting grain from trespass and theft, etc. (*MED*): C.13.46 If þe marchaunt make his way ouer menne corne And þe hayward happe with hym for to mete, Oþer his hatt or his hoed or elles his gloues The marchaunt mote forgo or moneye of his porse; C.5.16; C.6.368; C.13.44; B.19.332 (C.21.333). Cf. 'The Farmer's Complaint,' Sisam 111/15. For the duties of a hayward, see *Fleta* 2.84; *Court Baron* 102, 103, 120, 128, 141, passim; and H. S. Bennett 179.

***HANDI DANDI**   Covert bribe (something held or offered in the closed hand); as adv., with the secret conveying of money from one person to another: B.4.75 Thanne wowede wrong wisdom ful yerne To maken his pees wiþ his pens, handy dandy payed (A.4.61, C.4.68). Pearsall 91 n.: 'A game where children guess which hand a present is in. It came to mean a covert way of giving a present or bribe, as here.'

HANGEN   To execute (sb.) by hanging: B.18.379 It is noȝt vsed in erþe to hangen a feloun Ofter þan ones þouȝ he were a tretour. And if þe kyng of þat kyngdom come in þat tyme There a feloun þole sholde deeþ ooþer Iuwise Lawe wolde he yeue hym lif if he loked on hym (C.20.421); A.3.130 (B.3.141, C.3.177); B.5.234 (C.6.238); C.10.162; C.10.238; C.17.138; cf. B.5.279. On the custom referred to in B.18.379, Skeat's note is helpful (2:263–64), though he claims too much in saying that the historical incident there described 'can hardly be other than the very one of which William was thinking.' The prin-ciple was well-established; see *Writs* 101, and *K. Bench* 7:90: 'And thereupon, while Richard was in the process of executing the aforesaid judgement [the hanging of William], the king, happening to pass by, ordered Richard ... to delay execution and ... pardoned the said William.'

HANGMAN   A public hangman, an executioner: C.6.368 An hayward, an heremyte, the hangeman of Tybourne, Dawe þe dikere, with a dosoyne harlotes Of portours and of pikeporses. . . . *Jac.Well* 134/32 treats 'Hangemen, hauynge no pyte to hange men, ne to smyten of here hevedys, for ioye of here wynnyng' in the same class with prostitutes, harlots, beggars, etc. Apparently the office was sometimes a tenure: 'It seemeth in ancient times such officers were not voluntaries, nor for lucre to be hired, unlesse they were bound thereto by tenure' (quoted in Simpson 6 n.). TYBOURNE.

HANSELLE   An earnest (of good faith or fellowship): A.5.167 Vpholderis an hep . . . 3eue glotoun wiþ glad chiere good ale to hansele (B.5.318, C.6.375). Cf. *RR* 4.91: 'Some . . . were be-hote hansell if they helpe wold'; Dunbar's 'Presentation Verses with a New Year's Gift' (refrain): 'In hansell of þis guid new 3eir' (Robbins 91/4); *SGGK* 491: 'This hanselle hatz Arthur of auenturus on fyrst In 3onge 3er.' Pearsall 126: '*To hansull*: "as a gift or tip" (cf. *Lib.Alb.* 232), i.e., they bought his first drink, knowing they would profit in the end.' Pearsall explains in detail the game of exchange that follows. Blackstone traces the origin of the term as follows: 'Antiently, among all northern nations, shaking of hands was held necessary to bind the bargain; a custom which we still retain in many verbal contracts. A sale thus made was called *handsale*, '*venditio per mutuam manuum complexionem*'; till in process of time the same word was used to signify the price or earnest, which was given immediately after the shaking of hands, or instead thereof' (2:448). PLEGGE, WED.

HARM AND SHAME   'Damage e huntage,' a formula in civil actions: B.4.31 Oon waryn wisdom and witty his feere . . . riden faste for Reson sholde rede hem þe beste For to saue hemseluen from shame and from harmes (A.4.28). Often complainants sought compensation not only for harm but also for shame. There was a tendency, Plucknett observes, 'for ordinary persons to treat almost any tort as a personal affront: the abbot of Bury will complain in the King's Court that the bishop of Ely infringed his liberty "so that the abbot would not have the shame which the bishop did him for £100, nor the damage for 100 marks," and in local courts such allegations of shame are very common' (488–89). E.g., see *Court Baron*: 'The said John . . . surmised against him this villainy and slander in despite of the lord . . . to his damage of 20 s. and shame of a half-mark [damage de xx. s. e le huntage de demy mark]' (30); 'William Mercer . . . hath broken the assize of bread, whereby the lord and his good folk have damage to the amount of 100 s. and shame to the amount of 40 s. [damage de c. s. et huntage de xl s.]' (23). It is possible that 'waryn wisdom and witty his feere' are the defendants in a complaint alleging harm and shame. But given L's stress on the 'wiles in hire wordes,' their covetousness, and the fact that where 'wraþe and wranglynge is þer wynne þei siluer,' it seems more likely that they have conspired to bring suits themselves for profit. Thus 'to saue hemseluen from shame and from harmes' means to win compensation for the insult and injury supposedly done to them, so that (like the abbot of Bury) they should '*not have* the shame . . . nor the damage.' See also Helmholz, *Defamation* 28 (no. 32), 31 (no. 41), and li–lii (commentary).

HAROU A cry of distress; the exclamation in 'the hue and cry' raised by those threatened by, suffering, or witnessing a felony: B.20.88 There was 'harrow!' and 'help! here comeþ kynde Wiþ deeþ þat is dredful to vndo vs alle!' (C.22.88). P&M 2:578–79: 'When a felony is committed, the hue and cry [*hutesium et clamor*] should be raised. . . . Possibly the proper cry is "Out! Out!" and therefore it is *uthesium* or *hutesium*. The neighbours should turn out with the bows, arrows, knives, that they are bound to keep and, besides much shouting, there will be horn-blowing.' The authors add (579 n.): 'The famous Norman *Haro* seems to mean *Hither*.' Cf. the raising of the hue and cry in Chaucer's Nun's Priest's Tale (3380ff.) and the ensuing commotion; also *Lud. Cov.* 374/35, Skelton 237. The principal statute is Westminster 13 Edw. I, chaps. 1 and 4.

HAVEN AND HOLDEN A common phrase in conveyancing, derived from the *habendum et tenendum* of the old common law (Black): B.2.102 To haue and to holde, and hire heires after, A dwellynge wiþ þe deuel (A.2.67). Cf. Frisian *habba and halda* (Bethurum 278); *Abbey of H. G.* 339: '*Sciant presentes & futuri &c.*: Wetiþ зe þat . . . almiзti god . . . haþ зouen & graunted . . . to Adam . . . *Habendum et tenendum*: To hauen & to holden þis preciouse place wiþ þe noble abbeye & al þe holy couent.' Hall 1:25: 'The "Habendum et Tenendum" clause, which appeared in the reign of John, marks the division of the Dispositive Clause into two well-defined parts.' Bracton explains the first part of the phrase as meaning 'can be passed on to descendants,' and the second part as 'to hold of a lord' (67).

HEIR One who inherits or is entitled to inherit the property, title, honours, etc. of one who is deceased; an heir or heiress: C.5.163 Lytel hadde lordes a do to зeue lond fro her heyres (B.10.317); C.10.239 The eritage þat þe eyer [of a felon] sholde haue is at þe kynges wille; C.5.59 Eyres of heuene; A.2.67 (B.2.102); C.3.321; A.3.257 (B.3.279, C.3.431); C.6.255; A.9.80 (B.8.89, C.10.86); A.10.210; B.15.323; B.16.232; C.18.246. Blackstone 2:107: 'The word, heirs, is necessary in the grant or donation in order to make a fee, or inheritance. For if land be given to a man for ever, or to him and his assigns for ever, this vests in him but an estate for life.' HEIRS FOR EVER, ISSUE, LINAGE.

HEIRS FOR EVER A formula in bequests, conveyances, etc., importing tenure in fee simple (see FOR EVER): B.7.4 And purchaced hym a pardoun *a pena & a culpa*, For hym and for hise heires eueremoore after (A.8.4, C.9.4); B.3.279 God hated hym for euere and alle hise heires after (A.3.257, C.3.431); cf. B.10.331 And þanne shal þe Abbot of Abyngdoun and al his issue for euere Haue a knok of a kyng; B.2.103. *Nov. Narr.* 291: 'R. de M.

enfeoffed the said James of the manor of C. to him and to his heirs for ever [a lui et a ses heirs a touz iours]'; *K.Counc.* 71: 'Henry ... had by his charter enfeoffed the aforesaid William ... of the aforesaid manor ... to hold to him and his heirs forever [habendum sibi et heredibus suis imperpetuum].' Blackstone 2:104: 'Tenant in fee-simple ... is he that hath lands, tenements, or hereditaments, to hold to him and his heirs for ever.'

HERAUD OF ARMES An officer of a tournament who makes proclamations, conveys challenges, marshalls the combatants, etc.: B.18.16 Thanne was feiþ in a fenestre and cryde 'a! *fili dauid!*' As dooþ an heraud of armes whan Auentrous comeþ to Iustes (C.20.14); B.16.177 (C.18.186); B.16.247 (C.18.266); B.17.22, 55, 134; B.20.94 (C.22.94). Cf. *Jac.Well* 134/26: 'Herowdys of armys ... in iustyng or in turnementys wayten who doth best, & his name þei crye'; Vegetius, 'The Maner of Battale' (quoted in Neilson 227): 'The constable sall gar [cause] ane of his serjandis, or ane herald stand on a bar of the listis, or on ane stage at the entre of the barres, and call be name the prevare [appellant] or the defendour the quhilk that hapins to be absent, "Enter and appere to fulfill thine appele as thow art oblist;" or the defendour be name, "Enter within listis for to mak the defenss as thow art oblist."' See also *Fleta* 1.32, BATAILLE, CHAMPION, JUSTE.

HEREN AND SEN To know (something) first-hand, a phrase used of witnesses and in the opening of a letter patent: B.18.261 'Suffre we,' seide truþe; 'I here and see boþe A spirit spekeþ to helle and biddeþ vnspere þe yates' (C.20.269). *Court Baron* 75: 'If he denieth, wrongfully he denieth, for N. hath here A. B. C. who heard and saw [audientes et videntes]'; Stubbs 283: 'Johannes Dei gratia rex Angliae ... omnibus has litteras visuris vel audituris salutem.' See also the excerpt in Plucknett 122. WITNESSEN.

HERITAGE Inherited or inheritable property, right, office, etc.; also, the fact or right of inheriting: C.10.239 The eritage þat þe eyer [of a felon] sholde haue is at þe kynges wille; B.10.347 þei [the poor] han Eritage in heuene, and by trewe riȝte (A.11.231); C.3.242; A.11.239 (B.10.356); B.14.294 (C.16.128). *Lud.Cov.* 58/38: 'God of his high benyvolens ... wyll ... bye us all ffrom oure offens, in hevyn to haue his herytage'; Kail 41/28: 'Y dyed for ȝoure gylt ... ȝoure heritage y bouȝt ȝow newe'; Fisher 164/10: 'The forseyd Rauf be wey of Ryght entryd and took p[ossession] ... the which possessyon of Ryht herytage he kept.'

HIS (OWN) That which belongs, by law or justice, to a person: B.8.83 Whoso ... takeþ but his owene, ... dowel hym folweþ; B.Prol.122 The kyng and þe commune and kynde wit þe þridde Shopen lawe and leaute, ech life to knowe his owene; B.Prol.208; A.5.230 (B.5.458, C.6.313); B.15.159 (C.16.291); B.20.20 (C.20.20). Barbour 26: 'Debt represents an archaic conception. The active party appears at first as a demandant rather than a plaintiff, and ... claims what is *his own*.' As the highest representative of justice in the land, the king is bound by his coronation oath (*Fleta* 1.17) 'to award to every man that

70

which is his own' [vnicuique tribuere quod suum]. The phrase derives from the classical definition of JUSTICE, which appears most prominently in the opening sentence of the *Institutes* of Justinian: 'Justitia est constans et perpetua voluntas jus suum cuique tribuens' (ed. Sandars). Echoes of the definition are pervasive in legal records of the time; e.g., *Bor. Cust.* 1:251: 'They shall put stakes on the land . . . so as to give to each what is his [dandum unicuique quod suum est]'; 1:289: 'The bailiffs shall deliver to each what is his [liberabitur unicuique quod suum est]'; and so forth.

HOMAGE   Allegiance; 'to do homage,' to pledge or acknowledge one's fidelity to a king or feudal lord: B.12.154 Clerkes . . . comen wiþ hir presentʒ And diden hir homage honurably to hym þat was almyʒty (C.14.98). To accept homage was to acknowledge a person's freedom or right to tenure. Cf. *Writs* 192: 'The king to his beloved etc. Know that we have accepted the homage [homagium] of W., son and heir of A. deceased, for all the lands and tenements which the aforesaid A., his father, held of us in chief on the day he died, and we have restored to him those lands and tenements.' The oath of homage appears in *Mirror* 117.

HOUS HIRE   Rent for the use of a house: C.9.74 Pore folk in cotes . . . þat they with spynnyng may spare, spenen hit on hous-huyre. Cf. *Simonie* 159: 'For hous-hire ne for clothes he [Religioun] ne carez noht.' *Lib. Alb.* 204: 'Et si homme soit emplede par pleint de debt . . . pur la ferme des measouns allowez, appellez "househire," en tieux cas le defendaunt navera my sa ley'; see also 55, 220.

HOUVE   A lawyer's cap or coif: A.Prol.84 þere houide an hundrit in houuis of silk Seriauntis it semide þat seruide at þe barre (B.Prol.211, C.Prol.159); A.3.270 (B.3.295, C.3.447). Bennett 102.

*__HUKKERIE__   Retail trade, the business of a huckster: B.5.225 Rose þe Regrater . . . haþ holden hukkerye elleuene wynter (A.5.141, C.6.233). Skeat 2:84: 'A *huckster* was one who retailed ale, etc. from door to door. "Item, that no *brewer* or *brewster* sell any manner of *ale* unto any *huckster*," etc. – Liber Albus, p. 312. . . . *Huckster* is generally applied, in the City books, to females only.' Cf. *Cov. Leet* 111, 115, 139 passim.

I

IGNORANTIA NON EXCUSAT   'Ignorance (of the law) does not excuse,' a maxim of canon law: C.13.127 The bishop shal be blamed before god . . . That crouneth suche for goddes knyhtes that conne *sapientier* Nother syng ne rede ne seye a masse of þe day. Ac neuer noþer is blameles, the bischop ne þe chapeleyn, For *ignorancia non excusat*, as ych haue herd in bokes (B.11.316–

17). The passage recalls the opening of Peckham's *Constitutions*, 'Ne quis per ignorantiam se excuset . . . ,' where the essential points of knowledge belonging to priests are set forth (Lyndwood 1ff.). See also *CIC* 2:928, 1122.

IMAGINEN   *To contrive a plot or scheme, usually in conspiracy with others: B.13.357 Moore to good than to God þe gome his loue caste, And ymagynede how he it myȝte haue. Cf. *K. Counc.* 87: 'The said Anselm, imagining [imaginant] how he might secure for himself the aforesaid lands, tenements, goods and chattels, conspired with the said James . . . who by their false conspiracy and imagination [ymaginacion] procured a false inquest to indict the aforesaid John of felony.' Fisher 164/11: '[They] malycyouslych ymagenyd hym to Slee.' Barbour 181: 'Ymaginyng to putte þe seid suppliant fro his ferme [they] entretyd þe seid suppliant to leve þe terme þat he hadde in þe seid ferme.' CONSPIREN.

IMPUGNEN   To call into question the validity or authority of (a law, charter, document, etc.); to find fault with (a person or his actions), accuse: B.11.304 A chartre is chalangeable bifore a chief Iustice; If fals latyn be in þat lettre þe lawe it impugneþ (C.13.117); B.13.124 Piers þe Plowman haþ impugned vs alle...And no text ne takeþ to mayntene his cause But *Dilige deum* and *Domine quis habitabit* (C.15.131); B.Prol.109 (C.Prol.136); A.8.152 (B.7.153, C.9.303). Cf. Wright 47: 'Jam nil valet aliquis ni sciat litigare . . . Nisi sciat simplices dolis impugnare.' *Fleta* 1.32: 'Exceptions take the place of actions, since the one impugns [inpugnat] the other . . . (p. 81). ACCUSEN, ACOUPEN, CHALENGEN.

INCURABLE   (Of a fault) not able to be mended or pardoned; (of the punishment for a fault) unending, perpetual: B.10.332 And þanne shal þe Abbot of Abyngdoun and al his issue for euere Haue a knok of a kyng, and incurable þe wounde [trans. Isaiah 14:6 *plaga insanabili*] (C.5.177); B.13.13 Lewed men ben lad . . . Thoruȝ vnkonnynge curatours to incurable peynes (C.15.16). In the language of the penitential tradition, a sin absolved is a wound healed; e.g., B.14.97: 'Satisfaccion . . . to noȝte bryngeþ dedly synne That it neuere eft is sene ne soor, but semeþ a wounde yheeled'; also *Engl. Canons* 103: prelates should 'sometimes hear confessions and give penance; and frequently have their own sores healed by proper confessors'; *Spec. Sacerdot.* 71/4: 'Ȝif he [the sinner] be curable.' Similarly, in the law, a wrong mended was 'healed'; e.g., 'If the tenant does not appear when summoned . . . or fails to heal (*sanare*) his former default, then the land is adjudged to the demandant' (P&M 2:592). The legal meaning of B.10.332 is that the abbot's successors will not be able to recover the lost property.

IN DEI NOMINE AMEN   'In the name of God, Amen,' a formula often found at the beginning of a will: A.7.78 Forþi I wile er I wende do wryte my bequest. *In dei nomine Amen* I make it myseluen (B.6.86, C.8.95). See Sheehan 314, Barraclough 241, Holdsworth 3:671.

*INDULGENCE   A pardon or remission of the punishment due to sin; also, the document granting such a pardon: A.8.153 Dowel indulgence passiþ, Bienalis & trienalis & bisshopis lettres (B.7.175, C.9.321); B.17.257 Purchace al þe pardon of Pampilon and Rome, And Indulgences ynowe, and be *ingratus* to þi kynde, The holy goost hereþ þee noȝt (C.19.218); B.7.57 (C.9.52); A.8.177 (B.7.199, C.9.346); B.20.321 (C.22.321). *Cath. Encyc.* 7:783: 'The word *indulgence* [Lat. *indulgentia* . . .] originally meant kindness or favour; in post-classic Latin it came to mean the remission of a tax or debt. In Roman law and in the Vulgate of the Old Testament [Is., lxi, 1] it was used to express release from captivity or punishment. . . . [But in the technical sense] an indulgence is a remission of the temporal punishment due to sin, the guilt of which has been forgiven.' *A POENA ET A CULPA*, LETTRE, PARDOUN.

IN EXTREMIS   'In extreme circumstances,' that is, by necessity (e.g., on the point of death): B.10.352 [One who] is baptiȝed beþ saaf, be he riche or pouere. That is *in extremis* . . . as Sarȝens & Iewes Mowen be saued so (A.11.235). On baptism *in extremis*, see Lyndwood's *Provincial* lib. I, tit. 7; lib. III, tit. 24; and the Constitutions of Othobon lib. I, tit. 1 (Lyndwood 41ff., 241ff., 80f.); *Engl. Canons* 2:86, 110, 122.

INFAMIS   'Of ill FAME or repute,' a formal pronouncement in both canon and secular law made upon persons for egregious irregularities (esp. false oaths), and depriving them thereafter of certain legal rights and privileges (e.g., bringing suit, holding office): B.5.168 Seint Gregory . . . hadde a good forwit: That no Prioresse were preest [i.e., confessor]. . . . They hadde þanne ben *Infamis*, þei kan so yuele hele counseil. Gregory IX, *Decretals*, lib. 5, tit. 38, c. 10 (*CIC* 2:887), quoted in Bennett 162. *Cath. Encyc.* 8:1: 'Infamy in the canonical sense is defined as the privation or lessening of one's good name. . . . It constitutes an irregularity, i.e., a canonical impediment which prevents one being ordained or exercising such orders as he may have already received.' Cheney treats the concept of *infamia* among religious at length (77–83 passim). The concept derives from Roman law; see Buckland 91 and passim. It also figures in English legal procedure; e.g., a juror attainted of false swearing is declared *infamis*. Cf. *Mirror* 133: 'All who are lawfully attainted of a sin whence corporal punishment ensues are infamous [infames].' Additional citations in Alford 1984.

IN FAUTORES SUOS   'On their supporters or accomplices': B.15.215 Fy on faitours and *in fautores suos*! No exact precedent for the phrase has been found, but the word *fautor* itself (q.v.) is commonplace in legal complaints.

INGRATUS   'Ungrateful,' in civil and canon law a technical term applied to persons who, against the rule of natural justice, offend their lords or reciprocate kindness with contempt: B.14.169 Of þe good þat þow hem gyuest *ingrati* ben manye [cf. Luke 6:35]; B.17.257 Be *ingratus* to þi kynde, The holy goost hereþ þee noȝt (C.19.218). A serf is bound to his lord by a 'tie of gratitude' [cathena gratitudinis] in the same way that a knight is bound by his oath of fealty; cf. *Fleta* 2.51 (p. 173). In Roman law, ingratitude was a ground for revoking a gift or for restoring a freed slave to his servitude. Cf. *RR* 3.32: 'Propter ingratitudinem liber homo revocatur in servitutem.' The rule has significant theological implications (e.g., with respect to the gift of salvation and Christ's freeing man from the bondage of hell). Prosper of Aquitane's *Carmen de Ingratis* plays on the double meaning of *ingratus* as 'unprofitable' and 'despiser of grace' (see the discussion in Pierre de Labriolle, *The History and Literature of Christianity* [London, 1924], 430–31). Aquinas treats the sin of ingratitude in *ST* II–II, qu. 107. In *Mankind* 751–55 Mercy addresses Mankind: 'Thy peruersyose ingratytude I can not rehers. To God and to all þe holy cort of hewyn þou art despectyble . . . *Lex et natura, Cristus et omnia jura Damnant ingratum, lugent eum fore natum*' (EETS 262 [1969], 178). Further discussion in Alford 1984.

INQUEST   See ENQUESTE

INTENTIO I[U]DICAT HOMINEM   'The will or intent judges the man' (a maxim of canon law): A.10.90 ʒif clene consience acorde þat þiself dost wel Wilne þou neuere in þis world . . . for to do betere, For *intencio i[u]dicat hominem*. *Pace* Skeat and Kane, the reading should be *iudicat*, not *indicat*. Cf. *St. John the Evangelist* in Farmer 357: 'The courtesy of England is ofte to kiss, And of itself it is lechery where pleasure is. All young folk remember this – *Intentio judicat quenquam*. So great delight thou mayst have therein That afore God it is deadly sin.' Numerous additional citations in Alford 1984.

*INTESTATE   Deceased without having made a will or TESTAMENT: B.15.138 Curatours of holy kirke . . . endeþ intestate and þanne entreþ þe bisshop And makeþ murþe þerwiþ and his meyne boþe; And nempneþ hym a nygard þat no good myʒte aspare To frend ne to fremmed: 'þe fend haue his soule!'. The bishop was executor of the goods of all those who died intestate within his diocese. Cf. *Writs* 229 (quoted under ENTREN) and Woodcock 72–74. Normally a third of the deceased's movable goods were reserved for alms (prayers for his soul). In some dioceses 'members of the lower clergy were allowed to devote the income of their benefice for a year after death in alms and in payment of debt' (Sheehan 245 n.).

ISSUE   *Offspring, progeny, heir(s); legal successors in office: B.16.239 God . . . bihiʒte to me and to myn issue boþe Lond and lordshipe and lif wiþouten ende (C.18.256); B.10.331 þanne shal þe Abbot of Abyngdoun and al his issue for euere Haue a knok of a kyng; B.5.265 (Sk.); B.9.128; C.10.241; B.11.206 (C.12.112); B.16.196 (C.18.206); B.16.206; B.16.241 (C.18.258); C.18.235; B.18.344; C.20.197; C.20.303. Cf. Fisher 164/6: 'And be Cause the same Thomas deyde and al his Issew lyvyng the same Margaret Sche stood in hool possessyon of the forseyd tenement.' Grants made to religious houses were addressed to the abbot, abbess, etc. and their 'successors' (rather than their heirs); e.g., 'Dare possit et assignare dilectis nobis in Christo Abbati et Conventui de Dore; habenda et tenenda sibi et successoribus suis . . .' (Hall 2:72; 50, 67, passim); *Nov.Narr.* 244, 248. HEIR, HEIRS FOREVER, LINAGE.

74

J

JAILER   See GAIOLER

JEWISE   Judicial punishment or sentence (OF *juise* < Lat. *iudicium*): C.20.424 Yf þe kynge of þe kyngdoem come in þe tyme Ther a thief tholie sholde deth oþer iewyse. Cf. *RR* 3.341: 'Ther nas rial of the rewme that hem durste rebuke, Ne Iuge, ne Iustice that Iewis durste hem deme'; Reynes 137/373: 'He is noutȝ amercyable but mote haue iuyse'; *Lib.Alb*. 336: 'And if it be found that the bedel puts the mark upon a false measure, let him have judgment of the pillory (le juwyse del pyllorye).' DOM.

JUGGE   One with authority to hear and try causes in a court of justice: B.7.190 Ye maistres, Meires and Iugges (A.8.168, C.9.337); B.14.111 (C.15.289). On the evolution of judges from referees, concerned mainly with procedure, to judges in the modern sense, concerned as well with the substance of the law, see Harding 132–37 passim. According to Plucknett, the word *judge* (Lat. *judex*) 'is generally used only of judges in ecclesiastical courts, or by ecclesiastical writers' (91 n.); normally a secular judge was referred to as a 'justice' (*justiciarius*). CHIEF JUSTICE, DOMESMAN, JUSTICE.

JUGGEMENT OF ARMES   Judicial combat: B.16.95 Þanne sholde Iesus Iuste þerfore bi Iuggement of armes Wheiþer sholde fonge þe fruyt, þe fend or hymselue (C.18.129). BATAILLE, FIGHT, JUSTE.

JUGGEN   To try or pronounce sentence upon (someone) in a court of law; condemn; determine (an issue): B.14.289 Selde sit pouerte þe soþe to declare, Or as Iustice to Iugge men enioyned is no poore (C.16.124); B.12.89 Cristes caractes confortede ... The womman þat þe Iewes iugged; A.2.101 (B.2.137); A.2.121 (B.2.157, C.2.169); B.9.93; B.16.119; B.19.474 (C.21.474); B.20.29 (C.22.29). DAMPNEN, DEMEN, JUSTIFIEN, TERMINEN.

JUROUR   A sworn witness or recognitor; a layman summoned to assist a court in a disputed issue of fact: C.2.150 Iustices enioynen hem [Mede and Fals] thorw iuroures othes; B.7.45 Many a Iustice and Iurour wolde for Iohan do moore Than *pro dei pietate* pleden at þe barre. *Oxf.Comp.*: 'The origin of the jury is probably to be found in the importation, from Normandy, of a system of inquisitions in local courts by sworn witnesses. ... As originally established, the function of the jury was not to weigh evidence but to decide on the basis of their own knowledge, or the general belief of the district. ... They were accordingly witnesses to rather than judges of facts. ... So long as jurors were supposed to make findings from their own knowledge, they would be guilty of perjury if they gave a wrong verdict. They were liable to the writ of attaint whereby the cause was tried again by a jury of 24. If the verdict of the second jury differed from that of the first, the original (12) jurors were arrested and imprisoned, their lands and goods forfeited, and they became infamous' (686–87). Not until the early 18th century did the function of jurors as recognitors cease altogether. 'False jurors' were a major problem; see Statutes 1 Edw. III c. 6, 34 Edw. III c. 7, 8. On the development of the jury system, see Holdsworth 1:312–50, and Plucknett 106–38. FALS WITNESSE, PANEL, QUESTMONGER, SISOUR, WITNESSE; see also ATTEINT, SECTE.

JUSTE   A joust, a combat in which two knights on horseback encounter each other with lances; *pl.* a tournament; also a trial by battle: B.18.16 Feiþ . . . cryde . . . as dooþ an heraud of armes whan Auentrous comeþ to Iustes (C.20.14); B.17.54 (C.19.50); B.17.77. BATAILLE, FIGHT, JUGGEMENT OF ARMES.

JUSTEN   To joust: B.16.163 Iesus . . . on þe friday folwynge for mankyndes sake Iusted in Iherusalem, a ioye to vs alle. On cros vpon Caluarie crist took þe bataille Ayeins deeþ and þe deuel; B.16.95 (C.18.129); B.17.54 (C.19.50); B.18.19 (C.20.17); B.18.22 (C.20.21); B.18.27 (C.20.26); B.18.82 (C.20.85); B.18.181 (C.20.184); fig. B.20.134 (C.22.134). The Crucifixion is treated metaphorically as a judicial battle, in which Christ fights as the CHAMPION of mankind against the devil. The motif is a commonplace; see Wilbur Gaffney, 'The Allegory of the Christ Knight in *Piers Plowman*,' PMLA 46 (1931), 155–68.

JUSTER   One who fights in jousts, a CHAMPION: B.19.10 Is þis Iesus þe Iustere . . . Or it is Piers þe Plowman? (C.21.10).

JUSTICE   I. An administrator of justice, a judge: B.14.289 Selde sit pouerte þe soþe to declare, Or as Iustice to Iugge men enioyned is no poore (C.16.124); C.4.186 Y wolde...Consience in alle my courtes be a kynges iustice; B.2.48 (C.2.49); A.3.13 (B.3.13, C.3.14); B.3.155 (C.3.192); B.3.321 (C.3.473); B.6.329 (C.8.352); C.8.339; B.7.45; A.8.148 (B.7.171, C.9.316); B.11.303 (C.13.116); B.16.92 (C.18.126 = *sol iusticiae*); C.18.162; B.17.306 (C.19.281); B.18.38 (C.20.37); B.19.139 (C.21.139); B.20.134 (C.22.134). The phrase 'a kynges Iustice' (B.3.155, C.4.186, C.8.339, B.17.306) refers more specifically to a judge in the *Curia Regis* (Exchequer, King's Bench, Common Pleas). The oath of a king's justice is given in Hall 1:133–34. CHIEF JUSTICE, DOMESMAN, JUGGE.
    II. The moral principle which is the end of law, and the standard or criterion by which law is evaluated; the quality of being just or righteous; one of the four cardinal virtues: B.19.302 *Spiritus Iusticie* spareþ noȝt to spille þe gilty, And to correcte þe kyng if þe kyng falle in gilt (C.21.302); B.19.405 But þow lyue by loore of *Spiritus Iusticie*, The chief seed þat Piers sew, ysaued worstow neuere (C.21.405); B.19.297, 397, 402, 474 (C.21.298, etc.); B.20.24, 29 (C.22.24, 29); C.20.424 (jewyse). Like medieval thinkers in general, Langland regarded justice as the Idea from which all particular laws derive. What is not in

conformity with Justice is not law but rather an abuse of law (Aquinas, *ST* I–II, qu. 93, art. 3, and qu. 96, art. 4). Central to L's thought is the famous opening sentence of the *Institutes of Justinian*, 'Justitia est constans et perpetua voluntas jus suum cuique tribuens.' The definition is implicit in numerous passages (HIS OWN, NON DIMITTITUR) but nowhere more important than in the recurring phrase *Redde quod debes* (q.v.); to make restitution, to render to each what is his own, is essential to true penitence, hence the statement that *Spiritus Iusticie* was 'the chief seed þat Piers sew.' General studies of the theme of justice in *Piers* include P. M. Kean, 'Love, Law, and *Lewte* in *Piers Plowman*,' *RES* ns 15 (1964), 241–61, and 'Justice, Kingship and the Good Life in the Second Part of *Piers Plowman*,' in Hussey 76–110; Baldwin, *The Theme of Government in Piers Plowman*; Stokes, *Justice and Mercy in Piers Plowman*; John A. Yunck, 'Satire,' in Alford 1988, 135–54. EQUITE, RESOUN, RIGHT, RIGHTWISNESSE.

JUSTIFIEN To make just or do justice to (someone); to judge, rule or govern: B.Prol.130 Lewed men ne koude Iangle ne Iugge þat Iustifie hem sholde, But suffren and seruen; B.19.44 Iesus . . . Iustified [þe Iewes] and tauȝte hem The lawe of lif (C.21.44). The latter example may include the secondary meaning of 'to acquit or absolve by divine forgiveness and grace' (see *MED* [5]). *Bor.Cust.* 1:10: 'And if any fraunchysed man or forener do any felony . . . he most . . . be justified after his defautes acordyng to the laudable custome and antiquytie consuetude in dayes before tyme used.' Reynes 1/394: 'If he . . . wyll noȝt be iustyfyed, he mote haue the dome . . . þat is to wete þe baker on þe pylory, þe brewster on þe trubechet.' DEMEN, JUGGEN, LOKEN.

JUWISE See JEWISE

K

KEPEN AND DEFENDEN To guard and protect (laws, rights, property, etc.): C.21.42 Hit bicometh for a kyng to kepe and to defende . . . his layes and his large (B.19.42); C.22.257 Kynges and knyhtes, þat kepen and defenden, Haen officerys vnder hem (B.20.257). Statute 38 Edw. III st. 2 c. 4: 'The King [. . . et al.] are bound to keep and defend [garder & defendre] the one and the other from all damage, villainy, and reproof.' Hall 1:40 (grant of forfeited lands to another): 'Et nos et heredes nostri hanc nostram donacionem *defendere et conservare* tenemur, sicut nos et antecessores nostri alias donationes nostras et feoffamenta *conservare et defendere* consuevimus, et sicut ea *conservare et defendere* tenemur.'

KEPER Ruler, guardian, custodian (of a people or group of people): B.19.443 þe pope, þat pileþ holy kirke . . . cleymeþ bifore þe kyng to be kepere ouer cristene (C.21.443); B.20.72 Conscience þat kepere was and gyour Ouer kynde cristene and Cardynale vertues (C.22.72); B.12.126; C.16.273. B.19.443 is a skeptical allusion to the doctrine of papal dominion, addressed in Boniface VIII's bull *Unam sanctam*, which ends, 'We declare, state, define and pronounce that it is altogether necessary to salvation for every human creature to be subject to the Roman pontiff' (*CIC* 2:1245). By the phrase 'bifore þe kyng,' L means not 'in the presence of,' but 'ahead of, having precedence over.'

KING AND HIS COUNSEIL   The court of King's Bench, Common Pleas, or Exchequer; also 'the group of persons in the royal household, usually including the Officers of State, some of the judges, bishops, and barons, which gave the English kings advice and, notwithstanding the breaking away of the Exchequer, Common Pleas and King's Bench and their development into regular courts, advised him on the exercise of his personal jurisdiction, both appellate and, at first instance' (*Oxf. Comp.*, 'King's Council'); *gen.* Parliament: A.3.104 Panne was consience callid to comen & aperen Before þe kyng & his counseil, clerkis & oþere (B.3.115, C.3.150); A.7.298 Laboureris . . . þanne curse[n] þe king & alle þe counseil aftir Suche lawis to loke laboureris to chaste (B.6.317, C.8.339); A.5.38 (B.5.46, C.5.144); B.20.129 (C.22.129); cf. B.20.30 (C.20.30). Cf. Stat. 23 Edw. III c. 7 (Statute of Labourers): '. . . Regis & consilii'; Stat. 16 Ric. II c. 5, which provides that persons in violation of the Statute of Provisors are to be 'attached by their bodies . . . and brought before the King and his Council [le Roy & son Conseil], there to answer to the cases aforesaid,' on which language Blackstone comments: '. . . by the expression of king's *council*, were understood the king's judges of his courts of justice, the subject matter being legal: this being the general way of interpreting the word, *council*' (1:222). See J. F. Baldwin, *The King's Council*.

KING AND HIS CROUNE   The king and his office: C.21.465 And thenne cam þer a kyng and bi his corone saide: 'Y am kyng with crounc the comune to reule' (B.19.465); A.4.70 (B.4.83, C.4.79); A.4.121 (B.4.138, C.4.135). The phrase was used to distinguish the king's personal and corporate identities. The standard study is Ernst Kantorowicz, *The King's Two Bodies* (Princeton, 1957); see esp. pp. 364–72. Cf. Fisher 189/8: The insurrection was 'a yens the dygnyte of our soueraigne lord the kynge and his crowne.' *Fleta* 1.17: 'Nor can anyone give judgement in matters temporal except the king, either personally or by a delegate. For, by virtue of his oath, he is in especial bound to do this, and therefore the crown is a symbol that he will rule the people subject to him by process of law' (p. 35). See also *Mirror* 45, quoted below.

KING AND THE COMMUNE   The king and his subjects, the commonalty: C.15.169 The kyng and alle þe comune and clergie to þe loute As for here lord and here ledare (B.13.169); C.1.156 Forthi is loue . . . a mene, as þe mayre is, bitwene þe kyng and þe comune (B.1.160). Cf. *Mirror*: 'Torz fetz au Roi e al comun del poeple' (38); 'torz fez a eux e a la coroune e al comune del poeple' (45).

KINGES BENCH The Court of King's Bench: A.Prol.95 Archideknes & denis . . . ben clerkis of þe kinges bench. Cf. *Cov. Leet* 121: 'Laurence hathe reseyued of John Bristow . . . iij li. for poor men that weren endited in the kynges benche & might not pay her fynes.' The King's Bench was concerned primarily with criminal law; the Court of Common Pleas, with civil actions. See Blackstone 3:41–43, and Sayles's introductions to *K. Bench* (vols. 5–7). COURT.

KINGES COURT A royal court of justice (e.g., King's Bench, Common Pleas, Exchequer): B.3.319 Kynges Court and commune Court, Consistorie and Chapitle, Al shal be but oon court (C.3.472); C.18.95 In kynges court and in knyhtes, the clenneste men and fayreste Shollen serue for þe lord sulue; B.15.235 In kynges court he [charite] comeþ ofte þer þe counseil is trewe . . . In court amonges þe commune [q.v.] he comeþ but selde (C.16.357); C.2.22; A.2.152 (B.2.191, C.2.202); B.19.424 (C.21.424). *K. Counc.* 60: 'They should sue in the exchequer of the lord the king . . . or in the king's court [Curiis Regis] appointed for such causes.' COURT.

KNIGHTES COURT A feudal or manorial court, the Court Baron: C.7.33 Y can . . . holden a knyhtes court and acounte with þe reue; C.18.95 In kynges court and in knyhtes, the clenneste men and fayreste Shollen serue for þe lord sulue. The court was established by the lord of the manor, and presided over by his steward, 'for the maintenance of the services and duties . . . due from . . . tenants and for determining disputes where the debt or damages did not exceed 40 shillings' (*Oxf. Comp.*, 'Court Baron'). The terms 'court baron' and 'knight's court' are often used together or interchangeably; e.g., *Court Baron* 83: 'curiis baronum, militum et libere tenentium.'

KNIGHTES FEE An estate in land or tenements held in heritable or perpetual tenure to a feudal superior or the crown; 'knight's fee,' an estate held originally by the obligation of providing one knight for the lord's service (*MED*): C.5.77 Monkes and moniales . . . Imade here kyn knyhtes and knyhtes-fees ypurchased. Blackstone 2:62: 'The first, most universal, and esteemed the most honourable species of tenure, was that by knight-service. . . . To make a tenure by knight-service, a determinate quantity of land was necessary, which was called a knight's fee, *feodum militare*. . . . And he who held this proportion of land (or a whole fee) by knight-service, was bound to attend his lord to the wars for forty days in every year, if called upon: which attendance was his *reditus* or return, his rent or service, for the land he claimed to hold.' Gradually the obligation to fight was commuted to a money payment (scutage). Simpson discusses military tenures (ch. 1); and Hall prints several formulas (2:36–40).

KNOWEN I. To confess one's sins: A.11.281 A goode friday . . . a feloun was sauid . . . for he kneuȝ on þe crois & to crist shrof hym (B.10.422, C.11.257 beknew). Cf. *Jac. Well* 67/15: 'Knowe þi synne to vs, ȝif þou be gylty.' See also B.14.187 (confession and knowlichynge). SHEWEN.

*II. To confess someone, to hear confession: B.20.282 Persons and parissh preestes þat sholde þe peple shryue Ben Curatours called to knowe and to hele, Alle þat ben hir parisshens penaunce enioigne, And be ashamed in hir shrift (C.22.281); B.5.596 (C.7.244 hym knoweth). L's use of the word to signify the actions of both penitent and priest is analogous with *confessen* (cf. B.11.76 Ich haue muche merueille of yow . . . Whi youre Couent coueiteþ to confesse and to burye Raþer þan to baptiʒe). To translate B.20.282 as 'he must know all his parishioners and heal them' (Wells, Attwater, Goodridge) is to miss half the etymological point; see CUREN.

L

*LACCHEDRAWERE   One who causes the latch to be drawn or lifted (often by feigning injury or necessity) in order to beg, defraud, rob, etc.: C.8.287 Thouh lyares and lach-draweres and lollares knocke, Lat hem abyde til the bord be drawe ac bere hem none croumes Til alle thyne nedy neyhbores haue noen ymaked; C.9.192 Thise lollares, lache-draweres, lewede ermytes . . . ben but boyes . . . Noyther of lynage ne of lettrure; C.8.287. Skeat cites Statute 5 Edw. III c. 14 concerning 'divers manslaughters, felonies, and robberies, done by people that be called *Roberdesmen*, *Wastours*, and *drawlacches*' and the reconfirmation in 7 Rich. II c. 5. Cf. *Myrour* under the heading of avarice: 'Lacchedrawers or Roberdes men . . . comeþ homliche into mennes houses & feyneþ hem ibrente or wiþ some oþer chaunce com from richesse to pouerte, as robbed wiþ þeues, loste her catel by see, or lost hors or harneys by auenture of werre, as by enprisonynge or oþer wyse, or seiþ þat her londes beþ bynome hem by grete lordes, or elles þat þei haue leide hem to wedde to a certein day for seruice of þe kyng and of þe rewme, and many suche oþer lesynges makeþ forto gete good of pitevous men,' etc. (140). To a similar list of ploys used by 'lacchedrawerys þat vndon mennys dorys,' *Jac.Well* adds the conclusion '& so þei wyll noʒt go, tyl þei haue sumwhat' (134/16–21). *Pace* the *OED*'s definition, 'one who draws or lifts the latch to enter for an unlawful purpose,' breaking does not seem to be essential: L's *lacchedrawers* knock, and the *Myrour*'s 'comeþ homliche.' Deception is the key element.

*LACHES   Sloth, negligence; in law, the failure to assert a right or claim, which failure may later operate as a bar in a court of equity: C.9.279 Loke now for thy lachesse what lawe wol the graunte, Purgatorye for thy paie ore perpetuel helle; cf. A.9.32 (B.8.36); C.8.253; C.9.269. Black: '"Doctrine of laches," is based upon maxim that equity aids the vigilant and not those who slumber on their rights' (787). Gower refers to the maxim in *Mirour* 14138 (see John Fisher, *John Gower* [New York: New York University, 1964], 155), and plays on the idea in *Conf.Am.* 4.25ff.: 'As of lachesce I am beknowe . . . For whanne I thoghte mi poursuite To make, and therto sette a day . . . Laschesce bad abide yit, And bar on hond it was no wit Ne time forto speke as tho.' See also *Cov. Leet* 417: 'And yf the sherrefes be laches or defectyue in levyng therof, then the Meire for the tyme beyng shall rere of the seid Sherreffes be laches, so beyng laches at euery defalt vj d.' Although the *OED* cites Littleton's *Tenures* (1574) as the earliest occurrence of the word in its legal sense, Gower plainly knew this meaning; L's use is more general, but like Gower he seems to be playing on the technical meaning in C.9.279.

LATRO In the civil and old English law, a robber; a thief (Black): B.5.476 He hadde leyen by *Latro*, luciferis Aunte (A.5.250, C.6.330). The term seems to be used here mainly to support a pun: *latro / latere*, 'by the side, flank, body.'

LAWE **I.** A rule or system of rules governing human conduct, distinguished as: **A.** Positive law, that is, law that is 'posited' or legislated, esp. by a legally constituted authority, e.g.: **(1)** The laws of England, as contained in its customs and statutes: B.3.77 Maires and Maceres þat menes ben bitwene The kyng and þe comune to kepe þe lawes (A.3.66, C.3.78); C.10.237 Westminstre lawe [disinherits a felon's issue]; A.Prol.86 (B.Prol.213, C.Prol.161); B.2.22 (C.2.21); A.2.99 (B.2.135, C.2.148); C.3.88; C.3.120 (A.3.81, B.3.92 ayeins reson); A.7.299 (B.6.318, C.8.340); C.17.57; B.18.383 (C.20.425); B.19.469 (C.21.469). CUSTUME, STATUTE, WESTMINSTRE LAWE. **(2)** Ecclesiastical or canon law: C.17.283 Euery bisshope bi þe lawe sholde buxumliche walke And pacientliche thorw his prouynce and to his peple hym shewe; A.3.141 (B.3.152, C.3.188); C.9.328; B.15.240 (C.16.362); B.15.530 (C.17.280). BOTHE LAWES, CANOUN, DECREE, DECRETAL. **(3)** Civil or Roman law: B.20.274 Enuye . . . heet freres go to scole And lerne logyk and lawe (C.22.274). CIVILE, LAWE AND LOGIK. **(4)** Any body of legislated law: C.18.186 [Abraham as] An heraud of armes er eny lawe were; B.20.10 And nede haþ no lawe (i.e., natural law is not bound by positive law) (C.22.10); C.3.205; C.3.293; B.5.52; B.7.195; B.11.158 (C.12.88); C.17.133; B.16.119. **B.** The moral law, as seen in: **(1)** The Old Testament law of justice, the 'old law'; also Jewish custom as described therein: B.18.338 Þe olde lawe grauteþ That gilours be begiled and þat is good reson: *Dentem pro dente & oculum pro oculo* (C.20.381); C.5.55 By þe lawe of *Levyticy* . . . Clerkes ycrouned . . . Sholde nother swynke ne swete; B.12.73 In þe olde lawe as þe lettre telleþ, þat was þe lawe of Iewes, That what womman were in auoutrye taken, wher riche or poore, Wiþ stones men sholde hir strike and stone hire to deþe (C.14.38); C.9.212; B.11.205 (C.12.111); B.12.113 (C.14.58); B.13.185; B.15.466; C.17.70; C.18.222; B.18.348 (C.20.393); B.19.112 (C.21.112); B.19.310 (C.21.311). **(2)** The New Testament law of mercy, the 'new law': B.17.33 What neded it now a newe lawe to brynge Siþ þe firste suffiseþ to sauacion and to blisse? (C.19.32); B.18.260 (C.20.268); B.19.310 (C.21.311); B.19.446 (C.21.446). *LEX CHRISTI.* **(3)** The Judaeo-Christian law of love: C.14.38 For Moyses witnesseth þat god wroet and Crist with his fynger; Lawe of loue oure lorde wroet long ar Crist were; B.15.584 *Dilige deum & proximum* is parfit Iewen lawe; B.10.358; B.10.360; B.11.229, C.12.118). **(4)** Collectively, the moral teachings of the church, 'God's law': C.9.104 [Idlers] Lyuen aȝen goddes lawe; C.9.218; C.10.218; A.10.180; B.10.40; B.12.213 (C.14.152); B.15.93; B.16.6. **C.** Natural law, i.e., those rules of moral conduct which are self-evident to all rational beings, such as 'Contracts are to be kept,' 'God is to be honoured,' and so forth: C.17.152 [Even Saracens] Louen as by lawe of kynde oure lord god almyhty; B.20.18 þe lawe of kynde wolde That he dronke at ech dych er he deye for þurst (C.22.18); A.7.207 (B.6.221, C.8.231); C.17.160. RESOUN.

II. The law generally; right, justice: C.9.220 Holy churche hoteth alle manere peple Vnder obedience to be and buxum to þe lawe; B.20.266 Þe lawe wole and askeþ A certein for a certein (C.22.266); B.9.80 For moore bilongeþ to þe litel barn er he þe lawe knowe [i.e., before he reaches the age of discretion] Than nempnynge of a name; B.3.156 (C.3.193); B.10.25; C.10.95; C.10.125; C.17.136–37; B.18.285. EQUITE, JUSTICE, MESURE, RESOUN, RIGHT.

III. The legal process or system, esp. as represented in its officers and administrators: B.3.161 Lawe is so lordlich and looþ to maken ende (C.3.198); C.16.362 In constorie bifore commissarie a [charite] cometh nat ful ofte, For ouer-long is here lawe but yf þay lacche suluer (B.15.240); A.2.120 (B.2.156, C.2.169); A.2.159 (B.2.198, C.2.209); B.3.156–58 (C.3.193–95); B.4.174, 176, 180 (C.4.174); A.7.151 (B.6.166, C.8.163); B.11.91 (C.12.31); B.11.223; B.12.207 (C.14.146).

IV. Faith, doctrine: C.7.260 ȝef loue and leute and oure lawe be trewe; B.15.411 Makometh in mysbileue men and wommen brouȝte, That lered þere and lewed ȝit leeuen on hise lawes; C.14.9 Lowe the and leue forth in þe lawe of holy chirche; C.17.133; B.19.35 (C.21.35).

V. In phrases: **A.** 'As the law asks or demands': C.21.479 Than haue thow al thyn askyng as thy lawe asketh (B.19.479); C.13.49; B.20.266 (C.22.266). Cf. *K.Counc.* 83: '. . . that right and reason may be done, as the common law demands [sicome la commune ley demande].' **B.** 'Good law': C.17.57 Lewede consaylc hauc ȝc To fcffc suche . . . With þat ȝoure bernes and ȝoure bloed by goed lawe may clayme!' (cf. B.18.339). **C.** 'Against the law': C.3.120 Haue reuthe on this regraters . . . And soffre hem som tyme to selle aȝeyne þe lawe; C.17.280 To huppe aboute and halewe men auters And crepe in amonges curatours and confessen aȝeyn þe lawe (B.15.530); C.17.137; B.18.348 (C.20.393). To sell 'against the law' means to sell against the assize of bread and ale. See, for example, *Bor.Cust.* regarding women who sell beer 'extra domum suam contra assisam' (1:195); *LawMerch.* concerning a vintner who 'fregit assisam et vendidit pro xvj. d.' (19); *Fleta* 2.9–11 and *Lib.Alb.* 349–62, which set forth specific regulations governing the sale of victuals. To 'confessen aȝeyn þe lawe' means to hear the confession of someone who comes under another's jurisdiction; see below NOLITE MITTERE. 'Against the law' is a standard phrase in complaints, indictments, etc.; e.g., *K.Counc.*: 'John Knivett, chief justice, by the advice of all the judges, resolved that the said writ was contra legem' (55 n.14); 'The said John atte Wode and Alice his wife had been grievously and contrary to law [encountre la ley] ousted from their aforesaid lands and tenements' (89).

LAWE AND CUSTUME   A formulaic phrase in writs, charters, etc.: C.3.205–06 Wickede lawes And custumes of coueytise; B.12.97. Cf. *Jac.Well* 18/3: 'Swyche thynges as þey mowe lawfully beqwethe, by lawe or by consuetude.' Hall 1:87: 'leges et consuetudines'; *Writs* 17: 'secundum legem et consuetudinem' (also 45, 49, 55, 105); *Nov.Narr.* 309: 'encountre la ley et la custume du roialme.'

LAWEDAI   The day for the meeting of a court of law; hence, a court session; ?a LOVEDAI: C.5.158 Bothe monkes and chanons Haen ryde out of aray . . . Ledares of lawedays (A.11.212, B.10.312, C.6.159 [Sk.] louedaies). Cf. Fisher 188/16: 'At dyuers lawe dayes [he] stureth Tathing men [i.e., tithing-chiefs, constables] and also the xij men [i.e., questmen, jurors] that they shold no thyng presente and aftir his power of grete malice and euyll will wolde lette all the auantage that Sholde come of all the Courtes that ther ben holde.'

LAWEFUL   Just, equitable; living within the law; LELE, LELLI (< OF *loial*): B.11.145 Al þe clergie vnder crist ne myȝte me cracche fro helle, But oonliche loue and leautee and my laweful domes; B.15.308 Religiouses rightfulle men sholde fynde, And lawefulle men to lif holy men liflode brynge. 'Rightfulle . . . and lawefulle men' echoes the formula *probus et legalis homo* or *boun et leal homme*, applied to men of good fame (particularly to jurors and witnesses free from all exception). No person was to be made a citizen unless he was a 'boun et leal homme' (*Lib.Alb.* 268), and wardmoot inquisitions were to ascertain 'si ascun soit resident deinz la Garde qi nest my loial ou dessouz franc plegge' (*ibid.* 259).

LAWEFULLI   Righteously; in conformity with the law: C.9.59 Alle . . . þat lyuen . . . Lellyche and lauhfollyche, our lord Treuthe hem graunteth Pardoun perpetuel. Cf. Fisher 74/3: 'And if ye may lawfully doo al þat þe same bille conteneth we wolde ye dide hit.'

***LAWIER**   One versed in the law; a legal practitioner (advocate, attorney, pleader, etc.): B.7.60 Ye legistres and lawieres, if I lye witeþ Mathew: *Quodcumque vultis*, etc. (A.8.61). On ecclesiastical lawyers (proctors), see Purvis 65, Woodcock 40–45; on the profession generally, see Cohen.

LEAUTE   I. Lawfulness or respect for law (OF *leaute*, < Lat. *legalitas*): C.17.138 Oure lord aloueth no loue but lawe be þe cause: For lechours louyen aȝen þe lawe and at þe laste ben dampned, And theues louyen and leute haten and at þe laste ben hanged; B.15.468 The calf bitokneþ clennesse in hem þat kepeþ lawes, For as þe Cow þoruȝ kynde mylk þe calf norisseþ til an Oxe, So loue and leaute lele men susteneþ; B.Prol.126 (C.Prol.149); A.3.267 (B.3.291, C.3.443); B.4.180 (C.4.174); B.11.84, 85, 91 (C.12.23, 24, 31 passim); C.17.162. *Court Baron* 63: 'Sir, in God's name have pity of me and I will confess to thee the truth, and I will put me wholly upon thy loyalty [liaute].' 'William, by my loyalty [liaute] thou shalt have naught but justice!' (Cf. below). See LELE.

II. Justice; the principle of truth, honesty, equity: B.Prol.122 The kyng and þe commune and kynde wit þe þridde Shopen lawe and leaute, ech lif to knowe his owene; C.12.87ff. Lo, lordes, what leute dede and leele dome y-used . . . For lawe withouten leutee, ley þer a bene! (B.11.154ff.); B.2.21 (C.2.20); B.2.48 (C.2.49); C.3.196 (B.3.159 lawe); A.3.269 (B.3.294, C.3.446).

III. Loyalty, faith, fidelity (esp. in comb. with *love*); TREUTHE: B.12.32 He dooþ wel . . . þat dooþ as lewte techeþ. That is, if þow be man maryed þi make þow louye And lyue forþ as lawe wole; C.22.146 Coueytyse . . . leet Leautee a cherl, and Lyare a freman (B.20.146); C.3.378; B.4.36 (C.4.36); B.4.161 (C.4.156); C.6.195; C.7.260; C.10.171; B.19.89 (C.21.89). This meaning figures prominently in oaths, e.g., 'bi my lewte' (Wright 2:45), indentures for military service, e.g., 'en sa bone leaute,' 'par sa fey e sa bone leaute,' etc. (Denholm-Young 168) and in other contracts of allegiance, esp. oaths of fealty.

The word has occasioned much discussion. E.g., Donaldson: 'I suggest that the meaning is a good deal closer to the root meaning "legality" (Latin *legalitas*) than it is to Modern English "loyalty." I should define it as "exact justice; strict adherence to the letter of the law" ' (66 n.); P. M. Kean: '*Lewte* in Middle English can stand for virtue, for living well, in a wide sense' ('Love, Law, and *Lewte* in *Piers Plowman*,' *Review of English Studies*, ns 15 [1964], 241–61); George Kane (on B.Prol.126): '[A]s a personification it is untranslatable by "Loyalty": it seems to mean either "your loyal subjects" or, in my view more probably, "law-abiding people" ' ('Poetry and Lexicography' [see Introduction, n. 8], 40). Legal historians recognize the same latitude of meanings. Maitland and Baildon comment: 'The words "leute," "deleaus," seem to hover between "loyalty," "disloyal," on the one hand, and "lawfulness," "lawless," on the other hand. To say of a man that he is "deleaus" is to accuse him of something more definite than "disloyalty" in our sense of that word; it is to deny that he is a "lawful man": it is to suggest that he is a "lawless man," that is, an outlaw' (*Court Baron* 48 n.). No doubt, the rich ambiguity of the word partly explains its great appeal for Langland.

LEDE   **I.** *Pl.* Landed property, landholdings: C.11.69 Pe more a wynneth . . . And lordeth in ledes, the lasse goed he deleth (B.10.87); C.15.304 Lordes and ladyes ben cald for ledes þat they haue; B.15.558 (C.17.221).

II. One attached or belonging to the land of an estate (as a serf or villein); a vassal, one in the service of another; man, person (OE *leod*): A.4.147 It is wel hard . . . alle my lige ledis to lede þus euene (B.4.184, C.4.178); B.18.401 (C.20.444). Cf. *W&W* 501: 'I thynk to . . . giff giftes . . . To ledis of my legyance þat lufen me in hert.' BONDE, CHERL, LONDES AND LEDES, MAN, TENAUNT.

LEDEN   **I.** To direct the course of (the law): B.3.158 Mede . . . liþ ayein þe lawe and letteþ hym þe gate That feiþ may noȝt haue his forþ, hire floryns go so þikke. She ledeþ lawe as hire list (C.3.195). Cotgr.: *mener la loy* 'to proceed in a suit.' Cf. Kail 36/57: 'Auyse ȝow þat leden lawe, ffor drede of lordschipe or for mede Holde no pore in awe To storble here ryʒt or lette here nede'; 'Punctuation Poem, II,' Robbins 101/1: 'Nowe the lawe is ledde by clere conscience fful seld. Couetise hath dominacioun In Euery place'; *Lud.Cov.* 126/71: 'A ʒonge man may do more chere in bedde to A ʒonge wench þan may An olde þat is þe cawse such lawe is ledde þat many a man is a kokewolde.' *K.Counc.* 52: 'The aforesaid matter having been tried [deduci] before the lord the king'; *Writs* 120: 'That plea has been reasonably conducted [deducta] in the said county court' (also 125, 158, etc.).

    II. To bring (someone) before the court: C.3.128 The kyng fram conseyl come, calde aftur Mede And sente to se here – y myhte nat se þat ladde here. Cf. *Eyre* 67: The chief justice 'ordered the sheriff to lead [mener] John of Gisors to the bar'; 92: 'On which day the said Reymund comes, led [ductus] by the marshal'; Fisher 190/20: 'The same late Shirreves . . . arested the seide Gieffrey and hym inprisoned and hym so beyng prisoner ledde. . . .'

LEDERE OF LOVEDAIES   A person who arranges or conducts lovedays: B.10.312 Now is Religion a rydere . . . A ledere of louedayes and a lond buggere (A.11.212, C.6.159 [Sk.]). Cf. *ledere* as 'ruler, governor': B.1.159 (C.1.155), C.8.251; C.15.170; C.16.157; B.19.100 (C.21.100).

LEGATE   An ecclesiastic invested with papal authority: B.13.421 Ye lordes and ladies and legates of holy chirche That fedeþ fooles sages, flatereris and lieris (C.7.82). Cf. *Jac. Well* 33/8: 'And whanne a man is assoyled of þe court of Rome, or of a legat, of þe gret curse. . . .' *Engl.Canons* 2:151 distinguishes three kinds of legates.

LEGE   **I.** (Noun) A vassal, one who owes fealty to a lord; *gen.* a subject: B.19.60 Alle hise lele liges largely he yeueþ Places in Paradis (C.21.60); (Adj. as noun) C.3.316 [Rulers] ʒeue lond or lordschipe oþer large ʒeftes To here lele and to lege; B.18.349 (C.20.395). *K.Counc.* 70: 'Every liege of the realm [liege du roialme] should be free to sell.' MAN.

    II. (Adj.) Bound by a feudal tenure; owing allegiance to a lord or king; 'liege people,' subjects: C.3.414 God sente to Sauel . . . That Agag of Amalek and alle his leege peple Sholde deye derfly for dedes of here eldres; C.3.316–17; A.4.147 (B.4.184, C.4.178).

LEGGEN   See ALLEGGEN.

LEGISTRE   A legist, one versed in the law, esp. civil or canon law: B.7.14 Bysshopes . . . ben . . . Legistres of boþe lawes; A.8.61 ʒe legistris & lawieris, ʒe wyten ʒif I leiʒe (B.7.60). Usk 50/69: 'But among legistres there dar I not come.' DECRETISTRE, DOCTOUR, LAWIER, MAISTER.

*LEGITIME   Born in lawful wedlock; (as noun) those of legitimate birth: C.10.210 Men þat ben bygeten Out of matrimonye, nat moyloure, mowen nat haue þe grace That lele legityme by þe lawe may claymen. Cf. *Fleta* 1.14 ('De Legitimis') and *Writs* 92, 306. On the rights of illegitimate children, see

Blackstone 1:442–46. English law differed from Roman and canon law in denying legitimation to offspring born of parents who subsequently married; the policy is defended at length by Fortescue (chaps. 39–41). LAWEFUL, MULIER; see also BASTARD.

LEIAUNCE   The sway or jurisdiction of a sovereign over his subjects or 'lieges' (*OED*); also, the allegiance owed to a lord or sovereign (LEAUTE): C.18.201 Thre [things] bilongeth to a lord þat leiaunce claymeth. Cf. *W&W* 501: 'Ledis of my legyance þat lufen me in hert.' *Moots* 116: 'The defendant said that the plaintiff was born out of the allegiance [ligiance] of the king.' Blackstone 1:354: 'Natural-born subjects are such as are born within the dominions of the crown of England, that is, within the ligeance, or as it is generally called, the allegiance of the king.' But cf. *Lib.Alb.* 372 (privy letter): 'Edward, par la grace de Dieu Roy dEngleterre . . . si vous maundons et chargeons, sur la foi et ligeance qe vous nous devez . . .'; Statute 16 Ric. II c. 5: 'Les ditz Seignurs espiritueles . . . sount tenuz par lour ligeance.' LEAUTE, LORDSHIP.

LELE   **I.** Lawful, legally valid; within the law (as opposed to outside the law); law-abiding, respectful of law (OF *leal* < Lat. *legalis*): C.10.210 Men þat ben bygeten Out of matrimonye, nat moyloure, mowen nat haue þe grace That lele legityme by þe lawe may claymen; C.3.338 God gyueth to alle lele lyuynge, Grace of good ende and gret ioye aftur; C.Prol.146; A.2.31 (Sk.); C.8.261; B.19.250 (C.21.250). *Bor.Cust.*: 'If the goods of a good and lawful man be among the goods of a felon . . . [Si bienz d'ascun bon et leal soient entre lez biens d'un felon]' (1:71), 'Qwha sa ever comes to mak an acquitaunce sall . . . swere a lell othe' (179). LAWEFUL.
   II. Loyal, faithful; loyal to God, virtuous: B.19.60 Alle hise lele liges largely he yeueþ Places in Paradis (C.21.60); C.Prol.88; C.3.316; C.3.347; C.9.14; A.11.238 (B.10.355). Cf. the oath of fealty: 'Hear you my Lord R. that I P. shall be to you both faithful and true [foial et loial] . . .' (Statute 17 Edw. II st. 2. [Ruffhead]).
   III. Truthful, honest: B.11.69 Freres . . . loued me þe lasse for my lele speche; C.7.197; B.17.47 (C.19.43).

LELE WEDLOK   Lawful matrimony: C.10.291 For sholde no bed-bourde be, bote yf they bothe were Clene of lyf and in loue of soule and in lele wedlok. Cf. *Jac.Well* 21/20: 'Vnleefful matrimonye' includes 'alle þo þat . . . are weddyd to-gydere in ony degre of kynrede, or of affinyte, or of ony gossyb-rede.' *Writs* 325: 'She ought not to have dower thereof because she was never joined in lawful matrimony [legitimo matrimonio] to the aforesaid H.'

LELLI   **I.** Lawfully; sincerely, in good faith; virtuously: C.11.268 [David sent Uriah into battle] Lelly, as by his lokes, with a lettere of gyle ('In good faith, to all appearances, but with a letter full of deceit,' Pearsall); C.8.140; C.9.59; B.19.232 (C.21.232). *Court Baron* 101: 'Then shall be chosen four taxers [who . . .] shall lawfully [lealment] tax every man according to his trespass.'

II. Faithfully, loyally: A.3.29 Hendely þanne heo behiȝte hem þe same, To loue hem lelly & lordis hem make (B.3.30, C.3.31); A.1.76 (B.1.78); A.1.155 (B.1.181, C.1.177); C.7.208; C.8.255; A.8.160 (B.7.182, C.9.329); A.10.13 (B.9.13, C.10.139); B.10.240 (C.11.144); B.20.210 (C.22.210). *LawMerch*. 1:113: 'Martin said that he . . . had fully and faithfully [bien et loyalment] paid what he owed.'

III. Truthfully, accurately: C.8.298 Thow poyntest neyh þe treuthe And leelyche sayst; C.2.76; B.11.144, 148. *Lib.Alb*. 219: 'Trustworthy persons . . . who are ready lawfully to testify [loialment tesmoigner].'

LERED AND LEWED   Clergy and layfolk: C.16.34 Thise thre [contrition, confession, satisfaction] withoute doute . . . lereth lewed and lered, hey and lowe to knowe Ho doth wel or bet or beste. The pairing is a common alliterative formula, e.g., C.Prol.88; C.6.29; C.9.230; C.14.71; C.15.14; B.20.266 (C.22.266). The effort at inclusiveness in C.16.34 recalls the address of a royal proclamation: 'Henr' þurȝ Godes fultume king on Engleneloande . . . send igretinge to alle hise holde ilaerde and ileawede on Huntendon' schir' (Stubbs 387).

LETTEN TREUTHE   To impede or obstruct justice: B.4.176 Mede ouermaistreþ lawe and muche truþe letteþ (C.4.170); A.3.146; A.11.20 (B.10.20, C.11.17). Cf. *Jac.Well* 14/31: 'And be þis artycle are þei acursyd þat pursewyn wryttes or letterys in ony lay court, to lettyn þe process of lawe.' *Fleta* 1.20: 'Enquiry shall be made . . . of franchises that have been granted which obstruct the course of justice [inpediunt iusticiam].'

LETTRE   An official communication recording an agreement or granting certain legal rights, privileges, etc. **A.** CHARTRE: C.2.83 And Fauel . . . feffeth hem by þis lettre (B.2.78); B.11.304 A chartre is chalangeable bifore a chief Iustice; If fals latyn be in þat lettre þe lawe it impugneþ (C.13.117); C.2.107. **B.** A writ, brief, licence, warrant: B.20.325–26 The frere herof herde and hiede faste To a lord for a lettre leue to haue To curen as a Curatour; and cam with his lettre Boldely to þe bisshop (C.22.325–26); B.5.640; A.8.154 (B.7.176, C.9.332); B.9.39; B.10.92. For bishops' letters, see Bennett 225. BREF, BREVET. **C.** A bill of exchange (ESCHAUNGE), as in 'Lumbardes lettres': B.5.248 Wiþ lumbardes lettres I ladde gold to Rome (C.6.246). See Bennett 168. **D.** A privy letter (PRIVE LETTRE): B.7.23 Vnder his secret seel truþe sent hem [merchants] a lettre (A.8.25, C.9.27). **E.** A letter patent (PATENTE): B.17.10 'Lat se þi lettres,' quod I, 'we myghte þe lawe knowe.' He plukkede forþ a patente (C.19.11); C.19.4; B.17.36; B.17.120. Hall 1:53–74 prints a selection of letters patent. **F.** A pardon or letter of intercession: C.9.281 For shal no pardon preye for ȝow there [in hell] ne no princes lettres; B.18.182 (C.20.185); B.19.307 (C.21.308). **G.** Letter of fraternity: A.8.175 A pokeful of pardoun þere, ne þe prouincialis lettres, Þeiȝ þou be founde in þe fraternite among þe foure ordris, And haue indulgence double-fold, but dowel þe helpe I ne wolde ȝiue for þi patent on pye hele (B.7.197, C.9.344). See Bennett 225–26. **H.** Letter of appointment or authority; credentials: C.13.88 A trewe messager . . . sheweth be seel and seth by lettre with what lord he dwelleth; C.13.40; C.13.59.

LEVE Licence or permission; dispensation: B.11.128 For may no cherl chartre make ne his chatel selle Wiþouten leue of his lord (C.12.61); C.20.314 Thow gete hem with gyle and his gardyn breke; Aȝeyne his [God's] loue and his leue on his londe ȝedest; A.Prol.49 (B.Prol.49, C.Prol.50); B.2.114 (C.2.115); C.3.131; B.6.66 (C.8.67); C.13.82; B.16.47; B.18.267 (C.20.275); C.20.381; B.20.325 (C.22.325); C.22.286. LICENCE AND LEVE, LOVE AND LEVE.

LEX CHRISTI 'The law of Christ,' i.e., the New Law, the law of love: B.17.74 Þe Samaritan . . . ladde hym so forþ on Lyard to *lex Christi*, a graunge (C.19.71 lavacrum-lex-dei). LAWE (I.B.[2]), LOVE AND LAWE.

*LICENCE AND LEVE Formal permission, esp. for an otherwise irregular or wrongful action: C.6.121 Prelates pleyneth on hem [friars] for they here parschiens shryuen Withoute licence and leue; A.Prol.82 Personis & parissh prestis pleynide hem to here bisshop . . . To haue a licence & leue at lundoun to dwelle (B.Prol.85, C.Prol.83).

*LICITUM Lawful, permissible: B.11.96 It is *licitum* for lewed men to legge þe soþe If hem likeþ and lest; ech a lawe it graunteþ. Cf. Fisher 67/11: 'We wol þat ye . . . doo maake vnto þe forsaide priour . . . oure lettres patentes of confirmacion . . . leuyng out þe clause licet.'

LIEN Of an action, charge, claim, etc., to be admissible, to the point, or founded upon sufficient ground or cause: C.5.89 By Crist, y can nat se this lyeth; cf. B.3.176 (C.3.221). Chaucer *LGW* (F) 409: 'Syth no cause of deth lyeth in this caas, Yow oghte to be the lyghter merciable.' St. Germ. 103: 'The partie must haue his remedye by a wryt that called sub pena. Yf a subpena lye in the case.'

LIEUTENAUNT One who holds the place of another, a deputy; also, the governor of a town, prison, etc.: B.16.47 Þe fend . . . feccheþ awey my floures . . . Ac *liberum arbitrium* letteþ hym som tyme, That is lieutenaunt to loken it wel bi leue of myselue.

LIF AND LIM A formula used in oaths, charges, judgements, etc.: B.5.99 Bitwene meyne and meyne I make debate ofte That boþe lif and lyme is lost þoruȝ my speche; B.19.105 (C.21.105). Cf. *O&N* 1098: 'Vor riȝte niþe & for fule onde Let þane lutle fuȝel nime An him fordeme lif an lime.' *K. Counc.* 48: 'The said Sir William and others of his company threaten him in life and limb [de vie et de membre] so that he dares not go or be seen anywhere'; *Eyre* 32: 'This is a matter that touches life and limb [vie e menbre].'

LIMITOUR A friar licensed to hear confession within a certain jurisdiction: B.20.346 And at þe laste þis lymytour ... saluede so our wommen til some were wiþ childe (C.22.346); B.5.139; B.20.362 (C.22.362). The correct definition of this word was established by Arnold Williams, *Studies in Philology* 57 (1960), 463–78.

LINAGE Issue, descendants; ancestry, noble birth: C.13.110 Hit is a carfol knyhte and of a caytif kynges makynge That hath noþer lond ne lynage ryche (B.11.297); C.5.26; A.10.37 (B.9.49); C.9.195. HEIR, ISSUE.

LOGIK AND LAWE The law referred to is probably civil (unless the phrase is used merely for its alliteration): B.20.274 Enuye ... heet freres go to scole And lerne logyk and lawe (C.22.274). It may have been normal to take up the two studies together; Gower's *Vox Clamantis* refers to a clerk's studies as *civilia iura et logicam* (III.2105). Cf. A.11.128 (B.10.176, C.11.119); B.11.219, 220, 224. BOTHE LAWES, CIVILE.

LOKEN To ordain, decree, decide; keep or administer (the law): B.2.198 Shal neuere man of þis molde meynprise þe leeste, But riȝt as þe lawe lokeþ lat falle on hem alle (A.2.159, C.2.209); C.8.85 Hem þat han lawes to loke lacke hem nat; A.2.100 (B.2.136); A.7.299 (B.6.318); B.7.171; A.10.201 (Sk.). JUSTIFIEN.

LOND AND LORDSHIP Land and power, authority, jurisdiction: C.3.315 Thow the kyng of his cortesye ... ȝeue lond or lordschipe ... To here lele and to lege, loue ys the cause; C.9.202; A.11.14 (B.10.14, C.11.12); B.14.263 (C.16.103); B.14.330; C.16.159; B.15.555 (C.17.218); B.15.558 (C.17.221); B.16.240 (C.18.257); cf. B.11.23 Til þow be a lord and haue lond (C.11.185). See LORDSHIP.

LOND AND WATER A common formula expressing inclusive jurisdiction, possession, etc.: B.18.312 (Sk.) For thi last lesynge ylore we haue Adam, And al owre lordeship ... a londe and a water; cf. B.13.16; C.15.19; B.16.189; B.18.30 (C.20.29); B.19.236 (C.21.236). *Fleta* 2.52: 'The articles of the view of frankpledge are these. ... Concerning the concealment or alienation of the king's rights on land or sea [in terra vel in mari] ...'; *Lib.Alb.* 117: 'De purprestis factis super Regem in terris vel in aquis'; Fisher 225/16: 'The seid Iohn Davy ... hath no power auctorite ner Iurisdiccion ... withynne the body of this Reaume, neither on water ner on londe.'

LONDES AND LEDES Lands and tenements, a formulaic phrase in deeds, wills, etc.: B.15.558 Whan Costantyn of curteisie holy kirke dowed Wiþ londes and ledes, lordshipes and rentes (C.17.221). Cf. *Sir Tryamour* 1269: 'Y make the myn heyre Of londs and of lede' (*MED*); 'The Farmer's Complaint' (Sisam 112/27): 'Her landes and her ledes liggeth ful lene Thurgh bidding of bailifs such harm hem hath hight.' *Bor. Cust.* 1:68: 'If the man accused of the death flies, his lands and tenements [cez teres, tenements] and all his goods are forfeit'; *Lib.Alb.* 282: 'Ils . . . ne terres ne tenementz ount'; Reynes 333 (a will): 'Et quidem predicte terre et tenementa ad heredes meos proprios. . . .' Skeat notes, 'The word *ledes* = tenements, may be the same word as *ledes* = men' (2:383); hence, *londes and ledes* might also signify lands and the labourers belonging thereto. See also LEDE.

LONE   Lending (of money), USURIE; also, a loan: C.4.194 Loue wol lene þe seluer . . . More then alle thy marchauntes . . . Or Lumbardus of Lukes þat leuen by lone as Iewes; B.20.287 Fals folk . . . That borweþ . . . and þanne biddeþ frendes Yerne of forȝifnesse or lenger yeres loone (C.22.286 leue). DETTE, SUM CERTEIN.

LORD   I. One who presides at a judicial session; a judge or justice of the peace: A.3.24 Ientily wiþ ioye þe Iustices somme Buskide hem to þe bour þere þe burde dwelliþ. . . . Þanne lauȝte hy leue, þise lordis at mede (B.3.25); B.11.158 Wel ouȝte ye lordes þat lawes kepe þis lesson haue in mynde And on Troianus truþe to þenke, and do truþe to þe peple (C.12.88); B.5.96 I haue a neȝebore . . . To apeire hym bi my power pursued wel ofte, And bilowen hym to lordes to doon hym lese siluer; A.3.31 (B.3.32, C.3.3); B.3.298; B.10.25. Cf. *Gamelyn* 175/716: 'Gamelyn came well redy to the nexte shire And ther was his brother, both lord and sire.' Statute 34 Edw. III c. 1 (on justices of the peace): 'First, that in every county of England shall be assigned for the keeping of the peace one lord [Seignur] . . . with some learned in the law, and they shall have the power to restrain offenders . . ., to pursue, arrest, take and chastise them according to the law . . .'; Purvis 65: 'Officium domini [Office of Judge].' BAROUN, CHIEF JUSTICE, DOMESMAN, JUGGE.
    II. A landowner, esp. one having tenants attached to the land; a feudal lord: B.11.23 Til þow be a lord and haue lond (C.11.185); B.5.317 (C.5.163); C.9.73; B.10.477; C.15.14; B.15.309 (C.17.44); B.19.32 (C.21.32); B.19.459 (C.21.459). CHIEF LORD.
    III. A person of high rank or social position; a great lord or ruler: B.3.203 Hadde I ben Marchal of his men . . . He sholde haue be lord of þat lond in lengþe and in brede (C.3.259); A.4.101 (B.4.114, C.4.109); C.5.73; B.9.22; B.10.314 (C.5.160); B.10.321 (C.5.167); C.12.218; C.15.170; B.15.202.

LORDSHIP   I. The land or territory belonging to a lord; a manor, feudal estate, kingdom: B.2.89 Al I hem graunte . . . wiþ þe Burgh of þefte, Wiþ al þe lordshipe of leccherie in lengþe and in brede (A.2.61, C.2.93); A.12.64; B.15.555–58 (C.17.218–21). Cf. *K.Counc.* 96: 'Which wines . . . were brought within the lordship [seugneurie] of my lord the archbishop of Canterbury'; Fisher 163/75: '. . . tenentȝ of the Ryal lordshipe and tounshipe of Chestreton.' SIGNIURE, TOUN.
    II. The ownership of land or property: C.20.109 Alle ȝoure childerne, cherles, cheue shall neuere, Ne haue lordschipe in londe ne no londe tulye, And as bareyne be, and by vsure libbe (B.18.105); C.3.248; B.20.251 (C.22.251). Pearsall (on C.20.109): 'Jews were prohibited by law in Christian countries from owning land, which is one reason why they had to turn to moneylending as a profession' (324).

III. The rule, jurisdiction, or power of a lord: C.16.159 He þat hath lond and lordschipe . . . at þe laste ende Shal be porest of power at his partynge hennes; B.16.191 So þre [things] bilongeþ for a lord þat lordshipe cleymeþ; B.18.315 Ylorn we haue Adam, And al oure lordship . . . a londe and in helle (C.20.349); C.2.107; B.7.164; B.9.41; B.17.8 (C.19.10). REALTE.

IV. The household of a lord; retinue; company: A.2.28 Pere miȝte þou wyte ȝif þou wilt whiche þei ben alle Þat longiþ to þat lordsshipe, þe lasse & þe more (B.2.46, C.2.48). SECTE (II).

LOVE   Partiality; favouritism toward one of the parties in a legal suit (as in the oaths of judges, jurors and law officers that they will not be influenced by 'love or money [or friendship, hate, fear, etc.]'): B.1.103 [Knights should side with the true party] And neuere leue hem for loue ne lacchynge of yiftes (A.1.101, C.1.100). Cf. *Jac. Well* 95/26: 'Herkenbaldus of Bornayre . . . a gret iustyse . . . sparyd no persone, for loue, ne dreed, ne for wrethe, but þat in his demyng he dyde equite.' *K. Counc.* 105: 'And first was called . . . Thomas Wawton and sworne upon a boke to sey the playn trouth and nouzt to melle it with eny ontrouth for hate or euel will neither for loue ner fauour but plainly report as it was in dede'; *Eyre* 12: 'I will serve loyally in the office of sheriff . . . and will not cease to do this for gift nor for promise nor for love nor for anger [ne pur amur ne pur haungre] nor for anything . . .'; the oaths recorded in the *Liber Albus* afford numerous additional examples.

LOVE AND LAWE   A common formula in European legal tradition: B.7.63 Alle libbynge laborers þat . . . lyuen in loue and in lawe . . . Hadde þe same absolucion; B.11.171 Lawe wiþouten loue . . . ley þer a bene! (C.12.91 leutee); B.7.90 (C.9.166); B.9.191; B.11.229 (C.12.118); cf. B.11.223; C.17.130, 136, 139. The phrase covers two kinds of settlement. Disputants in civil cases might work out their differences either *per judicium vel per concordiam* (e.g., *Lib. Alb.* 71), that is, through litigation or through an amicable agreement such as a LOVEDAI; in canon law terms, *secundum amorem vel iustitiam* or *consilio vel iudicio*. The *OED* cites as the earliest example in English *The Laws of Aethelred* III.13 (c.1000) 'And þar þeȝen aȝe tweȝen costas lufe oððe laȝe, and he þonne lufe ȝeceose' (*OED* 1.d) and further notes that the phrase 'under love and law' came to mean 'under frankpledge.' Dorothy Bethurum takes the phrase to refer to a thegn's two alternatives: 'amicable agreement or recourse to the law' (274). An extremely common theme in medieval German literature, the contrast expresses itself in the formula *Minne und Recht*. See esp. Hugo Kuhn, 'Minne oder Recht,' *Dichtung und Welt im Mittelalter* (Stuttgart, 1959), 105–111; and Hans Hattenhauer, 'Minne und Recht als Ordnungsprinzipien des mittelalterlichen Rechts,' *Zeitschrift der Savigny-Stiftung für Rechtsgeschichte*, Ger. Abt. 80 (1963), 325–44. As Hattenhauer observes, there is an 'antithetische Spannung' between *minne* and *recht*, yet each corrects and takes its meaning from the other. So with Langland: C.17.136 Oure lord aloueth no loue but lawe be þe cause; B.11.171 Lawe wiþouten loue . . . ley þer a bene! As the fulfillment of the law and the incarnation of love, Christ combined both in a new 'law of love.'

LOVE AND LEAUTE   An alliterative formula used esp. to describe a vassal's duty to his lord: B.11.145 Al þe clergie vnder crist ne myȝte me cracche fro helle, But oonliche loue and leautee and my laweful domes (C.12.78); B.4.36 (C.4.36); B.15.468. The phrase translates such conventional formulas as *foi et loiaute* (Ganshof 94), *fide et dilectione* (Stubbs 481), etc. Cf. *RR* 1:44: 'With lewte and loue yloke to thi peeris'; Henryson, *The Taill of the Scheip and the Doig* 1301: 'Se how this cursit syn of covetice Exylit hes baith lufe, lawtie, and Law'; *Gorboduc* I.ii.366: 'I pray you all To beare my sonnes the loue and loyaltie That I haue founde within your faithfull brestes' (ed. J. M. Manly, *Specimens of Pre-Shakesperean Drama* [New York: Ginn, 1897], 2:228).

LOVE AND LEVE   Permission and leave (*MED*): C.20.314 For thow gete hem with gyle and his gardyn breke; Aȝeyne his loue and his leue on his londe ȝedest; C.20.381 Falsliche thou . . . my gardyne breke Aȝeyne my loue and my leue.

LOVEDAI   A formal meeting or time of meeting at which a dispute is settled out of court (often by leave of the court): B.3.158 [Mede] ledeþ lawe as hire list and louedaies makeþ (C.3.195); C.3.196; B.5.420; A.11.20 (B.10.20, C.11.17); A.11.212 (B.10.312, C.5.158 lawedays). Many aspects of the medieval loveday remain obscure. John Spargo derived the term from *dies amoris* and *jour d'amour*, and defined it as 'a day appointed by the express license or permission of a court for settling a case amicably out of court,' *Speculum* 15 (1940), 36–56. Josephine Waters Bennett, in *Speculum* 33 (1958), 351–70, rejected his argument. She extended the definition to include any meeting of contending parties for the purpose of settling a dispute; and concluded 'that Middle English *loveday* was formed on the analogy of *lawday*, and that the English is the older form, of which *dies amoris* and *jour d'amour* were translations.' Examples are plentiful: *LawMerch.*, 'A love-day is given [datus est dies amoris] to the parties on the morrow' (1:2; also 3, 5, 18, 36, 57, 58); *Bor. Cust.*, 'It is our wont in every plea to give a love-day [dies amoris] at the prayer of the parties' (1:90; also 229, 264); *Court Baron* 20, 47, 58, 74, 84, 88, etc.; *Wisdom* 137/698; *Lud. Cov.* 103/185; Ross, *ME Serm.* 132/18; *Upland* 77/140. Cambridge Univ. Lib. MS. Dd. 1.1 includes a 218-line poem in ME and Latin on the duties of arbitrators and litigants who take part in lovedays; ed. T. J. Heffernan in *Chaucer Review* 10 (1975), 172–85.

LUNATIK   Suffering from intermittent madness, believed to vary with the phases of the moon; as a noun: one subject to such recurrent attacks: B.Prol.123 Thanne loked vp a lunatik . . . And knelynge to þe kyng clergially he seide, 'Crist kepe þee, sire kyng, and þi kyngryche, And lene þee lede þi lond so leaute þee louye, And for þi riȝtful rulyng be rewarded in heuene'; C.9.107 Hem wanteth wyt, men and women bothe, The which aren lunatyk lollares and lepares aboute, And madden as þe mone sit . . . And aren meuynge aftur þe mone; C.9.137; cf. B.15.3. Medieval law distinguished between lunatics and natural-born idiots. Thus Blackstone 1:294: 'A lunatic, or *non compos mentis*, is one who hath had understanding, but by disease, grief, or other accident hath lost the use of his reason. A lunatic is indeed properly one that hath lucid intervals; sometimes enjoying his senses, and sometimes not, and that frequently depending upon the change of the moon. ... And therefore it is declared by the statute 17 Edw. II. c. 10 that the king shall provide for the custody and sustentation of lunatics, and preserve their lands and the profits of them, for their use, when they come to their right mind.' The especial dependence of persons *non compos mentis* upon the king's justice explains the lunatic's desire in the Prologue that the king govern with 'leaute' and 'riȝtful rulyng.' Persons were proved *non compos* on the basis of an inquisition (see Hall 2:86–87). The wardship of lunatics is discussed in Holdsworth 1:473–76.

*LUSHE-BURGH   A base coin made in imitation of the sterling or silver penny and imported from Luxembourg in the reign of Edward III (*OED*): B.15.349 As in lussheburwes is a luþer alay, and yet lokeþ he lik a sterlyng ... so it fareþ by some folk now; þei han a fair speche ... Ac þe metal, þat is mannes soule, myd synne is foule alayed (C.17.72); C.17.82; C.17.168. Statute 25 Edw. III (5) c. 2: 'It shall be called treason ... if a man bring false money into this realm, counterfeit to the money of England, as the money called Lushburgh [sicome la monoie appelle Lucynburgh].'

M

*MACERE   A mace bearer, a person who preceded and cleared the way for a dignitary or high public official; also any law officer (e.g., sheriff, bailiff, sergeant) authorized to carry a mace or *virga* as a symbol of office: B.3.76 Maires and Maceres þat menes ben bitwene The kyng and þe comune to kepe þe lawes (A.3.65). Cf. *RR* 3:268: Rulers were ordained 'to laboure on the lawe ... And to merke meyntenourz with maces ichonne.' Despite Bennett's view that 'mace-bearers were merely attendants, with no right to punish,' L might have had in mind a sheriff, bailiff, or sergeant-at-mace (*claviger*); indeed, *macere* is replaced in C by 'schyreues and seriauntes' (3.78). For references to the mace or rod of sheriffs, sergeants, bailiffs, etc., see *Eyre* 11, 40; *Bor. Cust.* 2:48; *Cov. Leet* 141: No bailiff to let to farm issues or fines to the sergeants-at-mace (clauigeribus).

MAINPERNOUR   *Lit.* a hand-taker or manucaptor; one who serves as surety that another (esp. a prisoner to be released on bail) will fulfil his legal obligation to appear in court when required; BORGH: B.4.112 That Mede moste be maynpernour [for Wrong] Reson þei bisouȝte (A.4.99, C.4.107); B.18.185 God haþ forgyuen and graunted me, pees, & mercy To be mannes meynpernour for eueremoore after (C.20.188). *Mirror* 193: 'Pledges and mainpernours are all one, though they have different names; but pledges are those who pledge something other than a man's body, as in real and mixed actions;

mainpernours are found in personal actions only, and they pledge a man's body.' *Bor.Cust.* 1:12: 'If he can fynde vi. maynpernours, that is to say vi. barons that wyll be bounde for hym to bryng his bodye to answere at all tymes within the seyd libertie whensoever ytt shalbe assigned, he shall goo to bayle.' Mainpernours who failed to produce the defendant when required could be amerced or imprisoned themselves. See *Lib.Alb.*, 'Quod arrestatus poterit invenire manucaptores,' 'De maynpernours' (200), 'Des mainpernours et attournez resceivers' (222) and passim. Discussion in *K.Counc.* xl.

MAINPRISE   The release of a prisoner to a MAINPERNOUR: B.4.88 And he amendes mowe make lat maynprise hym haue, And be borȝ for his bale and buggen hym boote (A.4.75, C.4.84); B.16.264 May no wed vs quyte, Ne no buyrn be oure borgh, ne brynge vs fram his daunger ... Out of þe poukes pondfold no maynprise may vs fecche (C.18.281); B.20.17 (C.22.17). Cf. *Pride of Life* 101/379: 'Þer [in hell] ne fallit no maynpris, Ne supersidias'; also *Gamelyn* 744. Fisher 216/28: '... the same ... to abide in þe kinges prison ... withoute þat þei or any of þeym be hade in baille or put to mainprise afore þende of suche determynacion hade.'

MAINPRISEN   To release or to arrange the release of (a prisoner) by surety, to be a mainpernour for; to secure pardon for (somebody): A.2.158 Shal neuere man of þis molde meynprise þe leste, But riȝt as þe lawe lokis let falle on hem alle (B.2.197, C.2.208); B.4.179 Mede shal noȝt maynprise yow (C.4.173); C.20.188. Cf. Fisher 162/8: 'I praye ȝou þat ... I myȝte Be brouȝte In to þe kyngesbenche and so I meinprised to go at large.' BORWEN (I), FECCHEN (III), RAUNSOUNEN.

MAINTENAUNCE   'Maintenance "signifieth in law a taking in hand, bearing up or upholding of quarrels and sides, to the disturbance or hindrance of common right" (Coke). It is the tort committed by a person who, having no interest in civil proceedings, and with no lawful justification, assists one of the parties, with money or otherwise, to institute, prosecute or defend the action. ... Maintenance includes champerty and embracery' (Osborn): B.5.250 Lentestow euere lordes for loue of hire mayntenaunce? (C.6.248). Schmidt: 'Either Cov[eitise] bought the protection of lords or lent to them to enable them to maintain their position' (317). Cf. *RR* 3.312: 'Thus is the lawe louyd thoru myȝhty lordis willys, That meynteyne myssdoers. ... ffor mayntenaunce many day well more is the reuthe!' *K.Bench* 7 includes a detailed record (together with verses in Middle English) of a suit for maintenance: 'Again, they present that John Berwald [et al.] ..., together with other malefactors of their covin to the number of eighty ... were dressed for the last six years in one livery of a single company by corrupt allegiance and confederacy, each of them in maintaining the other in all plaints, true or false, against whosoever should wish to complain against them or any one of them, in breach of the terms of the statute [i.e., 13 Ric. II st. 3]' (7:83–84). According to G. M. Trevelyan, 'The practice of maintenance had come in at least thirty years before the reign of Richard the Second, at a time when great armies of retainers were enlisted for the French war. It had been growing ever since, and continued to grow, until in the fifteenth century it was said to be impossible to get justice at all without the support of a lord and his following,' *England in the Age of Wycliffe* (New York, 1900), 58ff.

MAINTENEN   I. To aid or abet (somebody, esp. wrongdoers) in a legal action; to uphold (a wrong or a wrong cause): B.3.247 To mayntene mysdoers Mede þei take (A.3.226); B.4.55 He [Wrong] maynteneþ hise men to murþere myne hewen, Forstalleþ my feires, fiȝteþ in my Chepyng, Brekeþ vp my berne dores, bereþ awey my whete, etc. (A.4.42, C.4.58); A.2.157 (B.2.196, C.2.207); B.3.90; A.3.139 (B.3.150, C.3.186); C.17.234. Cf. *RR* 3.311 quoted above (lordis ... That meynteyne myssdoers). *Eyre* 40: 'Roger de Depham [et al.] ... were arraigned of conspiracy and of a false alliance to maintain [maintener] as well the plaints of others as their own plaints, by an oath taken between them.' CONSPIREN.
   II. To uphold (the law): B.3.216 [The pope] medeþ men hymseluen to mayntene hir lawes (A.3.203, C.3.271); B.2.37 Men of þis moolde þat maynteneþ truþe. See citation under MAN OF LAWE.

MAINTENOUR   One who is guilty of MAINTENAUNCE: C.3.286 Mede is euermore a mayntenour of gyle. Cf. *RR* 3.268: 'Rewlers of rewmes ... Were ... yffoundid ... to laboure on the lawe ... And to merke mayntenourz with maces ichonne'; *Jac. Well* 15/30: Accursed are 'alle comoun baratourys, felouns, and here mayntenourys, conspyratourys, confederatourys.' *K. Counc.* 82: 'It is testified that the said Percival is a common malfeasor and maintainer in the county' [meffesour et meyntenour]. Fisher 163/23: 'The wronges that we haue had by the Priour and Chanons of Bernewelle and her meyntenors' (also 164/16). *FAUTOR.*

MAIRE   The chief civil officer of a town, the mayor: B.1.160 Forþi is loue ledere of þe lordes folk of heuene And a meene, as þe Mair is, bitwene þe commune & þe kyng (C.1.156); A.3.83 Meiris and men þat kepiþ þe lawis (B.3.94, C.3.122); C.3.108 Mayres þat maketh fre men; A.3.65 (B.3.76, C.3.77); A.3.76 (B.3.87, C.3.115); B.3.315 (C.3.467); C.8.87; C.9.122; A.8.168 (B.7.190, C.9.337); B.13.270; B.14.290 (C.16.125). As Bennett notes (137): 'In the 14th c. the mayor's chief role was as a magistrate responsible for fair trade practices'; see also Cam 90ff.

MAISTER   A magistrate, a public civil officer having judicial or executive powers; 'master of the law,' one learned in the law (esp. civil and canon law): A.8.168 Be þou neuere þe baldere to breke þe ten hestis; And nameliche ȝe maistris, as meiris & iuggis (B.7.190, C.9.337); A.3.91 (Sk.) Now beoth ȝe war ... ȝe maysturs of the lawe; C.8.87 Maystres, as þe mayres ben ... What þei comaunde as by þe kyng countreplede hit neuere; A.3.225 (B.3.246); B.11.174 *Maister* often translates Lat. *magistratus* and is used interchangeably with ME *magistrat* (q.v. *MED*). LEGISTRE, MACERE, MAIRE.

95

MAKEN To establish, endow, provide expenses for (see *MED* 3): **A.** An institution, as a church, college, hospital: B.7.26 [Truth bad merchants] bug-gen boldely . . . And siþenes selle it ayein and saue þe wynnyng, And make Mesondieux þerwiþ myseise to helpe (A.8.28). DOWEN, FOUNDEN. **B.** A nun: B.7.29 [Truth bad merchants] Marien maydenes or maken hem Nonnes (A.8.31). *MED* 14 (a): 'To change (sb.) into (sth. else)'; however, the idea in lines 26 (to endow hospitals) and 29 (to 'marry' or provide dowries for poor maidens) is carried over as well. Like clerks who were given 'titles' (q.v.), nuns were usually required to bring an endowment or some guarantee of support with them into the convent. FINDEN, SETTEN.

MAN In possessive phrases ('your man'), the vassal of a lord or king; one who has taken an oath of homage to another: B.10.148 And whan I was war of his wille [Wit's] to his wif [Study] gan I knele And seide, 'mercy, madame; youre man shal I worþe . . . For to werche youre wille while my lif dureþ' (A.11.101, C.11.89); C.3.249; C.3.267; B.4.155; A.12.83; B.14.217 (C.16.59). The oaths of homage and fealty are recorded in Statute 17 Edw. II st. 2 (Ruffhead). See also Reynes 145: 'Whan a freman schall do his homage to his chef lord þat he halt of his chef tenement, he schal holden his handys togedyr betwyx his lordis handis, knelyng, he schall this seyn: "I become ʒour man fro þis day forward and feyth bere to ʒow for þat tenement þat I cleyme to helde of ʒow, sauyng the fewte wyche I owe to our lord the Kyng and oþer lordesheppes."' LEGE.

MANER A manorial estate, consisting of a manor house, service buildings, lands, and the tenants attached thereto; also a manor house or castle: B.5.243 I haue mo Manoirs þoruʒ Rerages; B.10.313 Now is Religion a rydere . . . A prikere on a palfrey fro place to Manere (C.5.159); A.6.73 (B.5.586, C.7.233); A.10.15. Blackstone 2:90: 'A manor, *manerium*, *a manendo*, because the usual residence of the owner, seems to have been a district of ground, held by lords or great personages . . . being occupied by the lord . . . and his servants.' For an account of the personnel and daily life on a manor, see H. S. Bennett. LORDSHIP, PLACE, SIGNIURE, TOUN.

MAN OF LAWE One in the legal profession, as a clerk, advocate, justice, etc.: B.4.152 I seiʒ Mede in þe moot halle on men of lawe wynke (C.4.148); B.7.40 Men of lawe leest pardon hadde (A.8.45, C.9.44); C.4.67; C.4.168; C.9.51; C.17.46; C.20.354. Cf. *D&P* 224/1: 'Also þese men of lawe þat for mede meynteþin falshed aʒenys þe trewþe or for mede hydyn þe trewþe þat þey schuldyn meynteþin . . . for[f]etyn aʒenys þis precept.' Statute 14 Edw. III c. 16: 'The *Nisi prius* shall be granted before the chief Baron of the Exchequer if he be a man of law [homme de ley]'; *Eyre* 102: 'You will never see the day among lawyers [gent de lei] when a deed of the King's can be vouched.' *Lib.Alb*. 33: 'Pluribus aliis in legibus tamen Sancti Edwardi, qui nunc "Justi-ciarii" dicuntur, vocabuntur "lagemanni," a *lage* Saxonice quod "lex" est Latine; unde "lagemannus" qui "legis homo"; quem dicimus nunc "jurisperi-tum," vel melius "legislatorem."' LAWIER, LEGISTRE, VOKETTE.

MANSLAUGHT   Homicide; the act of killing another human being, whether directly or indirectly (as by command, neglect, etc.): C.4.182 But ich ... brynge alle men to bowe withouten bittere wounde, Withouten mercement or manslauht amende alle reumes; C.17.241 Naught thorw manslaght and mannes strenghe Macometh hadde þe maistrie Bote thorw pacience and priue gyle. *Fleta* 1.23: 'Homicide is the slaying of man with evil intent, and there may be bodily slaying either by deed or by word: by deed, as in justice, by necessity, by chance or wilfully; by word, as by precept, by counsel or by forbidding.' Cf. *D&P* 2:1: 'Þe fyuete comandement is þis: Non occides [Ex. 20:13] ... in whiche precept God defendith us al maner manslauthe vnleful, boþin bodyly & gostlyche.'

*MARCHAUNDEN   To trade as a merchant, to bargain or exchange: C.6.280 Y sente ouer see my seruauntes to Bruges ... To marchaunde with my moneye and maken here eschaunges (B.13.393). Cf. Statute 2 Ric. II c. 1 against towns and cities that do not allow foreign merchants 'to go, travel, and merchandise [aler converser merchander] as they were accustomed to do.' See also A.3.236 (B.3.257, C.3.312) for *marchaundie* (trade, commerce); C.3.110 for *marchaundise* (commerce); and A.Prol.60 (B.Prol.63, C.Prol.61); A.5.120 (B.5.204, C.6.212); B.5.284 (C.6.340); C.13.50; C.13.52; B.13.361 (C.6.260) for *marchaundise* (goods, commodities). 'Fals marchaundyse' is divided by *Jac. Well* 133/17ff. into five categories. Other words used to describe commercial dealings include BARGAIN, BROKAGE, CHEVISAUNCE, ESCHAUNGE, MERCEDE, MERCIMONIE, PERMUTACIOUN, REGRATERIE.

MARIAGE   A woman's marriage portion in money or property given by her father (*MED*): A.2.37 Sire symonye is assent to asele þe chartres Pat fals & fauel be any fyn halden, And feffe mede þermyd in mariage for euere; A.2.47 Alle to wytnesse wel what þe writ wolde, In what maner þat mede in mariage was feffid.

MARIEN   **I.* To endow (a daughter); provide money for the marriage of (a maiden) (*MED*): A.8.31 [Treuthe bad merchants] Marie maidenis also or maken hem nonnes, Pore wydewis þat wiln not be wyues aftir (B.7.29). DOWEN, FINDEN.
    *II. To witness or attend the wedding of (someone): B.2.57 To marien þis mayde was many man assembled. WITNESSEN.

MARSHAL   Military commander, general: B.3.201 Hadde I ben Marchal of his men ... He sholde haue be lord of þat lond (A.3.188, C.3.257); C.3.256 For sholde neuere Consience be my constable ... Ne be marschal ouer my men there y moste fyhte. Ac hadde y, Mede, ben his marchel ouer his men in Fraunce ... He sholde haue be lord of þat lond. McKisack 265: The king's 'two principal military officers [were] the constable and the marshal, on whom rested responsibility for the maintenance of discipline in the army and for the enforcement of martial law.' *Fleta* 2.5: 'In every war in which the king is engaged, it is the duty of the marshal to be in the front line and to appoint the places in which the whole army and all concerned are to make their stay. . . . [E]very night at twilight he sets the watch and in the dawn he relieves it, and when the army is awake he goes forth in the vanguard, every day, with banner displayed, accompanied by foragers' (p. 114).

MATTER   See MOVEN A MATTER

MAUNDEMENT   A sealed writ, decree, directive: B.17.2 I am *Spes* . . . and spire after a Knyght That took me a maundement vpon þe mount of Synay To rule alle Reames wiþ; I bere þe writ riȝt here (C.19.2); B.17.63 (C.19.60). Fisher 171/6: 'That same dauyd . . . wald haue a maundement fro yowe . . . a wirtte [writte] sub pena direct to the said Dauid to apere be fore yow att a certein day forto declare the trewth in the matiers foresaide'; Hall 1:95: 'aquitance ou mandement'; Statute 20 Edw. III c. 1: 'letres ou mandementz'; *Lib.Alb.* 373: 'The effect or intention of our present command [de nostre present mandement] . . . given under Privy Seal'; *Bor.Cust.* 1:12: 'The warden of the v. portes sent maundement sertifying the cause.' LETTRE, WRIT.

MEBLE   See MOEBLE

MEDE   Compensation (for work or services), wages, salary; a gift, a bribe, any reward that is unearned or in excess of merit; hence, also the reward of salvation: A.3.218–35 Þere arn to maner of medis. . . . þere is a mede mesurles þat maistris desiriþ; To mayntene mysdoeris mede þei taken. . . . þat labour-eris & louȝ folk taken of here maistris Is no maner of mede but a mesurable hire; A.3.236 In marchaundie is no mede. . . . It is a permutacioun apertly, a penyworþ for anoþer (B.3.257, C.3.312); C.3.332 Thus is mede and mercede as two maner relacions, Rect and indirect; A.3.196–214 (B.3.209ff., C.3.264ff.); B.7.59 (C.9.54); C.7.203. Conceived of primarily in a legal context, Mede upsets the balance of justice. The promise not to take mede was a common element in the oaths of public officials, e.g., Hall, 'without favour, mede, drede or corruppcion' (2:64); *Lib.Alb.*, 'ne pur richesse, ne pur doune, ne pur promesse, ne pur favour' (306); 'Et qe vous ne lerrez pur doun, ne pur favoure, ne pur promesce' (308), etc. The word itself is closely associated with the satire of legal abuses. See esp. John Yunck, *The Lineage of Lady Meed* (Notre Dame, 1963); see also Yunck's essay on satire in Alford 1988 (which includes an overview of mede as a secular theme in the poem), and in the same volume Robert Adams's essay on L's theology (which discusses the notion of mede as 'spiritual reward').

MENDES   Amends, compensation: A.4.90 Mede haþ mad my mendis; I may no more axen (B.4.103 amendes, C.4.97). AMENDES, BOTE.

*__MERCEDE__   Pay or wages (< Lat. *mercedem*); in the civil law, reward of labour in money or other things (Black): C.3.290 Ac ther is mede and mercede, and bothe men demen A desert for som doynge; C.3.304 [Payment for work done] is no mede but a mercede, a manere dewe dette; C.3.311 *Amen Amen*, Matheu seyth, *mercedem suam recipiunt* [Matt. 6:2] (A.3.233a, B.3.254a); C.3.332. L's distinction between 'mede and mercede' is not absolute; the latter can also refer to bribery (see *Fleta* 1.20, 'De balliuis mercedem capientibus').

MERCI   Pardon or clemency for a wrongdoer, prisoner, etc.: B.3.319 After þe dede þat is doon oon doom shal rewarde Mercy or no mercy as Truthe may acorde (C.3.471); B.17.309 Þe peel is so huge That þe kyng may do no mercy til boþe men acorde (C.19.284); A.1.144 (B.1.170, C.1.166); A.4.63, 81, 125 (B.4.77ff., C.4.73ff.); A.4.86 (B.4.99, C.4.95); A.5.243 (B.5.469, C.6.324); B.5.479 (C.7.122); C.9.278; A.11.257 (B.10.376); B.11.136 (C.12.69); B.18.389 (C.20.431). *Cyclopedic Law Dictionary*: 'When the whole punishment is remitted, it is called a "pardon"; when only a part of the punishment is remitted, it is frequently a "conditional pardon"; or, before sentence, it is called "clemency" or "mercy"' (712). Use of the word in the sense of 'an amercement or arbitrary fine' (see MERCIMENT) does not occur in *Piers*. GRACE, MITIGACIOUN, *PARCE*, PARDOUN; see also CRIEN MERCI.

*MERCIMENT   A penalty imposed 'at the mercy' of the court (as distinct from a statutory fine), an amercement: B.1.162 Right so is loue a ledere and þe lawe shapeþ; Vpon man for hise mysdedes þe mercyment he taxeþ (C.1.158); C.4.182 [Reason engages to] brynge alle men to bowe withouten bittere wounde, Withouten mercement or manslauht amende alle reumes. *Mirror* 150: 'Pecuniary punishments we call amercements, which are real, personal, or mixed, and sometimes are certain and sometimes uncertain.' The *Mirror* goes on to set amercements according to the offence and the status of the offender. Technically amercements differed from fines. Thus *Lib.Alb.* 212: 'Et le defendaunt en tiel cas ferra *fyn* pur countredire de soun fait; et en les autres cases serra *asmercie*.' See Harding 56: 'A "fine" as we understand the word is also derived from "final concord." The man found guilty of an offence was in the king's mercy, and could be "amerced" to any sum: but he would normally be allowed to make a reasonable agreement of "fine" with the king.'

*MERCIMONIE   Reward, salary, hire (< Lat. *mercimonium*, 'merchandise; reward'): B.14.127 God is of a wonder wille ... To ȝyue many men his mercymonye er he it haue deserued. *Writs* 201: 'You have heavily distrained the aforesaid A. to pay toll to you for his goods and merchandise [bonis et mercimoniis]'; also *Lib.Alb.* 150, 165, 171, 493.

MESURE   Conduct in conformity with the principles of reason and justice; moderation: C.15.272 And yf men lyuede as mesure wolde sholde neuere be defaute (B.14.71); B.20.26 For *Spiritus fortitudinis* forfeteþ wel ofte; He shal do moore þan mesure (C.22.26); A.1.33 (B.1.35, C.1.33); B.14.75; C.17.52. Cf. Brown XV 287/16–18: 'Mesure is best of all thynge. To litill or to gret excesse, Bothe arne wike and vicyous.' Measure is a fundamental concept of medieval jurisprudence. The central maxim, Stoic in origin, is stated by Aquinas as follows: 'Law is a certain rule and measure [mensura] in accordance with which one is induced to act or is restrained from acting' (I–II, qu. 90, art. 1). Cf. *Fleta* 2.1: 'A trespass is an act where neither manner nor measure [modum . . . et mensuram] is observed, for everyone in what he does should have regard to manner and measure' (cf. B.1.19 mesurable manere). For other literary examples, see J. Crosland, 'The Conception of "Mesure" in Some Medieval Poets,' *Modern Language Review* 21 (1926), 380–84.

MINISTRE   **I.** Any official charged with carrying out or enforcing the law or the commands of a superior, esp. the king: B.14.290 Selde sit pouerte þe soþe to declare . . . Ne to be Mair aboue men ne Mynystre vnder kynges; Selde is any poore yput to punysshen any peple (C.16.125); C.5.60 (Cristes mynistres). Cf. *Myrour* 135/22, 25: 'Sompnoures and bedilles þat beþ mynistres to þis lawe . . .; schereues, baylyues & mynistres of þe lawe of the londe þat doth men be endited.' *Eyre* 11: 'The sheriffs are the King's servants [les ministres le Roi]'; *Mirror* 62: 'Juge, ou corouner, viscounte, baillif, ou tel autre ministre le roi.' OFFICER.
    *II.** The supervisor of a religious order: C.5.91 Ac it semeth no sad parfitnesse in citees to begge, But he be obediencer to prior or to mynistre; cf. B.15.419.

*MITIGACIOUN   Reduction of a fine or penalty; grace or favour: B.5.469 But for þi muchel mercy mitigacion I biseche (A.5.243, C.6.324). Jowitt: 'Where a defendant or prisoner proves facts tending to reduce the damages or punishment to be awarded against him, he is said to show facts in mitigation of damages or of sentence, as the case may be.' Cf. *Mirror* 121: 'Judgments . . . are not to be pronounced altogether according to the rigour of the Old Testament . . . but with mitigation [mitigacion] and temperament of grace and truth, of mercy and right, such as God Himself used upon earth, and in the New Testament commanded to be used'; see also 48, 136, 183. GRACE, MERCI.

MOEBLES   Movable goods and possessions; personal estate (as distinguished from real estate): B.17.278 Vnkynde cristene men, for coueitise and enuye Sleeþ a man for his moebles (C.19.254); B.9.85; C.9.272; C.10.96; C.13.6; C.14.181; C.15.168; C.16.12. Cotgrave: 'Les meubles suivant la personne.' Fisher 165/5: 'A ȝenste my wyll & wetynge . . . delyuered my mevable good . . . where hem leste.' CATEL, MOEBLES AND UNMOEBLES.

MOEBLES AND UNMOEBLES   Movable and immovable possessions, i.e., things personal and real: B.3.269 God hymself hoteþ þee . . . Weend to Amalec with þyn oost & what þow fyndest þere sle it . . . Moebles and vnmoebles . . . Bren it; bere it noȝt awey be it neuer so riche (C.3.421); C.10.186; Cf. *D&P* 2:131/30: 'As þe lawe seith, euery vnleful vsynge & takynge of anoþir manys good meuable or nout meuable is þefte'; Barraclough 244: 'Dedit et tradidit se et omnia bona sua mobilia et immobilia.' Blackstone 2:16:

'The objects of dominion or property are *things*, as contradistinguished from *persons*: and things are by the law of England distributed into two kinds; things *real*, and things *personal*. Things real are such as are permanent, fixed, and immoveable, which cannot be carried out of their place; as lands and tenements: things personal are goods, money, and all other moveables; which may attend the owner's person wherever he thinks proper to go.' A similar distinction appears in the Old English legal phrase *ne libbende ne licgende*, 'neither livestock nor other property' (Bethurum 274).

MORTHEREN   To kill (a human being), esp. in secret and with malice afore-thought: B.4.55 He maynteneþ hise men to murþere myne hewen (A.4.42, C.4.58); C.12.241 And so is many man ymorthred for his moneye and his godes; B.17.283 (C.19.259). Statute 52 Hen. III c. 25: 'Murdrum de cetero non adjudicetur coram Justiciariis, ubi infortunium tantummodo adjudica-tum est, sed locum habeat murdrum in interfectis per feloniam, & non aliter.' *Fleta* 1.23: 'Homicide is the slaying of man by man with evil intent . . . and if this is done secretly it will be accounted murder [pro murdro]'; see also 1:30. *Jac. Well* 20/1: Cursed are 'alle þo þat wrongfully slen or murderyn ony man'; *Simonie* 430: 'So the fend hem prokede uch man to mourdren other wid wille.'

MORTHERER   A murderer; a quack doctor: B.6.275 (Sk.) For morthereres aren mony leches . . . Thei do men deye thorw here drynkes ar destine it wolde; cf. A.7.257 (C.8.296).

MOTEN   To go to law, litigate; to plead a case: A.8.46 (Sk.) Men of lawe hedden lest [pardon] for heo beoth loth To mote for mene men but 3if thei hadde money; B.4.135 I shal no ruþe haue While Mede haþ þe maistrie to mote in þis halle (A.4.118, C.4.132 motyng); A.3.149 She let lawe as hire list & louedaies makiþ; Þe mase for a mene man þei3 he mote euere (B.3.160, C.3.197); A.1.150 (B.1.176, C.1.172). Cf. *Jac. Well* 130/34: 'A fals pleyntyf . . . sekyth a cause to moote a3ens resoun, & feynyth a fals accyoun.' ALLEG-GEN AND PREVEN, PLEDEN, SPEKEN.

MOTHALLE   A courtroom or an assembly hall: B.4.152 I sei3 Mede in þe moot halle on men of lawe wynke (C.4.148); A.4.135; B.4.159; C.4.163. Cf. *Simonie* 292: 'And justises, shirreves, meires, baillifs . . . maken the mot-halle at hom in here chaumbre'; *Gamelyn* 175/717: 'Gamelyn com boldelich into the moot-halle'; *Lud. Cov.* 279/218: 'Al heyl sere pylat . . . My lord busshop cayphas comawndyd hym to þe And prayd the to be At þe mothalle by þe day dawe.' *LawMerch.* 1:115: Thomas Carrier, catchpoll of the said town . . . arrested him and detained him in the moothall of the said court [in domo placitorum ejusdem curie] on the bridge of the said town. WESTMINSTRE (HALL).

MOTING   Legal plea or defence; proceedings at law: A.8.60 His pardoun in purcatorie wel petit is, I trowe, Þat any mede of mene men for motyng resceyueþ (B.7.59, C.9.54); C.4.132 Y shal no reuthe haue Whiles Mede hath the maistrie þer motyng is at barres (cf. A.4.118, B.4.135 moten). TALE, SPECHE.

MOVABLES   See MOEBLES

MOVENAMATTER   To argue a point, to engage in formal disputation; in law, to make a plea, put forth a petition: B.11.232 Why I meue þis matere is moost for þe pouere; A.9.113 (B.8.123); B.10.117; B.11.108 (C.12.40); C.15.130; B.15.71 (C.16.231). L's usage suggests mainly the practice of scholastic debate. However, the phrase also figures commonly in descriptions of legal suits (to move a debate, a plea, etc.); technically a 'matter' is a proceeding commenced by a bill or petition rather than by writ (*Oxf.Comp.* 193). Cf. *Assembly* 328: ' "Have ye brought any bille?" "Ye, ye," quod I, ". . . Where is ther on . . . To whom I may shewe my matiers playne?" '; Fisher 171/4, 'certeins matiers and debates mouyd be twyn thame two'; 225/16, 'for eny mater meved or don betwene partie and partie'; Statute 28 Edw. III c. 13, 'si ple ou debate soit meu'; *Bor.Cust.* 1:285, 'play seyt mu'; *Court Baron* 133, 'placitum motum fuerit.' PLEDEN, SPEKEN.

*MULIER   Legitimate, born in wedlock; also one born in wedlock (OF *moiller* < Lat. *mulier*): C.10.209 Men þat ben bygeten Out of matrimonye, nat moyloure, mowne nat haue þe grace That lele legityme by þe lawe may claymen; B.2.119 Mede is muliere of Amendes engendred (A.2.83, C.2.120); B.2.132 Fals is . . . a Bastard . . . And Mede is muliere, a maiden of goode (A.2.96, C.2.145); B.16.219 (C.18.221); B.16.221 (C.18.235). *Nov.Narr.* 287: 'He had legitimate issue [issue mullere] alive'; *Moots* 62: 'If the husband alleges bastardy and the demandant then is certified legitimate [est certifie mulier]. . . .' Black: 'The term is used always in contradistinction to a bastard, mulier being always legitimate.' LAWEFUL, LEGITIME, LELE; see also BASTARD.

N

NECESSITAS NON HABET LEGEM   'Need has no law,' a maxim of natural law: C.13.43a Thogh the messager make his way amydde the fayre whete Wol no wys man be wroth ne his wed take – *Necessitas non habet legem*. See below (NEDE NE HATH NO LAWE); also Gray; and for its special association with friars, Szittya 270, 277 passim.

NEDE NE HATH NO LAWE   *NECESSITAS NON HABET LEGEM*, a legal maxim:
C.22.10 Couthest thow nat excuse the . . . That thow toke to lyue by, to clothes
and to sustinaunce, Was bi techyng and by tellyng of *Spiritus temperancie* And
þat thow nome no more then nede the tauhte? And nede ne hath no lawe ne
neuere shal falle in dette For thre thynges þat he taketh his lyf for to saue
(B.20.10). The doctrine invoked here is fully explained in *D&P* 2:141: 'For ʒif
ony man or woman for myschef of hungyr or of þrest or of cold . . . take so
onyþing in peryl of deth or in gret myschef, nede excusith hym from þefte and
fro synne . . . for in gret nede alle þing is comoun. . . . And also for nede hat no
lawe. Example ha we in þe gospel, wher we fyndyn þat þe discyplis of Crist for
hungyr tokyn herys in þe feld & gnoddyn is & etyn is for hungyr [Matt. 12:1–8]
. . . . For it is a general reule in þe lawe þat nede hat no lawe.'

NE SITIS PERSONARUM ACCEPTORES   'Do not be respecters of persons,' i.e.,
do not show partiality or favouritism (a legal maxim): B.15.88 Ye [friars]
forsakeþ no mannes almesse . . . And louten to þise lordes þat mowen lene
yow nobles Ayein youre rule and Religion; I take record at Iesus That seide to
hise disciples, '*Ne sitis personarum acceptores*' (C.16.240a). Cf. Wright 225:
'Nam jubet lex naturae, Quod iudex in judicio Nec prece nec pretio acceptor
sit personae.' This *lex naturae* echoes a number of biblical texts, e.g., Prov.
24:23, James 2:1, Acts 10:34, but derives ultimately from Deut. 1:17 on the
institution of judges: 'Nulla erit distantia personarum; ita parvum audietis ut
magnum: nec accipietis cuiusquam personam, quia Dei iudicium est.' It became a central tenet of English judicial practice. The king swore in his coronation oath, 'that he would not be a *personarum acceptor*, that he would make
fair judgment between man and man' (Donaldson 117); the king's justices
swore in their oath of office to judge 'saunz resgard . . . de persone' (Hall
1:134); and it was a general rule of law that 'nule accepcion ne soit en persones'
(*Mirror* 195). For application of the words to friars in particular, see Szittya
98.

NOLITE MITTERE FALSEM IN MESSEM ALIENAM   'Do not put your sickle to
another man's corn'; a maxim of canon law prohibiting the violation of another's jurisdiction (e.g., in hearing confession or serving as judge in a legal
suit): B.15.530a [Some] crepe in amonges curatours, confessen ageyn þe
lawe: *Nolite mittere falsem in messem alienam* (C.17.280a). The maxim was
derived ultimately from Gregory's comment on Deut. 23:25, 'Falcem judicii
mittere non potes in eam segetem, quae alteri videtur esse commissa [Thou
mayest not put the sickle of judgement to the corn that is entrusted to
another].' See also Gregory's letter to Augustine, in Bede's *Historia Ecclesi-
astica* 1:27 qu. 7. For additional examples see Gray, and *Engl. Canons* 400,
413, etc.

NON DIMITTITUR PECCATUM DONEC RESTITUATUR ABLATUM   'The sin is not
forgiven until the thing taken has been restored,' a maxim of canon law:
B.5.273a Til þow make restitucion . . . I may þee noʒt assoille: *Non dimittitur
peccatum donec restituatur ablatum*; C.6.257a; B.17.310a (C.19.285a); cf.

B.20.321 (C.22.321). Cf. *Jac. Well* 66/17–18: 'Þe preest seyde: "and but þou restore aȝen as ferforth as þi good may reche, þou mayst noȝt be sauyd." ' The maxim, a central text in the penitential doctrine of restitution, derives ultimately from Augustine; see Lyndwood 333, St. Germ. 5; also Bennett 170, Alford 1975. REDDE QUOD DEBES.

NON LICET VOBIS LEGEM VOLUNTATI, SET VOLUNTATEM CONIUNGERE LEGI 'It is not lawful for you to make the law conform to your will, but (rather for you to conform) your will to the law': C.9.212a Thise ermytes þat edifien thus by the heye weye Whilen were werkmen, webbes and taylours ... [who] lefte ... here labour ... And clothed hem in copes ... Aȝen þe lawe of Leuey, yf Latyn be trewe: *Non licet uobis legem voluntati, set voluntatem coniungere legi*. Although the exact wording has not been found elsewhere, the substance of this maxim is common: e.g., 'Intentio inservire debet legibus, non leges intentioni' (Black 727); 'Et pro lege suum velle licere iubent' (Gower, *Vox* 1:832); other examples cited in Alford 1975.

NON MORABITUR OPUS MERSENARII 'The wages of him that hath been hired by thee shall not abide with thee until the morning' (Levit. 19:13), adopted into canon law as the rule enjoining prompt payment of wages: C.3.307a And but hit [mercede] prestly be ypayed þe payer is to blame, As by the book þat byt nobody with-holde The huyre of his hewe ouer eue til amorwe: *Non morabitur opus mersenarii*; C.7.195–96 He [Truth] is þe presteste payere þat eny pore man knoweth; He with-halt non hewe his huyre ouer euen (B.5.551–52). Cf. *Jac. Well* 129/15–17: 'Þou þat wyth-holdyst þi seruauntys hyre, þou art a raueynour be goddys lawe, þat wyth-holdyst þise dettys.' See De Roover 26; Walter Ullmann, *The Medieval Idea of Law* (1946), 184.

NOTARIE   A scribe authorized to draw up and authenticate documents and legal instruments, act as a witness, take depositions, etc. (*MED*): A.2.78 In þe date of þe deuil þe dede is asselid Be siȝte of sire symonye & signes of notories; B.15.32 And whan I chalange or chalange noȝt, chepe or refuse, Thanne am I Conscience ycalled, goddes clerk and his Notarie (C.16.191); B.20.272 I wolde witterly þat ye [friars] were in þe Registre And youre noumbre vnder Notaries signe and neiþer mo ne lasse (C.22.272); A.2.91 (B.2.127, C.2.139); B.2.143 (C.2.156); A.2.110 (B.2.146, C.2.159); A.2.131 (B.2.167); C.2.185. Cf. *Myrour* 136/22: 'A false notarie he is þat makiþ fals instrumentis, protegollis or libelles by whiche eny right is put down & falshede mayntened'; *Jac. Well* 131/20; *D&P* 2:203/76. References: C. R. Cheney, *Notaries Public in England in the Thirteenth and Fourteenth Centuries* (1972); Geoffrey Barraclough, *Public Notaries and the Papal Curia* (1934).

NOUMPERE   An arbiter, umpire, or mediator: A.5.179 Þei couþe not be here consience acorden togidere Til robyn þe ropere was red to arisen, And nempnide hym for a noumpere þat no debate nere (B.5.330, C.6.388). Cf. Usk 11/96: 'Maked I not a loveday bytwene god and mankynde, and chees a mayde to nompere, to putte the quarel at ende?' ARBITOUR.

O

OBEDIENCE Compliance with a rule or law; (of a religious) 'under obedience,' under the authority of a superior: C.9.222 For holy churche hoteth ... religious of religioun a reule to holde And vnder obedience be by dayes and by nyhtes; B.12.37 If þow be Religious ... hold þee vnder obedience; C.9.220; C.9.235; C.9.241; B.13.285. *Moots*: 'Gifts by a monk professed ... and by all others under profession and obedience ... are clearly void' (171); 'The pledges shall be sufficient. ... An infant within age, a married woman or a monk professed and under obedience [south obediens], is not sufficient.'

OBEDIENCER One who holds a subordinate office in a monastery: C.5.91 Ac it semeth no sad parfitnesse in citees to begge, But he be obediencer to prior or to mynistre.

OCCUPIEN To hold (a manor, land, estate); *reflex*. to dwell: B.16.196 God ... Sente forþ his sone ... To ocupie hym here til issue were spronge, That is children of charite, and holi chirche þe moder (C.18.206). Cf. Chaucer, *Complaint unto Pity* 90: 'Ye be than fro youre heritage ythrowe By Cruelte, that occupieth youre place'; *D&P* 1:320: '[Monks] occupyyn greter lordchepys þan don many dukys, arlys & baronys.' The word appears in legal documents as the technical term for 'be in possession of' as in the phrase 'hold and occupy': *K.Counc*. 87: 'He has held and occupied [tenuz et occupiez] all the said lands and tenements ... for seven years'; Fisher: 'Also longe as he shall haue And occupie þe said kepyng or ferme' (106/6); 'Suche Priouries and possessions...whiche any persone holdith hath or occupieth for terme of lif by the lawe of England' (151/10). Though L's *ocupie* could be taken in the ordinary sense of 'dwell,' its combination with 'issue' echoes the recurring metaphor of spiritual heritage.

OFFICE A position or place to which certain duties are attached, esp. one of a more or less public character (*OED*): B.3.100 Fir shall falle & forbrenne ... The hous and þe hom of hem þat desireþ Yiftes or yeresyeues bycause of hire Offices; A.7.184 Pieris ... putte hem in office, And ȝaf hem mete & monie as þei miȝte asserue. *Simonie* 45: 'No man may wel serue tweie lordes to queme. Summe beth in ofice wid the king, and gaderen tresor to hepe, And the fraunchise of holi churche hii laten ligge slepe ful stille.' Blackstone 2:36: 'Offices, which are a right to exercise a public or private employment, and the fees and emoluments thereunto belonging, are also incorporeal hereditaments: whether public, as those of magistrates; or private, as of bailiffs, receivers, and the like. For a man may have an estate in them.' DIGNITE.

OFFICER A high government official; *specif*. an officer of the court, a judge: C.4.195 The kyng comaundede Consience tho to congeye alle his offeceres And receyue tho that Resoun louede; cf. B.20.258 (C.22.258). Brown XIV 133/73: 'Ȝif þou beo mad an Offycer, And art a Mon of muche miht, What

105

cause þou demest, loke hit be cler, And reue no mon from him his riht'; *D&P* 2:157: 'And offycerys of kyngis . . . þat takyn ʒiftys of men . . . þat þey schuldyn meynteþin hem and ʒeuyn hem fauour in her causis . . . mon don elmesse of good so gotyn.' CLERK, MINISTRE.

OFFICIAL   An officer subordinate to an archbishop or bishop, esp. a bishop's chancellor, who presided over his consistory court; a canon-law judge: B.2.174 Denes and Southdenes, drawe you togideres; Erchedekenes and Officials and alle youre Registrers; B.20.136 And to þe Arches in haste he [Coveitise] yede anoon after And tornede Cyuyle into Symonye, and siþþe he took þe Official (C.22.137). One of the earliest references to officials is in Hubert Walter's legatine canons at York (*Engl. Canons* 1:75). Cf. *The Symonie* 332/192: 'And officials and denes that chapitles sholden holde . . . For have he silver, of sinne taketh he nevere ʒeme'; *Myrour* 135/14: 'Officiales & denes þat sitteþ & holdeþ her chapitles & concistories more forto wynne siluer þan forto destroye synne.' *K. Counc.* 7: 'The aforesaid bishop avowed and proved by his proctors that they excommunicated the aforesaid William . . . before the Official of the Court of Canterbury [i.e., the Arches].' See Woodcock 37–38.

ORDEINEN   To decree (something), make a law; to command: C.5.55 For by þe lawe of *Levyticy* þat our lord ordeynede, Clerkes ycrouned . . . Sholde nother swynke ne swete ne swerien at enquestes; B.5.167 (Sk.) Seynt Gregorie . . . had a gode forwit, That no priouresse were prest for that he ordeigned; B.Prol.119; C.3.240; C.10.218; C.17.16; cf. B.8.98 (Sk.). Cf. *D&P* 1:148/44: 'They haue ordeyned a comoun lawe.' *Lib. Alb.* 506: 'Item, come en lestatut fait a Westmestre . . . estoit ordeigne et acorde, qe. . . .'; *K. Counc.* 93: 'At Westminster . . . it had been ordained [ordinatum fuit] and made statute that . . .'; Fisher 80/4: 'We wol and charge yow þat . . . ye ordeyne þat deliuerance bee maad . . . of þe said temporalitees.' On Gregory's ordinance (B.5.167) see INFAMIS.

OTH   An oath to the truth of one's statements in a legal proceeding: C.2.150 Lawe may declare Where matrymonye may be of Mede and of Falshede. And thow iustices enioynen hem thorw iuroures othes ȝut beth ywar of þe weddynge; B.2.70 Lo! here a chartre That Gile wiþ hise grete oþes gaf hem togidere. *Writs* 127: 'A. complains that the jurors . . . have made a false oath [falsum sacramentum].' The false oaths of jurors and witnesses (including marriage cases) are a pervasive theme in the legal records of the time; see ATTEINT, DIVORCE, FALS WITNESSE.

OUTLAWE   A fugitive from justice; a miscreant or robber; *fig.* the devil: B.17.105 An Outlawe is in þe wode and vnder bank lotieþ. On the process of outlawry, see P&M 2:580–81, and *Fleta* 1.28; on the outlaws of the 'Greenwood' see Maurice Keen, *The Outlaws of Medieval England* (Toronto: Univ. of Toronto Press, 1961; rpt. 1977).

106

OUT OF TIME   During a period of time forbidden by ecclesiastical law: C.10.288 And ȝe þat han wyues, ben war and worcheth nat out of tyme (B.9.187 in tyme). Cf. the Old English legal phrase *inne tid and ut of tide* (Bethurum 274). UNTIME.

OUTRIDERE   An agent of a monastery who rides out to administer its affairs: C.4.116 'Rede me nat,' quod Resoun, 'no reuthe to haue Til . . . religious outryderes be reclused in here cloistres And be as Benet hem bad.' Cf. *CT.Prol.* 166: 'A Monk ther was . . . An outridere, that lovede venerie.' See John Reeves, *History of English Law*. 2nd edn, 4 vols. (Dublin, 1787; rpt. New York: Kelly, 1969), 2:404.

OVERLEDEN   To oppress or burden (someone) with legal suits and actions: B.3.314 (Sk.) Shal neither kynge ne knyȝte constable ne meire Ouer-lede the comune ne to the courte sompne (C.3.468 overcarken). *D&P* 2:9/59: 'Lordys . . . begynnyn warris, pleyys & debat . . . to ouyr-ledyn alle men til at þe laste þei ben distryyd hemself.'

OVERSKIPPEN   To skip over (material in a text); omit: B.11.305 A chartre is chalangeable . . . If fals latyn be in þat lettre . . . Or peynted parentrelynarie, parcelles ouerskipped (C.13.118). Writs may be void if they contain any 'omission ou transposicion de mot, sillable ou de clause' (*Mirror* 94); all writs issued from the chancery were to be examined by the clerks for accuracy 'in ratione, littera, diccione et sillaba' (*Fleta* 2.13). L compares overskipping in legal documents to the careless recitation of divine service, which, canon law stressed, should be said whole ('plene et integre'); see Lyndwood lib. III, tit. 23 ('*Plene.* sc. Absque omissione. *Integre.* i.e. Sine fractione verborum'). See also FALS LATIN, PARENTRELINARIE.

*OVERSKIPPER   A cleric who garbles his recitation by skipping over words: B.11.310 So is it a goky . . . þat in his gospel failleþ, Or in masse or in matyns makeþ any defaute . . . And also in þe Sauter seiþ Dauid to ouerskipperis (C.13.122). Continues the legal comparison from above, OVERSKIPPEN.

P

PAIEN   'To pay for,' to ransom (a prisoner); make amends or restitution: B.3.137 Mede . . . leteþ passe prisoners and paieþ for hem ofte, And gyueþ þe Gailers gold and grotes togidres (A.3.126, C.3.173); C.7.277 Largesse . . . payeth for prisones in puttes and in peynes; B.17.240 So wol þe fader forȝyue folk of mylde hertes . . . In as muche as þei mowen amenden and paien (C.19.201); B.17.320 (C.19.295); B.19.186 (C.21.186). RAUNSOUNEN.

*PANEL   A jury-list (orig. written on a panel), hence also the jury itself:
B.3.317 Shal neiþer kyng ne knyght, Constable ne Meire Ouercarke þe commune ne to þe Court sompne, Ne putte hem in panel to doon hem pliȝte hir
truþe (C.3.469). *Lib.Alb.* glossary 396: 'Panellum. A panel; *i.e.* a paper [or
perhaps originally, a board], on which the names of jurors were written.'
Bor.Cust. 1:41: 'He who is accused of the death . . . will make his panel at his
peril [fera son panel a son peril], and deliver it to the hand of the steward, and
as they of the panel are called [et com ils du panel soient demandes], each by
his name . . .'; *LawMerch.* 1:129: 'And the said John Wilkinson serjeant etc.
now and here has returned his writ of 'venire facias' together with the panel of
the names of the jurors etc. [cum panello de nominibus juratorum etc.].' A
writ of *Venire Facias* (to empanel a jury) is printed in Hall 2:177, together with
a panel of names (215, 218). Numerous complaints illuminate the meaning of
B.3.317. 'According to Britton, sheriffs and bailiffs were prone to summon
more people upon juries and inquests than were needed, with the intent to
oppress some of them and take bribes from others' (*K.Counc.* 10 n.); 'Concerning the sheriffs, who can relate with sufficient fulness how hard they are to
the poor? He who has nothing to give is dragged hither and thither, and is
placed in the assizes, and is obliged to take his oath, without daring to murmur' (Wright, 'Song on the Venality of the Judges,' trans. 228). The statute
De ponendis in assisis (21 Edw. I) was intended to correct such abuses, declaring, among other things, that no one should be empanelled unless he had
'lands and tenements to the yearly value of forty shillings' (cf. *Writs* 254).
Letters of exemption were common (example in Hall 1:71 [no. 68]). See also
ENQUESTE, JUROUR, SECTE, SISE.

PAPER   Written documents collectively (*OED*); *specif.* a written promise to
pay a debt, an 'IOU': C.13.37 The marchaunt mote nede be ylet lenger then
thc messager, For þe parcel of his paper and oþer pryue dettes Wol lette hym
. . . the lenghe of a myle. Cf. *CT.Cook* 4404: 'This joly prentys . . ., ny out of his
prentishood . . . his papir soghte. . . . Therefore his maister yaf hym acquitance, And bad hym go.' Statute 38 Edw. III c. 5 (1363): 'Whereas many
people are grieved and attached by their bodies in the city of London at the suit
of men in the same city, surmising to them that they are debtors and that will
they prove by their papers [par lour papirs], whereas they have no deed or
tally; it is assented that every man be received to his law by people sufficient of
his condition against such papers [countre tieles papirs], and let the creditor
take surety by another way. . . .'

PARCE   'Til *parce* it hote,' i.e., until the word *spare thou* commands an end:
B.18.392 They shul be clensed clerliche and keuered of hir synnes In my
prisone Purgatorie til *parce* it hote; cf. B.10.376 I shal punysshe in purgatorie
or in þe put of helle Ech man for his mysdede but mercy it make. The word is an
allusion to the *Dirige* or office of the dead for matins (see Alford, *Modern
Philology* 69 [1972], 323–25); however, the larger phrase repeats a common
formula in sentencings. E.g., *Court Baron*: 'The hayward is ordered to retain
his body *until he shall have made satisfaction* (120); 'He shall be put in the
stocks . . . *until he hath the grace of his lord*' (103).

*PARCEL   I. An estreat, abstract, or itemized list of commercial transactions, expenditures, payments, etc.; an account roll or 'parcel of account': C.13.37 The marchaunt mote nede be ylet lenger then the messager, For þe parcel of his paper and oþer pryue dettes Wol lette hym . . . the lenghe of a myle. Cf. *Cov.Leet* 501: 'Memorandum that these ben the parcels folowyng that þe seid Maire hath resceived and paide duryng the tyme of his office.' Statute 5 Ric. II c. 12: 'Item it is ordained and established that two clerks shall be assigned to make parcels of accounts [parcelles daccomptes] in the Exchequer to those who will demand the same.' Every account passed through several stages, of which the third was the making of abstracts called 'estreats' or 'parcels,' which could be communicated or preserved for official information (Hall 2:92, 108; Hall, *Studies* 309). See also the citation under DIS-CHARGEN.

   II. A part or section of a legal document: B.11.305 A chartre is chalangeable bifore a chief Iustice; If fals latyn be in þat lettre . . . Or peynted parentre-lynarie, parcelles ouerskipped (C.13.118).

   III. A share or allotted portion, as of an estate, bequest, etc.: B.20.292 And so it fareþ with muche folk þat to freres shryueþ, As sisours and executours; þei shul ȝyue þe freres A parcel to preye for hem and pleye wiþ þe remenaunt (C.22.291); A.11.50 (B.10.64, C.11.48). Cf. *Jac.Well* 199/20: 'Þou hast here a parcell of þi faderys good, wyttyng þat þi fadyr get þat good wyth gouyl . . .; þou art bounde to restore þat parcell of good, ȝif þou wylt be sauyd.'

PARDOUN   I. Remission of part or all of the temporal penalty in purgatory for sins already forgiven, INDULGENCE; also the document granting an indulgence (see *A POENA ET A CULPA*): B.7.58 Whan þei drawen on to þe deþ and Indulgences wolde haue, His pardon is wel petit at his partyng hennes That any Mede of mene men for motyng takeþ (A.8.59, C.9.53); B.13.246 And I hadde . . . Neiþer prouendre ne personage yet of þe popes ȝifte, Saue a pardon wiþ a peis of leed and two polles amyddes; A.8.3 (B.7.3, C.9.3); A.8.8 (B.7.8, C.9.8); C.9.60; A.8.86 (B.7.104, C.9.186); A.8.89, 91, 97 (B.7.107 etc., C.9.282 etc.); A.8.151 (B.7.174, C.9.320); B.11.57 (C.12.9); B.13.252; B.17.256 (C.19.217); B.19.183, 187, 188 (C.21.183, etc.); B.19.390 (C.21.390); B.20.308.

   II. Forgiveness of a crime or sin: B.15.183 [Charity] is woned to wenden on pilgrymages Ther poore men and prisons liggeþ, hir pardon to haue; A.11.78 (B.10.125).

PAREN   To clip (coins): B.5.240 I lerned among lumbardes . . . To weye pens wiþ a peis and pare þe heuyeste (C.6.242). Cf. *Jac.Well* 19/9: 'And we denounce acursed alle makerys of fals monye, & clypperys, & wasscherys.' See the writ *De bono et malo* for clipping of money ('pro retonsura monete nostre') in *Writs* 194. *Fleta* contains a chapter on money-clippers (1:20).

*PARENTRELINARIE   Between the lines: B.11.305 A chartre is chalangeable bifore a chief Iustice; If fals latyn be in þat lettre þe lawe it impugneþ, Or peynted parentrelynarie, parcelles ouerskipped (C.13.118). *Mirror* 94 notes that a judge's commission may be challenged 'because there is in it a rasure or an interlineation [*intreligneire*] or a diversity of handwriting or of phraseology, or because there is false Latin [faus latin].' Such challenges were not always effective. Thus *Yrbk.Edw.II* 120: 'Miggele challenged the deed because of an interlineation [Migg' chalengea le fet pur entrelinarie]; and this was not allowed, because it did not appear to be suspect.' The rule was enforced less rigorously in the common law courts than in the private courts, one reason for the displacement of the latter; as Denholm-Young observes, 'Few would willingly sue where a misplaced syllable might ruin their case, if they could afford to go elsewhere' (98). For a case involving the alteration of a document by rasure, see *K.Counc.* 97–101; the document itself, showing the rasure, survives. OVERSKIPPER.

PARLEMENT   The king's council; parliament sitting as a court of law: B.4.47 Thanne com pees into þe parlement and putte vp a bille (A.4.34, C.4.45); C.4.185 Resoun . . . [to] be my cheef chaunceller in cheker and in parlement. Precisely who constitutes these *parlements* is unclear. Pearsall glosses the first as 'the king and his council sitting as a court and listening particularly to complaints against the administration of law' (90 n.). Baldwin argues for much the same interpretation, describing L's *parlement* in both cases as a 'prerogative court' composed of the king [or chancellor] and his council, a smaller group than parliament but including many of the same lords (40–42); cf. Holdsworth 1:352. Fisher prints a large number of bills addressed to parliament beginning, for ex., 'To the moost noble & Worthiest Lordes moost ryghtful & wysest conseille to owre lige Lorde the king,' some of which are very similar to the bill 'put up' by Peace (e.g., no. 164). See the selections in *K.Counc.*; discussion in Holdsworth 1:352–56, Cam 106–31, Plucknett 151–55, and J. F. Baldwin, *The King's Council*. COUNSEIL, KING AND HIS COUNSEIL.

PARSON   See *RECTOR*

PARTIE   A person or group of persons involved in a lawsuit, dispute, betrothal, agreement, etc.: B.17.308 For þer þat partie pursueþ þe peel is so huge That þe kyng may do no mercy (C.19.283); C.1.95 Knyghtes sholde . . . halden with hem and here þat han trewe accion And for no lordene loue leue þe trewe partie; C.3.379; C.3.389; B.14.269 (C.16.109 persones); C.19.285. Cf. *D&P* 1:252: 'Of every controuersye . . . þat is in debat to confermyn þe trewe partye, þe laste ende is an oth.' Fisher 161/54: 'Al resoun wole: that no domesman stonde togidre Iuge & partye.'

PATEAT   'Let it be manifest,' the opening words of a deed: B.14.190a We sholde take þe Acquitaunce as quyk and to þe queed shewen it: *Pateat &c: Per passionem domini.*

PATENTE **I.** A letter patent; also a written document issued by the Crown (e.g., a grant, charter, statute), not sealed up but exposed to open view and usually addressed to all subjects of the realm: B.17.11 'Lat se þi lettres' quod I, 'we myghte þe lawe knowe.' He plukkede forþ a patente, a pece of an hard roche Wheron was writen two wordes on þis wise yglosed. *Dilige deum & proximum tuum* (C.19.12); B.14.192; B.18.186 (C.20.191). Cf. the close of Magna Carta: 'In cujus rei testimonium has litteras nostras fieri fecimus patentes.' Numerous samples of letters patent are printed in Hall 1:53–74. LETTRE, MAUNDEMENT.

II. A papal indulgence: B.7.200 I sette youre patentes and youre pardon at one pies hele.

PATRIMOINE An ecclesiastical living, benefice, endowment; *gen.* an inheritance: B.20.234 Þei [friars] are pouere, parauenture, for patrymoyne hem failleþ, They wol flatere to fare wel folk þat ben riche (C.22.234); B.15.246. Cf. *CT.Pars.* 789: '[Patrons] putten in theves that stelen the soules of Jhesu Crist and destroyen his patrimoyne.' BENEFICE, FINDING, TITLE.

PATROUN One who holds the right of presentation to an ecclesiastical benefice: C.5.78 Popes and patrones pore gentel blood refused And taken Symondes sones seyntwarie to kepe; B.12.227 (Nature as 'þe pies patron'). Cf. *Jac.Well* 15/22: Cursed are 'alle þo þat malycyously puttyn forth, or procuryn, ony stryif, debate, or ple, in patronage of ony cherch in tyme of voydaunce, wherfore þe verry patroun is lettyd þat tyme of his ryȝt.' Purvis 15: 'The "patron" of a benefice in his own right "advocat alium" to the Church being vacant and presents him to it in the place of the last holder on death, resignation or other cause of termination of incumbency. It is generally assumed that this right was acquired originally by founding, building or endowing of the church. There is then a reversionary right of presentation to an ecclesiastical benefice in a man and his heirs for ever.' Bribery could play a role in influencing a patron's choice, as L notes, so that like any other hereditable right the potentially lucrative right to present was often in dispute; e.g., *Moots* 114; *Writs* 128. On the system generally, see Addleshaw 17–23.

***PAULINES** Having to do with the consistory court held at St. Paul's (Cathedral) in London: B.2.178 Paulynes pryuees for pleintes in Consistorie Shul seruen myself þat Cyuyle is nempned; C.2.110 In wittenesse of þis thyng Wrong was the furste And Peres þe pardoner of Paulines queste (A.2.73 'poulynes doctor'; B.2.109 'of Paulynes doctrine'). Skeat observed, '*Of paulynes queste* apparently means, belonging to the inquest or jury of Paulines' (2:35) but took the word *paulynes* to refer to an order of friars, sometimes called 'Crutched Friars' (so also *OED* and *MED*). However, as subsequent editors have pointed out, the association of friars and pardoners is unlikely (Bennett 127, Pearsall 60). Though conceding that friars 'were not usually pardoners,' Schmidt says, 'but this one could have been, and the word *doctrine* strongly implies an order or profession – i.e. the Paulines' (309). But *doctrine* need signify nothing more than general instruction or knowledge in

111

any field, including the law. Far more crucial is the fact that every occurrence of the word *paulines* is in a legal context, pointing toward the ecclesiastical court of St. Paul's – or simply *Poules* as it was called in the vernacular until the sixteenth century (*Lib.Alb.* glossary 349, Fisher 181/14). The court had jurisdiction not only over spiritual matters (e.g., *Brut* 1447: 'Roger Norman . . . was . . . brought before the Bisshop of London and tofore the clergie in the Chapitre hous of Seint Paules, and there . . . conuicte in heresye') but also over divorces and the administration of wills, both of which invited false suitors, witnesses, etc. Cf. *Lib.Alb.*: 'Item, that if any one shall vouch two witnesses to bar a man of his law, or of Inquest, the same shall not be received unless they be folks of good report [de bon fame], and not common suitors or approvers before the Ordinaries at Saint Paul's or elsewhere [et ne pas comune seutiers ne proeves devaunt lez Ordinaries au Seint Poule ne aillours]' (1:475, trans. 3:192; also printed in *Bor.Cust.* 1:169). It is exactly such 'common suitors and approvers' that would have served Civil 'for pleintes in Consistorie' and that stood 'in wittenesse' of the marriage of Mede and Fals. See also PRIVE.

PAVELOUN *The fur-lined cloak worn by a serjeant-at-law: C.3.448 Shal no seriaunt . . . werie a selk houe Ne no pelure in his paueloun for pledyng at þe barre. Cf. *MED* '?A garment worn by lawyers; ?a coif.' *Coif* is unlikely; the usual headgear of a serjeant was a silk, not fur, 'houe.' The more general meaning of the word is 'tent or covering' (ModE pavilion), narrowed here to a specific article of clothing, a cape or cloak (cf. B.3.296 cloke, emended by K-D to *panelon*). L provides the only example in this sense. Fortescue describes the attire of a serjeant-at-law as follows: 'He was dressed in a long robe, like a priest's, with a furred cape [cum capicio penulato] about his shoulders, and above that with a hood with two tappets, as doctors of law customarily wear in certain universities, with a coif above described' (129).

PEEL See APPELE

PEINE Corporal or pecuniary punishment for a crime, sin, misdeed; the punishment of purgatory or hell (OF *peine* < Lat. *poena*): C.7.277 For she [Largesse] payeth for prisones in puttes and in peynes; B.14.54 Shul neuere gyues þee greue . . . Prison ne peyne, for *pacientes vincunt* (C.15.254); A.1.116 (B.1.127, C.1.128); B.2.104; C.4.101; A.5.29 (B.5.29, C.5.131); C.7.118; C.7.256; C.11.262; B.11.142, 153, 163; B.13.13 (C.15.16); B.18.144 (C.20.147); B.18.193 (C.20.198); B.18.200 (C.20.205). Cf. Fisher 163/146: 'They ben worthy to ben punysshed . . . and that vp on a suffisant peyne payinge to the king'; *Cov.Leet* 192: 'They ordeyn that Will. Powet, Capper, and his paromour be Caried and lad thorowe þe town in a Carre . . . and that alle other that be proved in the same syne, ffrom thys tyme fforward shall haue the same peyne.' Typical penalties meted out by ecclesiastical courts are described by Woodcock 97–102. PENAUNCE.

PELOUR One who accuses or appeals another (see APPELEN): B.18.40 Tho putte hym forþ a pelour bifore Pilat and seide, 'This Iesus of oure Iewes temple Iaped and despised, To fordoon it on o day' (C.20.39). The word translates the *falsi testes* (false witnesses) of Matt. 26:60.

PENA PECUNIARIA NON SUFFICIT PRO SPIRITUALIBUS DELICTIS 'Pecuniary penance does not suffice for spiritual faults,' a maxim of canon law: B.11.58a (C.12.10a). Cf. *Constitutio Domini Othoboni*, tit. 10 (Lyndwood 99): 'Et quia non sufficit pecuniaria poena, ubi est Spirituale delictum. . . .'

PENAUNCE Penalty, punishment; judicial sentence; 'to put in penance,' to subject to torture, hard punishment, or prison: A.9.95 Panne shulde þe kyng come & casten hem in presoun, And putten hem þere in penaunce wiþoute pite or grace; B.10.325 Ac þer shal come a kyng . . . And puten hem to hir penaunce (C.5.171); A.11.26 Pe penaunce þat pilatus wrouȝte To iesu þe gentil (B.10.34); C.3.101; A.8.88 (B.7.106, C.9.185); A.11.286 (B.10.427, C.11.262); B.13.88 (C.15.96). Cf. *K. Counc.* 56: 'The said sheriff took Robert Walman . . . and put him in durance [lui mist en penaunce] . . . whereby he was very near death for the durance [penaunces] that he suffered'; *Mirror* 185: 'The article [in the statute of Westminster I] about putting to their penance [mettre . . . a penaunce] men accused of felony . . . is so much disused that they are killed without regard to their condition.' L usually keeps distinct the notions of judicial penance and canonical penance, as prescribed by a priest (e.g., see B text 8.105, 10.125, 13.411, 14.10, 17.255, 19.376, 20.283, 20.306, etc.).

***PENSIOUN** A regular payment or stipend, often supported by an endowment, benefice, or other source of income: A.8.47 Of princes & prelatis here [lawyers'] pencioun shulde arise, And of no pore peple no penyworþ to take. The word is used by L to translate *merces* in the preceding quotation (*A regibus & principibus* [*erit merces eorum*], cf. B.7.44a), and may signify an allotment from the fines received by courts secular and ecclesiastical. Cf. *Fleta* 2.60: '. . . where a prelate or the patron of a church sues for a pension [pensionem] from the rector.' For documents relating to pensions, see Barraclough 217–220 ('Tractatus de pensionibus'). FINDING.

PENTAUNCER A priest appointed by a pope or bishop to administer the sacrament of penance, esp. in cases reserved to the bishop or pope; a penitentiary (*MED*): B.20.319 I woot no bettre leche Than person or parisshe preest, penitauncer or bisshop, Saue Piers þe Plowman (C.22.319); C.6.256 For þe pope with alle his pentauncers power hem fayleth To assoyle the of this synne *sine restitucione*. Cf. *D&P* 2:145: 'DIUES. Ȝif a þing be lost & he þat fyndyth it & kepith it stylle, is it þefte? PAUPER. He þat fyndith it is boundyn to retitucion . . . & ȝif no man ne woman chalange it he þat hat foundyn it may be autorite of his pentancer or of hys confessour kepyn it stille ȝif he be pore & nedy.' For a list of the greater sins reserved for confession before the pope or his penitentiary, see *Engl. Canons* 2:434–36.

***PERMUTACIOUN**   The exchange of one thing for another of equal value: B.3.258 In marchaundise is no Mede. . . . It is a permutacion apertly, a peny-worþ for anoþer (A.3.237, C.3.313). Bloomfield's comment cannot be supported: 'This idea of equal exchange as the basis in justice for trade is older than Duns Scotus, but I believe it was he who first actually used the term "permutacio" to describe it' (p. 166). The word has a long and complex history. Originally, in Roman law (e.g., *Digest* 19.4.1), it applied to barter only, but later came to include exchanges involving money, 'a penyworþ for anoþer' (see Buckland 523; J. W. Baldwin 19; De Roover 9, 19, 35, passim). Like Langland, Thomas Wilson later uses the term to contrast equal and unequal (or usurious) exchanges (292, 316). BARGAIN, ESCHAUNGE, THIS FOR THAT.

***PERMUTEN**   To exchange churches or benefices: C.2.185 Syuyle and Symo-nye . . . Wol ryde vppon *rectores* . . . And notaries on persones þat permuten ofte. The 'permuting' of benefices is classified in penitential treatises as a branch of simony, because it often involved a cash adjustment: *Myrour* 138/13–15: 'The þridde manere [of simony] is in chaungynge of benefice, as when two avaunced men of Holy Chirche lusteþ chaunge togidre here benefices & eny of hem ȝeue other eny worldly þyng for þe chaunge'; *Jacob's Well* 127/6: 'Þe thridde [kind of simony] . . . is chaungyng of benefyce, as to chaungyn a more & a lesse, & he þat hath þe lesse schal haue bote'; also *Ayenbite* 42. The practice was also called 'church-chopping'; e.g., *D&P* 2:183: 'Choppyng of chirchis withoutyn autoryte of þe buschop is symonye.' For sample documents seeking or granting such authority, see Purvis 26–27 and Barraclough 161, 203–06. L's use of *permuten* instead of 'chaungyn' suggests a first-hand knowledge of the canonical pronouncements on the subject; e.g., Gregory IX, *Decret*. III.19 (*De rerum permutatione*) in *CIC* 2:522–525.

PERPETUEL   Of punishment or pardon, 'for life' (or forever) as distinguished from a term of years: B.18.200 I, rightwisnesse, record . . . That hir peyne be perpetuel and no preiere hem helpe (C.20.205); C.10.8 (Sk.) Pardon with Peers plouhman perpetual he [Truth] graunteth; C.5.195; C.7.118; B.10.427 (C.11.263); B.14.215 (C.16.57). Cf. *Lib.Alb.* 370: 'Every person who shall be attainted three times [of usury] shall forswear the said city for ever without ransom, under penalty of perpetual imprisonment [sur peyne de perpetuele prisone].' FOR EVER.

***PERSONAGE**   A BENEFICE or maintenance granted to a parson: B.13.245 I hadde neuere of hym . . . Neiþer prouendre ne personage yet of þe popes ȝifte.

PES   **I.** The king's peace: B.4.47 Thanne com pees into þe parlement and putte vp a bille How wrong ayeins his wille hadde his wif taken, And how he rauysshede Rose. . . . He maynteneþ hise men to murþere myne hewen, Forstalleþ my feires, fiȝteþ in my Chepyng, Brekeþ vp my berne dores, bereþ awey my whete. . . . I am noȝt hardy for hym vnneþe to loke (A.4.34, C.4.45). Blackstone explains: 'In criminal proceedings . . . all offences are either against the king's peace, or his crown and dignity; and are so laid in every indictment' (1:258); e.g., *K.Bench* 6:37: 'The aforesaid evildoers . . . have behaved wickedly against the king's peace [contra pacem domini regis] and terrorised everybody else who quietly accepted the king's peace.' The author of the *Mirror* objects that 'in appeals one should have to . . . say "against the peace," for every sin is against the peace' (161). The complaint brought by Peace resembles countless petitions of the period, including his expression of fear ('I am noȝt hardy'), a formula in bills seeking equity or special relief: e.g., *K.Counc*. 48: 'The said Sir William and others of his company threaten him in life and limb so that he dares not go or be seen anywhere'; Fisher 164/40: 'Iohn Tyrell and othor mo all these wronges han doon to the forseyd Rauf And ȝet standith in dowte of his lyff ȝef he go to large.' F. Pollock, *The King's Peace* in *Oxford Lectures and Other Discourses*, London: Macmillan, 1890; *Oxf. Comp*. 703; Goebel 423–40; Baldwin 39–50.

II. 'To make peace,' to settle out of court (usually by means of a money payment): B.4.64 Wrong . . . souȝte To maken his pees wiþ hise pens (A.4.50); A.4.61 (B.4.75); C.13.75. Cf. *Jac.Well* 131/1: 'A fals pleyntyf . . . feynyth a fals accyoun, and so . . . puttyth þe trewe to trauayll & to gret exspensys, tyl he is fayn to make his pes.'

PESTILENCE   'Since the pestilence,' a conventional phrase in complaints on the times, echoing the opening sentence of the Statute of Labourers (1350): B.Prol.84 Persons and parisshe preestes pleyned hem to þe Bisshop That hire parisshe were pouere siþ þe pestilence tyme, To haue a licence and leue at London to dwelle To syngen for symonie (A.Prol.81, C.Prol.82); A.10.191 (B.9.170, C.10.269); A.11.59 (B.10.73, C.11.55). See the Statute (25 Edw. III): 'Whereas recently against the malice of servants who were idle and not willing to serve after the pestilence [apres la pestilence], without taking excessive wages, it was ordained . . .'; see also 25 Edw. III st. 2 and 36 Edw. III c. 8). L evidently knew the statute well (cf. STATUTE).

*PIKEHARNEIS   One who despoils those slain in battle of their armour: B.20.263 Pylours and Pykeharneys (C.22.263).

PIKEPORSE   One who steals purses or from purses; a pickpocket: C.6.370 Portours and . . . pikeporses. CUTTEPURS.

PIKER   A thief, esp. a petty thief or pilferer: C.5.17 Can thow . . . be hayward . . . And kepe my corn in my croft fro pykares and theues? RIFLERE, THEF.

PILEN   To rob (sb.), pillage, plunder: B.19.442 Þe pope . . . pileþ holy kirke (C.21.442). RIFLEN, ROBBEN, STELEN.

PILLORIE   A contrivance for punishment, resembling the stocks, in which an offender, with head and hands locked in place, was exposed to public ridicule, insult, and molestation: A.3.67 Meiris & maceris . . . punisshen on pillories & on pynyng stolis Breweris & bakeris, bocheris & cokes (B.3.78, C.3.79); A.2.168 (B.2.207, C.2.216). Cf. *Simonie* 345: 'The pilory and the cucking-stol beth i-mad for noht.' The pillory differed from the stocks mainly in the offender's standing rather than sitting, and in having the head secured. It was the standard punishment (see the statute *Judicium Pilloriae* in *Statutes* 1:201–02) for breaking the assizes of bread and ale in certain cases, e.g., where the offence was especially great, where the offender could not pay the fine, or where he or she had been convicted twice already. Thus Reynes 136/347: 'If the baker lakke an vnce in the wyght of a ferthyng loff, he be amercyed at xx d. . . . And if he lakke past [an vnce et dimidium], he mote haue iugement to the pelory' (also 136/358, 138/397).

PILOUR   A pillager, plunderer, or ROBBER: B.20.263 Alle oþere in bataille [i.e., unregistered combatants] ben yholde Brybours, Pylours and Pyke-harneys, in ech a parisshe ycursed (C.22.263); C.13.2 Pouerte . . . may walke vnrobbed Among pilours in pees; A.3.182 (B.3.195); B.18.40 (C.20.39); B.19.415 (C.21.415). Statute 34 Edw. III c. 1: 'pilours & robeours.' REVER, ROBERT, THEF.

PINFOLD   A pound for stray or distrained animals; *fig.* a prison: B.16.264 Out of þe poukes pondfold no maynprise may vs fecche (C.18.281); B.5.624 Largenesse þe lady . . . haþ holpe a þousand out of þe deueles punfolde. Cf. *Court Baron* 57: 'Nicholas of Hoo, that art attached to answer in this court wherefore and by what warrant thou didst take thy animals out of the lord's pinfold [ponefaude] where they were impounded for thy trespass because they were found in the lord's corn. How wilt thou amend the trespass?'

PINING STOL   A cucking stool: A.3.67 Meiris & maceris . . . punisshen on pillories & on pynyng stolis Breweris & bakeris, bocheris & cokes (B.3.78, C.3.79). Like the PILLORIE, the cucking stool was a standard form of punishment for those (esp. women) convicted of offences against the assizes of bread and ale. The offender was strapped in place and exposed to public ridicule in the market, town square, etc., and in some instances ducked under water. The device was also used to punish scolds (cf. Blackstone 4:169) and is probably alluded to in B.5.29: Tomme Stowue he tauȝte to take two staues And fecche Felice hom fro wyuen pyne (A.5.29, C.5.131). See also the punishment of a negligent reeve in *Court Baron* 103. STOKKES.

PIT   A dungeon or PRISOUN; *fig.* hell: B.5.405 I visited neuere feble men ne fettred men in puttes; A.11.256 I shal punisshen in purcatory or in þe put of helle (B.10.375); C.7.277; C.9.72; B.14.174.

PLACE   A manor; also the chief residence on an estate, a manor house: B.10.313 Ac now is Religion a rydere . . . A prikere on a palfrey fro place to Manere (C.5.159); C.21.61 Iesus . . . ȝeueth largeliche all his lele lege Places in paradys at here partyng hennes (B.19.61), an allusion to John 14:2, 'In domo Patris mei mansiones multae sunt.' Cf. *Abbey of H.G.* 339: 'To hauen and holden þis preciouse place wiþ þe noble abbeye & al þe holy couent.' *Fleta* 2.12: 'lord of the place' [dominus loci] (p. 121).

PLEDEN   To contend legally, as to bring suit, argue a case, offer a defence, etc.: B.Prol.213 Sergeantʒ . . . þat serueden at þe barre, Pleteden for penyes and pounded þe lawe (A.Prol.86, C.Prol.161); B.14.109 Ther þe poore dar plede and preue by pure reson To haue allowaunce of his lord; by þe lawe he it cleymeþ (C.15.287); B.4.54 Wrong . . . borwed of me bayard and brouʒte hym neuere ayein, Ne no ferþyng þerfore for nouʒt I koude plede (A.4.41, C.4.57), rendered by Bennett as 'And paid not a farthing in cash, no matter what legal claim I made' (145); B.3.296 (C.3.448); B.7.39 Sk. (C.9.44); B.7.43; B.7.46; C.9.54; B.14.189. Peace's lack of success in bringing Wrong to justice through the ordinary channels of common-law process is reflected in numerous records of the period. In a similar case, involving maintenance, the plaintiffs were forced to apply to the king's council (as in the Peace episode) because 'the said Percival will not come to answer any writ of the king that they can purchase against him' (*K.Counc.* 82). On pleading, see Henry John Stephen, *A Treatise on the Principles of Pleading in Civil Actions* (London: Saunders and Benning, 1838). ALLEGGEN, ANSWEREN, MOTEN, SPEKEN.

PLEDOUR   One who pleads in court, an advocate or lawyer: B.7.43 *Super innocentem munera non accipies. Pledours sholde peynen hem to plede for swiche and helpe. Lib.Alb.*: 'Item, it is ordained by the Mayor and Aldermen of the City of London, that all the attorneys . . . and other common pleaders [Comunes Pledours] . . . shall each year be strictly charged and sworn before the Mayor and Aldermen, for the time being, well and lawfully to do their duty' (525); (on the oath itself) 'Item, that the pleaders [lez Pleidours] who are commonly residing in the City for pleading, shall be sworn that they will not plead, or give counsel, against the usages and franchises of the City of London; but that they will maintain the same to the best of their power, within the City and without' (473). LAWIER, PROCURATOUR, VOKETTE.

PLEGGE   Something given as security, collateral: B.15.125a Sir Iohan and sire Geffrey haþ of siluer a girdel . . . Ac a Porthors þat sholde be his Plow . . . Pat is betake to tauerne hows for ten schelyng plegge. The line is rejected by K-D (p. 223). Cf. Edler, *pieggo.*

PLEINEN   To make a legal complaint or accusation; *reflex.* to lodge a formal complaint: A.3.155 Pouere men mowe haue no power to pleyne þeiʒ hem smerte, Such a maister is mede among men of goode (B.3.168, C.3.213); C.6.120 Prelates pleyneth on hem [friars] for they here parschiens shryuen; B.4.66 Hadde I loue of my lord þe kyng litel wolde I recche Theiʒ pees and his power pleyned hem euere (A.4.52, C.4.70); A.Prol.80 (B.Prol.83, C.Prol.81); C.4.30; A.7.146 (B.6.159, C.8.156); C.8.166; B.17.298. Cf. *D&P* 2:44/2: 'ʒif a clerk plenye hym to þe iustyce on hym þat robbith hym . . . þe clerk is nout irreguler.' The reflexive form follows the French; e.g., *Lib.*

Alb. 109: 'Adam Roem se pleinst de Johan Buquente, de felonie et de robberie'; *LawMerch*. 1:113: 'Hamond Elyot grocer de Loundres . . . se pleint sur Martyn Dyne.' APPELEN, PURSUEN, SHEWEN, SUEN.

PLEINTE A lawsuit, legal complaint, accusation: B.2.178 Paulynes pryuees for pleintes in Consistorie Shul seruen myself þat Cyuyle is nempned (A.2.139); C.3.213 Pore men dar nat pleyne ne no pleynt shewe. *K.Counc.* 70: 'The complaint [pleynte] is that the mariners are constrained so that they cannot sell their herrings.' *Mirror* 45: 'Plaintiffs are those who seek their own right or another's by plaints [par pleintis].'

PLIGHTEN To swear or pledge; to indenture (oneself); 'plighten treuth,' to pledge faith or fealty, to make a promise, to take an oath (as a juror); *reflex*. to make a vow of matrimony: B.3.317 Ne to þe Court sompne, Ne putte hem in panel to doon hem pliʒte hir truþe (C.3.469); A.7.36 Curteisliche þe kniʒt conseyuede þise wordis; 'Be my power, piers, I pliʒte þe my treuþe To fulfille þe foreward whiles I may stande' (B.6.34, C.8.33); A.5.116 I seruide symme at þe nok And was his prentis ypliʒt (B.5.200, C.6.208); A.10.191 In gelosie, ioyeles, & ianglyng a bedde, Manye peire siþen þe pestilence han pliʒt hem togidere (B.9.170, C.10.269); A.Prol.46 (B.Prol.46, C.Prol.47).

*****PLURALITE** The holding of two or more benefices concurrently by one person; a benefice held concurrently with another or others; *pl*. two or more benefices held together: A.11.200 Dobet doþ ful wel, & dewid he is also, And haþ possessions & pluralites for pore menis sake; C.3.33 And purchace ʒow prouendres while ʒoure panes lasteth And bygge ʒow benefices, pluralite to haue. Cf. *Jac.Well* 18/11: 'And alle þey bene acursed þat receyvin & holdyn pluralyte of cherchys, hauyng cure of soule, but ʒif it be by dyspensacyoun of þe court of Rome.' For formulas of dispensation, see Barraclough 146–47. The story of the clash between the Crown and the Papacy over the issue of pluralism is told by Maitland 148–57.

POSSESSION Property (esp. landed property) or ownership of property; an endowment, benefice: B.15.563 [Prelates] That sholden preie for þe pees, possession hem letteþ; Takeþ hire landes, ye lordes, and leteþ hem lyue by dymes (C.17.226); B.15.565 If possession be poison and inparfite hem make Charite were to deschargen hem for holy chirches sake (C.17.229); A.11.200 Dobet doþ ful wel, & dewid he is also, And haþ possessions & pluralites for pore menis sake; cf. B.11.273; B.14.271 (C.16.111).

*****POSSESSIONER** A beneficed clergyman or member of an endowed religious institution; one who holds a POSSESSION: B.5.145 Thise possessioners preche and depraue freres. *D&P* 1:316/7: 'Þese religious possessionerys enduyd in so gret richesse seyn þat it arn þe goodis of þe hous.' PROVENDRE.

POUNDEFOLD See PINFOLD

POWER   Legal power or authority; licence, authorization: B.6.149 Ac Robert Renaboute shal riȝt noȝt haue of myne, Ne Postles, but þei preche konne and haue power of þe bisshop; B.4.66 (C.4.70); B.13.254 (C.15.225); B.19.183 (C.21.183). Cf. Statute 14 Edw. III c. 5: 'Henceforth at every parliament there shall be chosen a prelate, two earls and two barons, who shall have commission and power [commission & poair] of the king to hear . . . complaints.' The writ *dedimus potestatem* conferred the right or power of attorney; the author of the *Mirror* complains of attorneys being received without it (166).

PRECEPTA REGIS SUNT NOBIS VINCULA LEGIS   'The commands of the king have for us the force of law,' a metrical variant of the Roman law maxim 'quod principi placuit legis habet vigorem': B.Prol.145 Thanne comsed al þe commune crye in verse of latyn To þe kynges counseil, construe whoso wolde, '*Precepta Regis sunt nobis vincula legis*.' An index of medieval glosses on the maxim can be found in Otto Gierke, *Political Theories of the Middle Age* (Cambridge: the University Press, 1913), 147. There is a close analogue to L's version of the maxim in Paris BN Latin 11867, 'Precepto regis mihi subdita sanctio legis' (Alford 1975).

PREIEN   To petition (for mercy, pardon, relief, etc.): B.4.98 Pees þanne pitously preyde to þe kynge To haue mercy on þat man; C.9.281 Loke now for thy lacchesse what lawe wol the graunte, Purgatorye for thy paie ore perpetuel helle, For shal no pardon preye for ȝow there ne no princes lettres; B.10.125. Brown XIV 99/48: 'Til þe iuge sal I come, bot I wate noght my day; Mercy es bath al & some, þar-in I trayst & after pray.' To 'pray' for mercy or remedy was the usual way of wording a petition in all equitable procedure; e.g., *Law Merch.* 1:113: 'And he alleged that the said Martin still owed him the balance, for which he prayed a remedy [pria remedie]'; *K.Counc.* 11: 'To our lord the king and his council . . . Hugh of Kent . . . prays you [vous prie] . . . to grant grace and remedy for this debt.' For a discussion of the 'prayer,' normally the third and last part of a petition, see *K.Counc.* xxxv–vi. BEDEN.

PREIERE   A plea for mercy, pardon, or special favour; an entreaty (on behalf of a defendant or prisoner): B.2.207 If ye lacche lyere lat hym noȝt ascapen . . . for any preyere (A.2.168, C.2.216); B.19.307 *[Spiritus Iusticie]* ne dide lawe For present or for preiere or any Prynces lettres (C.21.308); C.2.68; C.7.231; C.9.281; B.11.156; B.15.346; B.17.298; B.18.200 (C.20.205). Cf. *Jac.Well* 127/10: 'Whan a college or a couent schal chesyn here prelate, thurgh prayere or procuryng of a lord, þei schal chese one þat is onworthy.' *Lib.Alb.* 453: 'If any one shall make prayer [prie] for any person who shall do the contrary hereof, let him pay forty pence unto the Chamber for his prayer [pur sa priere]'; *Court Baron* 88: 'A love-day is given . . . on the prayer [prece] of the parties.' On the phrase 'for present or for preiere' (B.19.307), cf. the oath of sheriff: 'I will . . . not cease to do this [enforce the law] for gift nor for promise [pur doun ne pur promesse]' (*Eyre* 12); *Ayenbite* 38/19: 'Efterward þe kueade domesmen þet hise soffreþ oþer be yefþes oþer be biddynges. . . .'

119

PRE MANIBUS (Of contracts) 'Before-hand,' a term applied to payments in advance, often associated with usurious or unethical agreements: C.9.45 Men of lawe hadde lest [pardon] þat loth were to plede But they *pre manibus* were payed for pledynge at þe barre; C.3.299 Y halde hym ouer-hardy or elles nat trewe That *pre manibus* is paied or his pay asketh. Harlotes and hoores and also fals leches They asken here huyre ar thei hit haue deserued; cf. C.3.292–93, B.14.142, 149, etc. See *Nov.Narr.* 302 (a plea of covenant): 'It was agreed . . . that the aforesaid K. de P. should . . . enclose these twenty acres of land in B. with a wall . . . and to take for every acre twenty-two shillings, which money he received in full in cash down [auaunt la mayn]'; *LawMerch.* 1:36: 'John . . . complains of Roger Barber, for that he has unjustly broken a covenant with him, and unjustly because . . . the said Roger . . . undertook to cure his, John's, head of baldness for 9d., which the said John paid in advance [premanibus].' Payment in advance was required, typically, by those who operated on the fringes of the law – shysters, quacks, prostitutes. Because the law did not recognize contracts that were contrary to morals or 'good manners' (cf. *Mirror* 74), such persons had no legal recourse if their clients were dissatisfied and refused to pay; hence they demanded payment *pre manibus*. What made all payments in advance usurious was the lack of shared risk. In the words of Thomas Wilson, '[I]n lending for usury . . . the borower geveth a good assurance *before hand*, and abideth all the hazard and perill that may happen, the creditour susteining no adventure or damage at all' (300). ABOUGHT THE TIME; cf. SUM CERTEIN.

PREVARICATORES LEGIS Those who evade the law, esp. by means of their wealth or position: C.10.94 Dobest bere sholde þe bisshopes crose . . . And with the pyk pulte adoun *preuaricatores legis*. Lordes þat lyuen as hem lust and no lawe acounten, For here mok and here mebles suche men thenketh Sholde no bisshop be, here biddynges to withsite. The phrase is common in glosses on Psalm 118:119, where it is used to signify transgressors of the law in general (see Alford 1975).

PRISONER Prisoner: B.3.137 Mede . . . leteþ passe prisoners and paieþ for hem ofte, And gyueþ þe Gailers gold (A.3.126, C.3.173); B.14.174.

PRISOUN I. A prisoner: B.18.58 Pitousliche and pale, as a prison þat deieþ (C.20.59); C.7.277; C.9.72; B.7.30 (C.9.34); C.9.180; B.15.183 (C.16.322); B.15.346.
    II. A prison; *fig.* purgatory or hell: A.9.94 Þanne shulde þe kyng come & casten hem in presoun (B.8.104); B.18.392 They shul be . . . In my prisone Purgatorie til *parce* it hote; C.4.123; C.7.21; B.11.133 (C.12.66); B.15.265. PIT.

PRIVE Somebody who has an interest in a legal action (see *OED* B.I.2); 'Paulynes pryvees,' parties to suits in the consistory court of St. Paul's, London (see PAULINES): B.2.178 Paulynes pryuees for pleintes in Consistorie

120

Shul seruen myself þat Cyuyle is nempned. Black: 'Privies. Those who are partakers or have an interest in any action or thing, or any relation to another . . . . They are of six kinds' (list follows). See also 'Privity,' *Oxf. Comp.* (996). Cf. Statute 18 Edw. I st. 4: 'A fine [q.v.] is . . . of such great force . . . that it concludeth not only those who are parties and privies to the fine [parties & prives a la fine] . . . but all other people of the world'; *Moots*: 'Note that the mise shall not be joined . . . between privies in blood [privez de sanke]' (96); 'He shall have a writ of entry, but his successor shall not because he is not privy [prive] to the lease: he is not privy in fact [privey en feet] to the lease nor is he privy as heir [prive come heire]' (83). Privies or parties to an action are distinguished from 'strangers'; e.g., Simpson 117: 'So long as a fine was accompanied with proclamations it would bar strangers as well as parties and privies after a period of five years.'

PRIVE LETTRE   A letter close, as distinguished from a letter PATENTE, esp. one granting licence or favour: C.4.189 Y assente . . . And þat vnsittynge suffraunce ne sele ȝoure priue lettres. Possibly an allusion to the recent statute (1387) 11 Ric. II c. 10: 'Item it is ordained and established that neither letters of the signet nor of the king's privy seal shall from henceforth be sent in damage or prejudice of the realm, nor in disturbance of the law' (a confirmation of 2 Edw. III c. 8). For examples of letters sent under the privy seal, see Hall 1:91–113. CLAUSE, LETTRE.

PROCURATOUR   A person authorized to act for another; an agent, a proxy, proctor (attorney): B.19.258 I make Piers þe Plowman my procuratour and my reue, And Registrer to receyue *redde quod debes* (C.21.258); C.7.90. Cf. *CT. Friar* 1596: 'May I nat axe a libel, sire somonour, And answere there [in court] by my procuratour?' Given the common meaning of *procurator* as agent or attorney and its pairing in the present context with another ecclesiastical court official, the REGISTRER, it is clear that L is here describing 'the power of the keys' given to St. Peter as 'the power of attorney' in all matters relating to the church. Writs of procuration define the attorney's duties in detail; e.g., 'Be it known to all men by these presents that I, Geoffrey de Markel, rector of the church of St. Cride in the diocese of Exeter, do ordain, make and constitute my beloved A and B . . . my proctors or proctor in all causes and business, howsoever touching my person or church . . . whenever I shall be absent, giving them . . . full power and special mandate in my name to sue, defend, except, make replication, formulate and reply to allegations of fact, accuse of crimes and defaults, appeal, prosecute appeals. . . .; seek, receive and obtain improvement of my condition and full restitution with expenses and interest; perform canonical obedience in my name and do all and singular which can be performed and procured by true and lawful proctors or proctor' (*Writs* 133). All of these actions were regarded by the medieval church as its rights by virtue of its status as procurator of the Holy Spirit. The offices of registrar and procurator were closely related, the first often preliminary to the second (Woodcock 38–40).

PRO DEI PIETATE   'For the love of God,' a concluding formula in petitions of equity: B.7.46 Many a Iustice and Iurour wolde for Iohan do moore Than *pro dei pietate* pleden at þe barre; cf. B.4.39. *K. Counc.* 41: 'To their very excellent and very noble lord the king, . . . may it please you for the love of God [pour lamour de Dieu] and in way of charity . . . to grant, etc.'; *Chancery* 15: 'To the most gracious, the Lord Chancellor of England, Beseecheth humbly your poor servant, Andrew Ramsey . . . for the love of God and in way of charity [pur l'amour de Dieu et en oeuere de charitee].' The phrase, a standard part of a petitioner's 'prayer' (see *K. Counc.* xxxvi, and PREIERE), was a direct appeal to the king's or chancellor's 'grace' and indicated the petitioner's failure to get redress at common law 'because of the social standing of the defendant, his high rank or the protection afforded him by some powerful Baron,' etc. (Levy-Ullmann 299) – in other words the very sort of favouritism alluded to in B.7.46.

PROVENDRE   **I.** The stipend of a member of a cathedral or collegiate church, a prebend; also the land yielding revenue for such a stipend: C.3.32 Mede hendeliche behyhte hem . . . lordes to make, 'And purchace ȝow prouendres while ȝoure panes lasteth And bygge ȝow benefices, pluralite to haue'; B.13.245 I hadde neuere of hym . . . Neiþer prouendre ne personage yet of þe popes ȝifte. *Myrour* 138/10: 'Þe secounde manere [of simony] is in benefice, as when a man takeþ or ȝeueþ eny benefice of Holy Chirche, as cherche, prouendre, chapel, vicariage, chauntry or eny oþer for mede' (cf. *Jac. Well* 27/3); Usk 51/50: 'But now the leude for symonye is avaunced . . . and hath his provendre alone.' Statute 14 Edw. III c. 17 ('parsones des eglises ou provendres').

   II. One who holds a prebend, a prebendary: A.3.139 (B.3.150) She blissiþ þise bisshopis ȝif þei be lewid; Prouendrours, persones, & prestis she mayn-teniþ. POSSESSIONER.

*****PROVENDREN**   To provide (somebody) with a prebend: B.3.149 (Sk.) She blesseth thise bisshopes theiȝe they be lewed, Prouendreth [K-D prouendres] persones and prestes meynteneth (C.3.186 prouendreth). BENEFISEN, DOWEN.

*****PROVINCIAL**   The head of a province or district of an order of friars; 'prior provincial,' the director of all the houses of a religious order within a province: B.11.57 Freres wol . . . for þe biseke To hir Priour prouincial a pardon for to haue (C.12.9); A.8.175 (B.7.197, C.9.344).

*****PROVISOUR**   The holder of a provision or grant from the pope giving him the right to be appointed to a benefice as soon as a vacancy occurred: A.3.136 [Mede] is preuy wiþ þe pope, prouisours it knowiþ (B.3.147, C.3.183); A.4.116 And alle rome renneris . . . Bere no siluer ouer se . . . But it be marchaunt . . . Oþer prouisour, or prest þat þe pope auaunciþ (B.4.133, C.4.130); A.2.135 (B.2.171); C.2.182, 186. The system of papal provision aroused a great deal of opposition in fourteenth-century England. The common complaint, echoed in *Piers*, was that the buying and selling of such grants constituted simony; more to the point, probably, was that the pope's claim to make appointments conflicted with the claims of the king and of local patrons. The following petition came before the Chancellor in 1399–1401: 'Beseecheth your poor clerk, John Bremore, that whereas of late the church of Chesterton in the diocese of Lincoln being void and belonging to Richard, late King of England, the said late King presented the said John to the same church. . . . And Lewis Byford, clerk, by the abetment and maintenance of . . . many others, took the said church by virtue of a provision of the said church made to the said Lewis contrary to the Statute of Provisors [25 Edw. III, 1350–51],' etc. (*Chanc.* 96). See Maitland 51–99; Pantin 47–75, 82–98; G. Barraclough, *Papal Provisions* (Oxford, 1935). ROME RENNERE.

PURCHASEN   A. To acquire (land) by money, gift, or other legal means; 'purchased land,' acquired property as opposed to an inherited estate: C.5.158 Monkes and chanons Haen ryde out of aray . . . Ledares of lawedays and londes ypurchaced; C.5.77. Cf. 'Instructions for Purchasing Land,' Robbins 70–71; Statute 18 Edw. III c. 3 concerning 'gentz de religion qount purchacez terres et les ount mys a mort meyn.' Blackstone 2:241: 'Purchase, indeed, in its vulgar and confined acceptation, is applied only to such acquisitions of land, as are obtained by way of bargain and sale, for money, or some other valuable consideration. But this falls far short of the legal idea of purchase: for, if I *give* land freely to another, he is in the eye of the law a purchasor . . . for he comes to the estate by his own agreement, that is, he consents to the gift.' The context suggests, in fact, that religious come into land not through buying it but through more subtle, legal means. Cf. Chaucer's serjeant-at-law: 'So greet a purchasour was nowher noon' (*CT.Prol.* 318). **B.** To buy or acquire (sth.); 'to purchase a pardon,' to obtain a charter of pardon or an indulgence: C.3.32 And purchace ȝow prouendres . . . And bygge ȝow benefices; C.9.339 ȝe maistres, mayres and iuges, That haen the welthe of this world . . . To purchace ȝow pardoun and the popes bulles (A.8.170, B.7.192); A.8.3 (B.7.3, C.9.3); B.7.39 (C.9.42); B.17.256 (C.19.217). *Moots* 20: 'If in an assise outlawry of record be alleged in the plaintiff . . . and . . . the plaintiff purchases a charter of pardon,' etc. See PARDOUN.

**PURSUEN   *To bring charges against, prosecute, sue (sb.): B.17.308 For þer þat partie pursueþ þe peel is so huge That þe kyng may do no mercy (C.19.283); A.5.75 To apeire hym be my power I pursuide wel ofte, And belowen hym to lordis (B.5.95). Cf. *Jac.Well* 25/29, concerning persons 'þat ryȝtfully pursewyn in cristen court aȝens here aduersaryes'; Fisher 31/3: 'Lord ffiȝhugh oure Chamberlein is pursued and empleted . . . in certaine cause personneles'; *Court Baron* 65: [Bailiff] 'Qui pursuit vers cest homme?'; *Bor.Cust.* 27: 'If any wyll com to pursue in dewe forme ayenst the indited of his felony . . . he shalbe herd.'

**PURTINAUNCE   See APPURTENAUNCE

PUT   See PIT

*PUTOUR   A lecher, fornicator (OF *putour*, a whoremonger, brothel-keeper): C.6.172 Lady, to thy leue sone loute for me nouthe, That he haue pite on me, putour, of his puyr mercy. *Lib.Alb.* 179: 'Whereas in divers Wardmotes . . . there are indited . . . some men as common whoremongers [comunes putours], common adulterers, and common bawds,' etc.; *Mirror* 12: 'Widows should not lose their inheritance by unchastity [par putage].'

Q

QUASI MODO GENITI   'As newborn babes' (I Pet. 2:2), quoted in the Introit for Low Sunday after Easter: B.11.203 For at Caluarie of cristes blood cristendom gan sprynge, And blody breþeren we bicome þere of o body ywonne, As *quasi modo geniti* gentil men echone, No beggere ne boye amonges vs but if it synne made (C.12.109). The phrase is also used by Bracton to describe the readmission of an outlawed person to society. See P&M 1:477: 'If the king inlaws him, he comes back into the world like a new-born babe, *quasi modo genitus*, capable indeed of acquiring new rights, but unable to assert any of those that he had before his outlawry. . . . [T]he inlawed person is not the old person restored to legal life; he is a new person.' In quoting the phrase from Bracton, *Fleta* 1.28 obscures its biblical origin: 'per inlagacionem enim facti sunt quasi de nouo essent creati' (p. 75).

QUESTE   See ENQUESTE

QUESTMONGERE   One who profits from an inquest or a trial, esp. by giving false testimony; a corrupt and bribed juror: B.19.367 (Sk.) Lyeres and questmongeres that were forsworen ofte, Wytynge and willefully with the false helden. Cf. *D&P* 2:253/53: 'Many þeues & manqwellerys . . . hopyn alwey to ben sauyd be periurie and falshed of questemongeris þat for litil good wiln forsweryn hem.' See Arnold Williams, 'Middle English *Questmonger*,' *Mediaeval Studies* 10 (1948), 200–04. FALS WITNESS, JUROUR, SISOUR.

QUI PECUNIAM SUAM NON DEDIT AD VSURAM, ETC.   '[Lord, who shall dwell in thy tabernacle . . .?] He that hath not put out his money to usury, nor taken bribes against the innocent' (Ps. 14:5), a proof-text against usury and excessive legal fees: B.3.241a Lord, who shal wonye in þi wones. . . . [H]e þat vseþ no3t þe lyf of vsurie . . . . *Qui pecuniam suam non dedit*, etc. (A.3.221a); A.8.46a Men of lawe hadde lest [pardon] . . . For so seiþ þe sauter . . . *Super innocentem munera non accipies* (B.7.42a, C.2.40a). Cf. Hubert Walter's Legatine Canons: 'Since the Scripture testifies that he is blessed who withdraws his hand from accepting bribes, it is most carefully to be provided that justice be done gratis, and that no pay be taken for doing it, or laying it aside, or hastening, or delaying it in ecclesiastical cases' (*Engl.Canons* 2:78). See also *Vices and Virtues* (EETS 89) 76; Wilson 178; Yunck, in Alford 1988, 146. See ABOUGHT THE TIME, USURIE.

QUITEN   I. To satisfy (a claim); repay (a debt); 'quit' (p.pl., adj.): C.4.98
Mede hath made my mendes, y may no more asken, So alle my claymes ben
quyt; C.9.275 Thyn huyre . . . hath nat to quyte thy dette; B.6.98 Þouȝ I deye
today my dettes are quyte, I bar hom þat I borwed er I to bedde yede (A.7.90,
C.8.107); C.13.75; B.13.10 (C.15.12). The first citation suggests the term
quitclaim, 'a release or acquittance given to one man by another, in respect of
any action that he has or might have against him' (Black). Cf. 'Cursor Mundi,'
Sisam 140/25: 'The day is gan, the det unquit.' *Writs* 227: Defendant to render
his debts to the exchequer 'unless he can reasonably show . . . that he ought to
be quit thereof [quod inde quietus esse debeat].'
    II. To pay for, make amends, ransom; to expiate (a sin): B.18.340 *Dentem*
pro dente & oculum pro oculo. Ergo soule shal soule quyte . . . And al þat man
haþ mysdo I man wole amende . . . And boþe quykne and quyte þat queynt
was þoruȝ synne (C.20.386ff.); C.16.31 Satisfaccion . . . for soules paieth and
for alle synnes quyteth; B.16.262 May no wed vs quyte, Ne no buyrn be oure
borgh, ne brynge vs fram his daunger (C.18.279).

R

RAGMAN   In popular usage, a papal bull or any official document with seals
hanging from it: A.Prol.72 A pardoner . . . bunchide hem wiþ his breuet . . .
And rauȝte wiþ his rageman ryngis & brochis (B.Prol.75, C.Prol.73); B.16.89
(C.18.122). The first dated occurrence of the word is 1276, in the Statute of
Rageman (4 Edw. I), under which justices were appointed to hear and determine complaints in each hundred of each shire. Testimony was recorded on a
hundred roll or 'ragman roll' (> Mod.Eng. *rigmarole*). Bennett explains:
'The seals of the witnesses questioned were attached to these long rolls by
cutting the bottom edge of the parchment into strips, which thus formed a
tattered fringe; and the inquisitors who carried these ragged rolls came to be
known as ragmen. . . . The term became attached to the rolls themselves, and
thus to any documents presenting a similar appearance' (90).

RAIMEN   To have control over; to rule over (*OED*); to make a royal progress
(Skeat): A.1.93 (Sk.) Kynges and knihtes scholde . . . rihtfuliche raymen the
realmes a-abouten, And take trespassours and teiȝen hem faste (A.1.93,
B.1.95, C.1.91 riden & rappe). Possibly a reference to the General Eyre,
discontinued in L's day owing to the centralization of royal justice at Westminster (see Plucknett 145). Cf. *Mirror* 145: 'It was ordained of old that the
kings in person, or by their chief justices . . . should journey [errasent] every
seven years throughout all counties . . . to see whether any one had erred in
any point of law . . . and what they found undetermined they were to determine [q.v.] in their eyre . . . and punish neglects according to the rules of right.'
See also *TRANSGRESSOR*.

RAUNSOUN The action of procuring the release of a prisoner by the payment of a certain sum; a fine; *fig.* the redemption of souls through the payment of Christ's blood: B.18.352 Good feiþ me it tauȝte To recouere hem þoruȝ raunsoun. *Mirror* 182: 'It is not law that anyone should be punished for a single deed by imprisonment or any other corporal punishment, and in addition by a pecuniary punishment or ransom; for ransom is nothing else than the redemption of a corporal punishment [car ranceon nest autre chose qe rachat de peine corporele].' Cf. *Jac. Well* 129/33: 'Scherrevys & bayles puttyn often trewe men in gret dystres, & feteryn hem, tyl þei haue made a fyne, & payin a raunsoun'; *Hand. Synne* 5294: 'My blode y ȝaf for hys raunsun'; *Pr. Cons.* 77/2834: '*Quia in inferno nulla est redempcio*. In helle . . . es na raunceon. For na helpe may be in þat dungeon.' In law the idea of ransom (Lat. *redemptio*) is closely associated with that of grace, as in the formula 'without redemption or grace'; e.g., *Lib. Alb.* 361: 'la payne demprisonement par viii jours, sanz redempcioun ou grace du Mair.' BOTE, AMENDES.

RAUNSOUNEN To redeem (a prisoner) through the payment of RAUNSOUN: B.17.307 It is but selden yseiȝe . . . Any creature . . . Be raunsoned for his repentaunce þer alle reson hym dampneþ (C.19.282); B.18.349 Leue it noȝt, lucifer, ayein þe lawe I fecche hem, But by right and by reson raunsone here my liges (C.20.395); B.10.426 (C.11.261). PAIEN.

RAVENER One who ravens or takes goods by force; a robber, plunderer, despoiler (*OED*): C.17.42 Men of holy churche Sholde . . . refuse reuerences and raueners offrynges; C.17.47. Cf. *Jac. Well* 17/21: 'Raueynourys [& alle þat comaundyn oþere to don raveyn & thefte] . . . may noȝt ben assoyled, tyl þei haue made restitucyoun.' *D&P* 2:135: 'Sumtyme a þing is stolyn pryuelyche withoutyn wytynge of þe lord . . . and þan it is clepyd mecherye. Somtyme it is don opynly be myȝt & vyolence be wytynge of þe lord or of þe kepere aȝenys her wil, and þan it is clepyd propyrly *rapina* in Latyn, þat is raueyn in Englych.' PILOUR, ROBBER, THEF.

RAVISHEN I. To plunder, despoil: B.19.52 Mighte no deeþ hym fordo . . . That he naroos and regnede and rauysshed helle (C.21.52). DESPOILEN, REVEN.

II. To rob or deprive (one) of something: C.4.47 He raueschede Rose the ryche wydewe by nyhte And Margarete of here maydenhod as he mette here late (A.4.36, B.4.49). The *MED* defines the word as used in this passage: 'to carry off [a woman] by force, esp. for the purpose of rape.' This is possible, but L seems rather to be exploiting the double meaning of the word: Wrong ravished Rose the rich widow of her *goods* and Margaret of her maidenhead. Cf. *Jac. Well* 124/18: 'A gouelere [usurer] is a raueynere, for he . . . rauysschyth oþere men falsely of here godd.' ROBBEN, STELEN.

REALTE The rights and dignity of a lord or king; possession, LORDSHIP: A.11.228 Kinghod & kniȝthod . . . Helpiþ nouȝt to heueneward . . . Ne ricchesse, ne rentis, ne realte of lordis (B.10.340); B.14.210 Þe poore . . .

parauenture kan moore Of wit and of wisdom, þat fer awey is bettre Than richesse or reautee (C.16.52).Cf. *Writs* 125: 'If . . . one party in pleading claims property in the land, the court has the power to determine the question as to the realty [roialte],' i.e., ownership or possession; Fisher 163/81: 'The Priour and Chanons of Bernewell . . . cleymen the regalite and the frehold of the . . . tounshipe of Chestreton.'

RECEIVEN   To harbour (a criminal or wrongdoer), RECETTEN: C.3.497 He þat resceyueth here [Mede] or recheth here is rescettour of gyle; B.19.259 (C.21.259). Cf. *Jac. Well* 201/23: 'ȝif þou reseyue a theef wyttyngly, or defendyst hym, or kepyst treccherously in pryuite stolyn thynges . . . þou art bounde to restore þe hole of þat good.' The phrase 'resceyueth . . . or recheth' is formulaic: *Bor. Cust.* 1:62: 'Whosoever . . . will receave or resett any manner goods . . . or suspect persons,' etc.

RECETTEN   To harbour (a criminal or wrongdoer), RECEIVEN: C.4.501 (Sk.) Ac he that receyueth other recetteth hure [Mede] ys recettor of gyle; cf. C.3.497 resceyueth here or recheth here. Cf. *Myrour* 134/15: 'Þefes felawes beþ alle tho þat resetteþ þeues wittynglyche.' *Lib. Alb.* 283: 'Thieves and other persons of light and bad repute are often . . . received and harboured [recettes et herbergeez] in the houses of women of evil life.' Fisher 193/9: 'They herber and reset alle maner of myslyvers.' RECEIVEN.

RECETTOUR   One who knowingly harbours a criminal: C.3.497 He þat resceyueth here [Mede] or recheth here is rescettour of gyle. Cf. *Jac. Well* 30/10: Accursed are 'alle þat beryen . . . ony heretykes wylfully, or hem þat beleuyn on hem, or here receptourys, defenderys, or fauourerys, in cristen beryellys'; *D&P* 2:153/60. *Lib. Alb.* 276: 'And if any taverner shall receive any bad character, knowing that he has been a transgressor, let him have the imprisonment that is provided for all receivers of felons [recettours des felouns].' *Mirror* 45: 'utlaguez . . . e lur recettours.'

RECHEN   See RECETTEN

RECORD   Testimony; 'to take record,' to cite as evidence, call to witness: C.3.343 Relacoun rect . . . is a record of treuthe; B.15.87 I take record at Iesus That seide . . . *Ne sitis personarum acceptores. Lib. Alb.* 291: 'If any man feels himself aggrieved by a wrongful judgment, let those by whom the record is returned, forthwith cause the record to be brought in writing unto such place,' etc. RELACIOUN, WITNESS.

RECORDEN   'Recorder. In Norman law, to recite or testify on recollection what had previously passed in court. This was the duty of the judges and other principal persons who presided at the *placitum*; thence called *recordeurs*' (Black): B.4.172 The kyng . . . recordede þat Reson hadde riȝtfully shewed; C.4.29 Wareyn Wisman and Wily-man . . . Fayn were . . . To take reed of resoun þat recorde sholde Byfore þe kyng; C.20.373 Althouh resoun recordede, and rihte of mysulue, That if they ete þe appul alle sholde deye, Y behihte hem nat here helle for euere (B.18.330); C.3.470; B.4.157 (C.4.151); B.18.199 (C.20.204). In C.20.373 the image is that of God as judge and reason as his *recordeur*; the office of recorder is discussed by Cohen 244–48. Cf. *Launfal* 831: 'His borowes him [Launfal] brought befor the King. The King recordede tho. . . .' Fisher 163/12: 'Iohan Cokayn the Iustice recordede byfore the kyng'; *Bor. Cust.* 1:62: 'And if there come any persone that will recorde and justifie that he delyvered the goodes. . . .' REHERSEN, TESTIFIEN.

RECOVEREN To regain possession of (someone or something); to recover by law: B.18.352 Good feiþ me it tauȝte To recouere hem þoruȝ raunsoun; B.19.245 Grace . . . tauȝte . . . some to ryde and to recouere þat vnriȝtfully was wonne (C.21.245). Cf. Statute 3 Edw. I c. 48: 'The seisin shall be delivered by the justices, if it be recovered [si ele soit recovere], to the next friend of the heir'; *LawMerch*. 13: 'By the judgment of that court he recovered [recuperavit] against the said Hamon the said 2s. and his damages to the amount of 20s.' FECCHEN (II).

RECREAUNT Admitting defeat; surrendering oneself as a believer (with a pun on CREAUNT): B.18.100 For youre champion chiualer, chief knyȝt of yow alle, ȝilt hym recreaunt remyng, riȝt at Iesus wille (C.20.104); B.12.193 The þef . . . yald hym creaunt to crist & knewliched hym gilty (C.14.132). *SGGK* 456: 'Perfore com, oþer recreaunt be calde þe behoues.' The term belongs to the process of judicial combat. See the *Mirror* 109–112, esp. 112: 'And if the vanquished confesses his sin [conoisse sun pecchie; cf. 'knewliched hym gilty'] in the hearing of the people, or says the horrible word 'craven' [cravent] in sign of his recreancy [recreantise] . . . judgment is at once given upon the principal matter.' See BATAILLE, CHAMPION, FIGHT, JUGGEMENT OF ARMES, JUSTE.

RECT See RIGHT

RECTOR One who holds, as a benefice, a church and the whole or best part of the profits arising from its endowments: C.2.184 Syuyle and Symonye . . . Wol ryde vppon *rectores*. Addleshaw: 'The relationship of a rector or parson to the church which he had been given to rule or govern, was in the eyes of the canon law that of the holder of a benefice. The church and its endowments were his benefice, and he was entitled to enjoy for life the annual income and temporary profits from these endowments . . .' (9). For the presentation of a rector by a lay patron, see *Writs* 131–32. Cf. VICARI.

REDDE QUOD DEBES 'Pay what you owe' (Matt. 18:28), in *Piers* a formula standing for the notion of penitential satisfaction or restitution: B.19.187 Crist . . . yaf Piers pardon, and power . . . to assoille of alle manere synnes . . . In couenaunt þat þei come and kneweliche to paie To Piers pardon þe Plowman *redde quod debes* (C.21.187); B.19.193 (C.21.193); B.19.259

128

(C.21.259); B.19.390 (C.21.390); B.20.308 (C.22.308); cf. A.5.233 (B.5.461, C.6.316); A.5.241 (B.5.467, C.6.322). For a discussion of the central importance of the phrase in *Piers*, see J. A. Yunck, in Alford 1988, 149–52. NON DIMITTITUR, RESTITUCIOUN.

*REGISTRE   A. A record book: B.20.271 I wolde witterly þat ye [friars] were in þe Registre And youre noumbre vnder Notaries signe and neiþer mo ne lasse (C.22.271); B.5.272 I kan þee noȝt assoille Til þow make restitucion . . . And siþen þat Reson rolle it in þe Registre of heuene That þow hast maad ech man good. Fisher 26/12: 'We pray yow spekeþ vnto þarchebisshop of Canterbury þat . . . þe saide dymes and quinȝimes be entered in his Registre'; *Bor. Cust.* 1:308: 'Afore the same tenement they shall dryve a stake be the syght of neyghbours in warnyng of the tenaunte [owing back rent], and the day shalbe entred in the register'; *Cov. Leet* 33: '[The mayor and council agreed] þat all good ordynaunce of the leetys be sought up and wryton in a regestre, that they may be of record foreuermore.' B. A written chronology: C.11.276 Y . . . haue yrad registres and bokes And fonde y neuere . . . That clergie of Cristes mouthe comaunded was euere.

*REGISTRER   One who keeps a register; *specif.* the clerk of an ecclesiastical court, in charge of records, citations, receipts, etc.: B.2.174 Erchedekenes and Officials and alle youre Registrers, Lat sadle hem wiþ siluer oure synne to suffre, As deuoutrye and diuorses and derne vsurie; B.19.259 I make Piers þe Plowman my procuratour . . . And Registrer to receyue *redde quod debes* (C.21.259). Woodcock 38: 'If the efficiency of the courts depended on any one man, that man was the registrar. He determined the time and order of the hearing of cases; entered the *acta* of the court in the various registers; supervised the dispatch of citations, letters of suspension and excommunication, and directly controlled the activity of the apparitors [summoners]. He received the fees [cf. B.19.259 above], examined witnesses, and conducted inquisitions as ordered by the judge. A high standard of education and training was required for the efficient conduct of his office. He was of necessity a public notary. The registrar was the 'public person' and sufficient witness to the Acts of the court.' Cf. PROCURATOUR.

*REGRATER   A retailer who buys goods in order to sell them again at higher prices: C.3.118 Haue reuthe on this regraters . . . And soffre hem som tyme to selle aȝeyne þe lawe (A.3.79, B.3.90); C.3.113; A.5.140 (B.5.224, C.6.232). The term usually applies to retailers of victuals; e.g., 27 Edw. III c. 3 (1353): 'Les hostelers des herbergeries et autres Regraters de vitailles'; although regratery was perfectly legal (except for specified commodities like wool, certain kinds of fish, etc. [see 14 Rich. II c. 4]), it was subject to numerous regulations–e.g., *Lib. Alb.* 46, 271, 272, 275, 314, 353, 527, 657, 680, 689, 690, 693, 696, 700, 715.

*REGRATERIE   Retail selling, esp. of victuals (often at inflated prices):
A.3.72 Breweris & bakeris, bocheris & cokes . . . most harm werchiþ To þe
pore peple þat parcelmel biggen, For þei poisone þe peple preuyly wel ofte,
And richen þoruȝ regratrie (B.3.83, C.3.82). *Cov.Leet* 29: 'Allso we com-
maund þat no maner of fresche fysher by, ne take up, no maner of fresche
fysche of men of the contrey by way of regratry; þat is to witt, for to by hit of
men of the contrey, and aftur to sell hit agayn to hur neyghbures.'

REHERSEN   To recite aloud (a plea, list of charges, court record, etc.);
RECORDEN: B.7.196 What þow didest day by day þe doom wole reherce
(C.9.343); B.7.205 God gyue vs grace . . . That, after oure deeþ day, dowel
reherce At þe day of dome we dide as he hiȝte (A.8.183, C.9.352); C.4.150
Mede in the mot-halle tho on men of lawe gan winke In signe þat thei sholde
with som sotil speche Reherce ther anon ryhte þat myhte Resoun stoppe;
A.4.134; A.5.43 (B.5.60, C.6.1); C.12.34. *SGGK* 392: 'Sir Gawan . . . þou
hatz redily rehersed, bi resoun ful trwe, Clanly al þe couenaunt.' Cf. Reynes
144/16: 'Of how many articules ȝe schulne soth seyn þat here schall be put to
ȝow bytwyxe partye and partye . . . weche ple schal be rehersyd aforn ȝow.'
Eyre: 'Then the parties came, and Passeley rehearsed [rehersa] the plea' (90);
'Stanton, J[ustice] rehearsed all this process [reherca tut ceo proces]' (33);
K.Counc.: 'And the said John appeared in the said chancery at Westminster
. . ., the aforesaid process having been read and rehearsed [recitato] before
John himself' (38).

REKENEN   I. To make an accounting; to render an account (of one's stew-
ardship, deeds, etc.); to settle accounts (with somebody): C.11.300 Selde
falleth þe seruant so depe in arrerage As doth the reue or contrerollor þat
rykene moet and acounten; B.5.271 I kan þee noȝt assoille Til þow make
restitucion . . . and rekene wiþ hem alle; A.2.96 (Sk.); C.13.34; B.14.106
(C.15.283); B.14.211 (C.16.53). **TELLEN.**
   II. 'To reckon with,' to call to account: B.4.177 Ac Reson shal rekene wiþ
yow . . . And deme yow, bi þis day, as ye han deserued (C.4.171); B.11.131
(C.12.64).

REKENING   An accounting: B.5.420 I kan holde louedayes and here a Reues
rekenyng, Ac in Canoun nor in decretals I kan noȝt rede a lyne; B.5.427 Ruþe
is to here rekenyng whan we shul rede acountes (C.7.40); B.5.293 At þe heiȝe
dome . . . man shal yeue a rekenyng (C.6.348); B.14.108. Cf. *D&P* 2:249/19:
'At þe doom, God schal askyn of us rekenyng & answer of þe benefycis þat we
han takyn of hym.'

*RELACIOUN   A connection, correspondence, or association between
things, relationship; also, in law, the action of relating or narrating (an
account, plea, report, etc.): C.3.343 Relacoun rect . . . is a record of treuthe;
C.3.373 Relacoun rect is a ryhtful custume; C.3.387 As relacoynes indirect
reccheth thei [inparfit peple] neuere Of the cours of case so thei cache suluer;
C.3.332, 341, 360. Cf. 'A Dramatic Monologue by Law' (Robbins 114/38):

'To Israel [God] made playne relacioun, That the saide lawe, hadde in memory, Shuld gyde theym into eterne glory!' See also Fisher 163/65: Plaintiff prays for a copy of his bill and his adversaries' replications so that he can 'make trewe relacion vnto the kyng of her replicacions' (1414); *Cov. Leet*: 'And to mak true relacion to hym how many panyers . . . the forsaid fischers bryng in-to hur Innes ther hoost schal-be sworne to the maiour' (33); 'Ordinatum est . . . þat the comen sergeant goo aboute & serche euery weke þe forsaid Ryuer & make relacion to þe maiour of euery man þat is fond giltye' (91); 'fforalsomoche as hit was notiffied & Relacion made vnto þe maire . . .' (203), etc. Although the *OED* gives 1632 as the earliest instance of the word in a legal sense, the citations above date such usage to at least the first quarter of the fifteenth century. L's use of the word in a context saturated in legal terminology also suggests a play on its legal as well as grammatical meaning (cf. esp. the phrase, cited above, 'to make a true relation').

RELES AND REMISSIOUN   Release from an obligation; *fig.* forgiveness or remission of sin: A.7.82 He shal haue my soule . . . And defende it fro þe fend . . . Til I come to his acountes . . . To haue reles & remissioun (B.6.90, C.8.99). To 'remit and release' [remisisse et relaxasse] is the crucial phrase in deeds of release and quitclaim (Reynes 117/226, 117/238); the phrase appears also as a formula in pardons, 'perdonavimus, remisimus et relaxavimus' (Hall 71, 108).

RELESEN   To remit a debt or obligation; *fig.* to forgive (a sin): B.3.58 Lecherie . . . is synne of þe seuene sonnest relessed (C.3.62). Cf. Brown XIV 178/31: 'And haue relese of all trespace'; Fisher 164/31: 'I seled hem a Relees of all the wrong.'

REMISSIOUN   Release from a debt, duty, or obligation; *fig.* forgiveness of sin: A.11.285 A robbere hadde remission . . . Wiþoute penaunce of purcatorie to haue paradis for euere; C.3.357 Remissioun to haue, Of oure sory synnes; A.7.82 (B.6.90, C.8.99). RELES AND REMISSIOUN.

REMENAUNT   **A.** That which remains of an estate after all charges, debts, and bequests have been paid: B.20.292 Sisours and executours . . . shul ȝyue þe freres A parcel to preye for hem and pleye wiþ þe remenaunt (C.22.292). RESIDUE AND REMENAUNT. **B.** The balance remaining to be paid on a debt: B.17.242 And if it suffise noȝt for assetȝ . . . Mercy for his mekenesse wol maken good þe remenaunt (C.19.203). Cf. Fisher 222/10: 'She . . . paied of the dettes of hur seid late (husbondes) the summe of .xliiij. li and more and entendid to haue content the remenaunt not content.'

RENEIEN   To renounce or abjure (one's lord, faith, etc.): B.11.125–30 For þouȝ a cristen man coueited his cristendom to reneye, Riȝtfully to reneye no reson it wolde . . . Ac he may renne in arerage and rome fro home, As a reneyed caytif recchelesly rennen aboute (C.12.58–63). For writs issued against fugitive servants in arrerage, see *Writs* 70, 209. L's image fuses the secular and religious. Cf. *Myrour* 139/5: 'Reneyeng of þe lawe of Crist is when a man leueþ þe lawe of cristen men and turneþ to þe lawe of Saresynes, Iewes or eny oþer secte' (cf. *Jac. Well* 131/31). See also *Mirror* 59–60. The notion of irrevocable allegiance ('riȝtfully to reneye no reson it wolde') is elaborated in Blackstone: 'For it is a principle of universal law, that the natural-born subject of one prince cannot by any act of his own, no, not by swearing allegiance to another, put off or discharge his natural allegiance to the former' (1:358). DEFIEN; see also ARRERAGE, LEIAUNCE.

*RENTAL   A list or register of the rents due by tenants to a proprietor; a rent-roll (AF *rental*); *fig*. a record of sins on which payment (penance) is due: A.7.82 He shal haue my soule . . . And defende it fro þe fend . . . Til I come to his acountes . . . To haue reles & remissioun, on þat rental I leue (B.6.90, C.8.99). H. S. Bennett 154: 'The rental is a document, sometimes called an 'extent' – it set out in the greatest detail exactly what was to be demanded of every single landowner in the coffer.' Cf. *Jac. Well* 41: 'Ȝif a styward fynde in þe old court-rollys & rentallys, & in þe newe bothe, þat þou art behynde of þi rente to þi lord for þi tenement, and þou seyst þat þou wylt noȝt payin it, because þou vsedyst noȝt to paye before þat tyme; schal þin euyl vsage excuse þe, & proue fals þat is wretin in þe court-rollys & rentallys? I trowe nay. þou schalt paye it, or be put out of þi tenement. Ryȝt so, ihesu, þe styward of þe fadyr of heuen, whanne he sytteth in þe last court of þe doom, ȝif he fynde þe in þe old lawe, & newe, þat þou art behynde of þi tythe, schal þin euyl vsage excuse þe for to dystroye goddys lawe?' REGISTRE, ROLLE.

*RENTEN   To endow (somebody) with income property; *yrented*, possessed of property yielding income: A.8.35 Treuþe . . . bad hem . . . Releue religioun & renten hem betere (B.7.33, C.9.36); C.10.263 Late here be knowe For riche or yrented wel . . . Ther ne is squier ne knyhte . . . That ne wol . . . wedden here for here welthe. DOWEN.

RENTE   I. Income from property; also property that yields income: A.3.72 Breweris & bakeris, bocheris & cokes . . . richen þoruȝ regratrie & rentis hem biggen (B.3.83, C.3.82); C.3.322 That kyng . . . hem gaf catel oþer rente; C.5.73 Lordes sones . . . leyde here rentes to wedde; B.15.321 If lewed men knewe þis latyn þei wolde loke . . . Er þei amortisede to monkes or monyales hir rentes; B.15.558 Costantyn of curteisie holy kirke dowed Wiþ londes and ledes, lordshipes and rentes (C.17.221); A.11.15 (B.10.15); A.11.228 (B.10.340); B.13.233a (K-D, p.223); C.14.184; B.14.231 (C.16.73); B.15.176–77 (C.16.314–15). Cf. *D&P* 1:317/22: 'Religious . . . schewen wel þat al her besynesse is . . . to beggyn of lordis & ladyys & of oþer men londys and rentis'; Wright 230: Bailiffs or sheriffs' clerks, starting out poor, soon begin 'to buy lands and tenements and . . . rents [terras et domos emere, et redditus].' Blackstone 2:41: 'Rents are [a] species of incorporeal hereditaments. The word, rent, or render, *reditus*, signifies a compensation, or return . . . . It is defined to be a certain profit issuing yearly out of lands and tenements corporeal.'

II. A payment made periodically by a tenant to a landlord: C.9.73 Most neden aren oure neyhebores ... Charged with childrene and chief lordes rente; Pat they with spynnyng may spare, spenen hit on hous-huyre.

RERAGE   See ARRERAGE

RESIDUE   *The remainder of a dead man's estate after all debts and obligations have been discharged (see RESIDUE AND REMENAUNT): C.12.215 An unredy reue thy residue shal spene; B.20.290 (Sk.). Statute 9 Hen. III c. 18 (Magna Carta): 'If anyone holding of us a lay fee should die ... [in debt to the crown], nothing [of his goods] shall be taken away, until the debt owed to us has been paid, and the residue [residuum] shall remain to the executors to perform the testament of the dead.'

*RESIDUE AND REMENAUNT   That which remains of an estate after all charges, debts, and bequests have been paid: B.20.290 (Sk.) Sysours and excecutours thei wil ȝyue the freres A parcel to preye for hem and make hem-self myrye With the residue and the remenaunt; A.7.92 My wyf shal haue of þat I wan ... And dele among my frendis & my dere children ... And wiþ þe residue & þe remenaunt ... I wile worsshipe þerewiþ treuþe (B.6.100, C.8.109); A.5.231 (B.5.459). Normally the personal estate of a dead man, after all debts had been paid, was divided into thirds: a third for the widow, a third for the children, and a third for the dead man himself, to pay for alms, commemorative services, overdue tithes, etc. (see *Fleta* 2.57). The 'residue and remnant' referred to in the above examples is identified by Bennett as 'the dead's part' (203). For a full discussion of the disbursement of property in medieval wills, see Sheehan. REMENAUNT, RESIDUE, TESTAMENT, WILLE.

RESONABLE   Right, in accordance with law and RESOUN; having the quality of MESURE, proportion, justice: C.3.366 And þat is nat resonable ne rect to refuse my syre name; C.6.33 Me wilnynge þat men wente y were, as in auer, Ryche and resonable and ryhtful of lyuynge; B.13.285 Was noon swich as hymself ... Yhabited as an heremyte, an ordre by hymselue, Religion saunȝ rule and resonable obedience. Cf. *K.Counc.*: 'The suit ... is not reasonable [resonable] and is against the said statute' (60); 'It semeth to the kyng and his wise Counsaille that the patent be laweful and resonable' (92). See UNRESONABLE.

RESONABLE ACCOUNT   A formula in writs of account, 'to render a *racionabilem compotum*' (i.e., an orderly and accurate account): C.13.34 A marchant and mesager ... bothe mosten ... rikene byfore resoun a resonable acounte. *Fleta* 2.70 discusses the writ and the process. For examples see *Writs* 208: 'We command you to justice the merchant B. that justly etc. he render to the merchant A. his reasonable account for the time when he was receiver of the monies of the said A ...' (also 96, 204, 209, etc.); *LawMerch.* 2:lxxviii: 'The King to the Sheriff, greeting. Order John son of William of N. that justly, etc., he render to Ernald of N. his reasonable account of the time that he was his bailiff . . .' (also 2:lxxx). Cf. *Yrbk.Edw.III* 407: 'leal acompte.'

RESONEN   See ARESOUNEN

RESOUN   **I.** Law, equity, justice: **A.** As the principle of right or right order: B.17.307 Ac it is but selden yseiȝe . . . Any creature . . . Be raunsoned for his repentaunce þer alle reson hym dampneþ (C.19.282); B.18.339 Þe olde lawe graunteth That gilours be begiled and þat is good reson; B.14.109 Þe poore dar plede and preue by pure reson To haue allowaunce of his lord; by þe lawe he it cleymeþ (C.15.287, cf. C.16.100 Alle pore þat pacient is of puyr rihte may claymen Aftur here endynge here heuene-ryche blisse); B.4.153 Men of lawe . . . lope to hire [Mede] and lefte Reson (cf. Wright 225 on judges who for the sake of mede *cedunt a ratione*); B.10.347; C.11.100; B.11.126 (C.12.59); C.17.69; C.20.308. The identification of reason and justice reflects the basic premise of natural law theory – that the rules governing human conduct should be in conformity with the natural order. Reason is the name given both to that order [Lat. *ratio*] and to the faculty that apprehends it. The identification is commonplace; e.g., *Yrbk.Edw.III* 379: 'Hillary: [La ley est] volunte des Justices. Stonore: Nanyl; ley est resoun.' For a full discussion of L's use of the word, see Alford, 'The Idea of Reason in *Piers Plowman*,' *Medieval English Studies Presented to George Kane*, ed. by Donald Kennedy, R. A. Waldron, and Joseph S. Wittig (Cambridge: D. S. Brewer, 1988), 199–215. **B.** As personification: (1) A judge, steward, reeve, etc.: B.4.177 Ac Reson shal rekene wiþ yow . . . And deme yow . . . as ye han deserued (C.4.171); C.13.34 A marchant and mesager . . . moste . . . rikene byfore resoun a resonable acounte; A.4.95 (B.4.108, C.4.103); A.4.99 (B.4.112, C.4.107); A.4.145 (B.4.172); B.5.272; B.11.131 (C.12.64); B.18.330 (C.20.373). The recurring combination of 'reason' and 'reckon' is a pun; see *MED* 'resoun' 6(a): 'an account, a reckoning' (cf. C.9.274 *Redde racionem villicacionis*; Edler, *ragione*, 'account'). Brown XIV 97/26: 'Rekken þou mon, & ȝelde reson of thyng þat þou here thoght.' (2) 'Reason and Conscience': B.4.171 The kyng callede Conscience and afterward Reson (C.4.166); A.4.5 (B.4.5, C.4.5); A.4.7–11 (B.4.7–11, C.4.7–11); C.4.184–87. The words 'reason' and 'conscience' are associated in the early history of the chancery court, which came into being as an equitable alternative to the rigour of the common law. 'The mere fact, however, that the common law provided no remedy for a particular case was not in itself enough to induce the chancellor to intervene. Something else must exist. And so we find that a petitioner always bases his claim for relief on a principle, ordinarily expressed by two words, "reason and conscience" ' (Barbour 155); e.g., Fisher 197/28: 'Wherfore the seid suppliant bisecheth your gracious ffadorhode of remedie aftor reson & conscience'. The best discussion of the principle is St. German's dialogue *Doctor and Student*. See also Baldwin 42. **C.** In phrases: (1) RIGHT AND RESOUN. (2) 'Against reason,' against the law or fair play, unjust: B.3.92 [Mede besought the mayor to permit regrators] to selle somdel ayeins reson (A.3.81; C.3.120 aȝeyne þe lawe); B.18.334 Wiþ gile þow hem gete ageyn alle reson

134

(C.20.377); C.3.445 (A.3.268, B.3.393 ayein his wille); B.18.199 (C.20.204). In their oath of office, the King's Justices swore to sanction nothing 'countre reson et countre les leis de la terre' (Hall 1:134). Mede's request in B.3.92 is, more specifically, that the mayor allow regrators to sell 'against the assize' (*contra assisam vendiderunt*, Statute 51 Hen. III st. 6); see LAWE (V.C).

II. That which is within reason; MESURE, moderation: B.11.335 Reson I seiʒ sooþly sewen alle beestes, In etynge, in drynkynge and in engendryge of kynde (C.13.142); B.11.370 Reson rewarded and ruled alle beestes Saue man and his make (C.13.179); C.6.435 Y . . . fedde me with ale Out of resoun; A.1.25 (B.1.25); B.2.85 (C.2.89); B.5.36; C.13.153. As a principle that rules 'alle beestes save man,' *resoun* cannot possibly signify, except in an ironic sense, the faculty of reason; it is more the quality of reasonableness, of acting in accordance with nature. 'Reason' and 'nature' are often paired; e.g., *D&P* 1:86: 'a synne al aʒens resoun and aʒens kende.'

III. A ground or cause (for doing something); also a speech putting forth a ground or cause (such as an accusation, argument, advice): B.2.49 Lat hem worþe til leaute be Iustice And haue power to punysshe hem; þanne put forþ þi reson (C.2.50); C.16.144 Lordes alloueth hym [the poor man] litel or leggeth ere to his resoun (B.14.311); B.Prol.175 (C.Prol.190); A.11.41 (B.10.55, C.11.38); ?B.17.258. The phrase 'put forþ þi reson' reflects the language of procedure; e.g., *K.Counc.* 27: The defendants 'were charged and put to answer [ad racionem positi] before the king.' See also Statute 20 Edw. I st. 2: 'per diversas rationes asserentibus'; *Eyre* 89: 'Kelshall rehearsed the arguments [resouns] etc. as above' (repeated in *Nov.Narr.* 343). Acording to a well-known etymology, from Isidore of Seville: 'Oratio dicta quasi oris ratio.' Middle English grammatical treatises actually translate *pars orationis* as 'part of reason' (Alford 1982, 739–40).

*RESTITUEN   To restore property to a former owner, repay, make reparations: B.5.275 For al þat haþ of þi good . . . Is holden at þe heiʒe doom to helpe þee to restitue (C.6.299); B.5.289 If þow wite neuere to whom ne where to restitue Ber it to þe Bisshop (C.6.344); C.10.54; C.12.17. Cf. *K.Counc.* 72: 'The aforesaid manor with appurtenances . . . restored [restitui] and delivered to the said William Clopton.' RESTITUCIOUN.

RESTITUCIOUN   The restoration of ill-gotten money, goods, lands, etc. to the former or rightful owner; the making of amends for a sin, crime, debt, injury, etc.: B.5.271 I kan þee noʒt assoille Til þow make restitucion (C.6.297); B.5.230, 233, 235 (C.6.234, 237); B.17.239 (C.19.200); B.17.319 (C.19.294). A crucial concept in *Piers* and penitential theology: a sin cannot be forgiven until the penitent has made, or earnestly willed to make, restitution. Cf. *Jac.Well* 17/22: 'And þey may noʒt ben assoyled, tyl þei haue made restitucyoun.' *NON DIMITTITUR PECCATUM, REDDE QUOD DEBES.*

REVE   The manorial officer responsible for managing the lord's demesne farm, accounting for the yearly income and expenditures of the manor and representing the interests of the serfs; also, a steward, bailiff, an overseer

(*MED*): C.11.300 Selde falleth þe seruant so depe in arrerage As doth the reue or contrerollor þat rykene moet and acounten Of al þat they haen had of hym þat is here maister (B.10.477); B.19.460 I holde it riȝt and reson of my Reue to take Al þat myn Auditour or ellis my Styward Counseilleþ me bi hir acounte and my clerkes writynge (C.21.460); A.2.75 (B.2.111, C.2.112); C.2.180; C.3.308; B.5.420 (C.7.33); B.10.477; C.12.215; B.19.258. The office of reeve (*praepositus*) was sometimes combined with that of bailiff; normally reeves were elected by the other villeins, but bailiffs were appointed by the lord. For a reeve's duties, see *Fleta* 2.76; for his oath, *Court Baron* 103; for gen. discussion, H. S. Bennett 166–77. RIPEREVE.

REVEN To rob (sb. of sth.), to deprive or take away (cf. mod. *bereft*): C.16.1 Allas! þat rychesse shal reue and robbe mannes soule (B.14.132); C.18.122 Go ransake þat ragman and reue hym of his apples (B.16.89); C.3.326 As sone as god seyh a sewed nat his wille A refte hym of his richesse and of his ryhte mynde; C.4.180; C.20.299. DESPOILEN, PILEN, RAVISHEN, ROBBEN.

REVEN OF RIGHT To deprive (someone) of his right: C.20.308 Sethe he is a lele lord . . . he wol nat Reuen vs of oure riht; C.3.326 (above). Cf. Brown XIV 133/76: 'What cause þou demest, loke hit be cler, And reue no mon from him his riht.'

REVER A robber: C.13.57 The marchaunt . . . dredeth to be ded þer-fore and he in derke mette With robbares and reuares þat ryche men despoilen; B.14.182 *Conuertimini ad me & salui eritis*. Thus . . . Iesu crist seide To robberis and to Reueris. The alliteration of 'robber' and 'rever' is common; see C.16.1 (quoted under REVEN), B.16.89, and *MED* 'robber.' PILOUR, THEF.

REVES ROLLES The reeve's annual account of manorial receipts and expenditures: B.19.463 I holde it riȝt and reson of my Reue to take Al þat myn Auditour or ellis my Styward Counseilleþ me bi hir acounte and my clerkes writynge. Wiþ *Spiritus Intellectus* þei toke þe reues rolles (C.21.463). Skeat 2:274, quoting Whitaker: 'These Reeve-Rolls . . . consisted, for one year, of several sheets stitched together, and contained very curious and minute details of all the receipts and expenses of these officers.' ROLLE.

RIFLEN To rob (sb.); ransack or rifle (bags); ROBBEN: C.4.54 Wrong . . . aspyeth To robbe me or to ruyfle me yf y ryde softe; B.5.232 'Repentedestow euere,' quod Repentaunce, 'or restitucion madest?' 'Ȝis, ones I was yherberwed . . . wiþ an heep of chapmen; I roos whan þei were areste and riflede hire males' (C.6.236); B.5.235; C.10.194; B.17.102 (C.19.90). Pearsall 119 n. explains Coveitise's answer above as a deliberate confusion of *restitucion* and *areste*. However, the pun may lie instead, or in addition, on the word *riflen*, derived from French *rifler* ('I wende riflynge were restitucion . . . And I kan no frenssh') but confused by Coveitise, who spent his youth 'among lumbardes,' with Italian *rifare*, 'to restore, rebate, make amends' (cf. Edler).

RIFLERE A robber: C.6.316 Robert the ruyflare on *reddite* lokede; C.4.125 Alle Rome-rennares for ruyflares in France To bere no seluer ouer see þat sygne of kyng sheweth [an allusion to the papal court at Avignon] (A.4.111, B.4.128). PIKER, ROBBER.

RIGHT I. Interest or TITLE in an object or property; a just or legally enforceable claim; a right or privilege: B.10.347 [The patient poor] han Eritage in heuene, and by trewe riȝte, Ther riche men no riȝt may cleyme; C.16.100 Alle pore þat pacient is of puyr rihte may claymen Aftur here endynge here heuene-ryche blisse (B.14.260); C.17.69 Y dar nat carpe of clerkes now þat Cristes tresor kepe That pore peple by puyre riht here part myhte aske; B.18.277 If he reue me my riȝt he robbeþ me by maistrie (C.20.299); C.3.367 Y am his sone and . . . sewe for his ryhte (B.18.37); C.8.53; B.18.36 (C.20.36); C.20.308; C.20.371; B.18.278 (C.20.300); B.20.96 (C.22.96). *To claim as one's right*: 'clamat esse ius' (*Writs* 294), 'cleime cum son dreit' (*Court Baron* 62); *to sue for one's right*: 'pursuer lour droit' (*K. Counc.* 88), 'I . . . haue come to the kynges presence to pursue my right' (Fisher 163/51).

II. The virtue or power of justice; that which is right, law, truth: C.20.439 My rihtwysnesse and rihte shal regnen in helle, And mercy al mankynde bifore me in heuene (B.18.396); C.5.74; C.11.27; B.19.90 (C.21.90). EQUITE, JUSTICE, RIGHT AND RESOUN, TREUTHE.

RIGHT AND RESOUN Justice, equity, law; see RESOUN: C.3.293 [To pay] bifore þe doynge . . . is nother resoun ne ryhte ne in no rewme lawe; B.19.460 I holde it riȝt and reson of my Reue to take Al þat myn Auditour . . . Counseilleþ me (C.21.460); B.3.239; C.3.366; C.11.29; B.12.209 (C.14.148); B.15.550 (C.17.213); C.19.3; B.18.278 (C.20.300); B.18.330 (C.20.373); B.18.349 (C.20.395); B.19.83 (C.21.83); B.19.88 (C.21.88). Statute 1 Edw. III st. 2 c. 15: 'contre droit & reson.' The phrase is esp. associated with equitable law; e.g., *Chanc.*: 'Thomas . . . as right and reason demand, took the said Maude to wife' (44); 'Thomas Stones . . . hath disseised them . . . forcibly and without any right or reason or process of law' (82); 'The said Walter is so great in that country that no one can have right or reason against him' (127); Fisher 84/6, 164/34.

RIGHT OF THE REAUME The justifiable claims of the realm to property or authority; *gen.* justice: C.5.74 For the ryhte of this reume [they] ryden aȝeyn oure enemyes; B.15.525.

RIGHTWISNESSE A. Justice, esp. the principle or action of strict adherence to the law: B.17.319 Ac er his rightwisnesse to ruþe torne som restitucion bihoueþ (C.19.294); C.20.431 Y may do mercy of my rihtwysnesse (B.18.389); B.17.304 (C.19.279); C.20.189; B.18.396 (C.20.439); B.19.83 (C.21.88). Fisher 163/30: 'I am of no power to pursue these materes in any other Court saue in this heye Court of rightwisnesse [Parliament] where as most truste and hope to haue rightwisnesse and lawe rather than I shulde in

137

ony other Court.' LAWE, JUSTICE, RIGHT. **B.** One of the four daughters of God (based on Ps. 84:11): B.18.165 Rightwisnesse . . . woot moore þan we [Truth, Mercy]; heo was er we boþe (C.20.168); etc.

*RIPEREVE   A harvest overseer (*OED*); one who protects the lord's harvest from trespassers: C.5.15 Can thow . . . Mowen or mywen or make bond to sheues, Repe or been a rypereue and aryse erly. *Court Baron* 123: 'Geoffrey Knight, who was the reaping-reeve [qui fuit Ripereue], at harvest time took from diverse trespassers the gleanings wrongfully acquired by them.'

ROBBEN   To take from (another person) against his will: A.3.182 Wiþoute pite, pilour, pore men þou robbedest, And bar here bras on þi bak to caleis to selle (B.3.195); C.4.54; C.9.180; C.10.194; C.11.21; B.11.268 (C.12.150); C.13.1; B.14.305 (C.16.139); B.16.89; B.17.92; B.17.102; B.18.277 (C.20.299); B.18.338; B.19.444 (C.21.444). *Mirror* 178: 'There is no difference between taking what is another's against his will and robbery'; for the correct form of an appeal of robbery, see *Fleta* 1.37. FECCHEN, REVEN, STELEN.

ROBBER   One who robs; also, a thief or plunderer: C.13.57 The marchaunt . . . dredeth to be ded . . . and he in derke mette With robbares and reuares þat ryche men despoilen; A.4.111 (B.4.128); A.5.233 (B.5.461); B.5.233; B.5.467; A.11.285 (B.10.426, C.11.261); C.12.246. CUTTEPURS, PIKE-PORSE, PILOUR, REVER, THEF.

ROBERT   The personal name Robert, as a designation for a robber, vagabond, or lowly person (*MED*): A.5.233 Robert þe robbour on *reddite* lokide (B.5.461, C.6.316); A.5.241 So rewe on þis robert þat *reddere* ne hauiþ (B.5.467, C.6.322); A.Prol.44 (B.Prol.44, C.Prol.45); A.7.65 (B.6.73, C.8.75); B.6.148. See Wright, 'A Song on the Times': 'Competenter per *Robert, robbur* designatur' (49); and also the explanation given by a twelfth-century scribe for the name of one of his brothers (354): 'Secundus dicebatur Robertus, quia a re nomen habuit, spoliator enim diu fuit et praedo.' Cf. 'Roberdes men' as used in statutes 5 Edw. III c. 14 and 7 Ric. II c. 5 (quoted under LACCHEDRAWERE).

ROLLE   A scroll containing documents and records of various sorts; an account roll; a register of names (guild members, God's elect, etc.): C.3.111 Forthy mayres þat maketh fre men, me thynketh þat ȝe ouhten For to spyre and to aspye . . . Ar he were vnderfonge fre and felawe in ȝoure rolles; B.19.463 (C.21.463). *Writs* 212–13: 'And make known to the aforesaid B. that he should be there then with the rolls and tallies [cum rotulis et talliis] by which the aforesaid A. previously rendered his aforesaid account'; *Mirror* 108: 'He is not bound to account . . . for that the plaintiff is seised of the tallies and rolls [des tailles e des roulles].' RENTAL, REVES ROLLES, REGISTRE.

*ROLLEN   To record (a deed, title, action, payment, etc.) in an official roll or register: B.5.272 I kan þee noȝt assoille Til þow make restitucion ... and rekene wiþ hem alle; And siþen þat Reson rolle it in þe Registre of heuene. *Writs* 200: 'We ... command you to cause our aforesaid charter to be enrolled [irrotulari] without delay on the rolls of our said exchequer.'

ROME RENNERE   One who seeks a benefice, privilege, etc., at Rome; also, an agent at the papal court (*MED*): A.4.111 Rede me not ... no reuþe to haue Til ... alle rome renneris, for robberis of beȝonde, Bere no siluer ouer se þat signe of king shewiþ ... But it be marchaunt ... Oþer prouisour (B.4.128, C.4.125). L's distinction between 'Rome renneris' and 'provisours' is explained by Bennett: 'A *prouysoure* would go to receive benefices or offices already given' (148). On the subject of papal provisions generally see Pantin 47–75. PROVISOUR.

S

SALARIE   A fixed payment made periodically to a person as compensation for regular service; also, any wage for a specific task: C.7.39 Thus haue y tened trewe men ... And my seruauntes som-tyme here salerie is bihynde (B.5.426); B.14.142 Riȝt as a seruaunt takeþ his salarie bifore, & siþþe wolde clayme moore. Cf. *RR* 4.47: 'We beth seruantis and sallere ffongen.' Early instances of the word (only one earlier than *Piers*) echo the opening of the Statute of Labourers: 'Whereas etc., ... it was ordained [that labourers ...] should be bound to serve, receiving the salaries and wages [salaries et gages] customary in the places they are bound to serve.'

SAVEN   *Fig.* to redeem (a prisoner) by mainprise or payment of a fine or ransom: B.18.183 Loue ... lettres me sente That mercy ... and I mankynde sholde saue [and ...] be mannes meynpernour for eueremoore after (C.20.186); B.18.328 Oure lord ... seide to Sathan, 'lo! here my soule to amendes For alle synfulle soules, to saue þo þat ben worþi.' Here L revitalizes a theological term by restoring its literal meaning in the law. Prisoners freed by ransom were saved or 'redeemed'; those denied the possibility were said to be 'without redemption or grace' (see RAUNSOUN).

SAVEN RIGHT   To protect or safeguard a right against other claims: C.20.371 'Lo! me here,' quod oure lord, 'lyf and soule bothe, For alle synfole soules to saue oure bothe rihte.' Pearsall comments: ' "to preserve the right of both of us," i.e. to honour the just claim on all sinful souls of both Christ and Satan.' A 'saving clause' was routinely added to decrees, statutes, etc. *Mirror* 143: 'As to false justices ... they should first be adjudged to make satisfaction to the injured, and ... the remnant of their goods should be forfeited to the king, with a saving for the rights and debts of others [sauve autriz droiz e dettes]';

Statute 25 Edw. III st. 4: 'sauvant totefoitz a nostre Seignur le Roi & as autres Seignurs lour aunciene droit'; 5 Ric. II c. 14: 'toutdys le droit le Roi salvez'; *Court Baron* 47: 'sauue le dreyt le seignur en tutes choses'; *K.Counc.* 22: 'cuiuslibet iure salvo.'

SCIANT PRESENTES & FUTURI &C. 'Be it known to all present and to come,' the standard opening of a deed or charter of conveyance: B.2.74a Symonye and Cyuylle stonden forþ boþe And vnfoldeþ þe feffement that Fals hath ymaked. Thus bigynnen þe gomes and greden wel heiȝe: '*Sciant presentes & futuri &c.* Witeþ and witnesseþ þat wonieþ vpon erþe (C.2.78a). Cf. *Abbey of H.G.* 338: 'Here begynniþ þe forseyd chartre. *Sciant presentes & futuri &c.*: Wetiþ ȝe þat ben now here, & þei þat schulen comen after ȝou.' *Cov.Leet* 1. For a detailed explanation of each part of a charter (like the one beginning at B.2.74a), see *Fleta* 3.14.

SCLAUNDRE **I.** False accusation: B.2.82 And Fauel . . . feffeþ by þis chartre To be Princes in pride . . . To bakbite and to bosten and bere fals witnesse, To scorne and to scolde and sclaundre to make (C.2.86). Cf. *Jac.Well* 34/33: 'And alle þo arn acursed þat . . . castyn ony fals cause, dyspyȝt or slaundre.' *Cov.Leet* 331: 'Imaginacions, sclaundours, or feyned accusacions.' FALS WITNESS.

II. Disgrace, dishonour: C.3.61 Ho may askape þe sclaundre, þe skathe myhte sone be mended (B.3.57); B.12.46. Statute 5 Edw. III c. 2 (Ruffhead): 'Purveyors for the King's house . . . have committed such outrages in slander [en esclaundre] of the King, the Queen and their children.' DISCLAUNDRE, FAME.

SECRET SELE See SELE (II)

SECTE **I.** The 'following' of a party involved in litigation, compurgators, 'the witness of law-abiding men' (*Fleta* 2.63); 'to lead a sect' (*sectam ducere*), to produce witnesses; hence, a legal suit. Possibly L puns on the word in B.5.490: But in oure secte was þe sorwe and þi sone it ladde. For the collocation *secte . . . ladde* (*sectam ducere*) see *LawMerch.* 1:9, 13, 18, 22; *Court Baron* 133; cf. Baird, *Chaucer Review* 6 (1971), 117–119. On *secta*, see P&M 2:606–10, and Holdsworth 1:301–05.

II. A retinue, company of followers (as of a lord); followers of a particular patron or belief, a sect (e.g., the Franciscans): C.6.38 Was non such as mysulue . . . Summe tyme in o sekte, summe tyme in another; In alle kyne couent contreuede how y myhte Be holden for holy; B.15.232 In a freres frokke [Charity] was yfounden ones . . . in Fraunceis tyme; In þat secte siþþe to selde haþ he ben knowe (C.16.354) (also in sense III.A); C.15.79; B.14.257 (C.16.97); C.16.293. Cf. *D&P* 1:284: 'Anticrist schal do men halwyn boþe Sonday & Satirday, Sonday for to drawyn cristene peple to his secte . . . and þe Satirday to drawyn þe Iewys to his secte.' Fisher 218/9: 'Iohn Newport and oþur of hus secte . . . [threatened] þe kinggis pepil.' Szittya 182: '*Secta*, says Wyclif, is from *sequi*. All Christians are one sect, because all follow Christ.' LORDSHIP (IV).

III. A. The distinctive dress of a following, livery; a suit of clothing: C.12.131 In þe parail of a pilgrime . . . ac neuere in secte of riche (B.11.245); B.14.259 God is [the poor man's] grettest help . . . And he his seruaunt . . . and of his sute boþe. And wheiþer he be or be nouȝt, he bereþ þe signe of pouerte And in þat secte oure saueour saued al mankynde (C.16.99); B.15.232 (C.16.354). The pun on meaning II is common; cf. *Lud.Cov.* 193/159–163 which admonishes: do not follow 'þe fowle sute of þe devyl' but 'clothe the in clennes.' At the Last Judgement the saved may say: 'Lorde, I haue on þi leueree and I am þi man' (Ross 19/30). **B.** *Fig.* the flesh: C.7.141 Of thy douhtiest dedes, [all] was don in oure sekte. *Verbum caro factum est*; B.5.490; B.5.487 (C.7.130); B.5.496 (C.7.137). See SUTE.

SECUTOUR   Aphetic form of EXECUTOUR: C.6.254 Shal neuere seketoure wel bysette the syluer þat thow hem leuest Ne thyn heyres; C.2.189; B.15.132 (C.16.277); B.15.248.

SEISEN   **I.** To enfeoff or put (sb.) in legal possession of (land, estate, goods, etc.); (in passive constructions) to have or be put in legal possession: A.2.66 In al þe signiure of slouþe I sese hem togidere; B.18.284 And siþen I was seised seuene þousand wynter I leeue þat lawe nyl noȝt lete hym þe leeste (C.20.309). Hall 2:71: '. . . quod omnes terras et tenementa de quibus prefatus David fuit seisitus in dominico suo'; Fisher 105: 'And that grond that is not chalenged with ynne the saide day limited we wol ye ordeine that hit be saised in to oure handes.' Blackstone 2:209. See Alford 1977 for a discussion of the devil's seisin (B.18.274). FEFFEN, GIVEN AND GRAUNTEN.
   II. To take possession (of land, goods, etc.): C.6.271 Y . . . ȝaf hem red þat repe To sese to me with here sikel þat y ne sewe neuere (B.13.374).

SELE   **I.** A device (e.g., a heraldic or emblematic design, a letter, word, or sentence) impressed on a piece of wax or other plastic material as evidence of authenticity or attestation; also, the piece of wax, etc. bearing this impressed device (leaden seals, *bullae*, were used by the popes – whence the name of the document itself) (*OED*): C.13.88 A trewe messager . . . sheweth be seel and scth by lettre with what lord he dwelleth; A.Prol.66 A pardoner . . . Brouȝte forþ a bulle wiþ bisshopis selis And seide þat hymself miȝte assoile hem alle (B.Prol.69, C.Prol.67); B.Prol.79 (C.Prol.77); A.2.107 (B.2.143, C.2.156); A.2.183 (B.2.224, C.2.231); B.13.248. Cf. *CT.Pard.Prol.* 336: 'Thanne my bulles shewe I . . . Oure lige lordes seel on my patente, That shewe I first, my body to warente, That no man be so boold . . . Me to destourbe of Cristes hooly werk.' SIGNE.
   II. 'Secret seal,' the king's privy seal; any personal signet: B.3.146 She may neiȝ as muche do in a Monþe ones As youre secret seel in sixe score dayes (A.3.135, C.3.182); B.7.23 Ac vnder his secret seel truþe sente hem [merchants] a lettre (A.8.25, C.9.27); C.9.138 ȝe sholde . . . helpen . . . lunatyk loreles and lepares aboute, For vnder godes secret seal here synnes ben keuered. As L implies in both B.7.23 and C.9.138, letters sent under the king's secret seal sometimes included special dispensations (cf. *Lib.Alb.* 372).

141

Sample documents under the privy seal are printed in Hall 1:91–121. In strict usage, 'secret' and 'privy' seals are different; see Chrimes, who gives a full account of the development of seals of government in L's day.

SELEN To authenticate (a charter, bull, instrument of measure) with an official mark or SELE: B.3.148 Sire Symonie and hirselue seleþ þe bulles (A.3.137, C.3.184); C.3.88 Thei fillen nat ful þat for lawe is seled; C.4.189 Y assente ... by so ... vnsittynge suffraunce ne sele ʒoure priue lettres. ASE-LEN, ENSELEN; cf. FALS MESURE, UNSELED.

SENATOUR A member of a governing body (e.g., parliament); an alderman: C.8.87 Maystres, as þe mayres ben, and grete menne, senatours, What þei comaunde as by þe kyng countreplede hit neuere. Cf. Usk 26/62: 'And trewly, lady ... me rought litel of any hate of the mighty senatours in thilke cite, ne of comunes malice.' *Lib.Alb.* 32: '"Aldermanni" per etymologiam nomine seniores dicti sunt. *Alde* enim Saxonice "senex," et *alder* "senior" est; et sic, quia in senioribus plus viget consilium, quod apud Romanos "Consul" vel "Senator" dicebatur, apud nos dicitur "Aldermannus."'

*SENESCHAL An official in the household of a lord, to whom the administration of justice and entire control of domestic arrangements were entrusted; a steward: C.Prol.93 Summe aren as seneschalles and seruen oþer lordes And ben in stede of stewardus and sitten and demen. See H. S. Bennett 157–61: 'At the head of the lord's officials stood the seneschal or steward. ... To him was committed the management of the agricultural exploitation of the land. ... Every year he summoned before him those underlings whom he had charged with the day by day conduct of the manor, and extracted from them, in the presence of the auditors, a detailed account. ... [He] was the dispenser of justice and presided over the [manorial] court in the place of his lord,' etc. STIWARD.

SERGEAUNT I. An officer whose duty is to enforce the judgements of a court; one charged with the arrest of offenders or the summoning of persons to court; a bailiff: B.2.209 þe kyng comaunded Constables and sergeauntʒ Fals-nesse and his felawship to fettren and to bynden; B.3.102 The kyng ... called after Mede And ... sergeauntʒ hire fette (A.3.91); C.3.78. BAILLIF, CON-STABLE.

II. A serjeant at law (Lat. *serviens ad legem*); a member of a superior order of barristers; a chief justice: B.3.295 Shal no sergeant for þat seruice were a silk howue, Ne no pelure in his panelon for pledynge at þe barre (A.3.270, C.3.447); A.Prol.85 (B.Prol.212, C.Prol.160); B.15.8. Cf. *CT.Prol.* 309: 'A sergeant of the lawe, war and wys, That often hadde been at the Parvys, Ther was also. ... Justice he was ful often in assise.' Statute 36 Edw. III c. 15: 'The people ... have no understanding of that which is said for them or against them by their serjeants [lour Sergeantz] and other pleaders.' In L's day, the serjeant at law was 'the prince of his profession' (Harding 174). Induction into the order required a minimum of 16 years' apprenticeship and the private wealth to maintain an appropriate style of living. From the rank of serjeants were chosen the justices of the Common Law courts. Fortescue devotes a chapter (*De laudibus*, chap. 50) to praise of their training, position, integrity, etc. Plucknett 220–224.

SERGEAUNT OF ARMES An officer (usually armed) in the service of the king, a bishop, nobleman, etc.: B.19.339 [Pride] sente forþ Surquidous, his sergeaunt of Armes (C.21.340). *K.Counc.* 37: 'A commission was issued to Thomas atte Ferye, serjeant at arms [seruienti ad arma] of the lord the king, to take the said William and bring him to the Tower of London there to stay in prison.' As the name of Pride's serjeant implies, these officers were not popular with the people. 'At the grievous complaint of the commons made . . . of the excessive and superfluous number of serjeants at arms, and of many great extortions and oppressions done by them to the people,' Statute 13 Ric. II c. 6 says, 'the King therefore wills that they all be discharged, and that of them and of others there be taken good and sufficient persons to the number of thirty without more from henceforth.'

SETTEN To endow or provide support for (someone); FINDEN: B.10.173 [Dame Studie says concerning Clergie:] I sette hym to Scole; B.7.32 [Truth commands that merchants] Sette Scolers to scole or to som kynnes craftes. Cf. Usk 50/44: 'Poore clerkes, for witte of schole, I sette in churches, and made suche persones to preche.' DOWEN.

SHAME See HARM AND SHAME

SHERREVE The chief law officer of the county, responsible for conducting preliminary investigations of accused persons, trying minor offences, and detaining greater offenders for the king's justices (*Oxf.Comp.*): B.3.135 Sherreues of Shires were shent if she [Mede] ne were (A.3.124, C.3.171); B.2.59 (C.2.59); A.2.128 (B.2.164); C.2.177; B.2.259; C.3.78. Blackstone 1:328–334 gives a brief history of the office. The oath of sheriffs is given in *Statutes* 1:247.

SHERREVES CLERK See CLERK

SHEWEN *I. To put up (a bill), lay (a complaint or 'tale') before the court: C.3.213 Pore men dar nat pleyne ne no pleynt shewe, Such a maister is Mede among men of gode; C.12.171 Mo prouerbes y myhte haue . . . To testifie for treuthe þe tale þat y shewe (see TALE). Cf. Usk 50/39: 'The law was set as it shuld; tofore the juge, as wel the poore durste shewe his greef as the riche, for al his money' ('to show grief' = to lodge a grievance); *RR* 4.47: 'We beth seruantis . . . y-sent ffro the shiris to shewe what hem greueth.' The word is the conventional opening of a petition or complaint; e.g., 'Monstravit nobis' (*Writs* 11, 23, 55, 200, 247, etc.), 'Ceo vous moustre' (*Nov.Narr.* 178, 179, 180, etc.); 'Sheweth your most humble liege man Iohn Carpenter . . .' (Fisher

181/2, 174/1, 140/1, etc.). *Eyre* 3: 'All bringing complaints . . . [are] to show all their plaints there [querimonias ostendendas] and to receive due amends according to the law and custom of our realm.' PLEINEN, SUEN.

II. To handle, administer, or declare (the law); '*to show law*: to plead (*for* a suitor)' (*OED* 23e): B.2.134 (Sk.) For-thi . . . ledeth hire to Londoun there lawe is yshewed (B.2.135 K-D yhandled, C.2.148 there lawe may declare); A.8.52 He þat spendiþ his speche & spekiþ for þe pore . . . coueitiþ nouȝt his goodis, Ac for oure lordis loue lawe hym shewiþ (B.7.50, C.9.49 declareth); A.4.145 (B.4.172); C.12.171. LEDEN.

III. To confess (one's sins): B.11.54 Go confesse þee to some frere and shewe hym þi synnes; A.5.147 Now begynneþ glotoun for to go to shrift, And cairiþ hym to kirkeward hise coupe to shewe (B.5.297, C.6.351); A.5.59 (B.5.76); B.5.143; B.5.237 (Sk.); B.5.366. KNOWEN.

Si 'If,' a technical word used in grants, deeds, contracts, etc. to indicate a condition: C.3.328 So god gyueth nothyng þat *si* ne is the glose. The Middle English 'Charters of Christ' make the same point (see Spalding 30). Deeds are distinguished as either simple or conditional (*Yrbk.Edw.II* 121), the latter usually characterized by the presence of the word *si*. Cf. *Fleta* 3.15: 'The word *ut* . . . denotes a mode, *si* a condition, *quia* a cause'; Bracton notes several common conditions (144). For a sample contract, see *LawMerch.* 1:80: 'ex condicione quod *si* . . .' (cf. B.19.477 'In condicion þat . . .').

SIGNE   **I.** An official mark or SELE: C.22.272 Forthy y wolde witterly þat ȝe were in registre And ȝoure nombre vnder notarie sygne (B.20.272); C.2.156 Til he hadde seluer for the seel and signes of notaries (A.2.107, B.2.143); A.2.78; A.4.112 (B.4.129, C.4.126). Cf. Skelton 273: 'Under a notary's sign'; *K.Counc.* 22: 'cum signis . . . notariorum' (22 n.: 'The sign of a notary was a design more or less complicated, more or less artistic, which was his distinctive mark and personal property').

II. The badge or livery worn by the retainers of a lord: B.14.258 He bereþ þe signe of pouerte And in þat secte oure saueour saued al mankynde (C.16.98). Cf. *RR* 2.19–35: 'What kynnes conceyll that the kyng had . . . meued him most to merke his liegis, Or serue hem with signes. . . . They . . . schewed her signes ffor men shulde drede To axe ony mendis ffor her mys-dedis. Thus leuerez ouere-loked ȝoure liegis ichone.'

SIGNIURE   Territory under the dominion of a lord, esp. a feudal domain (*OED*): A.2.66 In al þe signiure of slouþe I sese hem togidere; Þei to haue & to holde & here eires aftir. Not in B or C, the word seems to have been unfamiliar to many scribes; variants include segoury, synge, synnes, seruyse. *Moots* 208: 'He who has a seignory [seigniorie] . . . shall avow on each tenant,' etc. LORDSHIP, MANER, TOUN.

SIMONIE   The sale of a church office or benefice; the granting of any spiritual benefit (prayer, confession, mass, etc.) in exchange for money or other forms of payment: B.2.126 [Theology:] Symonye and þiself [Cyuyle] shenden holi chirche (A.2.90); C.9.55 Beth ywar, ȝe wis men and witty of þe lawe . . . That mede of mene men for her motynge taken. For hit is symonye to sulle þat sent is of grace. A.Prol.83 (B.Prol.86, C.Prol.84); A.2.35; B.2.63 (C.2.63); B.2.67 (C.2.67); A.2.53–54, 78, 106, 132, 136, 165 (B.2.71–72ff., C.2.71–72ff.); A.3.137 (B.3.148, C.3.184); B.20.126 (C.22.126); B.20.137 (C.22.137). *Jac.Well* 126–27 lists six kinds of simony and concludes: 'All þis is symonye . . . ȝif þou bygge or selle þise gostly thinges forsayde, in couenaunt made beforn, and þe preest wyll noȝt don it, but he haue his couenaunt.' L's broader definition, which includes the sale of any divine gift intended for the common good (such as justice, knowledge, health, etc.), reflects the doctrine of *donum Dei*; see G. Post, K. Giocarnis and R. Kay, 'The Medieval Heritage of a Humanistic Ideal: "Scientia Donum Dei Est, Unde Vendi Non Potest,"' *Traditio* 11 (1955), 195–234.

SISE   An assize, a trial in which sworn assessors or jurymen (SISOURS) decide questions of fact; a judicial inquest: C.2.178 And [Gyle] shop þat a shereue sholde bere Mede . . . fram syse to syse, And Fals and Fauel fecche forth sysores. Cf. *Gamelyn* 870: 'Than saide Gamelyn to the justise, "Thou hast y-yeue domes of the wors assise; And the twelve sisours that weren of the queste, They shull been hanged this day"'; Brown XIV 99/42: 'Lord, lat it noght be aloynt, when þou sal sett þi gret assyse.' Blackstone 3:185: 'The word, *assise*, is derived by sir Edward Coke from the Latin *assideo*, to sit together; and it signifies, originally, the jury who try the cause, and sit together for that purpose. By a figure it is now made to signify the court or jurisdiction, which summons this jury together by a commission of assise . . . and hence the judicial assemblies held by the king's commission in every county . . . are termed in common speech the *assises*.' See also the elaborate distinctions given in *Mirror* 65. ENQUESTE.

SISOUR   An assizer, one of those who constituted the assize or inquest, whence the modern jury originated; a sworn recognitor (*OED*): B.20.161 Hir sire was a Sysour þat neuere swoor truþe, Oon Tomme two-tonge, atteynt at ech a queste (C.22.161); A.2.44 (B.2.59, C.2.59); B.2.63 (C.2.63); A.2.129 (B.2.165, C.2.179); A.3.123 (B.3.134, C.3.170); B.4.167 (C.4.162); B.20.291 (C.22.290); B.19.369 (C.21.370). Cf. *Jac.Well* 131/8: 'False cysourys gon vp-on qwestys, & puttyn a man fro his ryȝt thrugh a fals verdyȝte, & wytnessen aȝens trewthe'; see also *Gamelyn* (quoted above). JUROUR, WITNESS; see also PANEL, SECTE.

SITTEN   To occupy a seat in the capacity of a judge or with some administrative function (*OED*); to serve on a jury or inquest: B.Prol.96 And in stede of Stywardes sitten and demen (C.Prol.94); C.16.123 Selde syt pouerte þe sothe to declare, Or a iustice to iuge men (B.14.288); A.8.19 (B.7.17); B.19.304 (C.21.305); cf. B.18.36 Thanne cam *Pilatus* with muche peple, *sedens pro tribunali* (C.20.35). Cf. *D&P* 1:236: 'Whan þe juge schulde sittyn on þe cause'; *Lud. Cov.* 123: 'And lete my lorde þe buschop come And syt in þe courte þe lawes ffor to doo.' *K.Counc.* 79: 'And the said John Wadham . . . , while he was sitting [seaunt] in a session of the peace . . . holding process upon the said felons, the said John Grenville told him . . . that he should sit [dust seere] more uprightly without partiality [sanz enclyn] in this session than he had at the last session.' SISE.

SO ME GOD HELPE   An oath to the truth of one's testimony, the concluding words of a witness's oath: B.5.22 Of þis matere I myȝte mamelen wel longe, Ac I shal seye as I sauȝ, so me god helpe (A.5.22); B.15.158. Cf. *Court Baron* 77: 'Hear this sir N. that I, N. will speak the truth and no falsehood upon the matter. . . . So help me God [sic Deus me adjuvet], etc.' (The narrator represents himself as a witness of truth, simply reporting what he has seen and heard.) OTH; see WITNESS.

SOMNOUR   Apparitor, an officer who summoned defendants to an ecclesiastical court (mainly for moral offences): C.2.187 Somnours and sodenes that *supersedeas* taketh, On hem þat loueth leccherye; A.2.44 (B.2.59, C.2.59); A.2.134 (B.2.170); A.3.123 (B.3.134, C.3.170); B.4.167 (C.4.162); C.9.263; B.15.132 (C.16.277); B.19.369 (C.21.370). Cf. *Jac. Well* 129/29: 'Somnours & bedels, þat dwellyn in offyce vnder [offycyallys & denys], spare no conscyens to take what þei may getyn.' Chaucer's portrait, as Bennett observes, is the *locus classicus* (*CT. Prol.* 623–68). For a summons, see *Lud. Cov.* 123. The office is described in detail by Woodcock 45–49.

SOMPNEN   To order (a person) to appear in court by the issuance of a summons; also, to call together: C.3.468 Shal nother kyng ne knyght, constable ne mayre Ouerkarke þe comune ne to þe court sompne (B.3.316); A.2.123 (B.2.159, C.2.172); B.19.214 (C.21.214). Cf. *Jac. Well* 25/8: 'Lordys . . . forbydden here tenauntys þat þei go noȝt out of þe lordschip, for no somounyng, to appere before þe ordinarie, neyther for correccyoun of here synnes, ne for provyng of testamentys.'

SOUTHDENE   See SUBDEAN

SPECHE   A plea or suit at law: B.7.47 Many a Iustice and Iurour wolde for Iohan do moore Than *pro dei pietate* pleden at þe barre. Ac he þat spendeþ his speche and spekeþ for þe pouere That is Innocent and nedy and . . . lawe for hym sheweþ . . . Shal no deuel at his deeþ day deren hym a myte (A.8.49, C.9.46); C.4.149 (men of lawe . . . with som sotil speche). Cf. *O&N* 13: '& hure & hure of oþeres songe Hi holde plaiding suþe stronge. Þe Niȝtingale bigon þe speche' (see Intro. 28, '*Speche*, "law-suit, plea" '). To 'spend speech' is an alliterative formula (cf. *SGGK* 410). MOTING.

SPEKEN   To speak, plead, imparl: A.3.158 Panne mournide mede & menide hire to þe king To haue space to speke, spede ȝif she miȝte. Þe king grauntide hire grace wiþ a good wille: 'Excuse þe ȝif þou canst' (B.3.171, C.3.216); B.7.47. Cf. the formula 'Sire jeo enparlerai a vostre conge,' where *enparler* means 'to have licence to settle a litigation amicably' (*Court Baron* 54, 61, etc.). MOTEN.

146

SPIRITUALTE   An endowment, ecclesiastical property or revenue held or received in return for spiritual services: B.5.150 [Wrath speaking of friars and possessioners:] Til þei be boþe beggers and by my spiritualte libben (C.6.125). Cf. *Jac. Well* 215/31: 'Be ware ȝe þat takyn . . . good & possessiouns þat falsely is gett of temperalte or spiritualte . . . wyttynge þat it were vnryȝt-fully gett, and wyll noȝt restoryn it.' Fisher 226/3: 'The more part of spiritu-eltees and temporaltees of the seid monastery. . . .' Blackstone 1:368: 'During the vacancy of any see in his province, [the archbishop] is guardian of the spiritualties thereof, as the king is of the temporalties' (q.v.).

STATUTE   A declaration by the king and his council or parliament, addressed to all subjects of the realm and having the force of law; *specif.* the Statute of Labourers (1349–50): B.6.320 Laborers þat haue no land to lyue on but hire handes. . . . But he be heiȝliche hyred ellis wole he chide . . . And þanne corseþ þe kyng and al þe counseil after Swiche lawes to loke laborers to chaste. Ac whiles hunger was hir maister þer wolde noon chide Ne stryuen ayeins þe statut (A.7.301, C.8.342). In an attempt to control the steep rise in wages following the Black Death, the statute ordained that labourers were obliged to work for anyone willing to employ them at the wages paid between 1340 and 1346. L seems to have known the statute well: much of his account echoes its language (e.g., 'nec habens de suo proprio unde vivere possit, vel terram propriam,' PESTILENCE, SALARIE); see Baldwin 56–63. Suits brought under the statute were numerous; e.g., *K. Bench* 7:60. The standard history is Bertha Putnam, *The Enforcement of the Statutes of Labourers during the First Decade after the Black Death, 1349–59* (New York: Columbia Univ. Press, 1908).

STELEN   To take feloniously the personal property of another without his leave and consent: A.6.64 (B.5.577, C.7.224); B.13.366 (C.6.265); B.19.156 (C.21.156). The term was commonly used in indictments for larceny – 'take, steal, and carry away' – and denoted the commission of THEFTE. DESPOILEN, FECCHEN, PIKEN, PILEN, RAVISHEN, RIFLEN, ROBBEN.

STIWARD   The chief official in the household of a lord; one who transacted the legal and financial business of a manor on behalf of the lord, including the holding of the manor court: B.Prol.96 And somme seruen as seruauntȝ lordes and ladies, And in stede of Stywardes sitten and demen (C.Prol.94); B.19.461 I holde it riȝt and reson of my Reue to take Al þat myn Auditour or ellis my Styward Counseilleþ me bi hir acounte and my clerkes writynge (C.21.461); C.3.122; A.5.39 (B.5.47, C.5.145); C.15.40; B.19.256 (C.21.256). *Court Baron* 20 (beginning): 'Here one may find all sufficiently and all fully the whole course of a court baron . . . and the office of steward [le office du seneschal] how he shall speak when he holdeth the courts'; see also the duties of a steward described in *Fleta* 2.72. The steward *presided* over the manorial court; 'but the president was in no sense a judge as the word is understood to-day' (Plucknett 143). SENESCHAL.

STOKKES An instrument of punishment, consisting of a heavy timber frame with holes for confining the ankles and sometimes the wrists (cf. PILLORIE): C.8.163 [Knight to Wastour:] Y shal bete the by the lawe and brynge þe in stokkes; A.4.95 (B.4.108, C.4.103); B.7.30; C.9.34. Cf. *Jac.Well* 28/7: Acursed are 'alle þo lay-men þat wyth-holdyn ony clerk vnryȝtfully . . . or putte hem in fetterys or stokkys.' *Court Baron* 103: Robert the reeve, because 'he is negligent in all his duties . . . shall be put in the stocks upon a pining-stool [mis en cieps sur j. puner].' PINING STOL.

STOPPEN *To cause (someone) to desist in an argument, plea, complaint; to estop: C.4.150 Mede in the mot-halle tho on men of lawe gan wynke In signe þat thei sholde with som sotil speche Reherce ther anon ryhte þat myhte Resoun stoppe. The search for some legal strategem that might 'Resoun stoppe' evokes the procedural notion of *estoppel*, 'The principle which precludes a party from alleging or proving in legal proceedings that a fact is otherwise than it has appeared to be from the circumstances' (*Oxf.Comp.* 432). The fact that Reason is speaking in confirmation of Conscience's previous testimony makes the strategy of *estoppel* particularly feasible; for example, if 'men of lawe . . . with som sotil speche' can construe earlier testimony in such a way as to make a contradiction appear, they can 'estop' Reason. Cf. *Moots* 73: The wife 'shall not be estopped [serra estoppe] by any plea the husband pleaded earlier.' Cf. FALLAS.

***STREYVES** Lost property, esp. stray animals (usu. in comb. with WEY-VES): B.Prol.94 Somme seruen þe kyng and his siluer tellen, In Cheker and in Chauncelrie chalangen hise dettes Of wardes and of wardemotes, weyues and streyves (C.Prol.92). If after due notice at fairs, churches, markets, etc., the ownership of *streyves* could not be determined, it fell to the lord of the fee in which they were found or to the king; see Blackstone 1:286–88. Skeat gives a different meaning, however: 'The old sense of *stray* was property which was left behind by an alien at his death, and which went to the king for default of heirs.'

SUBDENE An official immediately below a dean in rank, acting as his deputy; also a rural dean, a parish priest chosen to assist the bishop in enforcing discipline in local testamentary, moral, and (originally) matrimonial matters (Bennett 129): C.2.187 Somnours and sodenes that *supersedeas* taketh (A.2.137, B.2.173); B.15.132 (C.16.277).

SUEN **I.** To sue for (sth.) at law; to make claim: C.3.367 And þat is nat resonable ne rect to refuse my syre name, Sethe y am his sone and his seruant sewe for his ryhte. 'To sue for one's rights': see *Jac.Well* 24/17, 29/18, 55/17; Robbins 169/1ff. Fisher 163/117: 'The forsaide Priour and Chanons of Bernewell han vs enprisoned . . . that we shulde not pursue oure right ne the kynges right aȝeyns hem.' CHALENGEN, CLAIMEN, PURSUEN.

II. To succeed or come after (as progeny): B.18.192 At þe bigynnyng god gaf þe doom hymselue That Adam and Eue and alle þat hem suwede Sholden deye downrighte . . . If þat þei touchede a tree.'

SUFFEREN   To indulge or tolerate (immoral or illegal actions): B.2.175 Erchedekenes and Officials and alle youre Registrers, Lat sadle hem wiþ siluer oure synne to suffre; A.3.81 For my loue . . . suffre hem to selle sumdel aȝens resoun (B.3.92, C.3.120); C.Prol.96, 101, 109, 119; B.20.293 (C.22.293); cf. B.20.322 (C.22.322).

SUFFRAUNCE   Improper indulgence; licence implied from the omission or neglect to enforce an adverse right (Black): C.4.189 [Let] vnsittynge suffraunce ne sele ȝoure priue lettres; C.Prol.124.; C.3.207; B.6.144. *Lib.Alb.* 284: Let those sworn to keep watch be imprisoned if they show any favour or leniency [desport] toward offenders by reason of any corruption, affinity, or indulgence [corrupcioun, affinitee, ou soeffraunce]; Hall 1:95: The sheriffs of London are to see that Crown debts are collected 'sanz desport ou soefferaunce.' The problem of 'vnsittynge suffraunce' authorized by letters sent under the king's seal is recognized in the oath of the justices (see Statute 18 Edw. III st. 4 [Ruffhead]) and addressed again in Statute 11 Ric. II c. 10: 'Item it is ordained that neither letters of the signet nor of the King's privy seal shall be from henceforth sent in damage or prejudice of the realm or in disturbance of the law.'

SUGGESTION   *An allegation or information not upon oath: B.7.66 Beggeres and bidderes beþ noȝt in þe bulle But if þe suggestion be sooþ þat shapeþ hem to begge (A.8.68, C.9.62). As Schmidt points out, 'Such beggars are guilty of *false* suggestion (a legal notion).' Cf. Fisher 32/5: 'Wheþer þe suggestion . . . be trewe'; *Lib.Alb.* 452 on serfs admitted to the freedom of the city *per suggestionem falsam*; *K.Counc.* 86: 'The said friar went to certain people of London and made an untrue suggestion [une suggestion nient verraie], submitting that [Nicholas Hogonona] was "a wild Irishman" and an enemy to our said lord the king.' Statute 17 Ric. II c. 6 provides that damages may be awarded for untrue suggestions ('suggestions nient vrais'). See also Statute 27 Edw. III c. 2. For discussion, see *K.Counc.* xxxvi–vii; Blackstone 4:305; Woodcock 65.

SUM CERTEIN   In law of negotiable instruments, the sum payable is a sum certain even though it is to be paid with stated interest, discount, exchange, or other differences (Black): B.13.376 And what body borwed of me abouȝte þe tyme Wiþ presentes pryuely, or paide som certeyn; cf. the pun in C.19.31 He can no certeyn somme telle and somme aren in his lappe. Barbour 34–35: In actions of debt, 'the claim must always be for a sum certain. The defendant could not owe a duty to pay an uncertain sum; it must be reduced to certainty. Thus, in case of a sale of goods, the vendee's promise to pay what the goods were worth would not support Debt.' *Lib.Alb.* 2:221: Let it be figured 'how much each . . . ought to pay to make up the sum expended, over and above the sum certain [outre le certain] which he ought to pay.' DETTE, LONE; cf. *PRE MANIBUS*.

149

SUPERSEDEAS   A writ that stayed or put an end to a proceeding: C.4.190 [Reason will serve as chancellor provided the king] no *supersedeas* sende but y assente; C.2.187; C.9.263. Cf. *Pride of Life* 101: '[In hell] þer ne fallit no maynpris, Ne supersidias'; *Respublica* 261: 'We must serve you with a super-sedeas'; *Moots* 76: 'In this case a writ in the nature of a supersedeas shall issue out of the chancery to the justices of the Common Bench to cause them to cease.' The writ was meant to protect individual rights (e.g., to keep a litigant in one court from being arrested by order of another court), but issuance of the writ, as Langland notes, was subject to abuses such as bribery, favouritism, etc. Sample writs of *supersedeas* are printed in Hall 2:150, *Writs* 147, 148, 223, etc.

SUREN   To pledge or promise (sth. to sb.): B.5.540 [Conscience and kynde wit] diden me suren hym [Truth] siþþen to seruen hym for euere (A.6.28).

SUTE   Apparel; *fig.* the flesh: B.5.487 Þi sone sent was to erþe And ... in oure sute deidest On good fryday for mannes sake. Bennett: 'In *sute* the primary reference is to the apparel of human flesh. . . . But there is doubtless a further allusion (1) to the sense "action at law, cause", and possibly (2) to the sense "suite of followers, witnesses": (1) is suggested by "for mannes sake" ' (184). See SECTE.

SWEREN   To take an OTH; to be sworn. C.5.57 Clerkes ycrouned ... Sholde nother swynke ne swete ne swerien at enquestes; B.20.161 (C.22.161). Fisher 192/10 on judgements 'returned by the shereve of the shire and other Bayllefs and sworen in enquestes.'

T

TAILLAGE   A tax levied upon feudal dependents by their superiors; a general name for taxes, prob. as being a part cut away (*taille*) from a man's substance: B.19.37 Now are þei [the Jews] lowe cherles. As wide as þe world is wonyeþ þer noon But vnder tribut and taillage as tikes and cherles. And þo þat bicome cristene ... Aren frankeleyns, free men þoruȝ fullynge þat þei toke (C.21.37). *Jac.Well* 42/12 explains taillages as a form of God's vengeance: 'God suffryth hem to be pyled of lordys wyth taxis, tallyagys, & extorcyouns.' For writs of talliage (De tallagio habendo), see *Writs* 65, 169, etc.; for a royal dispensation, see 103 ('Know that we have granted to P ... that he be free of all tallages and contributions assessed on the vill of N., for whatever cause, as long as he lives'). Part of L's point is that Christians have been granted 'dispensations.'

TAILLE   A tally, a proof of debt (Fr. *taille*), often in the form of a notched stick (the split halves given to debtor and creditor): B.4.58 Wrong ... takeþ me but a taille for ten quarters Otes (A.4.45, C.4.61); B.5.249 Wiþ lumbardes lettres I ladde gold to Rome And took it by tale here and tolde hem þere lasse; C.10.80 (A.9.74, B.8.83 tailende). Wrong's practice of paying by tally identifies him as one of the king's purveyors [FOREGOER]; cf. Statute 5 Edw. III c. 2: 'Between the purveyors and those whose goods shall be taken . . . tallies shall be made' (repeated 10 Edw. III st. 2 c. 1, 25 Edw. III st. 5 c. 1, etc.). The practice was extremely unpopular. E.g., Wright 186: 'Est vitii signum pro victu solvere lignum' (It is a sign of vice to pay for victuals with wood, i.e., with a tally). Upon satisfaction of a debt, the creditor's half of the tally was broken or given up to the debtor. A creditor's neglect or refusal to yield proof of payment often resulted in a law suit (e.g., *LawMerch* 1:23). A full account of the royal system of tallies is given in Hall, *Antiquities* 118ff.

TAILLEN   To tally or reckon by tally; to record (a debt) by notching a stick (see TAILLE): B.5.422 If I bigge and borwe auȝt, but if it be ytailed, I foryete it as yerne (C.7.35); A.9.74 Whoso is . . . Trusty of his tailende, takiþ but his owene . . . dowel hym folewiþ (B.8.83, C.10.80); C.3.369. REKENEN.

TALE   The plaintiff's account in a legal suit; 'Pleadings are the mutual altercations between the plaintiff and defendant. . . . The first of these is the *declaration*, *narratio*, or *count*, antiently called the *tale*; in which the plaintiff sets forth his cause of complaint at length' (Blackstone 3:293): B.11.99–100 It is *licitum* for lewed men to legge þe soþe . . . ech a lawe it graunteþ, Excepte persons and preestes and prelates of holy chirche. It falleþ noȝt for þat folk no tales to telle Thouȝ þe tale were trewe, and it touched synne; B.18.132 And þat my tale be trewe I take god to witnesse (C.20.136); C.3.390; B.9.74; C.12.171. Cf. *O&N* 53/140: 'Þos word aȝaf þe Niȝtingale, & after þare longe tale (see *O&N* Intro. 28). Harding 124: 'The first move in civil pleading was the plaintiff's "count" or "tale". . . . It might run like this: "This sheweth unto you John Smith by his attorney . . . that David Jones . . . wrongfully deforces him of the manor of Blackacre," ' etc. Cf. C.12.171: 'To testifie for treuthe þe tale þat y shewe.' The *OED* does not recognize a specifically legal meaning for *tale*, although it derives the word from OE *talu* [legal case, action at law] and includes citations that strongly suggest a legal interpretation, e.g., *Cursor Mundi* 8697 [MS Cott.]: 'O þiskin tall [MS Gött.: *playnt*] hym thoght selcouth, Als of a cas þat was vncuþ' [*OED* I.3]. ME *tale* not only retains the legal meaning of Old English *talu* but also translates the corresponding terms in Latin and Anglo-Norman: 'When the parties stand opposite to each other, it then behoves the plaintiff to state his case by his own mouth or that of his pleader. His statement is called in Latin *narratio*, in French *conte*; probably in English it is called his *tale*' (P&M 2:605); cf. Plucknett 217. See *Bor. Cust.*: 'Yf the playntyf tell in his tale ayenst the defendant . . .' (1:220); 'No man of lawe schold pled . . . for no maner of man bot gyf that the accyon pas 20s., bot every man to tell hys own tale' (2:15), etc.; Kail 22/240: 'What helpeþ his riches or wys counsaille? Hym self his owen tale shal say'; *Gammer Gurton's Needle* V.i.35: 'I warrant in this case she wil be hir owne proctor; She will tel hir owne tale, in metter or in prose.' For a compilation of legal 'tales' in Anglo-Norman, see Shanks, *Novae Narrationes*. See also SHEWEN.

151

TAXEN To assess (a fine, penalty, damages): B.1.162 Right so is loue a ledere and þe lawe shapeþ; Vpon man for hise mysdedes þe mercyment he taxeþ (C.1.158). *Lib.Alb.* 211: 'His damages shall be taxed for him by the Court [ses damages luy serrount taxez par la court]'; *LawMerch.* 52–53: 'It is awarded that the said Matthew make satisfaction to the same William for his damages, which are taxed at a half-mark, and he [Matthew] is in mercy 12d. for the trespass [que taxantur ad dimidiam marcam, et pro transgressione est in misericordia xij. d.' The word is not always neutral. The fact that the court might assess damages at a lower rate than those claimed by the plaintiff, e.g., in actions of debt, gave the term more positive connotations; thus Pollock and Maitland speak of 'mitigation or "taxation" of the amount that the plaintiff has mentioned' (2:215–16), and *Fleta* observes that 'the damages are not to be reduced unless the convicted party prays that they may be taxed' (2:203). L clearly means in both B.1.162 and B.6.39 (below) that the taxer [love, mercy] will not only assess the fine but will do so at a lower rate than strict justice would require.

TAXOUR One who determines the amount of a fine; an assessor: B.6.39 Þou3 þow mowe amercy hem lat mercy be taxour (C.8.37). A taxer might be the judge in a case, the jury, or persons chosen specially for the office. In a manorial court, it was customary to retain four taxers, two free and two bond, 'sworn to tax lawfully every man according to his trespass, saving to a gentleman the contenement of his house, to a merchant his merchandise, to a land-tenant his plough and cart' (*Court Baron* 101). Hall 2:46 prints the oath taken by royal assessors (*sacramentum taxatorum*).

TELLEN To count (money); reckon, keep an account: B.Prol.92 Somme seruen þe kyng and his siluer tellen, In Cheker and in Chauncelrie chalangen hise dettes (C.Prol.90); B.5.249 Wiþ lumbardes lettres I ladde gold to Rome And took it by tale here and tolde hem þere lasse [Bennett 168 'fraudulently paid in . . . less than he had received']; cf. C.19.31. Blackstone 3:44: 'The court of exchequer is . . . intended principally to order the revenues of the crown, and to recover the king's debts and duties' (cf. 'chalangen hise dettes'); see CHEKER. By those who 'tellen' the king's silver, L refers to the financial, as distinguished from the judicial, side of the exchequer, i.e., 'the receipt of the exchequer, which manages the royal revenue' (*ibid.*). Presiding over this side of the exchequer were four officers called *tellers*. REKENEN.

TEMPORALTIES The lay revenues, lands, tenements, etc. belonging to a prelate's office (bishop, archbishop, abbot, etc.), esp. as distinguished from the revenues arising from SPIRITUALTIES: B.20.128 Symonye . . . pressed on þe pope and prelates þei maden To holden wiþ Antecrist, hir temporaltees to saue (C.22.128). Cf. *Jac.Well* 215/31: 'Be ware 3e þat takyn ony . . . good & possessiouns þat falsely is gett of temperalte or spiritualte.' Blackstone 4:414: 'Henry I . . . gave up to the clergy the free election of bishops and mitred abbots; reserving however these ensigns of patronage, *conge d'eslire*, custody of the temporalties when vacant, and homage upon their restitution.' Statute

25 Edw. III st. 3 c. 6: 'The temporalities of archbishops and bishops have been often taken into the King's hands for contempts done to him upon writs of *Quare non admisit.*' For a writ of 'restitution of temporalities to the elect,' see *Writs* 101.

TENAUNT   One who holds or possesses lands or tenements: B.15.310 Þanne wolde lordes and ladies be looþ to agulte, And to taken of hir tenauntȝ moore þan trouþe wolde (C.17.45); A.7.39 (B.6.38, C.8.36). See also BONDE, BONDEMAN, COTER.

TENEN   To harass or oppress (sb.), esp. by fines, legal suits, etc.: C.8.36 [Piers to the knight:] Loke ȝe tene no tenaunt but treuthe wol assente (A.7.39, B.6.38). The word translates Lat. *vexare*, as used in the writ *ne iniuste vexes*: 'The king to B., greeting. We forbid you to vex A. unjustly or allow him to be vexed in regard to his free tenement, which he holds from you in N., or to exact from him, or allow to be exacted thereof, customs or services which he ought not to render and is not accustomed to render' (*Writs* 25, also 38, 46, 114, etc.); in the language of pleading, 'to vex' means to threaten with a suit (Barbour 137). *K. Counc.* 84 records a typical case. For the expression 'but treuthe wol assente,' esp. as it relates to lords who 'tenen' their tenants, see TREUTHE.

TERMINEN   To bring (a legal case) 'to an end,' that is, to judge or pronounce judgement: A.1.95 Kinges & kniȝtes shulde . . . taken trespassours & teiȝen hem faste Til treuþe hadde termined here trespas to þe ende (B.1.97, C.1.93). Cf. *RR* 2.97: 'Trouthe hathe determyned the tente [intent] to the ende'; Robbins 170/39: '[Venus] comawndes yowe apere afore Iuges tweyn to determyne yur matir & here al your pleeis.' The word is short for 'hear and determine' [*oyer e terminer*]; e.g., 'Matthew . . . prays that auditors may be assigned to him, knights who are not justices, to hear and determine [oier e terminer] the grievances whereof he complains against the bishop of Bath' (*K. Counc.* 15).

TESTAMENT   A document recording a person's wishes on the disposition of his personal property after death: A.7.78 (Sk.) For-thi I wole, ar I wende write my testament (A.7.77, B.6.85, C.8.94 biqueste). P&M 2:337–38: 'If in Latin, the document usually calls itself a testament – *Ego A. B. condo testamentum meum* is a common phrase – in French or English it will call itself a testament or a devise or a last will.' The two words *testament* and *will* (or *last will*) often appear together; e.g., Lyndwood lib. III tit. 13 ('De Testamentis'), Fisher 222/2, Reynes 518–19. As suggested by Piers's action, it was customary for pilgrims to make a will before setting out (see *Fleta* 2.57). Piers's will follows the usual form, in which the testator bequeaths his soul to God, his body to a particular church, and so forth; a typical fourteenth-century will is given by Holdsworth 3:671. On other literary uses of the form, see Eber Carle Perrow, 'The Last Will and Testament as a Form of Literature,' *Trans. of the Wisconsin Academy of Sciences, Arts, and Letters* 17, pt. 1 (1914), 682–753. BIQUESTE, TESTAMENTUM, WILLE; see also RESIDUE AND REMENAUNT.

TESTAMENTUM   A will or testament: C.9.94a (Sk.) For-thi ich wolle, er ich wende do wryten my byquyste. Testamentum Petri Plouhman. *In dei nomine, amen.*

TESTIFIEN   To bear witness to, attest, affirm the truth of (a statement); also, to make a solemn statement in support of an argument or position: C.11.308 All þat Treuth attacheth and testifieth for gode [Pearsall: All those that Truth claims jurisdiction over and testifies to be good]; B.13.94 Þanne shal he testifie of a Trinite, and take his felawe to witnesse What he fond in a forel of a freres lyuyng; C.12.171 Mo prouerbes y myhte haue of mony holy seyntes To testifie for treuthe þe tale þat y shewe. RECORDEN, REHERSEN, WITNESSEN.

THEF   One who commits theft: B.12.190–91 *Dominus pars hereditatis mee* is a murye verset That haþ take fro Tybourne twenty stronge þeues, Ther lewed þeues ben lolled vp (C.14.129–30); C.5.17 Can thow . . . be hayward . . . And kepe my corn in my croft fro pykares and theues? B.9.121; C.13.61; B.12.192ff. (C.14.131ff.); B.14.308; C.17.138; B.17.56 (C.19.52); B.17.92; B.18.71 (C.20.74); B.19.366 (Sk.); C.20.424; etc. RAVENER, REVER, ROBBER.

THEFLI   In a thief-like manner, stealthily, furtively: B.18.338 [Christ to Lucifer:] Thus ylik a Lusard wiþ a lady visage Thefliche þow me robbedest.

THEFTE   'Theft is the fraudulent appropriation of the property of another, with the intention of stealing, against the owner's will' (*Fleta* 1.36): B.5.233 'Ones I was yherberwed,' quod he, 'wiþ an heep of chapmen; I roos whan þei were areste and riflede hire males.' 'That was no restitucion,' quod Repentaunce, 'but a robberis þefte; Thow haddest be bettre worþi ben hanged þerfore'; C.6.349; A.11.280 (B.10.421). Repentaunce's words 'worþi ben hanged þerfore' were apparently proverbial, as Bennett notes (166), citing *Sir Gawain* and *Raif Coilʒear*. Closer to L's use, however, is *Jac. Well* 128/5, which distinguishes (like *Fleta* 1.36) *pryvy* from *opyn* thefte, 'þat is, whann þou opynly, thrugh wyll, canst stele, and often hauntyst it, to susteyne þe and þine, & were worthy, be londys lawe, to be hangyd.' Like many other medieval writers, L seems not to distinguish between theft and robbery (see ROBBEN); cf. *D&P* 2:131: 'As þe lawe seith, euery vnleful vsynge & takynge of anoþir manys good meuable or nout meuable is þefte.'

THIS FOR THAT   *Quid pro quo*: C.9.277 Haue this for þat tho þat thow toke Mercy for mede, and my lawe breke; cf. B.3.258 Marchaundise is . . . a penyworþ for anoþer (A.3.237, C.3.313). On the technical meaning of *quid pro quo*, see Barbour 36ff.

THRAL   A bondman, serf, slave: C.21.33 [A conqueror has the power] To make lordes of laddes of lond þat he wynneth And fre men foule thralles þat folleweth nat his lawes (B.19.33). Cf. *D&P* 162/61: 'Þe fend halt hem wol

harde boundyn in his bondis as hese cherlys & hese þrallys, for alle swyche . . .
forsakyn God.' BONDE, BONDAGE, CHERL.

THRALDOM The state or condition of being a thrall; bondage, servitude:
C.20.107 And ȝoure franchise þat fre was yfallen is into thraldoem
(B.18.103). Cf. 'A Dramatic Monologue by Law,' Robbins 113/18: 'The
children of Israel – to thraldom Institute In the land of Egipte. . . .'

TITHE The tenth part [DIME] of the annual produce of agriculture, livestock, net income, etc., or the payment thereof (as required by English law),
given for the support of the clergy; see DIME: B.6.76 Holy chirche is holde of
hem [Iakke þe Iogelour, Ionette of þe Stuwes, danyel þe dees pleyere, Denote
þe baude, et al.] no tiþe to aske (A.7.68, C.8.78); C.6.300; A.7.84 (B.6.92,
C.8.101); C.6.305–06; C.13.83; B.15.107 (C.16.259); B.15.488. Blackstone
gives a full definition: 'A . . . species of incorporeal hereditaments . . . which
are defined to be the tenth part of the increase, yearly arising and renewing
from the profits of lands, the stock upon lands, and the personal industry of
the inhabitants: the first species being usually called *predial*, as of corn, grass,
hops, and wood; the second *mixed*, as of wool, milk, pigs, &c, consisting of
natural products, but nurtured and preserved in part by the care of man; and
of these the tenth must be paid in gross: the third *personal*, as of manual
occupations, trades, fisheries, and the like; and of these only the tenth part of
the clear gains and profits is due' (2:24); there follows a legal history of tithes
(24–32). *D&P* explains further: 'Tyþis personalys, as of merchandye and of
craft, man shal payn to hys parych chirche þer he dwellyth . . . but tyþis
predyalys he shal payyn to þe chirche to whyche þe maner & þe lond longith
to, but custum be into þe contrarie' (2:168). Canon law was very precise about
how tithes should be calculated: to whom paid, of whom received, and so
forth. See *Jac. Well* 37–47.

TITHEN To pay tithes on (one's land, property, etc.): C.13.72 Men þat . . .
Tythen here goed treuthliche, a tol, as hit semeth; C.6.306 An hore or here
ers-wynnynge may hardiloker tythe Then an errant vsurer; A.8.65 (Sk.);
C.13.83.

TITLE **I.** Legal right to the possession of property: B.18.294 [Gobelyn to
Lucifer:] We haue no trewe title to hem [þe renkes þat ben here], for þoruȝ
treson were þei dampned (C.20.324). Cf. *D&P* 2:178: 'It is a general reule in
þe lawe þat hoso occupye onyþing withoutyn ryȝtful titele he is boundyn to
restitucion of alle þe harmys & of al þe profyth þat cam þerof.' A 'trewe title' is
a legal title, a *titulus iuris* (see TREWE). On the question of the devil's 'title'
from a canonist's viewpoint, see Alford 1977, 945.
  II. A certificate of presentment to a benefice, or a guarantee of support,
required (in ordinary cases) by the bishop from a candidate for ordination
(*OED*): B.11.290–92 And þe title þat ye take ordres by telleþ ye ben
auaunced: Thanne nedeþ yow noȝt to nyme siluer for masses þat ye syngen,
For he þat took yow a title sholde take yow wages (C.13.103–05); B.11.300

(C.13.113). Lyndwood lib. III tit. 6: 'We ordain that every bishop give to every clerk whom he admits to a church letters patent testifying his admission, and specifying among other things what orders he has received, and by what title [quo titulo] he is admitted to the benefice.' A clerk in lower orders who wished to proceed to the others or to Priest in another diocese was required to obtain Letters Dimissory from the bishop of the first diocese to the bishop of the second. Purvis prints an example (35) and comments: 'The "titulus" clause shows the usual method of ensuring that the ordained clerk would not be a financial liability to his Ordinary or to the Diocese by insisting that he must have a "title," that is, that either he himself possessed means, or that he was supported by some person or body (monasteries frequently gave "tituli," especially nunneries which wanted a Chaplain) who would be responsible for his necessary maintenance.' See R. N. Swanson, 'Langland and the Priest's Title,' *N&Q* ns 33 (1986), 438–40; and Carter Revard, '*Title* and *Auaunced* in *Piers Plowman* B.11.290,' *Yearbook of Langland Studies* 1 (1987), 116–121.

TOLL   A tax, tribute, duty, custom (Lat. *theoloneum*): C.13.72 Tythen here goed treuthliche, a tol, as hit semeth, That oure lord loketh aftur [expects] of vch a lyf þat wynneth Withoute wyles or wronges; C.Prol.98 Boxes ben yset forth ybounde with yren To vndertake þe tol of vntrewe sacrefice; C.13.50. The payment of a toll was evidence that a business transaction had been conducted, as L puts it, 'withoute wyles or wronges.' Cf. *Mirror* 14: 'It was ordained ... that buyers of corn and beasts should give toll to the bailiffs of the lords of the markets or fairs. ... This toll was ordained as evidence of the contract, for every privy contract was prohibited.'

TOLLEN   To pay a TOLL: C.13.50 For the lawe asketh Marchauntz for her marchaundyse in many place to tolle. The 'many places' where merchants might be tolled included fairs and markets, highways, and at gates to the city. The goods of religious houses, not for resale, were normally exempted. See *Writs* 200, 201, 214.

TOLLER   One who takes toll or duty; a customs collector: B.Prol.221 Tollers in Markettes (A.Prol.100). Cf. *Myrour* 141/3: 'The eighþe [branch of avarice] beþ tollers þat gadreþ tolle as wel vnrightfulliche as rightfulliche of þe people, & greueþ ofte þe peple wrongfulliche'; *Jac. Well* 134/31: 'Tollerys þat dystressyn men to payin aзen resoun, & takyn more toll þan trewth wolde.'

TOUCHEN   Mainly in legal usage, to pertain or relate to (sth.): B.11.100 It falleþ noзt for þat folk [clergy] no tales to telle Thouз þe tale were trewe, and it touched synne. Cf. 'A Dramatic Monologue by Law,' Robbins 114/26: 'But now as of my matere a remembraunce Towchyng his [God's] lawe.' *Mirror* 181: 'They charge the jurors with articles touching torts [tochaunz torz] done by neigbour to neighbour'; *K.Counc.* 77: 'Les Records et proces touchantz le Conte de Deuenshire'; Fisher 18/6: '... endentures ... touching certain money þat is due to her.' That 'touch' in this sense was identified mainly with legal usage is evident as well from other fourteenth-century citations of the word (see *OED* 20).

TOUN The enclosed land surrounding or belonging to a single dwelling; a manor, 'an estate with a village community in villenage upon it under a lord's jurisdiction'; the house or group of houses upon such enclosed land (*OED* 1, 2): A.10.138 Barouns & burgeis, & bondemen of tounes. Cf. *Jac.Well* 132/3 condemns those guilty of 'dystroying of towne or of place' (see PLACE). Plucknett 83–84.

*TRANSGRESSOR One who violates either human or divine law: B.1.96 Kynges and knyȝtes sholde . . . Riden and rappen doun in Reaumes aboute, And taken *transgressores* and tyen hem faste Til treuþe hadde ytermyned hire trespas to þe ende (C.1.92). In legal usage the word *transgressio* has both a narrow and a general meaning. 'Throughout the Middle Ages there is no such word as misdemeanor – the crimes which do not amount to felony are trespasses [*transgressiones*]' or less serious breaches of the king's peace (Maitland *Forms* 49; cf. *Fleta* 1.36). On the other hand, Kiralfy observes: 'The word "trespass" was given a wide meaning in medieval times. Crimes, slander, omissions, nuisances, were all loosely referred to as trespasses, in the broad sense of violations of law. The only common element was that they were cases where a wrong was to be remedied rather than a right vindicated' (37 n.). The passage recalls the language of Statute 28 Edw. I c. 1: 'There shall be chosen in every shire court . . . knights . . . to hear and determine [complaints]. . . . And the same knights shall have power to punish all such as shall be attainted of any trespass . . . by imprisonment or by ransom,' etc. The basic study is by Milsom, 'Trespass from Henry III to Edward III,' *Law Quarterly Review* 74 (1958), 195ff., 407ff., 561ff. See also TRESPASSOUR.

TRECHERIE The violation of faith, fealty, or TRUTH; deceit or perfidious conduct, TRESOUN: A.1.172 Þat is no treuþe of trinite but treccherie of helle (B.1.198, C.1.193); C.Prol.12 Treuthe and tricherye, tresoun and gyle; B.7.79 In hym þat takeþ is þe trecherie if any treson walke; C.20.319 Thus with treson and tricherie thow troyledest hem bothe And dust hem breke here buxumnesse thorw fals bihestes. 'Treason and treachery' is a common alliterative collocation: e.g., *SGGK* 4–5: 'Þe tulk þat þe trammes of tresoun þer wroȝt Watz tried for his tricherie'; *Havelock* 443–44: 'He thoughte a full strong trechery, A traison and a felony.'

TRESORER A person entrusted with the receipt, care, and disbursement of revenues: B.20.260 Wol no tresorer take hem [soldiers] wages . . . But þei ben nempned in þe noumbre of hem þat ben ywaged (C.22.260).

TRESOUN Orig., a breach of faith by a vassal or subject; later, any action of deceit or treachery: B.19.90 Gold is likned to leautee þat laste shal euere For it shal turne tresoun to riȝt and to truþe; B.5.49 Reson . . . counseiled þe kyng

157

his commune to louye: 'It is þi tresor if treson ne were'; B.18.290 Þow ...
toldest hire [Eve] a tale, of treson were þe wordes; C.3.87 And thow thei
[regrators] take hem [the poor] vntidy thyng no tresoun þei ne halden hit;
C.Prol.12; B.7.79; B.16.158 (C.18.176); C.20.319; B.18.294 (C.20.324). The
medieval notion of treason was founded on two traditions, the Germanic
(*treubruch*, 'the breach of a man's oath of fealty') and the Roman (*laesa
maiestatis*, 'insult to those with public authority'). The development of the
two strains of thought in English law, along with the less defined notion of
felony, is treated by J. G. Bellamy, *The Law of Treason in England in the
Later Middle Ages* (Cambridge: Cambridge University Press, 1970). The
primary document is the Statute of Treasons of 1352; see also Statute 25 Edw.
III st. 5 c. 2 (1350), which sets forth 'in what case treason shall be said and in
what not.'

TRESOUN AND TRECHERIE   See TRECHERIE

TRESPAS   In a wide sense, any violation or transgression of the law; *specif.*
one not amounting to treason, felony, or misprision of either (*OED*); 'A
trespass [transgressio] is an act where neither manner nor measure is observed' (*Fleta* 2.1): B.1.97 Kynges and knyȝtes sholde ... taken *transgressores*
and tyen hem faste Til treuþe hadde ytermyned hire trespas to þe ende
(A.1.95, C.1.93); B.19.300 (Sk.) *Spiritus iusticie* spareth nouȝte to ... cor-
recte The kynge, ȝif he falle in gylte or in trespasse. '*Trespass* appears *circa*
1250 as a means of charging a defendant with violence but no felony' (Maitland *Forms* 65). However, as Baker notes, 'Professor Milsom [*LQR* 74
(1958), 195 passim.] has been at pains to demonstrate that the medieval
concept of 'trespass' was no more technical than the modern concept of
'wrong': it was the colloquial equivalent of the Latin *transgressio* or wrong-
doing,' *An Introduction to English Legal History* (1971), 82. Cf. Harding
97.

TRESPASSEN   To commit a TRESPAS: B.3.293 Whoso trespaseþ to truþe or
takeþ ayein his wille, Leaute shal don hym lawe (A.3.268); B.12.287 Ac truþe
þat trespased neuere ne trauersed ayeins his lawe, But lyueþ as his lawe techeþ
(C.14.209); B.5.368 (C.6.426).

*****TRESPASSOUR**   One who commits a TRESPAS: C.2.92 (Sk.) Kynges and
knyȝtes shoulde ... take trespassours [Pearsall C.1.92 *transgressores*] and
tyen hem faste (A.1.94). *Mirror* 122: It belongs to the king 'to punish trespassers [punir les trespassours].' TRANSGRESSOR.

TRETOUR   One who is faithless, either to another that trusts him or to a duty
entrusted to him: B.18.380 It is noȝt vsed in erþe to hangen a feloun Ofter þan
ones þouȝ he were a tretour (C.20.422); B.19.438 Piers þe Plowman ...
trauailleþ and tilieþ for a tretour also soore As for a trewe tidy man
(C.21.438); A.2.174 (Sk.); C.19.237.

TREUTHE I. A. The principle of right or justice: B.11.159 Wel ouȝte ye lordes þat lawes kepe ... on Troianus truþe to þenke, and do truþe to þe peple; B.5.52 And ye þat han lawes to loke, lat truþe be youre couetise Moore þan gold ouþer giftes; B.20.135 [Coveitise] Iogged to a Iustice and Iusted in his eere And ouertilte al his truþe wiþ 'tak þis vp amendement' (C.22.135); C.21.478 Rewle thy rewme in resoun riht wel and in treuthe (B.19.478); A.1.95 (B.1.97, C.1.93); A.1.100 (B.1.102); B.2.37; C.3.144; B.3.243 (C.3.308); A.3.268 (B.3.293, C.3.445); C.11.27; B.11.152; B.11.156 (C.12.89); B.15.27 (C.16.186); B.15.471; C.21.90. Cf. the formula 'truth and justice,' e.g., *Eyre* 45: 'They ... maintain the false pleas of parties in the City, etc. by which truth and justice [veritas et iusticia] are suppressed.' LETTEN TREUTHE. **B.** 'As treuthe wolde,' as justice requires, in proportion, according to the degree of the offence: B.15.310 And þanne wolde lordes and ladies be looþ to agulte, And to taken of hir tenauntȝ moore þan trouþe wolde (C.17.45); C.3.350; B.3.319 (C.3.471); A.7.39 (B.6.38, C.8.36); B.6.139; B.19.194 (C.21.194). Cf. *Jac. Well* 134/31: 'Tollerys þat dystressyn men to payin aȝen resoun, & takyn more toll þan trewth wolde.' The phrase translates the idea of punishment in proportion to the deed: e.g., the writ *De moderata misericordia* (*Writs* 167), which ends, 'And therefore we command you to take from the aforesaid A. a moderate amercement according to the degree of his offence [secundum quantitatem delicti ilius]'; Statute 28 Edw. I c. 1: The knights chosen in every shire court shall have the power to punish wrongdoers 'according to the trespass [selonc ceo qe le trespass le demande].'

II. Conduct in conformity with right and justice; obedience, honesty, integrity, virtuous living: A.7.62 Crafty men þat conne lyue in treuþe, I shal fynde hem foode þat feiþfulliche libbeþ (B.6.68, C.8.69); C.3.136; C.3.348; A.4.101 (B.4.114, C.4.109); B.5.547, 548; A.7.53 (B.6.58, C.8.57); A.6.93 (B.5.606, C.7.255); A.7.88 (B.6.96, C.8.105); A.7.238; C.9.251; C.10.181; B.16.27 (C.18.31); C.21.230.

III. The quality of being true: **A.** Loyalty, fidelity: A.1.172 Þat is no treuþe of trinite but treccherie of helle (B.1.198, C.1.193); B.19.90 It shal turne tresoun to riȝt and to truþe (C.21.90); A.1.97 (B.1.99, C.1.102); A.1.107 (B.1.109); C.5.183; C.15.137. **B.** One's faith as pledged or plighted in a solemn agreement, as 'to plight one's troth'; the act of pledging one's faith, promise, covenant: C.2.124 For Treuthe plyhte here treuthe to wedde on of here douhteres; B.3.317 Ne putte hem in panel to doon hem pliȝte hir truþe (C.3.469); C.8.33 [The knight to Piers:] Y plyhte the my treuthe To defende þe in fayth (A.7.36, B.6.34); B.20.118 Manye brode arewes [of Lecherie], Weren feþered wiþ fair biheste and many a fals truþe (C.22.118). **C.** In oaths, 'have God my treuthe': C.11.112; B.13.244; B.14.274.

IV. A. True account or testimony; that which is true and accurate: B.20.161 Hir sire was a Sysour þat neuere swoor truþe (C.22.161); C.8.297; A.8.94 (B.7.112, C.9.287); B.10.22; C.11.277; C.12.27; C.12.36; C.12.232; B.14.312 (C.16.145); C.20.311. **B.** As a pun: B.9.101 Truþe woot þe soþe; A.2.86 (B.2.122); A.6.84 (B.5.597, C.7.245); A.7.122 (B.6.130); B.18.147 (C.20.150).

V. *Gen.* as a virtue or way of life incorporating most or all of the above: A.1.133 It is a kynde knowyng þat kenneþ in þin herte For to loue þi lord leuere þanne þiselue; No dedly synne to do, diȝe þeiȝ þou shuldist. Þis I trowe be treuþe (B.1.145, C.1.144); A.1.83 Whanne alle tresours arn triȝed treuþe is þe beste (B.1.85, C.1.82); A.1.124 (B.1.135); A.1.126 (B.1.137, C.1.135); A.1.181 (B.1.207, C.1.202); B.3.301 (C.3.453); B.5.57 (C.5.198); C.7.198; C.12.94; B.12.290 (C.14.212); C.17.141; B.19.261 (C.21.261); B.19.333 (C.21.334).

VI. As a personification: A.1.12 Þe tour on þe toft . . . treuþe is þereinne, And wolde þat ȝe wrouȝten as his word techiþ (B.1.12, C.1.12); A.1.95 Kinges & kniȝtes shulde . . . taken trespassours & teiȝen hem faste Til treuþe hadde termined here trespas to þe ende (B.1.97, C.1.93); A.8.25 Ac vndir his secre sel treuþe sente hem a lettre (B.7.23, C.9.27); B.18.295 Certes I drede me . . . lest truþe [Christ] do hem fecche. Thise þritty wynter . . . he wente aboute and preched (C.20.325); B.18.119 A comely creature and a clene; truþe she highte (C.20.123); C.Prol.15; A.2.81 (B.2.117, C.2.118); A.2.84 (B.2.120); C.2.136; C.3.132; C.3.139; A.6.20 (B.5.532, C.7.177); B.5.547, 548; A.6.46 (B.5.559, C.7.203); C.7.298, 303; A.7.66 (B.6.74, C.8.76); A.7.126 (B.6.134, C.8.141); A.7.194 (B.6.208, C.8.218); A.8.1 (B.7.1, C.9.1); B.7.8); B.11.39; B.12.287 (C.14.209); B.18.121–422 (C.20.125–468).

Treuthe is the focus of the poem. For a discussion of the word itself in fourteenth-century usage, see George Kane, *The Liberating Truth: The Concept of Integrity in Chaucer's Writings* (London: Athlone, 1980). For the importance of the concept in the design of *Piers Plowman*, see Alford 1988, 32–36.

TREWE   *Legally valid, rightful, legitimate, as a 'true action,' 'true title,' 'true right,' etc.: C.1.94 Kynges and knyghtes sholde . . . halden with hem and here þat han trewe accion And for no lordene loue leue þe trewe partie; B.10.347 [The poor] han Eritage in heuene, and by trewe riȝte, Ther riche men no riȝt may cleyme but of ruþe and grace; B.18.294 We haue no trewe title to hem, for þoruȝ treson were þei dampned (C.20.324). Cf. Statute 25 Edw. III c. 3: 'The clerks . . . had good and true title [bone & verrei title] to the said benefices'; *Cov. Leet* 302: 'true pleas [vera placita] and not false nor foreign ones'; Statute 14 Edw. III c. 3: 'sanz verroie et jouste cause'; *Writs* 115: 'Let execution of this writ be made if the cause is true [si causa sit vera]'; *Eyre* 16: 'All those who were attainted of . . . maintenance of any false party [fauce partie] . . . should remain outside . . . the Eyre.'

TREWE   (Noun) A cessation or absence of hostilities; truce or treaty; peace: B.18.416 'Trewes,' quod Truþe . . . 'Clippe we in couenaunt, and ech of vs kisse ooþer' (C.20.462); C.8.354 Famyne shal aryse . . . pestilences . . . bane and batayle . . . But yf god of his goodnesse graunte vs a trewe (B.6.331).

TRIEN   To judge (a cause or question): B.5.338 (Sk.) Robyn the ropere . . . nempned hym for a noumpere that no debate were, For to trye this chaffare bitwixen hem thre. *Pearl* 702: At the Last Judgement where 'alle oure cause3 schal be tryed.' Cf. *Bor. Cust.* 1:175: 'The issue shall be tried by a jury [trie par pais]'; *Mirror* 50: 'La lei court napent nient detrier quele fu sa femme de fet e quele de droit'; *K. Counc.* 64: It is 'against the law of the land that people of one county should try [trier] anything done in another county.'

TROTH   See TREUTHE (III.B)

*TUTOUR   A legal guardian, custodian, keeper: C.1.52 For ri3tfulliche resoun sholde reule 3ow alle And kynde witte be wardeyn, 3oure welthe to kepe, And tutor of 3oure tresor, and take it 3ow at nede (A.1.54, B.1.56). Cf. *D&P* 2:140: 'God ... hat put mankende & namely þe pore peple vndir þe gouernance of þe riche folc & of þe lordys whiche ben her toutours & dispensourys of goodis of þis world, to sauacion of þe pore peple.' The term is taken from civil law, where it means 'a guardian appointed to have the care of a minor and his estate' (Black); the Roman doctrine of *tutela* or guardianship is treated at length in Buckland 142–67. L's 'wardeyn ... and tutor' reflects the common formula *custos et tutor* (see WARDEN).

*TYBOURNE   The place of public execution for Middlesex: C.6.368 The hangeman of Tybourne; B.12.190 *Dominus pars hereditatis mee* is a murye verset That haþ take fro Tybourne twenty stronge þeues (C.14.129). *Oxf. Comp.*: 'A stream flowing into the Thames in London, now running in a culvert. The name is associated with the Middlesex Gallows which stood west of the stream near the modern Marble Arch. This was a place of public hanging of criminals from about 1300 till 1783. The gibbet was sometimes known as Tyburn tree.'

U

UMPIRE   See NOUMPERE

UNCHARGEN   To free (sb.) from a charge or burden; DISCHARGEN: B.15.345 For charite wiþouten chalangynge vnchargeþ þe soule, And many a prison fram purgatorie þoru3 hise preieres deliuereþ. Cf. *Ayenbite* 97: 'Þe oþere [lawe] chargeþ: and þis onchargeþ'; *Hand. Synne* 11942: 'Yn euery tyme þat þou shryuest þe, Of pyne shalt þou vncharged be' (*Manuel des Pechiez*: 'De ceste peine vus descharge3').

UNMOEBLES   See MOEBLES AND UNMOEBLES

UNRESONABLE   Lacking in order, discipline, or MESURE: B.15.461 Heþen is to mene after heeþ and vntiled erþe, As in wildernesse wexeþ wilde beestes Rude and vnresonable, rennynge wiþouten keperes; B.6.151 Thei shul haue payn and potage ... For it is an vnresonable Religion þat haþ ri3t no3t of certein. Schmidt glosses the passage: 'For it would not be reasonable to expect members of any religious order to possess absolutely no source of sure sustenance.' Expansion of the word *vnresonable* – 'not be reasonable to expect' – is unnecessary. The referent is not some implied mental process but simply, as the syntax declares, *religioun*, which, if it 'haþ riȝt noȝt of certein,' is unreasonable in and of itself, lacking the essential quality of RESOUN. See RESONABLE, and Alford, 'The Idea of Reason in *Piers Plowman*,' *Medieval English Studies Presented to George Kane*, ed. by Donald Kennedy, R. A. Waldron, and Joseph S. Wittig (Cambridge: D. S. Brewer, 1988), 199–215.

UNSELED   C.16.129 Wynneth he nat with wightes false ne with vnselede mesures (B.14.295). Weights and measures used commercially were supposed to show, by an official seal, that they had been certified as accurate by city authorities; see FALS MESURE.

UNTIME   The 'wrong time' for certain actions that would be otherwise permissible, e.g., a period of fasting or penitence; also referred to as CURSED TIME and OUT OF TIME: A.10.202 For in vntyme, treweliche, betwyn man & womman Shulde no bedbourd be; but þei were boþe clene (B.9.189). Cf. B.9.122–23 Wastours and wrecches out of wedlock ... Conceyued ben in cursed tyme as Caym was on Eue; C.10.288–89 And ȝe þat han wyues, ben war and worcheth nat out of tyme, As Adam dede and Eue; C.10.217; C.13.142–54; B.13.349–50; etc. Cf. *CT.Pars.* 1050: 'A man shall nat ete in untyme.'

USURER   One who practises USURIE: C.6.307 For an hore of here erswynnynge may hardiloker tythe Then an errant vsurer; B.11.284 If preestes weren wise þei wolde no siluer take For masses ne for matyns, noȝt hir mete of vsureres; B.15.85 Ye forsakeþ no mannes almesse, Of vsurers, of hoores, of Auarouse chapmen. Cf. *D&P* 2:204/17: 'Wherby schul men knowyn an oppyn usurer?'

USURIE   The lending of money (or other means of exchange) at interest: B.2.176 Lat sadle hem wiþ siluer oure synne to suffre, As deuoutrye and diuorses and derne vsurie; C.6.304 And what lede leueth þat y lye, look in þe sauter glosed, on *Ecce enim veritatem dilexisti*, And there shal he wite witterly what vsure is to mene; B.19.350 Conscience shal noȝt knowe who is cristene or heþene, Ne no manere marchaunt þat wiþ moneye deleþ Wheiþer he wynne wiþ right, wiþ wrong or wiþ vsure (C.21.351); A.2.63 (B.2.87, C.2.91); B.3.240; C.3.113; B.5.237 (C.6.239); B.5.239–249 (C.6.240–47 [describes various types of usury]); B.18.106 (C.20.110). Cf. *D&P* 2:195: 'Vsure is a wynnynge askyd be comenant [sic] of lendynge & for lendynge ..., & it is don mest comonly in þingis of numbre, of whyȝte & of mesure, as in monye þat is teld, in gold & syluer & oþir metal þat is weyn, or in corn, olee & wyn þat is mesured.... Reymund [of Pennafort] seith þat þer ben two spycys of usure. Or. is spiritual & ryȝtful, of whyche Cryst spekyth in þe gospel, Luce xix [23]: Quare non dedisti pecuniam meam ad mensam, etc. [see below] ... Anoþir usure is bodely usure & vnry3tful þat comyth of fals couetyse be comenant [sic] of lendynge. . . . No monye ne þing þat may ben mesuryd be monye, neyþer mete ne drynk no cloþ ne 3ifte of hond, of tunge ne of seruyce [may þe lendere askyn]. But oþir þing þat may nout ben mesuryd be monye he may askyn, as loue & charite, good wil and good frenchepe for his lendynge.' Because of statutory laws against usury, the simple lending of money at interest was less common than 'derne vsurie,' a phrase that covers a variety of usurious transactions hidden within an outwardly legal agreement. Some of these are referred to in B.5.237–49; for example, 'to legge a wed and lese it' refers to the practice (often a result of collusion between the lender and borrower) of putting up security for a loan and then losing it through a failure to repay or to repay on time. To expose the devices of 'derne vsurie' occupied many a moralist and canon lawyer; e.g., *Hand.Synne* 181–92; *Jac.Well* 122–24; *Myrour* 132–33; *D&P* 2:195ff.; Wilson 191ff.; R. H. Bowers, 'A Middle English Mnemonic Poem on Usury,' *Medieval Studies* 17 (1955), 226–32. The medieval doctrine of usury is discussed by R. H. Tawney, *Religion and the Rise of Capitalism* (New York: New American Library, 1960; orig. pub. 1926), 37–52; Tawney, intro. to Wilson; and Noonan, *The Scholastic Analysis of Usury*. See ABOUGHT THE TIME, BREKEN DAI, CHEVISAUNCE, LONE, MEDE, *PRE MANIBUS*.

II. Spiritual usury (see above): B.7.83 Beggeres borwen eueremo and hir borgh is god almy3ty To yelden hem þat yeueþ hem and yet vsure moore: *Quare non dedisti pecuniam meam ad mensam vt ego veniens cum vsuris exegissem illam?* (Luke 19:23).

V

VAUNCEN   To promote (a clerk); provide with a benefice, AVAUNCEN: C.3.36 Shal no lewedenesse lette þe clerk þat y louye That he ne worth furste vaunsed (A.3.32, B.3.33 auaunced). BENEFISEN, PROVENDREN.

VICARI   One who takes the place of, or acts instead of, another; a person acting as priest in a parish in place of the real priest or rector: C.14.70 For clergy is Cristes vycary to conforte and to cure; B.19.409 Quod a lewed vicory, 'I am a Curatour of holy kirke' (C.21.409); B.19.419, 480 (C.21.419, 480). Addleshaw 13: '[I]n a church where the rector [q.v.] is unable to reside, there should be appointed a clerk to take his place, a vicar. . . . A part of the church's endowment is set aside and formed into what is called a vicarage, for which the vicar on his appointment swears fealty to the rector.' R. A. R. Hartridge, *A History of Vicarages in the Middle Ages* (Cambridge: Cambridge Univ. Press, 1930).

VISITING   *The canonical inspection of a diocese by the bishop or his officers; an episcopal visitation: B.2.177 Erchedekenes and Officials and alle youre Registrers, Lat sadle hem wiþ siluer oure synne to suffre, As deuoutrye and diuorses and derne vsurie, To bere Bisshopes aboute abrood in visitynge. *Jac. Well* 129/21 condemns 'prelatys of holy cherch þat puttyn here sugettys to outrageous cost, þat is, in vysityng, & in raysinge of procuracyes vnleffully, & so what þei aske þei muste paye.' Although the *OED* interprets L's meaning as 'the action of calling upon others in a social or friendly way,' he is clearly referring to the bishop's regular inspection of his diocese as required by canon law. During these visitations the bishop would enquire into the spiritual condition of the churches and religious houses under his jurisdiction (often according to a set questionnaire), give correction, hear appeals, and so forth. The literature of the period is full of complaints about these 'visitings.' Bishops and their retinues are accused of using these tours as opportunities to indulge a taste for high living. Part of the cost, L suggests above, was met by bribes in the form of 'penances.' Cf. *Simonie* 49: 'And thise ersedeknes that ben set to visite holi churche, Everich fondeth hu he may shrewedelichest worche; He wole take mede of that on and that other, And late the parsoun have a wyf, and the prest another, at wille; Coveytise shal stoppen here mouth, and maken hem al stille.' Other writers complain of extortion and excessive charges: e.g., *Myrour* 135/9: 'Coueitous prelates of Holy Chirche beþ þei þat setteþ imposiciouns vpon her sugettes and chargeþ hem wrongfulliche in her visitaciouns'; *D&P* 2:19: 'Þe lawe byddith þat whan buschopes & her offyceris gon aboutyn for to visityn þat þey schuldyn don non tyrantrye in takynge of her costis but visityn with charite & lownesse, withoutyn pompe of gret array & of gret mene, besy for to amendyn defautis & to prechyn Godys word & to wynnyn manys soule, nout to robbyn folc of her good but takyn her costis in esy maner.' Purvis discusses the process of visitation and reproduces a number of records (46–63); the basic study is C. R. Cheney, *Episcopal Visitation of Monasteries in the Thirteenth Century* (1931).

VOKETTE   An advocate or professional pleader, esp. in a church court; a PROCURATOUR: B.2.61 Forgoers and vitaillers and vokettes of þe Arches (C.2.61). *Towneley* 367/9 [On the Last Judgement:] 'Ther may no man of lagh help with no quantyce. vokettys ten or twelfe may none help at this nede, Bot ilk man for his self shall answere for his dede.' Kiralfy 175: 'The terminology of the ecclesiastical courts differed from that of the common law. ... Legal representation was not by solicitors and counsel but by proctors and advocates.' Like their common-law counterparts, proctors were concerned mainly with fact, advocates with law. William of Drogheda sharply distinguishes the two offices and notes: 'A person is said to be client [q.v.] to an advocate, but master and mandator to a proctor' (Cohen 109 n.). In the lower diocesan courts, however, proctors and advocates were generally the same person (Woodcock 42).

164

W

WAGEN   **I.** To give (sth.) as a PLEGGE or security: C.18.284 Crist . . . shal delyuere vs som day out of þe deueles power And bettere wed for vs wagen then we ben alle worthy (B.16.267).

*II. To give security or pledge oneself for the fulfilment of (something promised): A.4.84 Haue þis of me . . . to amende þi skape, For I wile wage for wrong, he wile do so no more (B.4.97, C.4.93); A.4.87 Pees þanne pitousliche preyede to þe king To haue mercy on þat man þat mysdede hym ofte: 'For he haþ wagid me wel . . . I forgyue hym þat gilt wiþ a good wille' (B.4.100, C.4.96). BORWEN.

WARDE   **I.** A person, esp. a minor, legally incapable of conducting his own affairs; also, the guardianship of such: B.Prol.94 Somme seruen þe kyng and his siluer tellen, In Cheker and in Chauncelrie chalangen hise dettes Of wardes and of wardemotes, weyues and streyves (C.Prol.92). Bennett 94: 'As supreme feudal lord the king could claim this guardianship whenever one of his tenants-in-chief died leaving a minor as head: until the minor came of age all the revenues of the estate concerned went to the Crown, forming as a whole an important part of the revenues collected by the exchequer.' Cf. Statute 51 Hen. III st. 5 (Ruffhead): 'The King commandeth that . . . receivers of issues, wards [gardes], and escheats of their bailiwicks shall be answerable in the exchequer.'

II. One under the protection or control of another, a subject: C.5.185 Þe comune is the kynges tresor. . . . Lat no kyne consayl ne couetyse ȝow parte, That o wit and o wil al ȝoure wardes kepe.

WARDEN   One entrusted with the care or keeping of something: A.1.53 For riȝtfulliche resoun shulde rewele ȝow alle, And kynde wyt be wardeyn ȝoure welþe to kepe, And tutour of ȝour tresour (B.1.55, C.1.51). L's 'wardeyn . . . and tutor' reflects the formula *custos et tutor*, e.g., *Bor.Cust.* 1:63: 'No one under age can swear or bear witness or make answer in a borough, but his guardian or tutor [sed custos ejus sive tutor] in whose wardship he is shall answer for him.' Cf. *D&P* 1:247: 'Ne childryn withynne age schul makyn no vouh withoutyn assent of her fadir or of her tutour.' TUTOUR.

*WARDMOTE   A meeting of the citizens of a ward; the smallest of the many courts in London; 'the meetings held in each ward at which the exchequer clerks would claim the dues payable to the king' (Bennett 94): B.Prol.94 Somme seruen þe kyng . . . In Cheker and in Chauncelrie chalangen hise dettes Of wardes and of wardemotes (C.Prol.92). Cam explains wardmoots as follows: 'London was divided into wards, at first twenty, later twenty-four. . . . They were summoned by their alderman for police and military purposes, and they supplied juries to report crimes and nuisances and to meet other royal demands' (86). For a full account of the wardmoot, its duties, and its relation to the mayor's court, see *Lib.Alb.* 36–39.

165

*WARNER   An officer employed to watch over the game in a park or preserve, a warrener: B.5.308 Watte þe warner and his wif boþe (A.5.159 [Sk.], C.6.363). Statute 21 Edw. I st. 2: 'If any forester, parker, or warrener [forestarius parcarius aut warennarius] find any trespassers wandering within his bailiwick. . . .'

WED   A pledge, something deposited as security for a payment or the fulfilment of an obligation (*OED*); cf. BORGH: B.5.241 I lerned . . . to legge a wed and lese it (C.6.243); B.13.359 Moore to good þan to god þe gome his loue caste . . . Lened for loue of þe wed; B.20.13 Ne wight noon wol ben his boruჳ, ne wed haþ noon to legge (C.22.13); A.3.189 (B.3.202); C.5.73; B.16.262, 267 (C.18.280, 284); B.18.31 (C.20.30). Cf. *D&P* 2:148: 'And ჳif a man lende anoþir onyþing upon a wedde & he use þat wedde withoutyn leue of hym þat owith it, he doth þefte'; *W&W* 284: 'Bot when this wele es a-waye, the wyne moste be payede fore: Than lympis ჳowe weddis to laye, or ჳoure londe selle'; Fisher 14/3: 'Iohn Hull . . . haath compleined to vs he is endaungerd gretly and certein goodys of his leyd to wedde.' Plucknett 630: 'The *wed* in many cases became a form, very often consisting of a rod or stick which was handed over, or held, as a symbol of the transaction. . . . Typically mercantile forms were earnest money, and a drink' (cf. HANSELLE).

WESTMINSTRE   Westminster Hall, the judicial and administrative center of England in the late fourteenth century; also, the franchise of Westminster: B.20.133 Coveitise . . . boldeliche bar adoun wiþ many a bright Noble Muche of þe wit and and wisdom of westmynstre halle (C.22.133); B.20.285 Shame makeþ hem wende And fleen to þe freres, as fals folk to westmynstre That borweþ and bereþ it þider and þanne biddeþ frendes Yerne of forჳifnesse or lenger yeres loone (C.22.284); A.2.125 (B.2.161, C.2.174); A.3.12 (B.3.12, C.3.13); B.20.288 (C.22.287). Westminster Hall, so called for its proximity to Westminster Abbey, housed the chancery and royal courts of justice; it was also the meeting place of parliament. On the 'Westminster sanctuary' (B.20.285), see Statute 50 Edw. III c. 6: 'Because divers people inherit of divers tenements, borrowing divers goods in money or in merchandise of divers people of this realm, give their tenements and chattels to their friends, by collusion thereof to have the profits at their will, and afterwards flee to the franchise of Westminster . . . and there live a long time with a great countenance of another man's goods and profits of the said tenements and chattels, til the said creditors are bound to take a small parcel of their debt and release the remnant, it is ordained and assented that if it be found that such gifts are so made by collusion, the said creditors shall have execution of the said tenements and chattels, as if no such gift had been made.' For discussion of the practice, see Anna P. Baldwin, 'A Reference in *Piers Plowman* to the Westminster Sanctuary,' *N&Q* ns 29 (1982), 106–08.

WESTMINSTRE LAWE   The law administered by the king's courts at Westminster; the common law of England: C.10.237 Holy writ witnesseth þat for no wikkede dede That þe sire by hymsulue doth þe sone sholde be þe worse. Ac Westminstre lawe . . . worcheth þe contrarye. LAWE (I.A).

*WEYVES   *Pl.* property which is found ownerless and which, if unclaimed within a fixed period after due notice given, falls to the lord of the manor or to the king, e.g., an article washed up on the seashore, an animal that has strayed (usu. in comb. with STREYVES): B.Prol.94 Somme seruen þe kyng and his siluer tellen, In Cheker and in Chauncelrie chalangen hise dettes Of wardes and of wardemotes, weyues and streyves (C.Prol.92). *Bor.Cust.* 1:61: In the case of animals presumed stolen but for which no owner can be found, 'the goods shalbe forfayted to the king as weyff.' *Fleta* 2.45: 'If anyone, who claims the enjoyment of the franchise of waif [libertatem weyuii], find an animal wandering in his fee, he shall make it known forthwith to the adjoining townships and shall cause solemn proclamation to be made in fairs and parish churches and markets ... And if he do this, after a year and a day no action is available to anyone, but by the law of nations the animal becomes the lord's property.' For the phrase 'weyues and streyves,' see *Lib.Cust.* 486: 'Quod praedictus Dux ... haberet ... omnimoda catalla vocata "*Wayf*" et "*Stray*," deodanda, thesaurum inventum, ac alias res vel catalla inventa'; *Cov.Leet* 8: 'The prior as lord of Coundon has view of frankpledge ... waif and stray [vayvium & extrahuras]'; *Mirror* 102: 'the franchise of waif and stray' [de estrai ou de weif].

WILFULLI   With criminal intent; not accidentally or involuntarily: C.4.46 Pees ... putte vp a bille How Wrong wilfully hadde his wyf forleyn; B.17.290 wikkedliche and wilfulliche (C.19.266).

WILLE   I. The 'last will' of a person, as recorded in a will or testament: B.12.260 Executours, false frendes, þat fulfille noȝt his wille That was writen, and þei witnesse to werche as it wolde. BIQUESTE, TESTAMENT.
    II. Wish, desire, pleasure: A. 'Against one's will,' technical phrase used in framing an indictment for robbery from the person, rape and some other offences (Black): B.4.48 Thanne com pees into þe parlement and putte vp a bille How wrong ayeins his wille hadde his wif taken (A.4.35); A.3.268 (B.3.293); B.7.69 (C.9.65); C.10.216; B.18.88 (C.20.91); B.18.267 (C.20.275). Cf. *D&P* 1:74 'Þe housebounde may nout accusyn his wif of lecherie ... ȝif she be defylyd be strencþe & gret violence aȝenys hyr wil'; Chaucer, *CT.Pars.* 877: 'Thefte generally is for to reve a wight his thyng agayns his wille.' *Mirror* 103: 'No presumption arises that he took her against her will since there were no torn clothes ... or other evidence of violence.' B. 'At (someone's) will': C.10.239 The eritage þat þe eyer sholde haue is at þe kynges wille; A.Prol.37 (B.Prol.37, C.Prol.38); B.3.18 (C.3.19); B.6.206; A.10.31 (B.9.30, C.10.155); B.9.59; C.14.175; B.14.59 (C.15.259); B.18.344. Cf. *Mirror* 146: 'Officers guilty of wrongs against the king and the people were punished like other men, and in addition they were punished at the king's will [solom la voluntie le Roi].' C. 'With a good will': A.3.159 Þe king grauntide hire grace wiþ a good wille (B.3.172, C.3.217); A.1.119 (B.2.155, C.2.168); A.4.88 (B.4.101); C.7.296; C.9.111; B.14.20. D. 'With an ill or wicked will': B.5.428 So wiþ wikked wil ... my werkmen I paye (C.7.41); B.5.122 (C.6.87); B.10.440; B.15.123 (Sk.).

WITHSEGGEN To contradict (a person or statement), to counterplead: A.4.142 Waryn wisdom þo ... Couþe nouȝt warpen a word to wiþsigge resoun; B.10.349 *Contra*! ... þat kan I wiþseye, And preuen it by þe pistel þat Peter is nempned. Cf. *Chancery* 136: 'Wherefor, in asmoche as he withseieth not the matier conteigned in the seid bille of complainte ... he praieth that the seid John Wayte may be compelled bi the rule and discrecion of this Courte to restore him of his seid godes'; *Mirror*: 'This exception may be encountered [est encontrable] by this peremptory replication' (102); 'He is quit forever ... unless some reasonable exception encounters [encountre] him' (108). COUN-TREPLEDEN; see also STOPPEN.

WITNESS **I.** One who attests, gives evidence, or witnesses an event or trans-action (as a marriage): B.9.120 And þus was wedlok ywroȝt ... hymself was þe witnesse; C.6.53 Of werkes þat y wel dede witnesses take And sygge to suche þat sytte me byside, 'Lo, yf ȝe leue me nat or þat y lye wenen, Ascuth at hym or at here' (B.13.306); B.9.75; B.18.132 (C.20.136).
   II. A. Attestation of a fact, event, or statement (as in the phrases 'in witness of,' 'to witness,' 'to bear witness,' etc.): B.2.108 In witnesse of which þyng [the charter of Fals] wrong was þe firste (A.2.72, C.2.109); A.8.135 (B.7.157, C.9.306); B.11.269 (C.12.151); B.11.87; B.12.123 (C.14.66); B.13.94 (C.15.102); B.14.86; B.17.305 (C.19.280); B.18.232 (C.20.241); B.18.237 (C.20.246); C.20.311. **B.** (False) witness: A.2.111 (B.2.147, C.2.160); B.2.81 (C.2.85); B.2.147; A.6.67 (B.5.580, C.7.227); B.13.358. FALS WITNESS.

WITNESSEN **I.** To attest formally by signature, to sign (a document) as a witness of its execution (*OED*): B.2.161 Thanne was Fals fayn and Fauel as bliþe, And leten somone alle segges ... To wenden wiþ hem to westmynstre to witnesse þis dede (A.2.125); B.12.261 Executours, false frendes, þat fulfille noȝt his wille That was writen, and þei witnesse to werche as it wolde.
   II. A. To give formal or sworn evidence (of a fact, etc.); to testify: B.4.181 I wole haue leaute in lawe ... And as moost folk [i.e., 4.159] witnesseþ wel wrong shal be demed; B.4.91 (C.4.87); C.20.45. Cf. HEREN AND SEN, TESTI-FIEN. **B.** *Fig.* to furnish evidence or proof of: B.18.242 The water witnesseþ þat he was god for he wente on it (C.20.251); B.Prol.195 (C.Prol.205); C.2.129; B.11.39; C.12.153.
   III. To be formally present as a witness of (a transaction) (*OED*): B.2.75 *Sciant presentes & futuri &c.* Witeþ and witnesseþ þat wonieþ vpon erþe That Mede is ymaried moore for hire goodes Than for any vertue (A.2.57, C.2.79); A.2.46. Cf. MARIEN.

WITTING AND WILFUL Knowingly and with consent: B.19.370 A sisour and a somonour þat were forsworen ofte; Wity[n]ge and wilfully wiþ þe false helden (C.20.371). Cf. Fisher 165/4: 'Iohan ... a ȝenste my wyll & wetynge pot my land to fferme.' Bracton 74, 149, etc.: 'scienti et volenti.'

WORD AND WORK 'Word and deed,' an alliterative formula: B.15.198 Clerkes haue no knowyng ... but by werkes and wordes; B.15.210; cf. B.10.260. Bethurum calls attention to the phrase *word and weorc* in the laws of Aethelred (V.22.2, VI.28) and, after Liebermann, to continental parallels (272f.). She notes further that it translates 'a biblical opposition appearing in *verbo et factis* (Rom. xv, 18) or in *opere et sermone* (Luke xxiv, 19; 2 Thes. ii, 15)' (275). J. A. Burrow sees in the recurring triad *will*, *words*, and *works* the influence of 'the *thought*, *word* and *deed* of the Confiteor.' See his essay 'Words, Works and Will: Theme and Structure in *Piers Plowman*,' Hussey 112 and passim.

WRIT A legal document or instrument, as a CHARTRE, DEDE, PATENTE (cf. Lat. *scriptum*): A.2.46 Alle to wytnesse wel what þe writ wolde, In what maner þat mede in mariage was feffid; B.17.3 I bere þe writ riȝt here; B.17.18 (C.19.17). BREVET, CAPIAS, LETTRE, MAUNDEMENT.

WRITEN To draft or draw up (a document), to put into proper written form: B.6.85 I wole er I wende do write [cause to be written] my biqueste (A.7.77, C.8.94); A.8.43 Marchauntis ... ȝaf wille for his writyng wollene cloþis; B.19.462 I holde it riȝt and reson of my Reue to take Al þat myn Auditour ... Counseilleþ me bi ... my clerkes writynge (C.21.462); B.12.261; B.13.247. To 'write' often has in Middle English a more specific meaning than in Modern English; that Piers has his will drawn up by someone else (as most persons do today) is not evidence that 'Peres is illiterate' (Pearsall 150); cf. B.7.137ff.

WRONG As a personification: collectively, those actions defined by law as civil and criminal wrongs: B.4.48 Thanne com pees into þe parlement and putte vp a bille How wrong ayeins his wille hadde his wif taken, And how he rauysshede Rose. ... He maynteneþ hise men to murþere myne hewen, Forstalleþ my feires, fiȝteþ in my Chepyng, Brekeþ vp my berne dores, bereþ awey my whete, etc. (A.4.35, C.4.46); B.4.181. *Fleta* 2.1: 'Wrong [iniuria] is everything which is not done according to law.' However, the trial of Wrong (A.4.34–127, B.4.47–144, C.4.45–141) is aimed at a specific class of legal wrongs, not at 'wrongful' behaviour in general. The charges brought by Peace constitute a catalogue of crimes *contra pacem regis*, 'against the king's peace' (see PES). Such crimes were considered to be not only against the victim but also against the king himself, who would prosecute even if the wronged individual failed to do so. Thus, when Peace 'preyde to þe kynge To haue mercy on þat man ... "for he haþ waged me wel,"' the king rejected the petition and continued the action against Wrong. See Baldwin 39–50.

Y

YEMAN Yeoman; a freeholder under the rank of gentleman (Black): C.3.269 Alle manere lordes Thorw ȝeftes haen ȝemen to ȝerne and to ryde.

Cf. *D&P* 1:118: 'Þe kyng . . . hatȝ power and fredam of a page to makyn a ȝeman, of a ȝeman a gentylman, of a gentylman a knyȝt.' Fisher 186/7: 'Of the which mysdoers the names of certain gentilmen and yemen . . . ben conteyned in the bille.' See GENTILMAN.

YERE   *Fig.* the life of a contract; 'year's end,' the date fixed for the repayment of a loan or the fulfilment of an obligation: B.2.105 Yeldynge for þis þyng at one yeres ende Hire soules to Sathan (A.2.69); B.20.287 Fals folk . . . That borweþ . . . and þanne biddeþ frendes Yerne of forȝifnesse or lenger yeres loone (C.22.286); A.2.95 (Sk.); A.7.42 (B.6.44); A.11.227 (B.10.339).

YERESYEVE   A gift customarily given or exacted at the New Year or at the beginning of a year of office (*OED*); '*Yeresgive* is a toll or fine taken by the king's officers on a person's entering an office; or rather, a sum of money or bribe, given to them to connive at extortion or other offences in him that gives it' (quoted by Skeat 2:44 from *N&Q* 4th ser. 4 [1869], 560): B.3.100 [Conscience prophesies the punishment] of hem þat desireþ Yiftes or yeresyeues bycause of hire Offices; B.10.48 Ne holpe hir harlotrye . . . Wolde neuere kyng ne knyȝt ne canon of Seint Poules ȝyue hem to hir yeresȝyue þe value of a grote (A.11.34); B.13.184 What! . . . ar ye coueitous nouþe After yeresȝeues or ȝiftes? B.8.52 God . . . yaf þee to yeresȝyue to yeme wel þiselue Wit and fre wil. *Lib. Alb.* 138: 'Item, quod cives sint quieti de Childwyte, Yeresgyve, et de Scotale' (charter of Hen. III). Stubbs prints several examples of royal charters releasing towns from the obligation of *yeresyeve*; e.g., 'Concessimus, quod omnes sint quieti de jeresgieve et de scotteshale' (261, also 262, 307, 308).